Some of My Best Friends Are Books

Guiding Gifted Readers from Preschool to High School

Judith Wynn Halsted

Ohio Psychology Press
Dayton, Ohio

Quote on page iv is from *The Poetry of Yevgeny Yevtushenko, 1953 to 1965*, reprinted by permission of Marion Boyars Publishing Ltd. Copyright 1981 by M. Boyars Ltd., publishers of this book in the United States and Great Britain.

Quote on page 113 is from Arlene Hynes and Mary Hynes-Berry, *Bibliotherapy: The Interactive Process*, reprinted by permission of Westview Press. Copyright 1986 by Westview Press, Boulder, Colorado.

Quote on page 188 is from Elizabeth Cook, *The Ordinary and the Fabulous*, reprinted by permission of Cambridge University Press. Copyright 1969 by Cambridge University Press, London, U.K.

Quote on page 228 is from Marcia Sewall, *The World Turned Upside Down: An Old Penny Rhyme*, reprinted by permission of Little, Brown and Company. Copyright 1986 by Atlantic Monthly Press, Boston.

Cover Art Design: Kerry B. Causey
Interior Design/Art Direction: Spring Dawn Reader
Indexer: Joan K. Griffitts

Published by
Ohio Psychology Press
P.O. Box 90095
Dayton, OH 45490

copyright © 1994 by Ohio Psychology Press

First published in 1988 under the title, *Guiding Gifted Readers.*
Revised and enlarged.

Library of Congress Cataloging in Publication Data

Halsted, Judith Wynn, 1940 -
    Some of my best friends are books : guiding gifted readers from preschool to high school / Judith Wynn Halsted. -- Rev. And enl.
        p. cm.
    Rev. ed. of: Guiding gifted readers. c1988.
    Includes bibliographical references and index.
    ISBN 0-910707-24-3 : $15.00
    1. Gifted children -- United States -- Books and reading. 2. Gifted children -- Education -- United States. 3. Youth -- United States -- Books and reading. I. Halsted, Judith Wynn, 1940-   Guiding gifted readers. II. Title.
Z1039.G55H35   1994
025.5'35 -- dc20   94-32347
                                                         CIP

For my husband,
David W. Halsted
an exemplary parent
and my best teacher
with love and gratitude.

Be equal to your talent, not your age.
At times let the gap between them be embarrassing.
Fear not to be young, precocious.

— Yevgeny Yevtushenko
"Others May Judge You"

Table of Contents

INDEXES

PREFACE

I n 1992, not a single book was purchased in 35% of the homes in the United States. Although Americans bought 7% more books in 1992 than in 1991, book purchases by those under twenty-five dropped 27% ("Book purchases," 1993). Ten percent of the people read 80% of the books read in the United States each year, according to estimates. Chances are good that you, reading this preface, are from one of the 65% of households that bought at least one book last year, and among the top 10% of our nation's readers.

If you are a parent, you probably hope your children will join this small but influential group. If you teach, no doubt you want to inspire at least some of your students to become lifelong readers.

Your children and students may already give evidence of doing so, avidly reading all they can during their leisure time. Or they may be among the many who *can* read easily and well, but do not *choose* to spend their time with books, leaving you wondering how best to encourage reading.

Some parents and teachers of avid and excellent readers have been told that their children are gifted. Some have been told that their apparently bright children are not gifted, that they do not meet the criteria for entrance into the school gifted program. And some live and teach in areas where there is no gifted program, and no means of knowing whether their children are gifted, despite signals from certain children that cause adults to wonder.

For some adults in the 10% of the public that reads most of the books, *gifted* is an irrelevant term. They take great pleasure in the characteristics, shared by many bright, creative people, that make certain children especially good company—traits like an insatiable curiosity, a terrific sense of humor, and an eagerness to read and talk about ideas—but give little thought to whether or not a child should be labeled gifted.

If your child or student has been identified as gifted, whether or not he is a reader, this book is for you.

If your child or student is an avid reader, whether or not she has been called talented or creative, this book is for you.

This book is for parents and teachers and librarians and counselors of children and young people who are different from the norm by reason of giftedness or intense interests—intellectual, artistic, or musical.

For many of these children, at least for a portion of the time, it is quite true that some of their best friends are books.

The new title for this second edition of *Guiding Gifted Readers* reflects two new goals, both of which are based on the comments and requests of readers.

The first goal is to make the book more meaningful to parents. These beleaguered people are under many conflicting pressures today. Here are just two:

As more mothers work outside the home and the leisure time of American workers shrinks, quiet time with family becomes ever more rare and precious. Not only parents are busy, but children also are occupied with after-school activities. Chronic scheduling problems leave parents and children with little time to talk, and when they do have a few moments together, they may find it difficult to carry on a conversation of much depth.

At the same time, with our educational system in crisis, conscientious parents recognize that they must become more involved in their children's education by being more active at home, and if possible by volunteering at school, where they are certainly needed.

Unfortunately, as school districts tighten their budgets across the country, gifted programs that have been in place for a decade or more are threatened. In the near future, children identified as gifted may lose the special curricular offerings they need. Their parents, knowing how much their children have benefitted from programming designed for them, must find ways to compensate at home for the loss.

How will parents find the time? How will they use that time to make for the greatest impact? And how can parents who have no background in teaching enhance their children's educational experience with confidence that they are doing it well?

Some of My Best Friends Are Books outlines the reasons books are so important to gifted and capable students. It also proposes that by reading and discussing books with their children, parents can meet two needs in one pleasurable activity.

Books can provide a focus for discussions (non-threatening discussions, since, after all, they are about someone else) that touch not necessarily on plot and characterization but instead on feelings, values, and decision-making. Parents who have tried this tell me that they find books to be wonderful bridges for communication with their youngsters.

In addition, reading is a natural ally in the effort to improve the education of our students. In the past, many people who subsequently made important contributions educated themselves, an accomplishment made possible by their access to a public library. Today, one practical measure of the benefits of reading is the higher scores earned on college entrance exams by students who spend more time reading—fiction as well as nonfiction—than others. Parents can hardly go wrong by encouraging their children to read more, especially if they help select the books read and talk about them with their child.

Guiding Gifted Readers was written for parents and teachers, and both groups have found it useful. Teachers may find new incentive to use books with their gifted students if funding for more expensive gifted programming is curtailed. Accordingly, the suggestions on book discussion in a school setting have been expanded for this edition.

Additional new material is designed to help parents find ways to implement the ideas presented here in a variety of home situations.

The second goal is to broaden the target group of young readers to include not only those formally identified as gifted, but many others who may not be included in that category, especially

- the estimated one-half of our gifted students who have not been identified;
- the bright and eager learners who are not placed in a gifted program because they do not quite meet the criteria of the local schools;
- the many highly able children in rural areas of our country, or in larger schools where no gifted program is provided;
- all children who appear to have special ability, especially verbal ability, whether or not they could be identified as gifted.

Therefore I encourage any adult who senses a special spark in a child, even if "gifted" seems not quite the right word, to read this book. My hope is that parents and teachers will find, as readers of *Guiding Gifted Readers* have, that the ideas presented here benefit any child who is interested in reading and talking about challenging books.

One reason for this shift in focus is the growing recognition that an adequate definition of giftedness is elusive. In the past an IQ score sufficed; then the score was supplemented with a variety of inventories and forms to recognize behavioral characteristics; and now the works of Gardner (*Frames of Mind*) and Sternberg (*Beyond IQ: A Triarchic*

Theory of Human Intelligence), with their descriptions of various intelligences, highlight the complexity of the enterprise.

Another reason is that there are discrepancies in the procedures by which local school systems identify gifted students. Thus a child may be "gifted" in one school district but not in another. This book is for that child. It is also for those parents and teachers who suspect a child has special talents and want to offer him or her a chance to grow.

Most of the research cited in *Some of My Best Friends Are Books* describes studies of children identified as gifted. Curious, avid readers have not been singled out as a group for study. Adults who read this book with specific children in mind are encouraged to note when "the shoe fits" and when it does not, and to use the information and ideas presented here in creative ways to meet the individual needs of their children and students.

Clearly, it can be difficult to know for certain whether a particular child is gifted or not. Is it then better to do something, or nothing? This book offers a safe way of doing something. Parents and teachers who use it can be assured that there is nothing here that will hurt a child who is not gifted—if that child is interested in reading and talking about challenging books. The one caveat is that the interest must belong to the child, not just to the adult.

Some of My Best Friends Are Books has three parts and is divided into eight chapters. Part One, "The Children," offers updated background information on the emotional and intellectual developmental needs of children of high ability.

Part Two, "The Process," begins with a chapter about typical reading patterns and the need for reading guidance. The following chapters suggest methods for two approaches to discussing books with young readers: enhancing emotional development through bibliotherapy, and promoting intellectual growth through discussion of ideas. Chapter Four can be used as a primer on developmental bibliotherapy, with giftedness as the example of one use of this technique to meet developmental needs. Chapter Five, on book discussion for intellectual development, has been expanded, based in part on my recent experience working with a group of parent volunteers in a program that serves the gifted students in their children's school.

Part Three, "The Books," offers in the first two chapters criteria for selecting challenging books and a brief overview of children's literature, with special emphasis on gifted readers. The final—and longest—chapter is an expanded annotated bibliography listing over 300 books carefully selected for their usefulness in promoting the intellectual and emotional development of gifted children and young people. A new Index of Categories guides the reader to more issues of concern for gifted students than those offered in *Guiding Gifted Readers*, topics related to the emotional and intellectual characteristics outlined in the first part of the book.

There is nothing new about the idea that gifted children need good books or that books can be used to help children to build coping skills. The response to *Guiding Gifted Readers* suggests that there was something new and welcome in the ideas it presented for using books with *gifted* children to help them to develop optimally. The hope is that *Some of My Best Friends Are Books*, with its broader aim, improved organization, and enlarged bibliography, will prove even more helpful.

Again I want to thank the staff of the Traverse Area District Library in Traverse City, Michigan, especially Marlas Wyckoff for persistence with interlibrary loan requests, Theresa Schaub for diligence in locating errant children's books, Mary Franklin and the circulation staff for cheerful patience, and the entire reference staff for ready answers to last-minute telephone queries as I strove for accuracy.

Librarians and administrators for the Traverse City Area Public Schools agreed to read sections of the book in their areas of expertise. I am grateful to Dr. David Dean, Linda Barker, Jim Craig, Liz Messing, Linda Ligon, Cal Husby and Dawn Farley, whose comments go far to update and ensure the validity of this new edition.

Ideas for books to consider for Chapter Eight have come from many people who love to read and talk about books. In beautifully crafted and delivered lay sermons, Mark Gustafson has introduced me to artists both literary and musical. In addition to the students whose reading I have guided and discussed through the years I thank David Lemmen, Todd Ramlo, and David and Mark Halsted. Their stories add life and meaning to the theories presented here. One cold and rainy spring day, Nancy Lemmen, Michael Delp, and Claudia Delp—teachers of preschool through high school students—lengthened my list of prospective titles while waiting for a hatch on the opening day of trout season at the river cabin of Bill and Kathleen Porter. I thank them all for insight, suggestions, and comraderie.

And I want to thank all those who have used *Guiding Gifted Readers* and have written letters or stopped me on elevators and in the halls at conferences to tell me what the book has meant to them. Without their assurance that the ideas presented here are adaptable to many settings and are a contribution to the understanding and education of our brightest children, this second edition would not have been written.

I am grateful, too, to Dr. James T. Webb and Dr. Patricia A. Kleine of Wright State University, for seminal ideas and for reading and commenting on the manuscript; and to editor Linda Senter, whose efforts have made the book more readable.

Again and always, thanks to my husband, David, our sons, David and Mark, and our daughters-in-law, Keely and Barbara, for many conversations and vital encouragement; and to Christopher, our first grandchild, whose vibrant enthusiasm for books since the age of five months has been a pleasure and an inspiration.

Judith Wynn Halsted

References

Book purchases grew 7% in 1992, survey finds. (1993, March 31). *Wall Street Journal.*

Gardner, Howard. (1983). *Frames of mind: The theory of multiple intelligences.* New York: Basic Books.

Sternberg, Robert J. (1985). *Beyond IQ: A triarchic theory of human intelligence.* New York: Cambridge University Press.

INTRODUCTION

Steven is a joy! The preschooler is cheerful, curious, friendly, and bright. He talks easily with adults and seems quite mature, and his teacher relies on him as the most responsible child in his group. But other children are puzzled by him sometimes.

For Steven gets frustrated when his friends can't follow what he's saying. It bothers him that they don't share his amazed interest in the insects he brings to class. Adults help him find out about insects in books, and he is beginning to read about them himself.

Matthew is a smart, sullen high school junior. Social difficulties have left their marks on him, most obviously in the discrepancy between his ability and his performance. His PSAT scores qualify him to compete for a National Merit Scholarship, but his grades will keep him out of the better colleges. Teachers say that he doesn't measure up to his potential, refuses to do homework, and just doesn't study, particularly courses that require consistent daily effort like languages and math.

Matthew is defensive about his school record and confused about his future. He's so tired of hearing he's "not measuring up to his potential" that he has stopped listening. He wants to be part of the high school social life but doesn't fit in; he feels no one understands him. He knows he has mental ability that he does not use, at least not at school, but he has no idea how to "realize his potential." Matthew rationalizes that the world is in such a mess that no one can really change anything, so what he does with his life makes no difference.

He is depressed about his lack of direction, but the teachers see Matthew, who a few years ago was passionately concerned about national and international politics, as merely cynical and disinterested. They're concerned, but they don't know how to help him.

Amy is also a high school junior. She is active in sports, student government, and the school newspaper, and she keeps her grades at an honors level. Her special interest is biology, and she has arranged with the biology teacher to do a year-long independent study as a supplement to the regular classwork. Amy is quiet about her own excellent grades and is ready to help others who don't understand as quickly. In the summer she's a counselor at a day camp where the campers love her. She's always available for ping-pong or a quiet talk.

Despite her full schedule and many friends, Amy feels truly alone sometimes. Her concerns about the future are so much more intense than her friends' that she has never attempted to discuss them with anyone. Although she worries about the future of the world, Amy's plans for her own future are taking shape. She wants to go to a university with a strong biology curriculum and is looking forward to visiting campuses.

If we were to ask both Matthew's and Amy's parents what their children were like as preschoolers, they would describe someone remarkably like Steven. What happened in those twelve years to turn a Steven into a Matthew rather than an Amy?

Steven, Matthew and Amy are all gifted. This is an extra dimension in their lives, imposing on them certain developmental and intellectual tasks in addition to those all children face. Little has been written about the steps that lead a gifted child from a bright and curious preschooler to a well-adjusted high school student with a promising future. Based on a background of experience with gifted children and adults, this book attempts an answer to this question: If I'm fortunate enough to start with a child like Steven, what can I do to help him develop into a confident, productive young adult who remains as happy and responsive as Steven is now?

Beth is a conscientious ninth grader whose organization, discipline, and genuine interest in learning help her to maintain an A-average. Requirements for the gifted program at her school are unusually high, and her test scores have not qualified her to join. But her intellectual curiosity and her voracious reading habit set her apart from her classmates who are too busy for books. Sometimes Beth wonders why she has not been selected for special classes, but she is confident that she has a bright future nevertheless. To be honest, she is often relieved not to have the pressure of being labeled a "gifted" student.

In another school district, Beth might be eligible for the gifted program. With or without the label, she is a bright, intellectually curious girl whose development depends in part on nurturing adults who recognize and encourage these qualities.

Some of My Best Friends Are Books is written in the belief that books and book discussion can have a profound effect on the lives of children like Steven and Matthew and Amy and Beth. Parents and teachers can use books to guide bright and gifted children's intellectual and emotional development through book discussions and bibliotherapy— powerful tools for influencing the environment in which these exceptional youngsters grow.

Each stage brings a different challenge for children of high ability. Preschoolers need to develop a positive self-concept and grow toward a strong sense of self. In the early grades of elementary school, such youngsters begin to understand that people have different levels of abilities, and they must learn to value abilities that differ from their own. Although bright children need friends who share their own capabilities, they must learn to get along with all children.

In the later elementary grades, talented students often choose whether to acknowledge and follow their natural eagerness to learn, or to hide their abilities in order to fit in. This is one reason why it is so important for preschoolers to develop a strong sense of self, a confidence in their own worth.

Well-adjusted gifted children enter junior high school able to withstand the turmoil that typifies that age. If giftedness and intellectual curiosity are part of their self-concept, these aspects will remain intact—if temporarily submerged—as youngsters try on various personae. Ideally, they emerge from this stage knowing their capabilities, being at ease with their classmates, and having a few close friends.

Senior high students with this background, more aware of their individuality and responsibility for their own future, have a chance to accept and use their abilities without self-consciousness. If we have been able to follow Steven to this point, we will find him still happy but far more self-aware, conscious of both his abilities and his shortcomings. He's glad to be gifted and feels a sense of responsibility to himself—and to others—to fulfill his promise, although he doesn't know where his mind will lead him. He realizes that even though he is different, he is accepted by family and friends. He accepts and values others as well. He has the confidence to take risks, to allow himself to fail, and to pick up the pieces and try again. Steven's healthy development is more likely to occur if his parents, teachers, friends and school system value and nurture giftedness, whether or not they *formally* identify it.

In fact, only about half of our gifted children have been formally identified, according to estimates. That means that many exceptionally bright youngsters are instead being labeled "difficult" or "emotionally immature" or "too talkative" or "withdrawn." The unique, often intense emotional and intellectual needs of such children may never be accepted and understood, let alone met, either by the children themselves or by the adults around them. Other children too may be left out in the cold: those who aren't intellectually gifted but who are talented or creative in ways that can't be identified or for which no programs are available.

New developments in research are changing our definitions of giftedness. In *Growing Up Gifted* (1992), Barbara Clark defines gifted individuals as "those who are performing, or who show promise of performing, at high levels of intelligence." It is important to note that this definition includes those who show promise but may not yet show the fulfillment of it, due to environmental conditions that can be changed.

Unfortunately, "gifted" is a value-laden word, inviting charges of elitism that make students, parents, and teachers uncomfortable. But it is the best word we have to label a phenomenon we know exists, and we have plenty of Matthews to remind us that giftedness is no guarantee of a happy, productive life.

This book recommends that the adults most concerned with the development of gifted, talented, creative children consider very seriously the potential that books and reading have for helping these children understand themselves and become all that they can be.

Books for children are plentiful, and most bright children are good readers who find them easily. It may seem that *planning* to use books is unnecessary. Yet surprisingly often, where there is no planning even good readers are not introduced to the pleasures of leisure reading. Teachers struggling to meet basic requirements have little time to suggest and follow through with extra reading for brighter students. Parents may find it difficult to keep track of what their children are reading. Guiding children's reading appears to be one more unaffordable luxury in an increasingly busy world.

Yet books offer compelling advantages to parents and teachers who want to nurture the minds and hearts of highly able children. *Excellent books* are abundant, inexpensive, accessible sources of challenge and understanding. In fact, books should be the first choice of enrichment for these bright youngsters.

Merely providing books is not enough, however. A knowledge of gifted children, discussion techniques, and children's literature is necessary to make maximum use of the benefits books offer. By filling the gaps in their knowledge, parents, teachers, counselors and librarians can bring gifted children and books together more effectively. In so doing, they can help gifted children be themselves, comfortable in their present world and poised to grow into happy, productive adults.

References

Clark, Barbara. (1992). *Growing up gifted: Developing the potential of children at home and at school*. 4th ed. New York: Macmillan.

PART ONE

The Children

CHAPTER ONE

The Heart of the Child: Emotional Development

It's a persisting myth that gifted children have no trouble with emotional and social development, or that if they do have problems, they also have the intelligence to deal with them. Sensitive adults who work with gifted children realize that this is not true—that gifted children often are burdened with *extra* emotional and social needs and difficulties. In fact, being gifted truly complicates the usual problems of growing up.

In an article on the emotional needs of gifted adolescents, Frey (1991) names the general psychosocial needs of all adolescents, and then highlights the specialized *additional* needs of gifted students as identified by Buescher (1985). These special needs include the following:

- recognizing and owning their giftedness
- resolving the dissonance between their expectations of themselves and their actual performance

- taking risks (The reluctance of gifted adolescents to take risks can hamper their willingness to take appropriate but difficult courses.)
- determining how much to respond to others' expectations and how much weight to give to their own needs
- coping with their impatience with lack of clear-cut answers, especially in personal relationships and career choices
- meeting their inner demand for an identity, while avoiding the temptation to make premature decisions (usually regarding college and career) which would limit future access to their full potential

While Frey and Buescher show the difficulties of giftedness for teenagers, their point holds for gifted people of all ages: to understand their emotional needs, it is necessary to recognize the extras in the developmental tasks they face.

In this book five broad areas in which giftedness affects development will be proposed. One area, intellectual development, is reserved for the next chapter. In this chapter, four aspects of emotional development are presented:

- establishing an identity
- needing time alone
- relationships with others
- learning how to use one's ability

All children must establish their own identity; the gifted child must recognize and accept an identity that is different from the norm, which may not be popular or acceptable to peers or family.

Take a look at Matthew, the unhappy high schooler described in the introduction, when he was younger. As a seventh grader, Matthew has already figured out that his ideas seem weird to his classmates and even to his parents and teachers. Entering a new school, he's determined to be quiet and to keep his hand down. No more frantic arm waving when the answer is so very clear! Stifle, stifle, stifle. Stifle is the name of the game. At an age when he should be establishing *his sense of identity, he is denying a large part of himself. He is attempting to lose himself in the crowd called "normal." If he had been helped to understand and*

4

accept his differences when he first became aware of them,
he would be freer to acknowledge them now.

All children must learn to be alone at times; however, gifted children may actually *require* time alone, and they may need more of it than most people need or can understand. They may have to learn to cope with mixed feelings about their own need for time alone, aware that they also need time with other people, and uncertain how to balance these needs with the expectations of others.

> *Sara loves to read, play the piano, and sew—all solitary*
> *activities. After a day crowded with people at school, she*
> *enjoys coming home to these quiet pursuits. Her parents are*
> *worried, however, because she seldom invites friends home*
> *with her. Although Sara's happy with her friends at school*
> *and content with her activities at home, she senses her*
> *parents' concern and wonders whether there is something*
> *wrong with her. Her worries would be relieved if her parents*
> *recognized her need for time alone and encouraged her to*
> *take it.*

All children must learn how to get along with others; gifted children must find a few good friends and learn to value and respect others, even though they themselves may be rejected. Rejection sometimes results from the unusual intensity of many gifted children, a characteristic that is difficult for other children to understand. Gifted people also have heightened sensitivity to the comments and actions of others, so that being misunderstood or rejected is a more painful experience for them than for most. For gifted children the issues of friendship, so important to their healthy development, are much more complex than they are for most children.

> *Brian talks with enthusiasm to high school students and*
> *adults, but he can find no other grade school children who*
> *share his interest in biology. His sixth grade classmates are*
> *puzzled by the intensity that marks his oral science reports,*
> *and he mistakes their lack of understanding for rejection. In*
> *response, he is building a protective wall around himself,*
> *neither giving nor expecting friendship from people his own*
> *age. If he can be helped to respect his classmates' social or*
> *athletic skills as well as his own knowledge of biology—and*
> *if he can find just one or two friends his age who share his*
> *interest, perhaps at a community science center—he will*

avoid years of social isolation. Otherwise, Brian may not learn to make friends of his own age until he enters college.

All adolescents must make career and college decisions; gifted youngsters often have so many possibilities that choice paralyzes them. Unwilling to give anything up and unable to choose, gifted teenagers and young adults may find it difficult to take the steps that will enable them to make full use of their abilities.

Alex, a superior student in math and science, is considering a career in medicine. He also plays piano and guitar in a band that has performed at high school proms for the last three years. Music is so important to Alex that he wants to delay entering college while he tests his chances of finding work as a professional musician. But he's afraid that too much time away from science and math will dull his skills and ruin his chances of getting into medical school. As he weighs the decision, college application deadlines are passing by. He's beginning to panic about his future. Attention paid to preliminary college and career planning, beginning in the early adolescent years, would have helped.

Chapter One considers the emotional development of gifted children by further exploring each of these four aspects of development. Since this chapter serves as background for later sections, only brief mention will be made here of ways in which books can enhance that emotional development.

Establishing an Identity

A major task of growing up is the search for one's identity. Gifted children, in order to be wholly themselves, *must* recognize and accept their own giftedness. But giftedness is often more a burden than a blessing in our society, since many people are annoyed by and resentful of the precocious and verbal child whose abilities are above the norm. And so to fit giftedness willingly and comfortably into one's self-concept takes a degree of maturity that must develop over time.

6

Who They Are

Establishing an identity is a matter of discovering who we are, of learning what it is that makes us, like the Little Prince's rose, "unique in all the world." What gifted children discover may be a self that they know will not be popular. They may feel that they must choose between being themselves and being liked. Out of this conflict and the ways they choose to deal with it will emerge their identities. Several characteristics of typical bright children contribute to the conflict.

Difference. Gifted children realize fairly early not only that they are different, but also that there is something vaguely unacceptable about this difference. Our society is ambivalent about difference as well as intelligence, and children can easily develop the uncomfortable feeling that something is "wrong" with them. Usually they do not know what it is, or even why they are different. They only know that when they exercise their creativity or knowledge, they do not fit in. They then feel alone, wrong, even freakish; ironically, they may feel inferior to those around them.

At the same time, especially if their environment provides enough stimulation, they may experience the elation of the insights and awarenesses their giftedness makes possible. They can know the joy of discovering new ideas, new people with whom they can use their vocabularies fully, new stimuli such as museums, music or films that excite them.

They live with this paradox, and they must learn, in the "down" times when they are feeling different and alone, to trust that the "up" times, when they can enjoy the benefits of their extra measure of perception, will come again. Some of them must learn to make a little "up" time last over a long "down" period. One friendship established at summer camp may be what carries a child through the next school year; one understanding and stimulating teacher may keep another child going through two or three years with indifferent teachers.

Attending a high school that places more emphasis on sports than on academic achievement, Debbie finds her work with a statewide youth organization more stimulating than school. Although meetings occur only twice a year, the friendships she has made with other natural leaders, the creative energy she puts into planning conferences, and the experience of traveling to large cities around the state have compensated for her feeling of not fitting in at school.

Gradually she is learning to integrate the sense of being different and alone at school with the sense of inner delight and satisfaction that her giftedness brings in another setting. Her identity includes both.

Ambivalence about the Label. Middle-elementary children, just becoming aware of the concept of giftedness, may be ambivalent about having the label applied to them. If parents and teachers react positively and matter-of-factly to the idea of giftedness, children will probably do the same, accepting their abilities and learning to use them with enthusiasm. If anything in their environment causes them to be uncomfortable with the term, however, their responses may range from what appears to be showing off to denying their gifts with the responsibilities they imply.

Self-conscious about his lack of athletic ability, Derrick seeks approval by offering answers in class so eagerly and frequently that the other children think he is boasting about how much he knows. Meanwhile, Cheryl answers questions only when the teacher calls on her and even uses a doubtful tone of voice to give the impression that she knows no more than anyone else. Both responses indicate that these children need help in accepting who they are. Establishment of a healthy identity depends on that acceptance.

Emotional Overexcitability. It is often noted that gifted children, especially the highly gifted, have extraordinarily high degrees of emotional sensitivity and intensity. Piechowski's (1991) outline of Dabrowski's concept of "overexcitabilities" helps to explain this. Some people experience heightened degrees of excitement in any of five areas: psychomotor, sensual, intellectual, imaginational, and emotional. Piechowski defines emotional overexcitability as "great depth and intensity of emotional life expressed through a wide range of feelings, attachments, compassion, heightened sense of responsibility, and scrupulous self-examination" (p. 287).

Gifted people are often super-sensitive, sharply aware of their own and others' feelings. They are also often intense, not only in their depth of feeling but also in their commitment to an interest or a cause, and in their manner of expressing that commitment. In the adult world, the sensitivity and intensity of the gifted usually meet some degree of tolerance, but children are not always so understanding. Gifted children who exhibit emotional overexcitability need the support of an adult who takes Dabrowski's view that *the emotional extremes these children*

8

experience are not a sign of neurosis but an indication of potential for growth.

Awareness of Moral Issues. Gifted children read the newspapers and watch television news with comprehension earlier than most children. At an early age, they become aware of adult concerns about war, the environment, racial issues, and other social concerns. They may become deeply worried about the future of the world at a time when other children their age are unaware and uninterested—another difference between them and their classmates.

> *Richard will never forget hearing of the assassination of Martin Luther King, Jr.: the five-year-old was watching television when the news bulletin interrupted. He wasn't traumatized by the event, but he still remembers it as the awakening of the political awareness that is a major focus of interest for the 30-year-old.*

All of these characteristics of gifted youngsters—and the additional ones discussed elsewhere in this book—are aspects of the self that a high-potential child must learn to understand, accept, and balance as she develops a sense of identity.

Who They Will Become

Establishing an identity means more than merely discovering who we are. It also means creating who we will become through imagination, exploring available identities and choosing among them, and risking. Gifted youngsters may (and should) experiment with more identities than most children, displaying more imagination and less conventionality. Books offer possibilities they would otherwise not encounter and permit them to experience vicariously various roles and ways of living as they move through the process of creating a personal identity.

The search for identity raises some complex issues for gifted people. Some children deny the gift and avoid developing it fully. They may become restless adults, moving without a clear sense of direction from one pursuit to another. Because they have not trained themselves to use their abilities, they are often dissatisfied with the limited opportunities available to them. We are happiest when we know that our talents are being stretched and used; we feel best about ourselves when we know we are being useful. To reach that point, gifted children must develop the potential that lies within them.

Christopher was identified as gifted in junior high. Although he loved to read and talked glibly about ideas, he never learned to focus his thoughts sufficiently to complete written assignments on time. After graduation, he held a number of restaurant jobs, intending to save money for college but delaying application because he feared that his lack of study skills would lead to failure. Within two years he married a woman who met many of his emotional needs but did not share his intellectual interests. Soon supporting a wife and children took precedence over his education. Christopher might have become an excellent teacher, but his lack of training now confines him to work that offers no security and does not require him to think. With less time for reading now, and no one with whom to discuss his ideas, Christopher is lonely and resentful—an outcome that could have been prevented by early information about his ability and encouragement to use it well.

Other children feel that superior ability implies a responsibility. They see a gift as something to be developed so that they can pass it on by giving to others. These youngsters represent a happy middle ground; they can learn to rejoice in their gifts and to use them with humility and productivity.

Joyce grew up in a well-to-do family and enjoyed an excellent education. After her marriage there was no financial need for her to work. However, from her late elementary years she knew that she wanted a career that would serve other people in some way. She stayed home with her young children, but she continued her education as a part-time student while gaining experience as a volunteer in several community organizations. Fifteen years later she was ready to begin a career as a psychologist. Her present work includes helping gifted girls make appropriate educational and vocational decisions.

Another issue facing these children is their potential for leadership. Many of them are natural leaders, and developing a sense of identity means finding ways to explore and use their leadership ability. In some, the talent for leadership is so strong that if it finds no positive outlets, it will express itself in negative ways. They need adults who can see past the negative expressions and offer guidance in the constructive use of leadership ability. Since books provide examples of both negative and positive leaders, book discussion is one way of providing this guidance.

> *Unchallenged by his high school courses, Tad is not only refusing to do his assignments but is also loudly proclaiming to other students his low opinion of the teachers, the curriculum, and the school's requirements. Because Tad's voice carries some weight in his small high school, this gifted student is using his talent for leadership to encourage others to neglect their work, too. Tad and the others will all be happier if an adult can see what is happening and help Tad plan ways of redirecting his abilities.*

After exploring different roles for themselves, gifted students often discover that they can do so many things well that career choice is extremely difficult. Hence they need to develop superior self-knowledge and excellent decision-making skills. Multi-gifted young adults must face the fact that they will not have time to bring all of their talents to full flower. Again, books can help, enabling them to explore various options without spending months or years on each, helping them to establish priorities and make vocational and avocational choices.

Dyssynchrony

While gifted youngsters deal with these issues, they may also face the enormous task of integration. Different parts of themselves may develop at different rates, with academic interest and achievement far outstripping other areas of growth. The disparity between intellectual maturity and social, emotional, and physical development has been called dyssynchrony (Terrassier, 1985), a wonderfully descriptive term for what happens in children whose various developmental schedules are not in tune with one another. It simply expresses the fact that in gifted children intellectual development can move rapidly, while social, emotional, and physical growth remain tied to chronological age.

Dyssynchrony makes it difficult to know whether a child should skip a grade level in school. It is exemplified by a third grade boy who joined an enrichment class of fifth and sixth graders in the junior high library to work on a research project, but who had to tape record his report because his fine motor skills were not advanced enough to write all he had learned. Dyssynchrony causes surprise when the unusually tall, unusually verbal ten-year-old does not behave like the twelve-year-old she appears to be. We must consider dyssynchrony in choosing books for the second grader who is reading at the sixth grade level.

If a child's intellectual growth has far surpassed emotional and social development, there may come a necessary time of academic latency that allows social and emotional growth to catch up. This can happen during the high school years, after college, or any time in between.

> *One young man who began kindergarten at four and then was accelerated another year in high school entered college at sixteen. When he graduated from college at twenty he was sure of two things: he wanted to go to graduate school, and he did not want to go to graduate school that fall. He spent two years working at various jobs, learning to be self-supporting while consolidating his career plans. Now in graduate school, for the first time he is studying with his agemates, still occasionally restless at the pace of coursework but adapting to it with a new measure of self-understanding and maturity.*

Indeed, it may not be until the early twenties or later that the different aspects—intellectual, emotional, social, and physical—of a very complex person begin to come together. It will help the person living through this dyssynchrony if he and his parents recognize what is happening and know that the prognosis is good.

Establishing a Healthy Identity

For the gifted, establishing a healthy identity means discovering and accepting who one is and creating the person one will become, acknowledging and using giftedness unself-consciously. In addition, the gifted person needs to develop a protective attitude toward her abilities. On the one hand, she must integrate giftedness into her self-concept, and on the other she must be able to see it, with humility, as a separate entity to be nurtured. Only when she can do this has she fully accepted herself as a gifted person.

How does a gifted youngster reach this point? By admitting that she has many of the characteristics of gifted people, including some that are unpopular or misunderstood, such as being hypercritical or talking too much in class or wanting more time alone than most people do; by understanding the positive and useful sides of those unpopular characteristics; by forgiving herself for having them and bringing them under control to make good use of them; by recognizing the advantages of being gifted and learning to enjoy them; and by realizing that high intelligence is useless without training and self-discipline.

These attitudes cannot easily be taught by precept. Example is far superior, and examples can come from role models, gifted people whose lives are based on these understandings. Such role models can be alive or imaginary: parents, teachers, and friends—or characters in books.

Of course, some gifted children have so many barriers in their way that developing a healthy identity may be beyond their reach. The fortunate ones will have a good chance of becoming what Abraham Maslow (1962) called self-actualized adults: giving, productive people who make full use of their potential and gain deep satisfaction from doing so.

Being Alone

"Being alone" is an ambiguous term. It can mean being alone and liking it, being alone and lonely, or being alone and different. A gifted child can experience all of these, and can also develop conflicting emotions about being alone.

The child's confusion is compounded by the reactions of other people to those who appear to be "loners." Human beings are social animals, suspicious of those who choose to be less social than the norm. The gifted child is aware of this, and his own feelings about being alone are colored by his assumptions of the feelings of others.

Being Alone and Liking It

It has been estimated that only 25 percent of the general population is made up of introverts, while of the gifted population, the number is as high as 60 percent (Smutny, Veenker and Veenker, 1989). Characteristics of introversion include the following:

- needing time alone
- wanting one best friend rather than many friends
- being slow to respond to people and situations; needing time to think
- preferring to read rather than to be with others

None of these characteristics is "wrong," yet introversion may worry parents and teachers who don't know it is prevalent among the gifted.

> *In the question period after a parents' meeting on stress in gifted children, a mother expressed concern because her son resisted her attempts to sign him up for a full schedule of after-school programs. "Maybe he's an introvert," the speaker suggested. "Oh, no," the mother responded. "He gets along very well with people!" The speaker explained that many introverts do, only they need to do so for less time than extraverts. In fact, the speaker revealed, she herself was an introvert, and yet here she was, voluntarily speaking to a group. Once the mother realized that introversion is not a negative and certainly does not preclude getting along with people, she was ready to accept her son's need for alone time after school.*

Gifted children, and adults too, may need what seems to be an inordinate amount of time alone, and they can use it productively; in fact, they may well be far less productive if they do not have it. Those who gather large amounts of information require more time to assimilate it; those who are more creative require more incubation time. However, the gifted child who enjoys being alone may feel an underlying sense of guilt, secretly believing that something is wrong with her. Is she really alone by preference, or did she somehow send potential friends away? And yet it is so delicious to have quiet time to read, or build, or plan, or dream. Maybe tomorrow she will invite someone over. But she would really rather have this time to herself. Is that all right?

It *is* all right, of course, and she should be reassured about that. Caring adults should support this legitimate need to be alone. Parents must learn to be patient with a child who spends hours apparently doing nothing, playing with blocks, taking things apart, daydreaming seemingly without purpose while chores remain undone. One such child, now a college junior working on a medical research project at a major teaching hospital, contributes his ability to "play" freely with computers as he develops new ways to graph test results. He links this ability to the hours he spent happily alone in a garage filled with treasures, experimenting to learn how things worked—"useless" alone time that fathered his present productivity.

Gifted people who have developed a sense of inner-directedness and a protective attitude toward their own abilities may sense that time

14

spent with other people can hold them back. Their characteristic intensity may keep them at their work for long periods of time, and time spent socializing can seem to them to be wasted. It may take years for them to recognize the value of relaxed time with other people, and they may always struggle for a satisfactory balance between time alone and time with others.

> *Jesse came home from school every day to lose himself in books. For him this was replenishment for his soul; for his mother it was a source of concern. Usually she was silent, reflecting that after an hour or so of reading Jesse was glad to go outside and play, and he was a welcome friend both at school and in his neighborhood. One afternoon, however, she ventured, "Jesse, you're always reading. Why don't you invite a friend over tomorrow?" Looking up in surprise from his book, Jesse said, "But Mom—some of my best friends are books!"*

> *Pondering his words later, she realized that Jesse was right. Through books he communed with authors whose interests and intensity matched his—something he found in no child in the neighborhood. In coming home to read after school, Jesse was finding his own balance.*

Being Alone and Lonely

Adults who watch a child spend time alone often fear that the child is lonely. However, gifted children who are busy with books, collections, music, or other favorite pursuits may not feel lonely. Rather, they are likely to sense that they do not fit in with other children, and it is their response to this feeling of not belonging that adults must monitor and try to guide. The following are some typical behaviors.

Fitting In. Gifted youngsters may respond by trying to fit in. Without guidance, however, these attempts often do not work. Some try, often successfully, to hide their ability by producing mediocre work in school. By the time they complete sixth grade, this can become a pattern—one that becomes difficult to change as time goes on. Girls are especially likely to lower their aspirations during the junior high years in ways that will profoundly affect their futures (Kerr, 1985).

Drawing Attention. Children who wish to belong to the group sometimes use another ploy: attracting attention to themselves. Capitalizing on their differences may be the only way they know to do this. For gifted children, this can mean showing off their knowledge or using sarcasm or condescension with other children—behavior that can cause real rejection.

> *Amanda was a mature second grader with the highly critical nature gifted children sometimes develop. Feeling insecure when she entered a new school, she adopted the role of class police officer, letting her classmates know when they did not measure up to her standards and too often informing the teacher, too, of their failings. What began as her own fear of rejection led quickly enough to actual rebuff from her new classmates. A sympathetic adult can help lead Amanda toward self-understanding, and enhance her social skills.*

Arrogance. In a few cases, a gifted child will display a sense of elitism or arrogance toward others who are not as able. Such an inappropriate response to a feeling of not belonging is more likely to occur in gifted children who do not understand giftedness. Self-acceptance must precede acceptance of others. If parents and teachers cannot help gifted children to understand themselves, the children are hampered in developing self-acceptance, and an *appearance* of arrogance may result. It is in truth a defense, of course; the child is really feeling uncertain of how to relate to others.

Withdrawal. Other gifted children make no attempt to fit in, but withdraw instead. They may spend much time reading, which causes concern for adults. (The negative aspects of reading too much are discussed in Chapter Three.) However, spending large amounts of time reading is not necessarily unhealthy for gifted youngsters. They may use this time as part of their identity search, reading for various role models, identifying with different characters, working out the basic question: Who am I? They may identify with undesirable characters some of the time, but usually this is only temporary.

The Need to Learn Friendship Skills. Children who do not feel part of a group may need to develop social skills. This can be especially difficult for those who were rejected by other children or by parents when they were young, and learned to protect themselves by getting along on their own. It is hard for these children to recognize that they do indeed need others, and that they can take the first steps toward being a friend. However, they can be helped by school gifted programs that devote time to discussion of friendship skills, and by parents who teach the concepts at home. The books listed under "Relationships with Others" in the bibliography are recommended because they portray children learning how to be friends or, in the case of nonfiction, they directly teach about friendship.

Being Alone and Different

Being alone and different—that is, standing apart, being alone because one is different, and quite deliberately being oneself—is something that almost all gifted children will have to accept at some time. They know that they are different, but they may not know, unless a trusted adult tells them, *why* they are different. Knowledge of their giftedness and acceptance of their differences are very important steps in the search for identity.

It takes courage to be oneself, to be different, to like oneself despite the difference. This courage takes time to develop, and it must be done during that stage in life when conformity seems most important. Some gifted children need a great deal of support from parents, teachers, and other adults to move through this period successfully. Their independence and autonomous style must be incorporated into their identities, while at the same time they must learn to get along with others. Fortunately, the worth of standing alone is a common theme in literature, and books can easily be found to promote discussion and guidance.

Relationships with Others

For all of us, one key to emotional well-being is to strike a balance between knowing who we are as individuals and how we fit into our society. This is harder for gifted people, yet they need as much as anyone the nurturing warmth of good relationships.

Gifted children often see things from unusual points of view that others cannot share, and so they are misunderstood. They are even different from other gifted children: people at the upper ranges of intelligence differ from one another far more than do people in the middle and lower ranges.

At the same time, friends are extremely important to most gifted children. The eagerness to communicate with others can show itself very early. One gifted toddler would stand up in his stroller, wave his arms, and crow in delighted greeting whenever he saw another baby being pushed toward him—the very picture of emotional overexcitability. The response was usually a languid glance from the other child, yet until he outgrew his stroller, he continued his enthusiastic greetings.

Parents often worry that their gifted child will have trouble fitting in socially, and they sometimes encourage educational decisions that are detrimental academically in order to favor social development. However, according to Pendarvis, Howley, and Howley (1990), there is

> *"no empirical evidence to support the belief that gifted children are socially incompetent. Rather, it seems that they are socially competent but that some gifted children, because of their preference for activities that engage their intellect, avoid social interaction with age-mates. They may prefer the company of older children or adults; or they may prefer solitary activities, such as reading. These preferences do not indicate emotional problems, nor do they appear to have a detrimental effect on gifted children's emotional well-being"* (p. 234).

It seems, then, that parents should not worry, but should accept the child's pattern of friendship, which may differ from parents' expectations but may suit the child very well.

Parents can play an important role in helping a gifted child accomplish the two most important tasks he faces in building relationships with others: finding peers, and getting along with people of widely varying abilities.

Finding Peers

The special problem gifted children have in finding friends is not that they are loners, but that they need at least a few friends who can function on their level, with whom they can speak as equals. As Kerr (1991) points out, "Whenever verbally gifted students find themselves in conversations with individuals of lower verbal ability, they may be constantly trimming their conversation to fit the group. Particularly tactful verbally gifted students may conscientiously avoid using long words and discussing topics about which their agemates are ignorant. However, years of attempting to relate to people of lesser verbal ability may transform the talkative and friendly gifted student into a sarcastic cynic" (p. 125). Most of all, they need a friend who can listen with understanding.

Therefore, although they differ markedly from one another, their greatest social need is for friendships with other gifted children. Given the opportunity, gifted children may choose friends of their own mental age, rather than their own chronological age. Without such friendships, they may shrivel emotionally and intellectually; with them, they can thrive.

Getting along with others, then, means first finding appropriate others. The stratified grading arrangement in most schools makes it difficult for gifted children to find one another unless special arrangements are made by their parents or teachers. A gifted child may need to belong to several different groups, not necessarily of her own age, that will challenge her intellectually and introduce her to people with whom she can share her passionate interests.

This can be demanding and exhausting for parents. For a junior high student to join an adult astronomy group, his mother drove him to weekly meetings at a planetarium an hour away, driving home between one and two in the morning. Another family drove a daughter five hours each way, every other week for two years, to allow her to play in a university youth symphony. These parents understood their children's need to share their interests with other youth, and they were willing to sacrifice in providing for that need.

Other Children

Getting along with others also means getting along with those who don't share, let alone understand or respect, one's abilities and interests. In classrooms where there are only one or two gifted students, the gifted child is likely to alienate his classmates because he can do schoolwork so easily.

A subtler cause of resentment may be the intense interest gifted children have in topics that do not interest their classmates. If they talk too long about their shell collections, or use words that are too big, they can bore and finally turn away other students without understanding why. A lack of interest in seashells can quickly become a lack of interest in Tim, who talks about seashells all the time. And even before this happens, Tim may feel that it has happened—that the rejection of seashells is a rejection of him.

Gifted children are usually extremely sensitive, and remarks that most children toss off and forget can truly hurt them. They do not understand how lightly other children may make a cruel remark, and others have no idea how long and deeply the gifted child may brood over what is said. But the gifted child, who may have been as eager for friends as the baby in the stroller, begins to build a wall of defense, making it even harder to develop friendships.

Moreover, team sports are not interesting to some gifted children, and if they've been academically accelerated, their physical coordination doesn't match that of their classmates. In most schools, a lukewarm attitude toward team sports or lack of athletic ability can be another wedge between gifted children and their peers.

So gifted children can begin to feel rejected for a variety of reasons. And since giftedness does not necessarily include social maturity, these youngsters react in the same ways that most children do to feelings of rejection: they withdraw or act out. Either choice brings further rejection, and a downward cycle begins.

To reverse this cycle, children must take several steps that require maturity as well as adult guidance: they must develop empathy with those who are not as quick as they are, they must learn to cope with being misunderstood and teased, and they must recognize and modify the behavior that leads to rejection and teasing—all of this while retaining their own identities.

Parents and Teachers

Getting along with peers is the most obvious problem of getting along with others; however, gifted children can find themselves in other situations that may cause emotional problems, both at home and at school. These youngsters are vulnerable, and the attitudes they perceive in significant adults can make a tremendous difference in their attitudes toward themselves and their giftedness.

Parents. Parents who accept their child's giftedness may be relieved to have the school confirm what they have suspected, especially if a suitable program is available, and they may join other parents to support programs for the gifted students in the community.

Undeniably, parenting a gifted child properly places an extra strain on the parents' time, energy, and money. If parents have enough of these resources, their support can make all the difference. In some cases, memories of their own gifted childhoods can add richly to the support they offer to their child. If a gifted child has difficulty in finding peers, his parents may be his best friends for a time.

A child in such a family sees that giftedness is worthy of the effort needed to develop it. But there's a fine line between encouragement and pressure.

Scott has studied piano for six years and his teacher is pleased with his progress. When he enters ninth grade, however, homework, soccer, and the ski team will all demand more time, and he is considering dropping piano lessons. His parents are proud of his musical talent, which they believe is greater than his athletic ability, yet if they urge him to continue with piano, are they pressuring him to work beyond his endurance? Or are they encouraging him to develop a talent that could be a satisfying source of pleasure, relaxation and artistic expression throughout his adulthood? To find an answer they must take time for careful discussion with Scott—discussion which includes plenty of listening to Scott's ideas and reassures him of their support.

By contrast, some parents want their child to be just like everyone else, and they try to ignore the evidence that she is gifted. Such parents may refuse to place their child in a gifted program, preferring to believe that the school has made a mistake. Or parents may acknowledge signs of giftedness in their child but still refuse appropriate educational programs, in the hope that avoiding a special program will help the child to be "normal."

Either of these responses amounts to rejection of the child as she is, and insistence that she be someone else. It can also mean failure to provide opportunities for enrichment or college. The effect on the child's life can be devastating. Giftedness may appear to some to be a "high-class problem," but parents of gifted children know that it is also exhausting, sometimes frightening, and always challenging. As awareness of giftedness grows, more books for parents are published. One in particular that helps parents meet the emotional needs of their gifted children is *Guiding the Gifted Child* by Webb, Meckstroth, and Tolan (1982). This seminal book has been significantly updated in a 1993 article by Webb.

Teachers. Gifted children can make themselves unpopular with teachers, especially with those who do not know about or are not sympathetic to the special characteristics and needs of the gifted. One middle-aged woman still recalls with an inner cringe the scorn in her second-grade teacher's voice when she foolishly gave an answer from a few pages beyond the assigned reading. "You read ahead!" the teacher accused. She had, but she hadn't learned yet that in some classrooms, it is necessary to conceal such out-of-bounds curiosity.

Teachers whose energies are stretched as they try to meet the needs of a wide range of students may not always appreciate bright children who come up with many creative responses instead of the one "right" answer. Such students can see to the heart of a lesson plan while the teacher slowly presents it to the rest of the class, and their enthusiasm—or lack of tact—makes it hard for them to keep their insights to themselves.

Consider the fifth grader who announced that the book the class had read was so simple it would be easy to write a sequel. He then proceeded, on the spot, to outline a very plausible plot, making both the original and the sequel sound laughably trivial. How could a teacher lead a serious discussion after that? The group laughed, of course, and the teacher wisely waited until everyone had enjoyed his humor.

Even teachers who seek out and encourage gifted students find them frustrating at times. An exasperated teacher told a gifted fourth grader's mother after a field trip, "He was at my elbow talking the whole day. I wanted to listen because everything he says is worth hearing, but I have to listen to the others, too!"

Many gifted children are analytic thinkers, highly critical of the status quo and only too willing to express an opinion about how things are being run. It is especially important for them to learn early how and when to question authority, and how effective politeness and respect can be. Teachers have the potential to be a great influence, positively or negatively, on gifted children. *Guiding the Gifted Child* can help educators as well as parents better understand the emotional characteristics and needs of these children.

The gifted child is responsible for getting along with other children, but her parents and teachers are responsible for her relationships with *them*. If the adults around her can enjoy her giftedness yet also can understand—and gently modify—the negative traits that can go along with giftedness, her self-acceptance and ability to get along with others will be greatly enhanced.

Using Abilities

Humanistic psychologist Abraham Maslow (1962) developed a framework he called the hierarchy of needs, which is especially relevant in understanding gifted people. Maslow arranged human needs into five levels, from those so basic that life depends on them to those so advanced that only a few can feel and meet them. He makes the point that these needs must be met in a certain order: until the lowest ones are met, we are not free even to sense the higher ones.

Physiological needs are the most fundamental. Safety and security needs come next. Only if we feel that we are safe and secure can we experience the next needs, belonging and love. When we are sure that we belong and are loved, we are ready to sense the need for self-esteem. Those who achieve a healthy self-esteem are able to move to the highest level of need, self-actualization, the full use of one's resources and the fulfillment of potential.

Gifted children, as already mentioned, are especially prone to feelings of not belonging. After all, they're "different," and a sense of fitting in and being appreciated can be hard to come by. Self-esteem can also be a problem. Yet if, despite obstacles, the needs at these levels are met, the gifted person may still have great difficulty with self-actualization, the full use of abilities—a paradox, since in the gifted person the potential for self-actualization is so great. These issues have a profound impact on the gifted child's ability to lead a satisfying life as an adult. The foundations for self-actualization must be laid in childhood.

In reaching toward full use of their abilities, gifted students may find that some of their personal characteristics can paralyze them, making progress difficult. The following are some barriers that may hinder them.

Reluctance to Take Risks

To become a self-actualized adult, the high-ability child must make decisions that enable him to develop his potential. Often, especially among young children, the child is not aware that he is making life-shaping decisions. But choices made at an early age, seemingly minor at the time, have a cumulative effect on how well-prepared a person will be to take advantage of opportunities in his college years and beyond.

A junior high boy attending a weekend statewide church youth meeting felt out of place and wanted to leave early. A counselor spent an hour talking with him about his concerns and finally persuaded him to stay through the weekend. By the next day, he was comfortable enough to volunteer for a minor position in the organization.

After a year of involvement at the state level, he was chosen to attend a national meeting, where he was selected to serve on the national council. Holding leadership positions at two annual meetings gave him the confidence and experience to win a scholarship for a summer program in Japan before his senior year in high school. This experience helped him gain a merit scholarship at a highly-ranked university.

Although much of this might have happened in any case, he still traces his rich experiences to a Saturday afternoon in junior high when he was persuaded to see the weekend through, and he still makes risk-taking decisions with that example in mind. These decisions have kept options open for him and have put him in a position to become a self-actualized adult.

Whether or not to use all of one's potential becomes an issue early in the educational process. Gifted children often feel society's ambivalence toward those of high intellectual ability, and they may decide to understate their ability in order to get along (Pendarvis, 1991). The second grader who read ahead was faced with a decision: would she read ahead again? The fifth grader who becomes aware that she answers too many questions in class and begins rationing how many she will answer per day is dealing with this issue, although she does not see it that way. The junior high student who lets his grades slide because fitting into a social group is more important is facing decisions that ultimately affect self-actualization. All of these children are making choices based on their reluctance to take the risk of social failure, giving little or no thought to the long-range consequences.

Perfectionism

A related problem is perfectionism, another common characteristic of gifted people. Perfectionists have unrealistically high standards for their performance and may feel worthless if they do not meet these standards. Impelled by their own inner drive more often than by over-ambitious parents, they equate flawless performance with self-worth, and they're afraid to attempt a task that they might not perform well from the start. Their perfectionism puts them under severe stress.

Eventually they may try only those activities they know they will do well. To counteract perfectionism and learn to risk, they must see that failure is not disastrous. They must think of themselves not as perfect, but as experimenters.

> *Lisa has always been a superb student, but now in the eleventh grade she has to work harder than she has in the past to maintain her A average. She spends extra hours on her homework, leaving little time for social activities. She's become tense and has frequent headaches. The debate coach has been looking forward to Lisa's joining the team this year, but now Lisa is reluctant: she's never spoken in public and isn't sure how she'll do. If she doesn't join the team, she'll be narrowing her experiences when she should be broadening her outlook and options. If she joins, she probably will make valuable mistakes, and she can learn that life goes on after a defeat. And having to manage her time more carefully will make her establish priorities. She may see that she is valuable to the team, even when she doesn't win.*

One possible cause of perfectionism offered by Kerr (1991) is an inborn tendency in the child's personality. Kerr's statement is a relief to parents who wonder if they are responsible and a concern to parents who try to help their child achieve a better perspective. A music teacher relates this story:

> *One of my most talented violin students tied himself up in knots over studying, staying up till midnight to finish homework he said none of the other sixth graders ever did. He felt extraordinarily pushed at science fair time and said the pressure was just too much, but he placed second in his entire middle school! His parents worried about balancing violin enrichment for this gifted musician with his maniacal study habits.*

Other causes listed by Kerr are the child's unawareness of her giftedness, which may lead her to believe that her superior performance is based entirely on her own efforts; and overemphasis by parents or schools on systems of rewards or "points" for achievement, rather than on doing well for the pure pleasure of it.

Bibliotherapy is one way to break the perfectionist habit, according to Adderholdt-Elliott (1991), who recommends two nonfiction titles, *Gifted Kids Survival Guide* and *Perfectionism: What's Bad about Being Too Good?* These books are listed here in Chapter Eight, along with many fiction titles for use with gifted youngsters. In addition,

Chapter Four offers a broader conception of bibliotherapy than that intended by many writers, and methods for using this model with gifted children are thoroughly discussed.

Underachievement

Another problem directly related to the full use of ability is underachievement, which has several possible causes. One is children's fear of rejection for being out of step because of their intelligence. They can learn fairly early to hide their abilities in order to conform. After several years of not performing, they may miss some basic skills, so that they are not able to perform at all. Suspecting that they cannot do what is asked, they resist trying.

There are other, and far more complex, reasons for underachievement. For more information on this difficult problem, see Kerr (1991), Richert (1991), Rimm (1986, 1991), and Whitmore (1980).

Multipotentiality

According to Kerr (1991), multipotentiality first shows up in elementary school, when students who perform well in many or all school subjects have great difficulty choosing a topic from several options, and then have trouble finishing a project.

This pattern of excellence in school subjects combined with difficulty in making choices and following through continues through junior high. In senior high, multipotential students may have problems with college and career decisions, as well as "high flat profiles" on aptitude and interest tests. These profiles lack the peaks and valleys of students who display areas of strength and weakness to guide them in life decisions, and they lead adults to make the obvious but unhelpful statement, "You can do anything you want to do!"

"Multipotentiality is most commonly a concern of students with moderately high IQs (120-140), those who are academically talented, and those who have two or more outstanding but very different abilities such as violin virtuosity and mathematics precocity" (Kerr, 1990). Choosing among areas that offer equal promise of different success experiences is surely painful, but one lifetime does not provide time for excellence in several demanding fields of endeavor.

If these students resist the narrowing of their activities which is required in order to make a choice, they jeopardize their chances of achieving significantly in any area. The result can be poor career decision-making and, ultimately, dissatisfaction with career choice.

Low External Expectations

Finally, gifted youngsters may fail to make full use of their abilities because they are never given a chance to appreciate their own potential. A gifted student in a typical classroom can make *A*s without much effort, and both the student and his parents may believe that the grade means the student is doing as well as he can. In fact, the grade may mean only that the student has met the highest expectations set by that teacher or has performed at the top of what may be an average class.

Lack of Appropriate Internal Expectations

Earning the best grade available does not necessarily equate with doing the best work a gifted student is capable of doing, but what that "best" would be is never pointed out to some students. Since high grades and other measures of external expectations are not a reliable guide, it is desirable for a gifted student at an early age to learn to assess his or her own potential and then to be the judge of whether it has been realized. This is a complex process, requiring guidance from adults who recognize high ability, even if latent. With such guidance, the student can learn to recognize the feeling—the joy—of doing well for its own sake.

Why is it important that a gifted person use all his resources? One answer, of course, is that we need all the talent we have available to help us solve the world's problems. For the gifted individual, it is more to the point to recognize that he will simply be happier and more satisfied—life will be much more interesting—if he learns to understand and manage his intensity and creativity. Little research has been done on the gifted adult, so we have no clear idea of the long-term impact of not making full use of one's abilities. But Maslow's hierarchy, affirming that self-esteem and self-actualization are needs, points up the importance of being accepted, useful, valued, and free to use whatever talent one has.

To do this the gifted child must identify his talents, accept them, and then make a decision about whether to use them or not. The first steps in this decision can be made in the early elementary years. At this point the child begins to see some of the disadvantages of being gifted, some of the conflicts it brings him. He may also run into barriers, external limitations like the absence of educational opportunities, and make a decision (consciously or not) about how hard he will work to overcome them.

Whether a gifted child will use her abilities depends to a large extent on how successfully she establishes her identity, learns to be alone, and learns to get along with peers, family, and teachers. This is the crux of the matter: Can this person, who has the potential to become a self-actualized, fully-functioning and contributing member of society, content with herself and giving to those around her—can this person actually do it? How can we guide our gifted children to grow up happy with themselves and prepared to give to others?

How Books Can Help

Books can help us guide the emotional development of our gifted children far more than intellectual discussion precisely because stories touch the emotions. A skillful author can make us care about characters who have the same problems presented in this chapter. If a book can "hook" a child emotionally, he may be far more receptive to the ideas than if they are presented in a lecture by a concerned adult.

A child who is unwilling or unable to talk about things that are bothering him, or perhaps even to admit them to himself, often can identify with a character in a book strongly enough to experience an emotional release, a catharsis (*"He's* bored in school, too!"). He can also acquire some insights into his own situation. This is the process—often called bibliotherapy—which is discussed in detail in Chapter Four.

References

Adderholdt-Elliott, Miriam. (1991). Perfectionism and the gifted adolescent. In Marlene Bireley and Judy Genshaft (Eds.), *Understanding the gifted adolescent: Educational, developmental, and multicultural issues* (pp. 65-73). New York: Teachers College Press.

Adderholdt-Elliott, Miriam. (1987). *Perfectionism: What's bad about being too good.* Minneapolis: Free Spirit.

Buescher, Thomas M. (1985, September). A framework for understanding the social and emotional development of gifted and talented adolescents. *Roeper Review, 8,* 10-15.

Delisle, James and Judy Galbraith. (1987). *The gifted kids survival guide II.* Minneapolis: Free Spirit.

Frey, Diane E. (1991). Psychosocial needs of the gifted adolescent. In Marlene Bireley and Judy Genshaft (Eds.), *Understanding the gifted adolescent: Educational, developmental, and multicultural issues* (pp.35-49). New York: Teachers College Press.

Galbraith, Judy. (1983). *The gifted kids survival guide (for ages 11-18).* Minneapolis: Free Spirit.

Galbraith, Judy. (1984). *The gifted kids survival guide (for ages 10 and under).* Minneapolis: Free Spirit.

Kerr, Barbara A. (1985). *Smart girls, gifted women.* Columbus: Ohio Psychology Publishing Co.

Kerr, Barbara A. (1990). Career planning for gifted and talented youth. In Berger, S. (Ed.), *Flyer files on gifted students.* Reston, VA: ERIC Clearinghouse on Handicapped and Gifted Children.

Kerr, Barbara. (1991). *A handbook for counseling the gifted and talented.* Alexandria: American Association for Counseling and Development.

Maslow, Abraham. (1962). *Toward a psychology of being.* Princeton: VanNostrand.

Pendarvis, Edwina D., Howley, Aimee A., & Howley, Craig B. (1990). *The abilities of gifted children.* Englewood Cliffs, NJ: Prentice Hall.

Piechowski, Michael M. (1991). Emotional development and emotional giftedness. In Nicholas Colangelo and Gary A. Davis (Eds.), *Handbook of gifted education* (pp. 285-306). Boston: Allyn and Bacon.

Richert, E. Susanne. (1991) Patterns of underachievement among gifted students. In Marlene Bireley and Judy Genshaft (Eds.), *Understanding the gifted adolescent: Educational, developmental, and multicultural issues* (pp. 139-162). New York: Teachers College Press.

Rimm, Sylvia. *(1986). Underachievement syndrome: Causes and cures.* Watertown, Wis.: Apple Publishing Co.

Rimm, Sylvia. (1991). Underachievement and superachievement: Flip sides of the same psychological coin. In Nicholas Colangelo and Gary A. Davis (Eds.), *Handbook of gifted education* (pp. 328-343). Boston: Allyn and Bacon.

Smutny, Joan Franklin, Kathleen Veenker, and Stephen Veenker. (1989). *Your gifted child: How to recognize and develop the special talents in your child from birth to age seven.* New York: Facts on File.

Terrassier, Jean-Charles. (1985). Dyssynchrony—uneven development. In Joan Freeman (Ed.), *The psychology of gifted children: Perspectives on development and education* (pp. 254-274). New York: John Wiley.

Webb, James T. (1993). Nurturing social-emotional development of gifted children. In K. A. Heller, F. J. Monks, and A. H. Passow (Eds.), *International handbook of research and development of giftedness and talent* (pp. 525-538). Oxford: Pergamon Press.

Webb, James T., Meckstroth, Elizabeth A., & Tolan, Stephanie S. (1982). *Guiding the gifted child: A practical source for parents and teachers*. Dayton: Ohio Psychology Press.

Whitmore, Joanne Rand. (1980). *Giftedness, conflict, and underachievement*. Boston: Allyn and Bacon.

CHAPTER
TWO

The Mind of the Child: Intellectual Development

T he first edition of this book went to press in 1987, the year Diane Ravitch and Chester E. Finn, Jr. published *What Do Our 17-Year-Olds Know? A Report on the First National Assessment of History and Literature*. The increasing awareness of crisis in our educational system has generated a storm of studies, programs, efforts to reform and restructure the schools—and priority setting and budget cuts.

With no clear resolutions in sight, any consideration of the intellectual needs of high potential youngsters must be set within the context of the world in which they live and go to school. What do these children need for optimum intellectual development? What obstacles face teachers and school administrations as they try to meet those needs? How can parents identify gaps and compensate for them at home? And what is the role of books and reading?

The Need for Intellectual Development

Much more is known about the intellectual development of bright and gifted children than about their emotional development, and much has been done to help them meet their intellectual potential. In many school districts, tests and inventories help determine IQs and learning characteristics. Universities throughout the country have developed programs to prepare teachers in gifted education. Curricula designed to tap the reasoning powers of high potential students appear in professional journals. Programs like Future Problem Solving and Odyssey of the Mind have sprung up to fill extracurricular time.

Still, our high-potential students face increasing odds as they attempt to find their place in the sun. According to the first national report on the education of gifted children since 1972, written with a focus on anti-intellectualism in American society, these students receive mixed messages from the world around them (Office of Educational Research and Improvement, 1993). "As a culture, we admire and reward the brilliant, creative mind after it has invented something practical or produced tangible results. Yet we are not inclined to support those who want to pursue an artistic or intellectual life, and we find ways of discouraging those who wish to do so ... [Responding to this discouragement] students say they want to do well, but not exceptionally well, because it is more important to be accepted by the 'in crowd (which) is not the brain crowd'" (p. 13). Regardless of their inborn motivation, our most able students may need our encouragement to resist the cultural message.

The highly-able child, like other children, is a blend of emotions and intellect—with artistic, physical, social, and spiritual dimensions. Because the intellectual aspect stands out (as does the physical with athletes), school programming for these students has typically aimed at meeting intellectual needs. If, in the past, gifted programs erred in ignoring other facets of children's lives, in the last decade much has been done to correct this. This book is part of that attempt, taking the approach that intellectual development is just one part of the total person.

And yet intellectual development is an emotional need for some intellectually gifted people, especially the highly gifted. In fact, Webb (1992) states that "profoundly gifted children are ones for whom intellectual stimulation and/or creative expression are clearly emotional needs that may appear to be as intense as the physiological needs of hunger or thirst" (p. 12). For them, meeting intellectual needs is not a purely intellectual task: there is deep feeling behind it. Adults who seek to promote the intellectual development of their children will be more effective if they acknowledge and reinforce this driving need to learn.

To have curiosity satisfied, to experience a wealth of diversity in ideas, places, and people, to explore all of the world and find a place in it—all of this is truly a *survival issue* for these youngsters. They must be able to grow, to learn, to develop their capacities, or they will wither intellectually and emotionally.

Intellectual Needs as Emotional Needs

A bright or gifted child has extraordinary abilities, each accompanied by needs: a need for the ability to be developed and used, and a need for the child possessing it to become creative and eventually able to produce something of value to himself or others. For unusually talented people, the impetus is not merely that where there is an ability, it is best to develop it. Rather, an intellectually gifted child will not be happy or complete, and certainly not self-actualized, until he is using his intellectual ability at a level approaching his full capacity.

Imagine the frustration of an athlete who isn't allowed to run, jump, move. This gives some inkling of the frustration of a bright child denied the chance to challenge her mind. Underachieving gifted students may not display such restlessness, but this doesn't mean they don't need intellectual stimulation.

It is important that parents and teachers see intellectual development as a requirement for these children, and not merely an interest, a flair, or a phase they will outgrow. A painting student is quoted (Piechowski, 1979) as saying, "I have a hard time not painting. I paint about 10 hours a day. Painting is my life." Another student says simply, "I read because I can't help it." Gifted adults who relax by playing a musical instrument, reading in a foreign language, or experimenting with computer programming are expressing the same drive for mental stimulation. These activities are not work for them; they are paths to being fully alive.

Recognizing intellectual development as a need can help parents cope with inevitable frustration caused by a child who reads or tinkers or practices an instrument for "too many" hours per day. It can help teachers find patience when a child insists on working endlessly on a project or report, threatening to hold up the progress of the rest of the class.

Intellectual Overexcitability

Another way of thinking about the drive to understand comes from Kazimierz Dabrowski's intriguing ideas about developmental potential, which were introduced in Chapter One. Piechowski's work with Dabrowski's concept of intellectual overexcitablity can help adults appreciate not only the need for intellectual development, but also the strength of feeling behind it.

In 1979, Piechowski listed characteristics of intellectual overexcitability that may be familiar to those who deal with gifted youngsters: probing questions, problem solving, curiosity, concentration, capacity for sustained intellectual effort, voracious reading and starting on difficult books at a young age, a wide variety of interests, theoretical thinking (thinking about thinking, moral thinking, development of a hierarchy of values), independence of thought (often expressed in criticism), and processes of self-monitoring and self-evaluation. All of these characteristics are part of the drive to learn, to know, to understand.

Piechowski (1979) also states that intellectual overexcitability has more to do with "striving for understanding, probing the unknown and love of truth than with learning per se and academic achievement" (p. 34). More recently, he describes it as "an avidity for knowledge and the search for truth—expressed as discovery, questioning, and love of ideas and theoretical analysis" (1991, p. 287).

It is this extra sense of urgency about knowing that underlies the need of some gifted children for intellectual development, that causes them to say, "I read because I can't help it."

Like emotional overexcitability, intellectual overexcitability is not always understood or valued by others, but it contributes to the development of gifted individuals. Reading and book discussion are natural avenues of furthering their self-understanding.

"Can you tell the readers how awful it feels when you have to go for two days without reading?" said one young man when he knew I was writing this book. A 19-year-old German student described why he was drawn toward a career in university teaching: "When I read about culture, then I am happy!" Both of these young men exhibit the unusual intellectual intensity Piechowski describes.

Not everyone who has the potential for high intellectual achievement also possesses a passionate interest in intellectual pursuits. For those who do have such strong interests, however, learning about the work of Dabrowski and Piechowski often brings a reassuring shock of self-recognition.

The Child in Charge

Some bright children seem to lose touch with their drive to understand. Although as preschoolers they may have been as eager to learn as Steven, who was described in the Introduction, by the middle elementary grades their intellectual curiosity appears to be dulled and they are willing to settle for half-hearted efforts in school. What makes the difference between those who gradually reject and those who continue to be nourished by the pleasures of learning?

Just as gifted children must achieve a sense of identity that incorporates their unusual abilities, so must they recognize early that the drive to understand is part of who they are (Halsted, in press). At the preschool and primary levels, parents and teachers should help talented children know this about themselves: that learning is a source of pleasure for them. The knowledge that they enjoy learning should be integrated into their developing self-concepts.

Whatever steps adults take to satisfy the child's curiosity and enrich her experience, their underlying attitude that learning is important—for its own sake and to the child—is critical, and must gradually be adopted by the child. Ultimately, the responsibility for keeping curiosity both satisfied and piqued must shift to the child, as she makes decisions that enable her to continue learning. The knowledge that she *needs* to learn and that it is up to her to meet that need is part of her survival kit.

This largely intellectual challenge can be added to the four emotional needs presented in the first chapter. For satisfactory development, then, gifted and talented children must accomplish the following five tasks as they grow up:

- Achieve a sense of identity which includes their giftedness
- Understand and make positive use of their need for time alone
- Learn to get along with others of all ability levels
- Determine how to make use of their abilities
- Acknowledge and learn how to satisfy their drive to understand

Because reading and talking about books can help children cope with these five broad developmental tasks, many books that show characters dealing with these tasks are recommended in the Bibliography, Chapter Eight, in this book. But for now, we will focus specifically on the intellectual characteristics of gifted students and on necessary conditions for their optimal development.

Optimal Intellectual Development

Parents may notice signs of high ability in very young children, but if they are inexperienced observers, it may be some time before they grasp the meaning of these behaviors. A long list of such traits is provided by Smutny, Veenker, and Veenker (1989). Here are a few that relate to verbal development and reading:

- Likes to play with words
- Uses proper grammar and structure earlier than age-mates
- Uses rich language, with methaphor and analogy
- Asks about new words, learns and practices them
- Learns to read without instruction before starting school
- Makes up stories and songs

Once these children start school, it becomes clear that their abilities set them apart from their classmates. Because they have different abilities, they learn differently—not only more and faster, but also "in different modes and at greater depth"(Kerr, 1991, p. 23). Kerr also points out that "capable learners learn most effectively when appropriately challenged and tend to become bored and frustrated when the *pace* and *complexity* of material is below their ability" (p. 22, emphasis mine).

Their intellectual characteristics, then, dictate their intellectual needs. What are other needs related to their intellectual ability?

They need to be with others of their own ability level. Grouping gifted children together is controversial, but research indicates that it provides the optimum learning situation for them. Kerr (1991) cites research concluding that "ability grouping has minimal effects, either positive or negative, on the achievement of average or below-average students. Substantial evidence shows, however, that ability grouping has a positive effect on the achievement of gifted students" (p. 23).

In addition, they need teaching techniques that rely on the higher levels of thinking (Amidon, 1991), that is, on analysis, synthesis, and evaluation, rather than primarily on knowledge, comprehension, and application. Using the higher levels of thinking as a method of talking about books is discussed in Chapter Five.

If just these four general intellectual needs—

- pace of learning
- complexity of material
- being with other bright learners
- higher levels of thinking—

are considered, we can see how books and book discussion can meet the special needs of bright and gifted children. A reader can choose her own pace of reading; books are available at every degree of complexity; a discussion group can bring together learners of like ability (just two, a child and an adult, are enough); and the questions can elicit higher levels of thinking.

There are many lists that describe the intellectual characteristics of gifted children at all ages. These lists are typically used in conjunction with intelligence and achievement test scores to determine eligibility for school gifted programs. They offer more than that, however, if the intellectual characteristics are used as a springboard for identifying the intellectual needs they imply.

The following is a compilation of three of these recent lists (Clark, 1992; Ehrlich, 1985; Webb, Meckstroth, and Tolan, 1982). The listing here eliminates overlap and groups intellectual characteristics of gifted youngsters into three categories: verbal, thought-processing, and performance characteristics.

After each list of characteristics is a list of related intellectual needs, derived in part from Clark's examples of problems that may appear in work patterns or in getting along with others if the needs are not met.

Verbal Characteristics and Needs

Gifted children in general display the following verbal characteristics:

- They have a large vocabulary and are able to use advanced terminology correctly.

- They read early and may be self-taught; they read enthusiastically and widely, often above grade level; they select reading material purposefully and enjoy challenging books.

- They understand language subtleties and use language for humor.

- They write words and sentences early, and they produce superior creative writing (poetry, stories, plays).

- They display verbal ability in self-expression, choice of colorful and descriptive phrasing, and ease in learning a second language.

To challenge verbal abilities, gifted students need to do the following:

- Use their full vocabulary and develop it further with intellectual peers.

- Read books at an appropriate intellectual and emotional level.

- Be introduced to books that represent a variety of literary conventions and styles and that use language gracefully.

- Express ideas verbally and in depth by writing or speaking with others who challenge and thus refine their views and concepts.

Thought-Processing Characteristics and Needs

As a group, gifted children display the following traits in thought processing:

- They enjoy experimenting and can generate original ideas and solutions.

- They give evidence of divergent thinking.

- They accept open-ended situations and questions at an early age and do not require immediate solutions; they can accept ambiguity.

- They enjoy complexity and may try to create it, for example, by adding rules to games.

- They have unusual power to process information, using logic, abstract thinking and symbolic thought.

- They show flexibility of thought, seeking alternatives; they are able to see all sides of an issue.

- They synthesize well, seeing relationships others miss; they transfer past learning to new situations and draw generalizations.

To develop thought-processing potential, gifted students need to do the following:

- Consider alternatives and possible consequences of choices in an accepting environment.

- Be exposed to a great variety of vicarious experiences.

- Test new ideas without required conclusions or products.

- Discuss ideas with intellectual peers.

- Be exposed to many ideas at different levels.

- Take plenty of time for incubation of ideas.

Performance Characteristics and Needs

The following performance patterns are characteristic of gifted children:

- They show great curiosity and unusual persistence in efforts to gain answers.

- They have a wide range of interests and information.

- They comprehend new concepts rapidly at an advanced level; they have little or no need for drill.

- They display creativity and imagination, enjoy fantasies and science fiction, may have an imaginary playmate in their preschool years, can develop a variety of solutions to problems, and generate original ideas.

- They are persistent and goal-directed; they have a long attention span and may want to spend more than the time allotted to complete a project.

- They show unusual intensity regarding school projects, political or environmental issues, religion, world events, intellectual inquiry into an area of special interest, interpersonal relationships, and abstract values.

To enhance performance characteristics, gifted students need to do the following:

- Have curiosity met with exposure to varying styles of life, values, and approaches to problems.

- Be exposed to new information and new issues.

- Be presented with material at their own rate of learning.

- Develop skills in creative thinking and problem solving.

- Pursue interests beyond the time desired by most students.

- Learn skills for dealing with intensity by exploring ways by which others cope with it.

Reading such a list of ideal conditions should not lull us into the comfortable assumption that all of our bright and gifted children are having these experiences at school. While many of them are, it is safe to assume (since it is estimated that only half of our gifted children are identified) that most are not, and the programs now in place are threatened by budget cuts. What stands between our brightest children and the full realization of their potential?

Obstacles in the Way

Most educators want to do all they can to meet the educational needs of every student, and in recent years awareness has grown that this includes the special needs of gifted children. However, regardless of their desire to provide an appropriate educational environment for everyone, teachers and administrators are thwarted by economic and social conditions over which local schools have little control. Above average students are often the losers.

Economic Barriers

One result of the recession of the early 1990s was a weakening of resolve to provide special programs for gifted students. Since programs for mentally and physically handicapped youngsters are mandated by federal and state governments, they cannot be cut, leaving gifted programs open and vulnerable as one of the few ways to reduce costs. Parents and teachers have seen gifted programs trimmed or eliminated as state aid designated for them is frozen or dropped entirely. Sometimes the children who are highly able but not identified as gifted suffer the most from budget cutting and increased class size (Nordheimer, 1992).

The outlook is not good for the early reinstatement of this lost support, since the level of funding for gifted programs varies with political and educational trends. Interest and funding surged after Sputnik, when the nation needed scientists who would help us compete in space exploration. The urge to be competitive is still paramount, but in the 1990s the perceived need is different: now we lack a workforce with basic technological skills, and money can be expected to flow in that direction for the near future.

Parents who watch gifted children move rapidly through their school years during a time of financial retrenchment occasionally resort to legal action, as they attempt to force school systems to meet their children's special needs. To help such parents save both time and money, Karnes and Marquardt (1991a) discuss the advantages of me-

41

diation and due process over litigation. A companion volume (1991b) presents parents' stories of their efforts to use the legal system to ensure appropriate education for their youngsters.

Social Conditions

Alarming statistics revealing disturbing social trends in our children's lives and schooling are reported so relentlessly that we may become numb to them. Without question, children's potential for intellectual development is affected by divorce, poverty, malnutrition, a lack of health care, struggling single parents, frazzled parents in two-income families, and other social problems.

In her book, *Endangered Minds: Why Our Children Don't Think* (1990), Jane M. Healy looks behind these factors to two others that also characterize our children's world: the rapid pace of living and reliance on instant sensory gratification. She expresses deep concern that the stresses and deprivations our children experience are actually changing their brains and capacity for sustained analytical thought.

Citing research into physical changes that occur in the brain as a result of learning, Healy suggests that our processing of language is an important part of the development of our ability to think. It is at risk if appropriate language experiences are not available—and reinforced through practice—at the optimum time in the brain's development. Among her concerns is the interplay between the developing brain and reading.

With this in mind, let's look at how two major contemporary forces, television and video games, affect our children's reading and thinking—and the implications for their intellectual growth.

Television and Video Games

Without even considering the questionable *content* of many television programs, two compelling objections are immediately obvious to many experts: watching television is passive; and it steals time in which a child could be active. By contrast, reading is active, requiring the brain's involvement to interact with the words and to create the pictures that television provides for us.

Healy (1990) quotes a personal communication from M. Russell Harter, who is researching reading and the developing brain at the University of North Carolina: "Reading triggers certain experiences in the brain that just don't happen if you don't read. I think our brains are designed to symbolize and represent information in the way that we call language. If we don't exercise it, we lose it. Television, even *Sesame Street*, is not very symbolic. It makes things very tangible and easy to understand, but reading is the kind of exercise that causes the brain to develop differently because it uses that symbolic capability" (p. 208).

Jerre Levy, a biopsychologist at the University of Chicago, states, "The main thing that worries me about TV is not even its intellectual level. To the extent that children commit time looking at TV, they're not spending time reading. When a child reads a novel, he has to self-create whole scenarios, he has to create images of who these people are, what their emotions are, what their tones of voice are, what the environment looks like, what the feeling of this environment is. These self-created scenarios are important, and television leaves no room for that creative process. I think brains are designed to meet cognitive challenges. It's just like muscles; if you don't exercise them they wither. If you don't exercise brains, they wither" (Healy, 1990, p. 214).

Reading is not the only activity preferable to watching television. Vivian Paley, teacher of young children at the University of Chicago Laboratory Schools, points out that "none of the [television] programming—simply by virtue of what the medium is—suits the way a child learns. The child is simply not a passive creature. If you leave a child just sitting alone in his room with his toys, there's an active monologue going on there . . . The more opportunities for the child to play, and to play with other children, the better—and also to have open-ended conversations between parents and children about everything that's on a child's mind. And of course to be read to, just to be read to from all the wonderful prose and poetry that is available for children" (Obermiller, 1989, p. 16).

The lack of reading skills, and of the critical and analytical thinking they empower, should be recognized as a danger to our nation equal to a lack of technological skills, but more insidious. "The survival of our kind of democracy requires the ... active mind that the print culture produces and that [the] television spectator habit does not," according to Librarian of Congress James H. Billington (1990). "The controlling element of the electronic culture is television ... and this represents a threat of passivity that can block the effective functioning of an active citizenry that our democrary requires. Both our educational and political institutions and traditions are imperiled over the long run."

Video games demand more participation than television, but parents are justifiably uneasy about them nevertheless. Nintendo alone dominates children's play, with a Nintendo set in nearly one third of the nation's homes (Winn, 1991). The activity required is narrowly focused and without creativity, and Winn worries that "children accustomed to the quick gratifications of video games may not be willing to put up with the arduous efforts necessary to learn to play a musical instrument well, or to excel at tennis, even though their manual dexterity may indeed have been improved by all those hours steering little figures around on the video screen."

Addressing the question of whether there is any value in Nintendo—such as good eye coordination—Sylvia Rimm (1992), a child psychologist who specializes in underachievement, suggests that while video games may improve visual-motor integration, the same benefit, as well as many others, is gained by working on a computer. She goes on to list disadvantages of Nintendo: "Some games are violent and seem to encourage aggressive behavior in children. Furthermore, children spend so much time playing these games, that it may seem difficult to lure them away for healthier outdoor play, their chores and responsibilities, reading, and/or homework." She recommends limiting video-game play to weekends and allowing no more than 45 minutes to an hour, to "minimize any damage" (p. 5).

In a chapter titled "TV, Video Games, and the Growing Brain," Healy (1990) states, "It seems fairly safe to say that much of children's experience with such games will have little, if any, transfer value to traditional school tasks ... we do know that lack of use can definitely affect potential for brain connections. If a child spends an inordinate amount of time on video games (or television, or even other types of computer use) instead of playing and experimenting with many different types of skills, the foundations for some kinds of abilities may be sacrificed. These losses may not show up until much later, when more complicated kinds of thinking and learning become necessary. Tender young brains need broad horizons, not overbuilt neural pathways in one specific skill area" (p. 206).

All of these experts, and many others, are concerned not only about the direct negative effects of television and video games, but also about the time they take from reading. Healy (1990) reports that a study of fifth graders showed they watch television for an average of 2 hours and ten minutes a day. Of these same children, 50% read four minutes a day or less outside of school, 30% read two minutes or less, and 10% do not read at all outside of school. For older students, these percentages are no doubt lower, as will become clear in the next chapter.

Implications for Intellectual Growth

This is not a problem parents and teachers of gifted and talented students can ignore. Declining test scores tell us that even the brightest students are reading more poorly (as well as handling math and science less expertly) than their counterparts did in the past. Even among college students who have majored in verbal areas—most of those taking Graduate Record Examinations in English, French, Spanish or German—test scores have dropped (Healy, 1990).

Nor can we assume that technology alone will save us. Effective management of business requires verbal skills, as recognized by *Fortune Magazine* in an article called "America Won't Win Till It Reads More" (1991). Stating that the average adult American reads just 24 minutes a day, a 25% decline since 1965, the article goes on to discuss the business skills fostered by reading: speaking, writing, and linking unrelated events. Reorganizing business for more productivity means giving more authority to front-line workers, in jobs that demand thinking, judging, and decision-making. A consultant "worries that workers who don't read well, and therefore don't think well, may not be able to handle the added responsibility" (p. 202).

Reading seems so simple that it can easily be taken for granted. In fact, we may need to worry less about illiteracy than about aliteracy—citizens who know how to read at a functional level but who do not choose to read, thereby avoiding the mental demands of reading and losing the benefits of the mental exercise. Gifted students as well as average ones are at risk. The difference can be in their awareness of their need to learn and their responsibility for their own education.

The Importance of Parents

This review of the difficulties parents, teachers, and their talented students face is intended not to discourage but to set the ideal conditions outlined early in this chapter into a larger context. Perhaps dismaying realities will firm our resolve to do all we can to help high potential students set and meet appropriate goals.

Parents should be active in seeking three pieces of information:

- What sort of education is best for your child?
- How much of the desired program is he or she receiving in school?

- What can you do to compensate for any missing elements?

Developing complete answers to all three may be a long-term project. The first part of this chapter provides a brief discussion of the first question, and information to help parents evaluate school programs is found in Chapter Five. The remaining chapters offer one response to the last question. While books are not a panacea, using them effectively is one of the best ways to fill gaps left in the school program or to counteract distracting social influences.

How Books Can Help

Whatever the problems or trends in education, the innate traits of gifted and talented children remain the same. A glance back over the list of intellectual characteristics and needs found earlier in this chapter should confirm that reading and book discussion are ideal ways to respond to the characteristics and meet the related needs.

Many bright and gifted people suppress awareness of their need to learn. Teaching these children to use books is one way of demonstrating that learning is important to them, and that books can be a significant part of their lives. When teachers go to the trouble of establishing book discussion groups, or parents take the time to read what their children are reading and talk to them about it, it becomes clear that significant adults value and encourage reading. If reading and book discussions are happy and successful experiences, children learn to love books.

Especially where special programs for gifted children are unavailable, a vigorous use of books can be a real contribution to children's growth. Few activities are as available, inexpensive, and richly rewarding. No wonder some of their best friends are books!

References

America won't win till it reads more. (1991, November 18). *Fortune Magazine*, pp. 201-204.

Amidon, Susan R. (1991). Encouraging higher level thinking in the gifted adolescent. In Marlene Bireley and Judy Genshaft (Eds.), *Understanding the gifted adolescent: Educational, developmental, and multicultural issues* (pp. 91-103). New York: Teachers College Press.

Billington, James H. (1990, September). The electronic erosion of democracy. Inaugural C. Walter and Gerda B. Mortenson Lecture, Urbana, Illinois.

Clark, Barbara. (1992). *Growing up gifted: Developing the potential of children at home and at school*. 4th ed. New York: Macmillan.

Ehrlich, Virginia Z. (1985). *Gifted children: A guide for parents and teachers*. New York: Trillium.

Halsted, Judith Wynn (in press). [The young gifted child and the motivation to learn]. In Joan Smutny (Ed.), *Anthology on pre-primary and primary gifted children*. Cresskill, NJ: Hampton Press.

Healy, Jane M. (1990). *Endangered minds: Why our children don't think*. New York: Simon and Schuster.

Karnes, Frances A. and Marquardt, Ronald G. (1991a). *Gifted children and the law: Mediation, due process and court cases*. Dayton: Ohio Psychology Press.

Karnes, Frances A. and Marquardt, Ronald G. (1991b). *Gifted children and legal issues in education: Parents' stories of hope*. Dayton: Ohio Psychology Press.

Kerr, Barbara. (1991). *A handbook for counseling the gifted and talented*. Alexandria: American Association for Counseling and Development.

Nordheimer, Jon. (1992, November 29). Gifted education, seen as a luxury in hard times, encounters cutbacks. *New York Times*.

Obermiller, Tim. (1989, Summer). All in a day's play." *The University of Chicago Magazine*, *81*(4), pp. 14-19.

Office of Educational Research and Improvement. (1993). *National excellence: A case for developing America's talent*. Washington, DC: U.S. Government Printing Office.

Piechowski, Michael M. (1979) Developmental potential. In Nicholas Colangelo and Ronald T. Zaffrann (Eds.), *New voices in counseling the gifted* (pp. 25-57). Dubuque, Iowa: Kendall/Hunt.

Piechowski, Michael M. & Colangelo, Nicholas. (1984, Spring). Developmental potential of the gifted. *Gifted Child Quarterly*, *28*, 80-88.

Piechowski, Michael M. (1991). Emotional development and emotional giftedness. In Nicholas Colangelo and Gary A. Davis (Eds.), *Handbook of Gifted Education* (pp. 285-306). Boston: Allyn and Bacon.

Ravitch, Diane & Finn, Chester E. (1987). *What do our 17-year-olds know? A report on the first national assessment of history and literature*. New York: Harper and Row.

Rimm, Sylvia. (1992, Autumn). "Sylvia Rimm on raising kids." Grandville, MI Public Schools: *IMAGE Informer*, p. 5.

Smutny, Joan Franklin, Veenker, Kathleen, & Veenker, Stephen. (1989). *Your gifted child: How to recognize and develop the special talents in your child from birth to age seven.* New York: Facts on File.

Webb, James T. (1992). Assessing gifted and talented children. *Illinois Council for the Gifted Journal, 11,* 10-21.

Webb, James T., Meckstroth, Elizabeth A., & Tolan, Stephanie S. (1982). *Guiding the gifted child: A practical source for parents and teachers.* Dayton: Ohio Psychology Press.

Winn, Marie. (1991, December 22). Nintendo and the challenges of life. *New York Times Book Review,* p. 2.

PART TWO

The Process

CHAPTER
THREE

Reading Guidance

One of the changes my husband and I noticed when our younger son departed for college, along with how long it takes the dishwasher to fill up and how often the trash has to be taken out, was the loss of the sense of urgency about each day that we had felt when we had children in residence. Almost always now, whatever doesn't get done today really can be put off until tomorrow.

With growing children this is not so. Especially in the early years, each day is important, and if the needs at a given stage are not met at that time, the child cannot conveniently make up for the loss later on. The child's changing developmental requirements march on, regardless of parents' commitment, energy, patience, presence, income, and whatever else makes the difference between good and inadequate parenting. Thus the sense of urgency: the need, the readiness, is *now*, and the attentive parent senses the demand for an immediate response.

The principle extends to children's reading. Each stage of childhood lasts a breathlessly short time, and so also does the period of peak response to the literature appropriate to that stage.

As adults we feel a certain leisure about our reading, assuming that two or five years from now we can read a given book and expect much the same emotional and intellectual response we would have if we read it this week. Not so with children. They can, of course, read

Mother Goose rhymes much later, but after the age of four or five the emotional response to the rhythms and the intellectual response to the word play are dulled. They can read fairy tales even as adults, but after the middle elementary years the intense interest—the magic—is gone, and with it the power of the tales to enrich the growing imagination of the child. There are far too many excellent books available for the late elementary and junior high reader to have time to read them all. No wonder the thoughtful school librarian feels a sense of urgency, trying to expose children to the best of the wealth before they are too old—that is, before they are fourteen or fifteen!

Using books with bright and curious children requires knowledge of the needs of these youngsters (Part One), the books available to them (Part Three) and the processes of change, presented in this section. We begin with reading guidance: how to help them seek out the best books *for them* among the wide range of literature available.

Fundamentals of Reading Guidance

Reading guidance may be defined as "the right book for the right child at the right time." It means being aware of what a child is reading, in terms of quality, content, and age-appropriateness, and being ready to offer suggestions for further reading that will move that child along with good literature at each stage of development.

Watching the reading patterns of children, we know that the type of books they enjoy alters as they grow, from nursery rhymes to a wide range of adult fiction and nonfiction. While this change in their *interests* occurs naturally, it does not follow that a maturing of their *literary taste* is just as natural. The steps from grocery store picture books to well-written, insightful fiction and sophisticated, demanding nonfiction almost always require guidance.

Practicing reading guidance means watching a child read through the Hardy Boys series and being ready at the right time with a suggestion that he might also enjoy Alfred Hitchcock's short stories, and a few years later a Leon Garfield novel and then Edgar Allan Poe—all filled with suspense but moving up the ladder of age-appropriateness and literary quality. Or noticing that a third grader has reread Laura Ingalls Wilder until it may be time to tell her about *Caddie Woodlawn*, and then the historical fiction of Scott O'Dell and Betty Baker. Later she might enjoy *Johnny Tremain* or *Across Five Aprils*, and eventually Willa Cather's novels of the American West. In addition, she could be encouraged to branch out horizontally, with biography or fiction about the history of other countries.

Parents are in the best position to offer such long-range reading guidance. Teachers and librarians usually see only one to six or seven years of a child's development, so they must work harder early in their relationship with a child to learn what he has enjoyed reading, gaining the background information needed to suggest books that will interest and delight him and keep him coming back for more good literature.

Reading guidance involves stretching a child's mind and spirit, always trying to suggest a book that meets her where she is in the hope that when she has read it, she will have grown a little. Those who guide reading do not deny the use of escape literature, but they want the child to learn to use it appropriately. This means learning to recognize when she wants something easy and when she wants to be challenged—and then be able to find the more growth-enhancing literature.

Adult influence on the priority a child places on reading is limited primarily to the four years from second grade to sixth. Our influence on the *quality* of children's reading lasts perhaps two more years—the important junior high years (longer for those who continue leisure reading). Thus, time is precious indeed, and there isn't very much of it to introduce them to the wealth of children's literature. These are crucial years to stimulate imaginative thinking, to ensure that they will know some of the classics when they enter college, and to help them establish a pattern of reading to last a lifetime. The early years are a time for subtle intervention, for suggestions, for sharing and passing on the enjoyment of reading. It is no time for well-intentioned adults to watch passively as mediocre reading habits unfold and stabilize.

Reading guidance takes many forms. It can be so informal as the casual mention of a title or an author a parent has enjoyed, or the "floor work" that librarians do, talking with students as they browse the shelves. It can be a book talk carefully planned by a librarian or a teacher, or even a list of books from which students are required to select five to read each semester for an English class. Or it can be subtly woven into the fabric of family life:

> *Although she is now the mother of teenagers, Ginny has warm memories of summers spent reading when she was a child and adolescent. Her mother had always enjoyed reading, and she was ready each year with suggestions of*

books Ginny might enjoy that summer. They were books she might otherwise have missed: Too Late the Phalarope: My Name is Aram; Madame Curie; Wind, Sand and Stars; A Death in the Family. *Some were in her mother's library; she found others in the public library at her mother's suggestion. She has less time now, but reading is still a source of immense pleasure for Ginny, in part a result of her mother's gentle reading guidance.*

The relationship between the student and the guiding adult is important for the success of reading guidance, as is the genuine love of the adult for books and the natural wish to share this pleasure. If these are present, then an adult can establish a reading guidance relationship with students even without a formal program. Any adult who listens to a student talk about books she is reading, and is ready with suggestions for more good reading at appropriate times, is offering reading guidance.

Reading Patterns: What to Expect

As they grow from preschoolers to high school seniors, from nonreaders to independent and voluntary readers and perhaps even to mature readers, children's interest in reading as a leisure activity ebbs and flows in predictable patterns. Through research in children's reading we also see a clear pattern in the types of literature and topics that appeal at different ages, so that it is possible to say, for example, that students in the early grades enjoy fairy tales while sixth graders prefer mysteries.

The best way to learn what any child likes to read is to ask, but a direct question may not elicit clear information. A bit of probing may be necessary. What does he do with leisure time? What are his favorite television programs? The last good book he read? Identifying his own reading interests is part of each child's learning who he is, and that takes time. The third grader probably doesn't yet know what he likes to read; the ninth grader may, if she is lucky enough to have been introduced to a variety of good books and has had some intelligent, perceptive reading guidance.

When using an informal interview to determine a child's reading interests, it is important to remember that she cannot be interested in literature she hasn't met. It does not mean much if a fourth grader says that he doesn't like fantasy, if he hasn't read or heard anything that he recognizes as fantasy. It is necessary to learn not only what he has enjoyed, but also what kinds of books he has in his background.

One research finding that may surprise us in this liberated age is that as children grow older, the reading interests of boys and girls diverge. Reading studies have shown this divergence for a long time. It might be expected that the pattern would have changed in recent years, but Glazer (1981) and Hawkins (1983) found that this is not the case. Studying a group of gifted children, Hawkins found, for example, that girls in the upper elementary grades chose biography, poetry, fairy tales, and animal stories, while boys selected science, science fiction, and "how-to" books.

A more recent study cited by Langerman (1990) shows that boys in the primary grades prefer nonfiction while girls prefer fiction, but the boys are more flexible, more willing to try fiction than the girls are to try nonfiction. The experience of enlightened teachers and librarians bears this out, as they disprove the old belief that while girls would read "boys' books" (books in which boys are the main characters), boys would not read "girls' books." Teachers who read girls' books to a class—Jean Fritz' *Homesick: My Story*, Jane Langton's *The Fledgling*, or Avi's *The True Confessions of Charlotte Doyle*, for example—report that boys' interest equals the girls'. It is relatively easy to build on this response to encourage boys to read on their own some of the fine literature about girls. Adults choosing books to use for discussion with gifted children should not worry too much about the gender of the main character.

Preschool

Few school districts provide programs for gifted preschoolers. Therefore, the characteristics and needs of these children are not as carefully documented as those of school age children. Yet more people are becoming aware of their special needs—and of the immense importance of reading and talking to preschoolers.

Recent research indicates that between the ages of one and a half and four years, children's brains are especially open to learning language (Clark, 1992). During this time they gain language skills more easily than they ever will again. It is a critical period for parents to provide rich language experiences for their child, by talking directly to him and reading aloud. This is especially so for unusually bright and curious children, who respond eagerly to the stimulation and the exposure to new ideas that reading aloud can provide.

Nothing in a preschooler's life can quite match the warmth of being held and read to, and if the one who is reading loves not only the child but also the literature and the experience of sharing it, so much richer are both reader and child. Since the child's attention span is short at this age, it is best if there can be several brief "story hours" a day.

It is impossible to overemphasize the importance of reading aloud to children of any age, but especially to preschoolers. Any parent who doubts this, or cannot find time for reading aloud, should read *Babies Need Books* (Butler, 1985; regrettably out of print at this writing, but try the library), an eloquent statement of the pleasures and advantages of growing up in a family where reading aloud is valued. Butler can make a believer of anyone, and she gives plenty of suggestions for books to help those unfamiliar with children's literature.

Numerous studies document the fact that children who are read to as preschoolers are better prepared for learning to read when they enter school. Since their language skills are superior, they do well in any area that depends on language, and what area does not? Some parents read to their preschoolers specifically to build language and pre-reading skills. Books such as *Getting Ready to Read* (Boegehold, 1984) offer ideas on reading aloud to preschoolers for this purpose.

In addition, parents may read to their preschoolers simply to enrich the children's store of knowledge. An ever-increasing supply of information books for young children makes this an easy project, one which is sure to interest the parents as well as the child. In the process, the child is learning that books are an infinitely varied source of fascinating information.

But a more fundamental reason for making time to read to a preschool youngster, several times a day if possible, is to instill the sense that reading is a source of pleasure. By sitting with a child, cuddling, enjoying a good story and lovely illustrations, talking about the pictures and characters and imagining what would happen if this child were in the story, or had the same choices to make, adults lay the foundations for a lifetime of reading for pleasure and information. Reading at its best, even for adults, is an emotional response to the art of literature. The openness to the emotional response begins here, in a loving environment, when children's imagination is most accessible and flexible. Children who miss books at this age will never be able to make up entirely for the loss, because never again will they be so receptive.

They will not miss them if Jim Trelease has his way. The author of *The New Read-Aloud Handbook* (1989) works full-time addressing parents and teachers on children and literature, and he speaks like the man with a mission that he is. His book offers over ten pages of information and suggestions just on reading to preschoolers. Parents who are reluctant to begin reading to a newborn could do no better than to start here.

In addition to having loving adults who enjoy reading to them, preschoolers should attend a library story hour where they can experience literature with other children. The children's librarian knows the range of children's literature and understands how to make it live. Skilled librarians use music, puppets, and storytelling as well as reading aloud, and they involve the children as participants, making the literature an immediate experience.

This approach is perfect for preschoolers, who are still delighted with the sheer joy of language and who will respond well to cumulative tales like "The House That Jack Built" or the nonsense syllables in Mother Goose or the rhythms in Dr. Seuss. Stories that allow the children to join in the repetition are favorites, as are books without words that allow them to tell the story themselves. For content, preschoolers enjoy stories with simple plots about everyday experiences, and about "things that go" such as trucks, trains, and cars. They like stories with talking animals or toys, or with characters their own age. Funny creatures appeal to them, but they are also ready to begin hearing folklore like "The Three Billy Goats Gruff," "The Little Red Hen," and "The Gingerbread Boy."

Teaching Preschoolers to Read. Some gifted children of this age teach themselves to read, often to the alarm of parents who have been told not to push. If the children have indeed only been encouraged and not forced, but have learned spontaneously from being read to and asking questions about letters and words on signs, there is no cause for alarm. As many parents have learned, there is not much a parent can do to prevent a child from teaching herself to read if she is ready.

The harder question is whether parents should respond to the obvious interest of a gifted child by teaching him to read. This is one of the unresolved issues in education: teaching preschoolers to read is frowned upon by some educators and encouraged by others. Clark (1992) goes so far as to write, "I am convinced that reading is a natural, happy event if introduced during this...period [18 months to four years of age]. What we do at 6 years of age may be remedial reading." While she is not suggesting that parents engage in formal teaching, she goes on to say, "...if allowed the opportunity to play with words, if read to or shown any of the ways letters can be used to represent sound, children find their own way to learn. In an environment that responds *as the children direct* [emphasis mine], that is rich in good language experiences, children enjoy learning in their own way. Learning to read is no exception" (p. 103).

The parent of a gifted child may reason that knowing how to read could keep the child occupied in school while the teacher works with slower learners, preventing the disruptive behavior that accompanies boredom. Certainly it is difficult to withhold information from a child who clamors for it.

> *A mother who reluctantly admits that she taught her two children to read when they were three and four recently asked her younger son, now in college, how he felt about his reading lessons at the time. His surprising answer was that it was confidence-building for him, not because he would start school already reading, but because the time she spent teaching him was proof that "I was worth being taught to read." For him, learning to read was a rite of passage, a welcome into the circle of his reading family.*

It is possible for parents to teach their own gifted children to read without undue pushing. The question to answer before making this decision is that of motivation: Are the parents truly hoping to meet the child's need, or is a secret need of their own being met? For most parents, answering this question honestly will require some soul searching. One clue to parental need is this: have they imagined telling a friend or relative that Jennifer is now reading? The brief pleasure of that conversation is surely not worth risking the possibility of turning reading into a chore for Jennifer.

Yet even when parents conclude that their motives are pure, if they then begin to teach their child to read, they should continue to monitor their own behavior. Lessons should be very brief, and if there is any hint of impatience or stridency in their voices or in the child's, they should stop.

Sensible guidance is available in *Reading Begins at Home* (Butler and Clay, 1987). The authors offer prereading activities, pointing out the importance of parental sensitivity to any anxiety on their part or their child's. Then they go on to suggest one method of teaching that can be used by parents who decide it is appropriate for their family.

Joy is the only really good criterion for judging the value of preschool reading lessons at home. Is there joy in doing it, for the child and the parents? If not, it would be better not to bother. Continue to enjoy reading aloud, continue weekly trips to the library, and wait for nature to take its course.

Early Elementary (Grades K-2)

These are the years when most children learn to read, that is, learn the techniques of interpreting the words on a page. As they gain reading skills in the classroom, they eagerly come to the library. A group of first or second graders swarms over the shelves of easy-to-read books. They select a wide range of books, some of which they can read themselves but most of which they will have to find an adult to read. Whatever the library's limit on books per child, they will come to the circulation desk with that number or more.

As they become independent readers they become more selective. They learn to use the "five finger test," reading a page and putting one finger down for each word they do not know. If by the end of the page fewer than five fingers are down, probably the book is close enough to their reading level for comfort. They begin to recognize authors' names and may want to read all of the Encyclopedia Brown books, or all of Beverly Cleary.

Gifted children, and those most enthusiastic about reading, often become independent readers earlier than most. When they do, they should have free access to books at their reading level in the school library. It is a proud day when a second grader comes home to announce, "I can read chapter books now!"

As they become independent readers, primary children choose realistic animal and nature stories as well as adventure and mystery. They continue to enjoy folklore of increasing complexity, and they love fairy tales.

Their enthusiasm for the library story hour is undiminished, and as important as it is for parents to continue to read aloud at home, it is also important for teachers to find time to read aloud daily to the class. One primary teacher greets the children as they return from their library time and selects one book that has been checked out for immediate reading to the entire class. Then, all the children have quiet time to read their library books. These children look forward to library hour as one of the most important times of the week.

Upper Elementary (Grades 3-5)

A surge in reading begins at about fourth grade and carries through into junior high. Most children's reading is done between fourth and eighth grade, and these few years are vital in forming the reading patterns which will continue in adulthood. If at this time they have access to good books, time to read, and an enthusiastic adult, gifted children in particular have an excellent chance of joining that fortunate group of adults whose lives are immeasurably enriched by the pleasure they find in reading.

By fourth grade, readers have usually identified their favorite authors and ask for their books in the library. The gender split widens here: boys start to look for sports and war stories, while girls still enjoy fairy stories and begin an interest in books about interpersonal relationships. For both boys and girls in the upper elementary grades, mystery stories are the most popular literature.

Most young readers become interested in fantasy and science fiction at this age, often introduced to it through C. S. Lewis's Narnia series. A few children will show an interest in biographies or historical fiction. One study (Swanton, 1984) indicates that gifted students are more likely than their classmates to select fantasy, science fiction, and history.

By the fifth grade, the reading habit is becoming well fixed. Fifth and sixth graders may add the Greek and Roman myths and the legends of King Arthur and Robin Hood to their list of interests. Adventure, mystery, and fantasy remain on the list for gifted and average students alike.

Problem Novels. At this late elementary stage, children begin to read contemporary realistic fiction, including the "problem novels"— books about problems they or their friends may be experiencing. There are books for this age group about young people coping with physical or mental disability, divorce, drugs, aging, and death, as well as books that deal with the typical questions and concerns of growing up, finding friends, moving through puberty, and developing a sense of one's own identity. An excellent source for such reading is *The Bookfinder* (Dreyer, 1989) which lists books for children and young adults, summarized and cross-referenced according to topic and feelings exemplified in the book's story.

Young people know that they can read about someone their age coping with problems they themselves face, and this may cause gifted students to turn more readily to books for an understanding of difficul-

60

ties related to being gifted. Ironically, however, there is some evidence that gifted students do not perceive books as a source of problem solving as much as average students do (Martin, 1984). It is possible that because they choose books at a higher reading level, they don't see those that deal with problems of people their own age. Reading guidance can point them to useful books that they would otherwise miss.

Unfortunately, some gifted children lose interest in reading as a leisure activity sometime during these years (Martin, 1984). There seem to be two major reasons for this. One is that some youngsters become deeply involved in computers, video games, or sports and do not want to spend time reading; the other is that gifted students may resent being forced to read material not of their own choice. They want "interesting" and "exciting" reading, and their opinion of what is interesting and exciting often does not coincide with the material to be found in elementary reading texts.

Reading guidance to help them find appropriate books can help, along with open-ended assignments that encourage them to read books and also allow them some choice. It's a good idea to begin with books about computers or sports, so that reading can complement their areas of major interest rather than compete with them. And it is still important, difficult as it may be, for the teacher to find time in the school day to read aloud, and for the students to read silently.

Middle School (Grades 6-8)

At the beginning of this period, youngsters may still be at the peak of interest in reading, exploring every field of literature. By the end of it, however, other activities and interests take over, and most young people find little time for unassigned, leisure reading. What happens to young adolescents in other aspects of their lives occurs in their reading lives too: they are leaving childhood and the literature appropriate to it. If they continue leisure reading, they will increasingly choose adult literature, and their interests will become so individualized that general statements no longer apply. Anyone hoping to guide or influence their reading will have to know them as individuals, and know their reading background as well.

At this age boys are less flexible than girls in their reading choices. They will read about female characters as long as the plot provides suspenseful action in an outdoor setting. Girls prefer internal action focused on what a character thinks and feels, not just on what she does;

and they are willing to experiment with a wider range of reading (Carlsen, 1980).

Although reading tapers off for most students in the junior high years, gifted students are more likely to continue reading avidly. One study (Carter, 1982), designed specifically to determine leisure reading interests of gifted junior high students, reports that the gifted students read more than twice as much as the students in the control group, choosing more science fiction and fantasy, fewer problem novels, and a wider range of historical fiction than students in the comparison group. Of the students in the study, only the gifted showed the pattern of moving toward reading adult fiction; this shift began to occur at the end of the eighth grade.

As they begin the transition to adult literature, young people need reading guidance more than at any other time. Perhaps surprisingly, gifted students are no more skilled than others at selecting excellent literature without adult help.

Girls are likely to discover the more simplistic, sentimentalized romantic adult novels, while boys tend toward sensationalized, violent adventure. Without direction, they may never find the superb adult literature that can fill their present need for romance and adventure, while enhancing their taste for good literature. If they don't learn the difference between sentimental or sensational novels and good litera-ture at this age, chances are dim that they will eventually develop into mature readers of fiction.

Ironically, one barrier to this development can occur in an honors English class, according to middle school teacher Susan Rakow (1991). Noting that gifted adolescents experience the same emotional and social problems that their peers do, she presses for the use of young-adult literature to help them understand and discuss their experiences—yet honors courses frequently offer them only the classics, cutting them off from the opportunities for self-discovery that are made available to their classmates. "When teachers and parents discourage gifted adolescents from reading young-adult novels, they fail in their responsibility to provide appropriate reading guidance," she writes (p. 49).

Carlsen (1980) agrees. "Accelerating the intelligent child by giving him or her the adult classics of literature will not increase enjoyment of reading" (p. 34). Rather than being asked to read adult classic literature before they have developed social and emotional maturity to match their cognitive level, these students should be given age-appropriate literature by the best of the authors writing for them: Cooper, Garfield, Hamilton, LeGuin, Paterson and many others.

Senior High (Grades 9-12)

By the freshman year, the reading peak is past for most students, and those who still do unassigned reading choose books focused on very specific, individual interests. Their motivation is likely to be related to their interest in philosophical issues and their attempts to formulate their own opinions and value systems. For gifted high schoolers, this may raise special considerations that are discussed in Chapter Four under "Goals of Bibliotherapy with Gifted Students."

Senior high readers prefer protagonists who are making the transition which they face, from adolescence to adulthood; they are not interested in books with middle-aged characters, but do enjoy stories about the elderly, who face some of their problems: a changing peer group and adjustment to physical and mental changes (Carlsen, 1980).

Some senior high students become interested in reading the classics, out of a self-discipline that impels them to do "college-bound reading" or out of genuine intellectual curiosity. If such a student is fortunate enough to work with a mentor who possesses a broad knowledge of books as well as a sympathetic understanding of the student, this can be an extremely rewarding endeavor.

For the most fortunate, the reading experience at this age is one of long, leisurely discovery. In the autobiographical book *Self-Consciousness*, John Updike writes, "...certain kinds of novel, especially nineteenth-century novels, should be read in adolescence, on those dreamily endless solitary afternoons that in later life become so uselessly short and full of appointments, or they will never be read at all" (1989, p. 109).

Special Characteristics of Gifted Readers

Alison, a nine-year-old growing up in a midwestern university town, exemplifies the characteristics of gifted readers (Swinger, 1989).

Alison read before she entered kindergarten, and according to school and home records she read at least 73 books in the third grade, including Little Women. *She has also read* Charlotte's Web, Anne of Green Gables, Peter Pan, Heidi, *and* Alice's Adventures in Wonderland, *most of them recommended to her by her mother or a teacher.*

Alison looks for books by her favorite authors: Patricia MacLachlan, Patricia Reilly Giff, and L. M. Montgomery. When she discovered the Babysitters Club Series, she read several in a row, then immediately reread Charlotte's Web.

At school she reads constantly, even during math and spelling tests.

Everyone in Alison's family reads, including all the grandparents and her great-grandmother, who uses talking books for the blind. Alison still enjoys having bedtime stories read to her, and she sometimes reads the bedtime story to her younger brother. She "appears to belong to that group of people for whom reading is as natural and necessary as breathing" (p. 51).

Only a few studies, including those mentioned under the age groupings above, consider the points at which gifted readers differ from the average, but they provide information which may apply equally to intellectually curious children, whether or not they are identified as gifted.

Gifted children read earlier, better, and more than most children. In what they choose to read, however, differences are not so great. Gifted youngsters read a greater variety, and they may be more adventurous in exploring different types of literature, but in general their reading interests closely parallel those of other children their age (Hawkins, 1983). They want to read about the same subjects, although the specific books they read may vary.

They read three or four times as many books as most children, and some continue to do a great deal of reading after the time when children's reading typically tapers off (Russell, 1961; Whitehead, 1984).

When Melissa was in fifth and sixth grades, she typically read a book each day. In junior high, reading longer and more demanding books, her reading diminished to an average of three books a week. Now in senior high, when most of her friends find no time for unassigned reading, Melissa still reads a book every week or two; in the summer she systematically lists the books she plans to read, and she finds time to read fifteen to twenty adult books in addition to working.

A summary of reading patterns of gifted youngsters indicates the importance of guiding their reading early and consistently:

- They may teach themselves to read before they start school.

- Whether or not they are reading in kindergarten, they are probably independent readers by second grade at the latest.

- By third grade, they may have identified their favorite authors.

- By fifth grade, the habit of reading is well established, if it is going to be.

- By sixth grade, their reading may diminish if they are among the many gifted younsters who become involved in sports, computers, or video games.

- By late middle school, extracurricular reading may well have disappeared for some, although it may reappear later.

- Others spend extraordinary amounts of time reading, but need guidance to identify good literature.

- Capable of reading sophisticated literature, they have the potential to gain a great deal from the best books if they are directed to them.

For the adult who works with such children, reading guidance is especially rewarding, because they are likely to respond with great enthusiasm and develop a close relationship with the adult who talks about books with them.

Reading Aloud

When their children learn to read, parents should give some family reading time over to hearing the children read aloud—but they should also continue reading aloud to children.

Unhappily, most parents stop this practice by the time youngsters are eight or nine. In November of 1992, the Associated Press reported the findings of a study by the American Federation of Teachers: soon after parents stop reading aloud, their children begin to spend more hours in front of the television set. The study showed that 52 percent of parents read daily to children under eight, but only 13 percent continue to read every day to children aged nine to fourteen—and that children under ten spend more time reading than watching television, while older children reverse their priorities.

In addition to promoting a continued interest in reading, parents who read aloud can introduce their children to literature they might not find on their own, such as classic children's stories, folklore, poetry, and mythology.

Children will happily listen to adults read not only more advanced literature than they can read themselves, but also books they can read but would not choose. Slower-paced books of real quality lend themselves to reading aloud. *Old Ramon*, by Jack Schaefer, is a quiet book about a wealthy boy's relationship with a shepherd as they take the sheep to the high ground one summer, a trip arranged by the boy's father precisely so he could learn from the wise, unlettered older man. This is not initially an exciting book, and children who want adventure will not choose to read it themselves; however, fifth graders will sit silently day after day and listen, coming to love the book and identify with the boy, and they will be sorry to have the story end.

The story hour at home remains important for the warmth provided by the luxury of reading in a frenetic world, and it can answer a crucial need: unhurried, quiet time for reflection. The longer parents keep up the tradition of story hour, the better, both for the quality of family life and for the intellectual development of their children. Some families continue reading aloud until the children are in middle school. How much would have been missed if they had stopped when the children learned to read!

Books listing literature for reading aloud (and suggestions for choosing books especially for this purpose) include *For Reading Out Loud! a Guide to Sharing Books with Children* (Kimmel and Segel, 1983), *Books Kids Will Sit Still For* (Freeman, 1990), and *The New Read-Aloud Handbook* (Trelease, 1989).

Avid Readers and Resistant Readers

As readers, gifted children can be considered in two groups: those who pick up a book in their free time, and those who find something else to do. Members of the first group seem to have copious reading as a life goal. Reading comes naturally to them, and when tasks must come first, they feel distracted and annoyed. Those in the second group usually *can* read quite adequately (unless there is a learning disability); they simply do not choose to read *much*.

Avid Readers

Voracious in the pursuit of books, avid readers often keep several going at once. For a period of several years, Kevin could be traced through the house by the open books spread face down on the floor of each room he had left. He exemplifies those who learn early how to use the local library and the school library, becoming personal friends of the librarians who, in turn, are delighted with such enthusiastic patrons.

Such children may read with amazing speed and comprehension, or they may pore over a passage, savoring the beauty of words. They know how to skim and when to study. These are often the early readers, teaching themselves before they start school, or being taught by parents who respond to their interest.

It is important to remember that "read" in the early stages can mean something closer to "decode"—children can understand the words, pronounce most of them, and glean meaning from the sentences and paragraphs. They may be able to read a book of a hundred or more pages and summarize the story at a time when most of their classmates are still reading the early readers with controlled vocabularies.

However, these young readers may not be emotionally ready to comprehend what they read—to understand the symbolism, or grasp everything the author says about human relationships.

> *Seven-year-old Andrea is reading at the sixth grade level. Therefore, she can read* The Witch of Blackbird Pond. *While she can follow the story line and answer fact questions about the plot, Andrea is not ready to understand why the old Quaker woman who lives at the pond is feared as a witch, or appreciate the courage shown by Nat and Kit in befriending her.*

Children like Andrea, especially those who know how proud their parents are of their reading ability, need guidance to help them find appropriate reading. In some cases, it seems that more than anything else they need permission not to stretch too far, to enjoy the books that are appropriate for their level of emotional development.

In working with gifted readers, there are three potential problems. One is that they may push themselves, or be pushed by their perception of the pride others take in their reading, to read whatever they can decode before they have developed the emotional readiness to comprehend. They may then not read a book when they are emotionally ready for it because they have already "read" it. They do not realize, of course, that it would be an entirely different book for them at the right time. Such children in the sixth grade sometimes choose books normally read by third graders, perhaps trying to catch up on what they missed three years ago, when they were in such a hurry.

A second problem is to know what books to suggest. It is a great challenge to find a book for a second grader who reads at the sixth grade level. In general, it seems best to match fiction with his emotional level, while guiding him toward nonfiction at his reading level.

> *In the second grade Doug is reading Mary Norton's* The Borrowers, *E.B. White's* Trumpet of the Swan, *and George Selden's* The Cricket in Times Square. *At the same time he is pursuing his interest in computers and lasers by reading books on these topics written for middle school children. By the time he is in the upper elementary grades, he will be able to find more challenging fiction.*

Good sources for recommendations of intellectually challenging books are *Books for the Gifted Child* (Baskin and Harris, 1980; and Volume 2, Hauser and Nelson, 1988) and books listed under "Drive to Understand" in Chapter Eight of this book.

A third concern for those who work with gifted readers is to recognize that constant and prolific reading may not always be desirable. Occasionally the motive is not thirst for information or enthrallment with the world of the imagination, but simply the need of a gifted child to fill time he would prefer to spend playing with neighborhood children, if he only knew how to be accepted.

It is best to respond to this situation positively. The child should not be told he is reading too much or playing with others too little, but he should subtly and persistently be led to increase time with other children to achieve a better balance. It's quite likely that this child sees himself as a "reader"; that is, "I am a reader" is a positive part of his self-concept. Anything that makes him feel guilty about the time he spends reading may convince him that reading is somehow wrong; he may also begin to believe that he himself is not quite acceptable as the reader he is. Therefore, no connection should be made between time spent with other children and time spent in reading. Each should be valued independently.

How much is too much time spent in reading? That varies with the child. Those who tend toward introversion may spend more time alone than adults anticipate—and enjoy it. Remembering that reading is a productive and restorative way to spend time alone, parents and teachers must determine how much is appropriate for an individual child, basing their evaluation on how much time she spends with other children, how content she seems to be with herself, and how happily she spends time alone. If reading is an escape because interpersonal skills are lacking or because of depression or fear, then some intervention—perhaps professional—should be considered.

However, in our socially-oriented society, it is quite possible that adults are overly zealous to see children relate to others. If a child relates well with other children when he does play with them, and seems happy with himself in general, then it probably should not be of great concern if he spends less time with other children than adults think necessary.

Resistant Readers

Some highly intelligent and able children simply don't choose to spend their leisure time reading. They may be quite capable of reading to gain information, and they certainly have the potential for success in college and career, but they aren't people who enjoy literature as an art form. In the long run, this is no more alarming than the fact that some children never learn to enjoy music or dance or theater, or participate in sports or car repair. No matter how much we want our children to be well-rounded, they retain the right to develop their own interests. All we can do is to expose them to the world around them and accept the total package the child represents, without unduly imposing our values as we watch them make their choices.

Nevertheless, in the short run it is to the child's advantage to read, both to hone the skill and for the vast amount of information he can gain. Therefore, adults should avoid the tendency to view the middle-grade child—and to allow him to see himself—as a nonreader. It may help to understand what is going on if adults recognize that the roots for his resistance to reading may have been established long ago, in the preschool years, especially if an older sibling has pre-empted the reading role.

Consider the plight of the two- or three-year-old younger child growing up in a reading family. It is known, of course, that parents who are readers are good models for their children. Children growing up in homes where reading is valued are more likely to be good readers themselves than those in homes where little reading is done. But for this child, whose older siblings are also reading, there is a negative side: everyone in her world takes pleasure from an activity not yet available to her, inevitably ignoring her in the process. Frequent read-aloud sessions can only partially atone, and if the older children read when she wants to play with them—as they will if they are avid readers—it seems natural that she will resent reading to some degree. She learns to capitalize on what she *can* do, and so may begin her self-image as one who does rather than one who reads. Regardless of this child's ability to read by the time she is a third grader, the doer identity will have had a significant head start over the reader identity, and the reader may never catch up.

> *Jessica's parents and her older brother, Michael, had open books in every room. She, too, was included in the reading orgy, having been read to in the womb and the crib long before she could pick out her own books in the library. But if she wanted Michael to play with her, his invariable response was, "Jessica, I'm READing." When she wanted her mother's attention, it was "When I'm through with this chapter," and Dad's was an absent-minded, "That's nice, dear," as he turned a page.*

So Jessica began to draw. Her wallpaper still shows evidence of her early interest in art. Then she turned to clay and from there, as a teenager, to beads. While her family read, she sat among them working with tiny crystals and wires. Her giftedness found its outlet in the handiwork of her fingers as she created beautiful, intricate designs for necklaces and earrings. At twenty, she has already sold her work at local art fairs and planned a career in jewelry design. While she enjoys reading, she spends leisure time with beads, not books.

Jessica is proof that gifted nonreaders can be productive and happy. Nonetheless, because reading is such an important skill for success in school, it is important that adults in reading families not give up on their young children as potential readers, particularly during the peak reading period in the elementary grades.

At School. Because some bright children who do not choose to read in leisure time are conscientious about completing assignments, it is critical that teachers include full books in the curriculum as well as fragments of literature. If this is not happening, it may help if parents ask the teacher to do what they cannot do at home—assign a book.

The assignment may be all the incentive necessary, and it need not add to the teacher's burden. A simple notebook for recording titles of books read may be enough to keep them going if the teacher has no time for reading logs or more elaborate book-reporting procedures; in fact, this is something that not every child in the class would have to do. The book assignments should be free choice, from a list of recommended titles for quality control. Suggestions for the list can come from the school librarian, from Chapter Eight in this book, or from *Books for the Gifted Child, Volume 2* (Hauser and Nelson, 1988).

There are many ways for a teacher, with the help of the school librarian, to bring children's literature into the classroom. But when there are too many children and not enough time to meet the pressing curriculum requirements in every subject, literature may seem like a luxury. In these classrooms, it is especially important that reading be assigned to competent but resistant readers.

At Home. Parents can also gently build reading time into the schedule. One common way of doing this is to set bedtime a half hour earlier than necessary, with optional reading time. Limiting television is commendable for a variety of reasons; reading at bedtime is an excellent substitute.

If parents are aware of the child's reading—occasionally reading one of his books and talking with him about it, asking his opinion, and listening well—he will benefit in several ways. He will begin to think of himself not only as a reader, but as one who can respond to books and make judgments about them, judgments that others value. Parents usually find themselves truly enjoying children's books, giving him something of importance to share with them. Most important, books can become a bridge for more real communication than would otherwise occur. The elementary years are the ideal time to build these bridges—they will be needed during junior high school!

Finally, parents as well as teachers can help keep gifted children from prematurely deciding that they do not enjoy reading by continuing to read aloud.

Older Resistant Readers. As these children reach junior high, they may yet begin to enjoy reading, even if not as much as avid readers do. It will help if reading continues to be assigned. When these youngsters understand that a background in literature is part of a good education, some highly motivated and curious students, avid readers or not, will read from lists of classics or suggested pre-college reading during the summers simply to gain that background. Some will turn to reading even later: her mother reports that Jessica is now reading Dostoevski.

Some children will never be avid readers, and those of us whose business or interest it is to push books will do better if we can accept that gracefully. They can grow into happy, productive adults anyway, and there is nothing to be gained if they feel guilty about their lack of interest in reading. If our goal is simply their joy in the literature that we have been able to introduce, and if we achieve that, it is enough.

Mature Readers

Gifted and intellectually curious children have an opportunity to develop into what is known as a "mature reader." Mature readers consider reading an integral part of life. It is not something they do only to relax or to escape or if there is nothing good on television. It is something they plan for in each day, and if the day develops so they have no time for it they may become restless, rather like joggers who miss their run. Some, busy parents for example, stay up late at night to read their daily quota after the house is quiet.

The time spent reading each day may not be measurable in hours, especially for individuals leading active family and professional lives; however, the reading material will be carefully chosen with a long-range goal in mind, if only vaguely so. Reading will be a fairly important part of their pursuit of needs or interests they have identified, and the material they read will be appropriate to that pursuit.

They read about a variety of subjects, but with particular depth and perception in one or more interest areas. The gender gap has closed by now, and individual interests predominate. Seen as a tool for individual growth, their reading is purposeful, not random or accidental.

Reading is enjoyed not only for the characterization and story line of a novel or the information gained from well-chosen nonfiction, but also for the aesthetic pleasure found in language presented as the art form it can be. Mature readers may read slowly, savoring sentence structure and descriptive passages. While not everything they read is written on a high level, much of it is, and their competence in the skill of reading is superior at all levels.

Among mature readers, differing patterns emerge, reflecting personalities and life stages. A sixteen-year-old who would begin his freshman year in college in the fall showed his idiosyncratic taste in his summer reading list. Not following any of the college-bound lists but pursuing reading he had not had time to complete in a shortened high school career, he read *The Idiot*; *1984*; *Jude the Obscure*; *Tom Jones*; *Tales of the Mabinogi*; *The Journey through Wales* and *The Description of Wales* by Gerald of Wales; *Macbeth*; and Bulfinch's *The Age of Chivalry* and *The Legends of Charlemagne*.

An older but less focused reader, a graduate student in anthropology, wrote a series of letters to his sister and brother-in-law, both medical students, during a period when he was deliberately expanding his reading range:

> *"Perhaps I could pursue [French] as a form of personal entertainment [rather than as a course of study]. My other three courses are extremely interesting to me, so I spend a lot of time reading related books and articles, recommended by the professor or those I find on my own. If I only stuck to the course syllabus, I'd have enough time for French, etc...*

> *"... In this week's* U.S. News and World Report *is a biographical article on an architectural historian, Vincent Scully ... he recently published* Architecture: The Natural and the Manmade *... I mention it in case architecture is/becomes one of your reading interests.*

> *"I'm excited that you find* The Limits of Art *useful. Though it is often quickly buried beneath a pile of other books and papers in my room, it is never "lost." I always know where it is—unlike most other books I have, excepting the dictionary, of course.*

> *"Thinking about the major influences during the last few years, I realized that several lead back to the bookshelf in [his brother-in-law's] parents' home ... At the time ... I was beginning to feel ... a rebirth of interest in reading. I spent a couple of nights before falling asleep reading the house copy of T.S. Eliot ... I asked your mother about a book she had called* Good Reading *... I still occasionally refer to it. Books like* The Limits of Art *... have now assumed some of the responsibility (for older Western lit, anyway)."*

A different style of mature reading belongs to the brother-in-law in medical school. Seeking a balance to the daily diet of science, he pursues music avocationally. Without a musical instrument available at present, he has begun a planned program of reading and listening, reading about the structure in Bach's music, for example, and then listening with an informed ear. He also consults an art history text, adding "his" composers to the time line in the book to aid in placing them chronologically in his mind. At one time a resistant reader, he now uses reading systematically, as a tool to enrich his intellectual life.

In a small town near a river known to fly fishermen around the world lives a mature reader in his mid-forties. He gave up an academic career in order to have time for the outdoor activities he loves, and found work compatible with a sportsman's schedule. His reading interests encompass modern fiction, nonfiction, and poetry, and he and his wife have belonged to a book club for ten years. Books they have discussed that have been particularly meaningful to him include Moon's *Blue Highways*, Freud's *Future of an Illusion*, Kerouac's *On the Road*, *The Sportswriter* by Richard Ford, Joseph Campbell's *The Power of Myth*; *Christabel* and *This Boy's Life* (both of which are annotated in Chapter Eight) and *The Last Lion*, the second volume of Manchester's biography of Winston Churchill.

The list reveals the breadth and depth of interests of a thoughtful, open-minded adult—characteristic not only of this fly fisherman, but also of the friends with whom he and his wife have discussed books for ten years. The unexpected existence and longevity of the group in this remote town testifies to the value of reading in an enriched adult life—a possible future for students who list books among their best friends and who may worry that their love of books sets them apart. In the tiny town near the river, a love of books brings friends together.

Furthermore, the concept of mature reading as an adult can be useful in guiding the careers of multi-talented teens. Such gifted students must make a choice among interests, keeping one as a vocation and the others as avocations. It can be easier to give up the full-time pursuit of a favorite interest if one understands that he can continue to follow it through reading. In fact, he may make a career choice partly on the basis of which interests are most accessible through a program of planned and deliberate reading.

Therefore, the possibility of becoming a mature reader should be introduced in high school, so students can consider how to make use of it in their lives. It will be helpful if they realize that mature reading is an acceptable and enjoyable life pattern. With this reassurance, dedicated readers who have reached the age when few of their peers still enjoy leisure reading can avoid any concern about their own continuing interest in books.

References

Baskin, Barbara H. & Harris, Karen H. (1980). *Books for the gifted child*. New York: Bowker.

Boegehold, Betty D. (1984). *Getting ready to read*. New York: Ballantine.

Butler, Dorothy. (1985). *Babies need books*. New York: Atheneum.

Butler, Dorothy & Clay, Marie. (1987). *Reading begins at home: Preparing children to read before they go to school*. Portsmouth, NH: Heinemann Educational Books.

Carlsen, G. Robert. (1980). *Books and the teenage reader: A guide for teacher, librarians and parents*. 2nd rev. ed. New York: Harper and Row.

Carter, Betty. (1982, Summer). Leisure reading habits of gifted students in a suburban junior high school. *Top of the News, 38*, 312-317.

Clark, Barbara. (1992). *Growing up gifted: Developing the potential of children at home and school*. 4th ed. New York: Macmillan.

Dreyer, Sharon S. (1989). *The bookfinder*. Circle Pines, Minn.: American Guidance Service.

Freeman, Judy. (1990). *Books kids will sit still for: The complete read-aloud guide*. 2nd ed. New York: Bowker.

Glazer, Joan L. (1981). *Literature for young children*. Columbus: Merrill.

Hauser, Paula & Nelson, Gail A. (1982). *Books for the gifted child, Volume 2*. New York: Bowker.

Hawkins, Sue. (1983). Reading interests of gifted children. *Reading Horizons, 24*, 18-22.

Kimmel, Margaret and Segel, Elizabeth. (1983). *For reading out loud! A guide to sharing books with children*. New York: Dell.

Langerman, Deborah. (1990, March). Books and boys: Gender preferences and book selection. *School Library Journal*, 132-136.

Martin, Charles E. (1984). Why some gifted children do not like to read. *Roeper Review, 7*, 72-75.

Rakow, Susan R. (1991, January). Young-adult literature for honors students? *English Journal, 80*(1), 48-51.

Russell, David. (1961). *Children learn to read*. Boston: Ginn.

Swanton, Susan I. (1984, March). Minds alive: What and why gifted students read for pleasure. *School Library Journal, 30*, 99-102.

Swinger, Alice K. (1989, Winter). Portrait of a gifted reader: Alison. *Ohio Media Spectrum, 41*, 46-51.

Trelease, Jim. (1989). *The new read-aloud handbook*. New York: Penquin.

Updike, John. (1989). *Self-consciousness*. New York: Knopf.

Whitehead, Robert J. (1984). *A guide to selecting books for children*. Metuchen, N.J.: Scarecrow.

CHAPTER FOUR

Emotional Development Through Books

On the surface it often appears that most eager learners have everything going for them, that they can handle any difficulties on their own. They themselves help to perpetuate this myth: they are quick to perceive what is expected of them and to produce it, so that even alert adults may not be aware of these children's specific problems.

The discrepancy between a carefree appearance and painful reality was demonstrated by Beth, a bright, happy sixth grader. Telling about being accelerated into a fifth and sixth grade reading group when she was in fourth grade, she cheerfully recalled, "They hated me." Her voice revealed nothing of the pain of rejection by older children.

What prompted her comment was a discussion of *(George)*, a book in which Ben Carr, a seventh grader whose imaginary playmate, George, still lives inside him, is accelerated into a science class with seniors. With older students, he encounters an ethical situation that temporarily proves to be too much for his level of maturity. Discussion about the book led naturally to a conversation about how it feels to be accelerated, reminding Beth of her own experience.

Books like *(George)*, and conversations about them with understanding adults, can become catalysts to help children recognize and talk about some of the experiences—joyful and painful—that are part of growing up different, whether the difference is due to giftedness or to unusual intellectual or artistic interests. Such discussions offer adults a low-key method of informing children about their differences and the problems they may encounter. As with Beth, such reading and discussion can also lead to a new understanding of experiences they have already faced.

Books in which characters struggle with some of the same problems the reader has experienced can give assurance that someone else has had similar difficulties, and the reader can solve the problems vicariously with the character. If a trusted adult reads the same book and then discusses it with a child, an intimate problem can be discussed at third-person distance. If it is a group discussion, the child can benefit from the experiences of other children.

Many gifted children, for instance, try to hide their intelligence as Henry does in *Henry 3*. Although they may not wish to admit openly that they do this themselves, they can talk freely about why Henry does. In a group discussion, Patrick may recall that in first grade (now comfortably in the past) he pretended he couldn't read. Patrick's revelation surprises Holly, who thought she was the only one who had tried to conceal her ability. Holly may not add a word to discussion, but she feels less alone as a result of it and perhaps, too, more willing to answer difficult questions in Patrick's presence.

Individual or group discussion can lead to fresh insights that will help the child cope with difficult situations in her own life. This process is especially effective for gifted children because so many of them are enthusiastic readers.

The rewards are in the reading, in the discussion, and most of all in the response from the children. After a series of four discussions, Heather said, "I learned that being gifted is important." Her statement needed further clarification, but she had taken a step toward accepting her unusual talent as part of her identity.

The many gifted children who have not been formally identified have the same emotional needs as those who have been, and they too can benefit from discussions that will help them to establish an identity, recognize their need for alone time, learn to get along with others, develop their full potential, and take responsibility for their drive to understand. This chapter offers theoretical and practical information on using books to enhance the emotional development of children who are

different from the norm by reason of giftedness or intense interests—
through bibliotherapy.

Bibliotherapy

Webster's Third New International Dictionary defines bibliotherapy as "the use of selected reading materials as therapeutic
adjuvants in medicine and in psychiatry; also: guidance in the solution
of personal problems through directed reading." Cornett and Cornett
(1980, p. 8) quote one of the classic definitions among those who use
bibliotherapy: "A process of dynamic interaction between the personality of the reader and literature—interaction which may be utilized for
personality assessment, adjustment, and growth."

Webster's reference to medicine has a long and honorable history.
Libraries in the ancient world bore inscriptions such as "Medicine for
the Mind" in Alexandria and "The Healing Place of the Soul" in Thebes.
In America, the use of bibliotherapy goes back at least to Dr. Benjamin
Rush, who recommended the reading of books as part of a treatment
regimen for hospital patients in the early part of the 19th century.

The two definitions in Webster's point out the ambiguities in the
word. In fact, three types of bibliotherapy are recognized: institutional,
clinical, and developmental (Rubin, 1979). As the name implies, institutional bibliotherapy is used in hospital settings, following the lead of
psychiatrist William Menninger in the 1930s. It uses literature designed
to teach, and the discussion that follows the reading is typically between
an individual patient and his doctor. This type is less commonly used
at present than the other two (Rubin, 1979).

Clinical and developmental bibliotherapy can best be defined by
contrasting them. In clinical bibliotherapy, people who have emotional
or behavioral problems meet in a clinical setting such as a drug treatment center. With a psychiatrist, psychologist, nurse, or social worker
serving as facilitator, they hold a discussion or counseling session
designed to address their problems, in the hope of bringing about
changes in attitudes and behavior.

In developmental bibliotherapy (the most commonly used type),
ordinary people who are facing a normal life stage or transitional period
meet in community settings such as schools or libraries. Facilitated by
a teacher, librarian, or social worker, their discussion aims to provide

insight to help them resolve normal developmental issues of adjustment and growth.

Both types of bibliotherapy can be used with individuals or with groups.

Literature for Bibliotherapy

Both nonfiction and fiction are used for bibliotherapy, but they are usually used in different ways and for different purposes.

Nonfiction

Those who recommend nonfiction frequently hope that the inter-action between the reader and the information in the book will be sufficiently powerful to bring about attitudinal and behavioral changes, without the need for a discussion after the book is read.

Many therapists recommend nonfiction titles—often self-help books (Riordan and Wilson, 1989)—to their clients in the hope that with more information, clients will achieve a better cognitive grasp of their problems. If therapist and client discuss the book following the reading, the discussion begins at the cognitive level and the therapist attempts to help the client shift from an intellectual to an emotional under-standing.

Nonfiction is often recommended reading for gifted students, with or without a follow-up discussion. Reis and Dobyns (1991) point out the value of biographies of eminent women in providing role models for gifted girls, who may not be personally acquainted with women who are active in the high-level careers they hope to pursue. Adderholdt-El-liott (1991) recommends bibliotherapy for perfectionists, citing two non-fiction titles: Galbraith's *Gifted Kids Survival Guide* and her own *Perfectionism: What's Bad About Being Too Good* (both listed in Chapter Eight).

Fiction

Robert Coles, the psychiatrist who has written with such insight of children's responses to traumatic situations (*Children in Crisis*), draws on his teaching experience at Harvard for a more recent book: *The Call of Stories: Teaching and the Moral Imagination*. In seminars on "Literature and Medicine" and "A Literature of Social Reflection," Coles encourages medical, law and business students to explore how a thoughtful reading of fine novels, poems and plays can affect their lives. The stories he tells of the emotional impact of fiction on the developing values and goals of college students provide an excellent starting point for anyone considering bibliotherapy.

A child's response to fiction typically begins at the emotional level. For this reason, fiction is ideal for developmental bibliotherapy, especially when reading is accompanied by an opportunity to discuss the book with someone else who has read it. Hearing the comments of others enables the child to see that their responses are similar to his, that he is not alone in his feelings.

Using fiction for bibliotherapy, then, is not simply a matter of handing a child a book about a problem he is facing himself. A story is not a pill that will cure if administered at the proper time; it is a starting point. To be most effective, the reading must be followed by discussion with a concerned adult who has also read the book. This statement cannot be made too strongly: *the adult must read the book too*, and be prepared with his or her own response to the literature, and a few key questions to promote discussion.

The delightful surprise in store for adults unfamiliar with current children's literature is its high quality. There is no need to settle for the mediocre; there is plenty of the good and the excellent, and it is not boring, no matter what the age of the reader.

Nevertheless, a warning: with the rising concern over the number of social problems facing today's children, we have seen an increase in didactic fiction, stories designed to teach a lesson. At first glance, these books may seem ideal for bibliotherapy. However, fiction written for bibliotherapeutic purposes usually fails as literature—it is too earnest, and since discerning readers see through it quickly, it cannot bear the weight of serious discussion. To speak authentically to the emotions, and to reflect truly the human condition, fiction chosen for bibliotherapy must exemplify literature as the art form it was meant to be.

Nonfiction and fiction are both listed in the bibliography in Chapter Eight. However, the emphasis throughout this book is on the use of fiction in bibliotherapy.

Developmental Bibliotherapy

Participants in developmental bibliotherapy may be in a group assembled by a school counselor to help students cope with a current crisis situation such as parental divorce, or by a public librarian to help patrons meet a new life stage such as aging. They may be a classroom of children whose teacher believes they need to gain empathy for a handicapped classmate and who uses a story to try to move them to awareness, possibly without recognition on her part or theirs that they are experiencing bibliotherapy. Or they may be children in a family whose parents read and discuss books with them in ways intended to help the children grow.

Developmental bibliotherapy is used preventively, attempting to anticipate and meet needs before they become problems. The goal is to help people to move through life's predictable stages by providing information about what to expect and examples of how other people have dealt with the same developmental challenges.

Several psychologists have created lists of developmental tasks that everyone must meet. In an article about bibliotherapy in public libaries, Lack (1985) summarizes Zaccaria's (1978) compilation of such lists:

Infancy — Achieving a sense of trust

Middle childhood — Achieving a sense of initiative

Late childhood — Achieving a sense of industry

Adolescence — Developing a sense of identity

Early adulthood — Achieving a sense of intimacy

Middle adulthood — Achieving a sense of generativity

Late adulthood — Achieving a sense of ego integrity (p. 29)

Those who are interested in the development of gifted children will see immediately how important are the tasks for middle childhood, late childhood, and adolescence. A sense of initiative, industry, and identity are essential to enable gifted youngsters to avoid underachievement and develop their abilities to their own full satisfaction. Yet for some gifted children, the response of others to their giftedness makes it especially difficult for them to move through these developmental stages with complete success.

Todd showed a sense of initiative when he asked his fourth grade teacher for harder math problems. Busy with thirty-two other students and unable to believe that Todd wanted to work harder, she brushed aside his request.

When her sixth grade class studied ancient Egypt, Kirsten became so interested that she persuaded her family to travel to a nearby city one weekend to visit the museum, delaying the completion of her report. Her parents encouraged Kirsten's sense of industry; the teacher, who would not accept a late report, discouraged it.

Jason knew that he was unusually bright, but because his parents wanted their son to be "just normal, like everyone else," he had difficulty accepting his own ability. It was a junior high teacher, patiently working with Jason as he built a project for a science fair, who enabled him to enjoy his talent and develop a sense of identity that incorporated his intelligence.

Todd, Kirsten, and Jason exemplify the impact of adults' responses to gifted children's attempts to establish a sense of initiative, industry, and identity. The reactions of other children can also encourage or thwart the healthy growth of these children. Developmental bibliotherapy can help make the difference.

Typically, when used by teachers and school counselors bibliotherapy focuses on events that are difficult for a child to comprehend, such as death or divorce, or tasks that every child faces in the process of growing up, such as making friends or accepting differences among people. But developmental bibliotherapy can also be used by teachers, libarians, counselors, and parents to help gifted youngsters recognize and articulate their feelings, and to prepare them for the particular spins that being gifted puts on the normal developmental tasks faced by all children.

Therefore, in this chapter bibliotherapy is seen more specifically as a way of helping gifted and talented children understand and cope with growing up different in a world that is geared to the average. It can be used to help them anticipate difficulties as well as give them a basis for self-understanding when they feel alone and misunderstood, or are reluctant to use their abilities because it is not popular to be smart.

Through bibliotherapy, adults hope to encourage them to build a strong enough self-concept to develop their full potential despite the inevitable pull toward the peer group, or to resist pressures from inside and outside toward perfectionism. Developmental bibliotherapy can be part of a planned effort to help them meet their childhood and adolescent tasks.

Studies of Bibliotherapy

Bibliotherapy is based on the belief that our lives can be changed by what we read, particularly if there is an opportunity to discuss what we read with others. Although difficult to document, this belief persists, perhaps because of the inner certainty of those who love books; we may feel that we do not need scientific proof of what we so surely know. Each of us has identified so strongly with a character that we made him a part of ourselves or adopted his attitude toward a situation. We have all been comforted by knowing that an author has perfectly described our innermost feelings; and developments in psychology over the last two decades have shown that group discussion can be a therapeutic process.

Research results confirming this intuitive evaluation of the effectiveness of bibliotherapy would be welcome, but studies in the field yield ambiguous results. Bibliotherapy is an emerging discipline, and there is not yet enough research to confirm the theories behind it. Nearly every article on bibliotherapy closes with a plea for further study.

In the 1970s, research focused on whether reading had the power to change attitudes, specifically attitudes of white children toward black children who were being bused to white schools. Schrank and Engles (1981) and Schrank (1982) reviewed the research studies of that period and reported that while the effectiveness of bibliotherapy in some other areas was not supported, "research in this category suggests an overwhelming Yes to the question of whether bibliotherapy is effective" (Schrank and Engels, 1981, p. 144).

But it is difficult to point to research findings that verify or refute the effectiveness of bibliotherapy with bright and gifted children. The reasons for this may have more to do with the mechanics of research than with the topic under investigation.

First, inconsistencies in definition and method weaken the collective impact of findings. In an article reviewing earlier studies, Tillman

(1984) reveals the difficulties of using them to make definitive statements about the effectiveness of bibliotherapy. For example, some studies have gathered information simply through a checklist that asks students how reading has affected them. In others, the effect of reading on attitudes is studied by administering a pretest, a reading, and a post-test.

Second, in these types of research there is no discussion of the book or of students' reactions to it, although other studies do include discussion as a part of bibliotherapy. If the definition of bibliotherapy includes a follow-up discussion of the reading, as it does here, then research will have to attempt to assess the entire process.

Third, most recent research studies reflect the work of counselors and other mental health practitioners who typically use bibliotherapy as an adjunct to therapy. This research has concentrated on self-help books rather than on fiction, and the effectiveness of fiction remains unvalidated (Riordan and Wilson, 1989).

Fourth, research investigating the use of bibliotherapy with gifted children is rare, in part because of the failure of researchers to recognize that gifted children have problems that might be addressed through bibliotherapy (Hebert, 1991).

And finally, the impact of a book varies significantly from one reader to another, determined by an overwhelming number of variables. Attempts to measure and quantify the effect of art on personality will always be thwarted to some degree by the elusiveness of the concepts involved.

Therefore, current studies can point toward but not confirm the effectiveness of using carefully selected books and well-planned discussion to help gifted students cope with giftedness. At present, only the experience of educators and children support the assertion that bibliotherapy is valuable for gifted students. Children probably say it best when they affirm, time after time, that they would want to be in a discussion group again and that it is definitely worth the time it takes from their regular schedule—typical responses when they are asked to evaluate the experience at the end of a discussion series.

Continued and expanded use of developmental bibliotherapy with gifted youngsters should be encouraged. The research we do have indicates that the process has potential; connecting gifted children with books and giving them a chance to talk about their responses makes intuitive sense. From the knowledge now available, it seems safe to assume that developmental bibliotherapy is a promising technique still in the theoretical and experimental stages. Adults who work with books and gifted youngsters can do so with the knowledge that they are creating a new method of guiding gifted children. They must proceed with caution, with respect for the infinite variability of human nature, and in the knowledge that they are practicing an art and not a science.

Training in Bibliotherapy

Currently there are only two positions in the country for full-time bibliotherapists, both clinically oriented: at the D.C. Commission on Mental Health Services (formerly St. Elizabeths Hospital) in Washington, D. C., and at the Santa Clara County Free Library in San Jose, California. The many others who practice bibliotherapy use it as a tool in their work as librarians, social workers, nurses, counselors, or teachers.

Many who work in clinical settings are certified poetry therapists (CPT) or registered poetry therapists (RPT). These designations are awarded by the National Association of Poetry Therapy (NAPT) through its credentials committee. Information about requirements can be found in *Trainees' and Trainer's Guide to Requirements for CPT and RPT Designation*, which can be purchased through Peggy Heller, 7715 White Rim Terrace, Potomac, MD, 20854.

Training geared toward fulfilling requirements for the designations of CPT or RPT is available at the D.C. Commission on Mental Health Services. The program offers part-time poetry therapy/bibliotherapy training with peer groups, didactic work, and clinical experiences supported by individual and group supervision. Information on this program can be obtained from Kenneth Gorelick, M.D., R.P.T., Barton Hall, St. Elizabeths Campus, Washington, D.C., 20032.

Dr. Gorelick can also supply a list of other training opportunities around the country.

There is no separate certification at this time for developmental bibliotherapists, but some training is available. Graduate schools in library science sometimes offer courses in bibliotherapy, and Rhea Rubin, an independent library consultant and author of books on bibliotherapy, offers workshops in various locations. She may be contacted at 5860 Huron Drive, Oakland, CA 94618. Another source of current information on such offerings is The Association of Specialized and Cooperative Library Agencies (ASCLA) of the American Library Association, 50 East Huron Street, Chicago, IL, 60611.

The University of South Florida in Tampa's School of Library and Information Science has temporarily suspended its program in bibliotherapy, but may reinstate it in the near future. This program offers two courses on developmental bibliotherapy and an opportunity for supervised field work, in VA and children's hospitals as well as in schools and public libraries. Those interested in this program should contact the School of Library and Information Science, HMS 301, University of South Florida, Tampa, FL, 33620.

For discussion leaders who cannot take a course or attend a workshop, *Bibliotherapy: The Interactive Process: a Handbook* (Hynes and Hynes-Berry, 1986), offers a thorough and thoughtful explanation of the process and is highly recommended. Hynes established the St. Elizabeths training program, and while her book emphasizes clinical work, it also provides a good basis for developmental bibliotherapy.

Students who cannot find desired courses in bibliotherapy sometimes use this book as a resource for independent study. (Rhea Rubin, personal communication, November 5, 1992)

Do parents, teachers, or librarians who lack special training have the expertise to lead a bibliotherapeutic discussion? Smith (1989, Spring) asserts that "Any group may be conducted by a *knowledgeable* librarian alone or with a counselor or social worker, other therapist, or similar professional person who will not want to probe too deeply into the members' emotions" (p. 248).

This book takes the view that many parents, teachers, and librarians are already practicing bibliotherapy in various degrees, perhaps without knowing it and almost always without formal training. The information provided in this chapter is offered in the belief that the more these discussion leaders can learn about what they are doing, the more effective they will be.

Those who are interested in doing bibliotherapy probably already have some of the qualifications. Hynes and Hynes-Berry (1986) list the personal characteristics required of a bibliotherapist:

- Maturity: self-awareness, self-acceptance, tolerance of others
- Integrity: respect for self and others that enables the therapist to avoid exploitation of emotions
- Responsibility: an attitude of responsiveness as well as willingness to guide group participants through potentially difficult discussions

- Adaptability: the ability to adjust plans to meet the needs of the group at the moment, and to allow participants their own interpretations

In addition to these inherent characteristics, the authors point out that the bibliotherapist must acquire and develop therapeutic attitudes:

- Empathy: the ability to understand another person's feelings without actually experiencing them
- Respect: the recognition of the value of another person's feelings, and of his or her inherent worth and uniqueness
- Genuineness: sincerity, spontaneity, openness; awareness and acceptance of one's own inner experiences

To use developmental bibliotherapy with gifted children, leaders should also know and enjoy children's literature, understand child development in general and that of gifted children in particular, have the trust of the children with whom they are working, and know something about counseling and discussion techniques.

The Bibliotherapeutic Process

Present theories about what happens in bibliotherapy go back to 1949 when educator Carolyn Shrodes studied the relationship between bibliotherapy and psychotherapy for her doctoral dissertation. She identified three phases of the bibliotherapeutic process, corresponding to phases of psychotherapy: these form the basis of subsequent concepts of bibliotherapy.

The three stages of bibliotherapy are identification, catharsis, and insight. Another phase, less often mentioned but especially interesting for work with gifted children, is universalization (Slavson, 1950), the recognition that our difficulties and sense of difference are not ours alone.

Bibliotherapy depends on the dynamics set up among the reader, the literature, and the discussion. It begins with *identification*, when the reader identifies with a character in the book, recognizing something of herself and so coming to care what happens to that character. Mollie

Hunter (1990), author of several books listed in Chapter Eight, describes identification with the understanding and skill of a fine writer:

> *... even the most superficial reader will follow the incident by identifying with the character concerned in it; and so, willy-nilly, there comes a point when reader and character are involved in the same emotions ... the reader ... glimpse[s] a reflection of himself in another young person caught in a situation that demands the enunciation of some value, the setting of some standard. Temporarily at least, he will have had a sense of participating in the decision taken, and the process of thought set unconsciously in train may yet surface in his mind ... the reader will still be essentially free to formulate his own eventual philosophy; but [he will have been shown] something of what may be implied by the choices occurring in those adolescent years* (p. 28).

It may sound improbable that identification with a fictional character can be such a powerful experience. Book characters are real people to most children, however, and children continue to see them as real people even under the close scrutiny of discussion. Coles (1989) indicates that this is true of college students as well.

At the same time, the child's awareness of the distancing effect of literature provides a sense of safety. Lerner and Mahlendorf (1992) point out that "it is for the reason of emotional safety by proper distancing that literary works can do more than merely instruct us ... they ... make us more sensitive to [our] feelings and ourselves. In this way, we gain an emotional awareness that transforms us and gives us the motivation to change ourselves" (p. x).

Universalization is behind Delisle's description (1990) of "John," in an article recommending bibliotherapy as one means of preventing suicide among gifted young people. John

> *... probably does not realize that thousands of other persons throughout the centuries have wrestled with the same types of issues that he now confronts...More than anything else—anyone else—what John now needs is someone to tell him that it is OK to be confused, anxious, and ambivalent. This person may be a teacher, a counselor, Holden Caulfield from* Catcher in the Rye, *or the protagonist in* Zen and the Art of Motorcycle Maintenance. *To gifted students like John, getting the answers to timeworn philosophical issues is less*

important than merely being told that his questions *are legitimate* (p.223-224).

Catharsis occurs as the reader follows the character through a difficult situation to a successful resolution. Spache (1974) defines catharsis:

> *...sharing of motivations, conflicts and emotions of a book character. Defined in psychological terms, catharsis is an active release of emotions, experienced either first-hand or vicariously. Catharsis goes beyond the simple intellectual recognition of commonalities as in identification ... It involves empathetic emotional reactions similar to those that the reader imagines were felt by the book character. Or, in another sense, the reader relives, insofar as his own emotional experiences permit, the feelings he attributes to a character in a story* (p. 242).

One quiet summer morning years ago I was working contentedly in the kitchen, the children still in bed upstairs, when from Mark's room came the sudden heart-stopping sound of deep sobbing. He had been awake for some time, reading *Julie of the Wolves,* and had reached the cruel and emotionally painful point in Julie's conflict between two cultures. Anyone who knows that book will recognize that Mark was experiencing catharsis. It is not a bad thing, after all, to be able to cry over a book.

Insight is the reader's application of the character's situation to her own life. If identification and catharsis have occurred while reading the book, insight may occur during discussion or even later, as the reader reflects on the story. She may transfer his understanding of the character's personality and motivations to herself, increasing self-understanding and bringing her own options into sharper focus.

Insight does not necessarily lead to immediate action, nor does it need to. The discussion leader may not even always know whether it has occurred. Assumptions can be made, however. What insights might have resulted from Mark's reading of *Julie of the Wolves*? A confirmation of his sensitivity to cruelty and his tender-heartedness toward animals; a reluctant recognition that true endings are not always happy ones; and the new-found confidence that he could accept this fact, if with sadness. A growing experience for a ten-year-old.

This process, of course, does not take place with every reader and every book. A discussion leader can help to bring it about by asking questions that focus first on identification with one or several characters (and on the universality of the experience if that is appropriate); then on the critical situation, the way the story character handled it, and the feelings stirred in the reader in response; and finally on ways in which all this relates to the reader's own life. A demonstration of this process will be found in the sample questions given later in this chapter.

Nor do all of these steps necessarily fit neatly into a half-hour discussion session. Many readers continue to mull over books long after they have finished them. If there is not a good response to one of the deeper questions during the discussion, a seed may nevertheless have been planted that will lead to thought later on. Like parents and teachers, bibliotherapy discussion leaders will know only a small portion of the impact they have on children's lives.

Caution with Bibliotherapy

As with any helping relationship, bibliotherapists must exercise caution, always aware of the possibility that deeper problems may be present, and remembering that developmental bibliotherapy is meant to help prevent problems, not to cure them. Anyone who encourages children to discuss their feelings should know when to refer a child to a mental health professional. Children may exhibit any of several warning signals that the bibliotherapist should discuss with the child's parents or a psychologist.

There may be underlying problems if a gifted child or her parents appear to be denying giftedness. If the child shows unusual reluctance to be placed in the gifted category, or if the parents are unable or unwilling to allow the child to participate in enrichment activities, there is some cause for concern. Comments from the child may indicate prejudicial treatment at home, in the form of parental attitudes disclosed in statements like "If you're so smart, why can't you remember to take out the trash?"

If a child seems unable to relate to the purpose of the book discussion group, or unable to relate meaningfully to at least some of the other children in the group, there may be a problem.

Bruce made it clear that he didn't want any part of a book discussion group: he slumped in his chair and glowered at

91

the floor except when spoken to directly. He spoke as little as possible, contributing one comment that revealed very low self-esteem. After three sessions he stopped attending, and after the discussion leader called his mother for a conference, the mother made arrangements for individual sessions for him—a much more appropriate arrangement in this instance than group discussion.

Responses can indicate much more than low self-esteem. There is reason to be concerned about students whose responses reveal excessive anger, aggression, anxiety, depression, fear, preoccupation with sexuality, inability to have empathy for others, little or no social life, or inordinately high or perfectionistic standards for themselves. School performance that is far below ability level, or a lack of investment in achievement in any area, even those of high ability, are further signals of underlying problems that might be helped by therapy.

Anna has been invited to join a bibliotherapy discussion group because her test scores indicate that she is gifted. Her academic performance has never measured up to her potential, and teachers hope the group will bring about changes in her behavior. Although the other students in the group are her friends, Anna does not join in the discussion. It is clear by the second session that she has transferred her attitude toward schoolwork to the group; she will not read the books not because she is too busy but because she has decided not to participate. Recognizing that the bibliotherapy group is not appropriate for Anna, the leader refers her to the school psychologist.

Of course, a leader must be concerned about a student who gives evidence of physical or psychological abuse or neglect, who shows signs of drug or alcohol abuse, or who is carrying a weapon. She may be alerted in discussion, for example, by a student who strongly defends the right of individuals to use drugs.

A bibliotherapist must also be aware of the possibility of serious depression or even potential suicide. Indications of depression include insomnia or other sleep disturbances, lack of interest in life or in any number of activities that formerly were motivating and exciting, emotional outbursts, noticeable weight gain or loss, and changes in clothing and dress standards. Direct mention of suicide and a strong defense of suicide as a desirable choice are clear danger signs.

These warning signals do not occur often, but bibliotherapists should be aware of them and realize they are in a unique position to help. A discussion leader's best contribution to some children may well be a referral to a competent psychologist.

In addition to watching for signs of deep emotional problems, discussion leaders should be careful to control the depth of the discussion. It is not necessary that everything be explicitly said; participants can be trusted to take and use what they can. If a discussion at greater depth seems potentially beneficial, a teacher or librarian could ask the school guidance counselor or psychologist to serve as co-leader. Unless a mental health professional is present, discussion leaders without training in psychology should not attempt to invite self-disclosures that would make participants feel exposed.

Setting Up Discussion Groups at School

When teachers or librarians use book discussion with high-ability students, they are most likely to do so with a group, although they may occasionally hold informal talks with individual students. This section provides detailed information on selecting children to join discussion groups, on choosing books for groups to read, and on setting a place and time for book discussion at school.

Before a leader can sit down with a group of youngsters, all of whom have read the same book and are eager to discuss it, there is much work to be done. Setting up a group means bringing appropriate children and appropriate books together, in sufficient numbers of each, at a time and place that will suit everyone's needs. The advance planning will vary considerably, depending on such factors as how the school identifies gifted students, the academic structure of the program for them (if any), the flexibility in the schedule, and how important the faculty and administration feel it is to deal with the emotional needs of gifted youngsters.

The Children

It is easier to hold effective discussions if the children are close in age. Students from two grade levels can meet together, but a wider age range makes it difficult to choose literature that will appeal to everyone.

They should also be relatively close in ability level. Like academic programs for the gifted, a book discussion group that combines students in the superior range with those who are highly gifted will probably fail to meet the needs of the highly gifted members; it would be better to have a separate group for them if possible.

Remembering that highly gifted people differ from one another more than do people in the superior or average ranges, the leader for this group should keep the individual characteristics of each reader in mind while selecting books. For the same reason, discussion should be specifically planned for the individual students rather than for the group in general. In addition, the books chosen for them should offer examples of highly gifted people.

With any discussion group for highly able children, the leader should know how much the children understand about their selection for the group. If the term *gifted* is used, the comfort level of the students will depend largely on how the use of the term is handled within their school. It may be a good idea in the first session to discuss how members will describe the group for children who are not included. The leader can help them avoid hurting others without downplaying their own abilities: "We're going to read books and talk about them. It's a group for good readers who like to read a lot. We're going to learn ways to think about a book after you've read it, and how to discuss the ideas in the book."

The leader should consider whether the self-concept and personal strength of each potential member is sufficient to allow participation in the group without inappropriate self-revelation or hypersensitivity. If the leader knows that a child has a specific problem that may be discussed and that it is so close to the surface that the student will be unable to think or speak about it objectively, then for the protection of the child an individual discussion would be preferable to a group experience.

Tracy's parents have recently divorced, and her mother has asked Tracy's school counselor to include her in a support group for children of divorced parents. In talking with Tracy, however, the counselor has learned that she is not yet ready to discuss her experience in a group of peers. Rather than participate in a group discussion of A Girl Called Al *or* The Boy Who Could Make Himself Disappear, *both about children dealing with the emotional aftermath of divorce, Tracy should be given the option of meeting individually with the counselor for a time.*

Unexpected self-revelation may well occur during group discussion, and the leader can deal with it at that time through reassurance, redirection of the topic, or by offering to talk about it after the meeting; it is better if selection of group members can minimize its occurrence. Members of a book discussion group designed to help them cope with developmental issues of giftedness should be children not currently in crisis. A group for children in crisis should be planned and led differently, probably with a counselor as co-leader.

A group size of six to eight is optimum. Even with eight, there may be some who will be able to remain silent because the group is large enough for them to do so. With fewer than six, the group can become ineffective if two members are absent or have not read the book.

Should group membership be optional for those eligible to join? If it is, there will be better potential for good discussion. However, if it is required, the group may include students who would not otherwise join, but who may benefit greatly once they are involved. Those who know the students best should make this decision.

Consider forming a group specifically for those who would not join if given a choice, such as future scientists who scorn fiction and do not think of themselves as readers. Certainly this would benefit leaders who are nonscientists who could do with some stretching in that direction, and it would help them to develop a participatory rather than authoritarian leadership style, since they would need help from the students. A good start might be to ask potential group members for suggestions of book titles, including biography and other nonfiction as well as fiction, from which to develop a book list.

Another issue is what to do about students who come to the discussion without having finished the book. One way of alleviating this problem is to request that the classroom teacher accept books read for group discussion as book reports to meet the curriculum quota, so the books do double duty.

The Books

In some contexts, bibliotherapy is practiced with little regard for the quality of the literature chosen. The only requirement is that the subject of the literature be appropriate to the goals of the discussion. For a couple of reasons, this cannot be the case in bibliotherapy with especially bright students.

First and most practical, inferior literature will not lend itself to discussions that will touch and challenge gifted students. They may not recognize the technical differences between good and bad literature, but they will certainly recognize (and mention with notable lack of grace) when a book is "bor-ing." Discussion about books perceived as boring is bound to be boring itself, for any age group.

Second, it is a disservice to skilled and enthusiastic readers to encourage them to spend their time on less than the best. Of course they will experiment with escape literature from time to time, but they can learn to recognize it and how to find good literature when they want it. Parents and teachers who are guiding them in the larger sense of helping them develop their potential must have the courage to differentiate the inferior from the good, and must take the time to find the best for them. There is plenty of excellence in literature for children and young people as well as for adults.

To find good literature, make use of as many sources of book lists as possible. Parents and teachers should have access to *Booklist, School Library Journal*, and other selection aids librarians use in considering books to buy. Journals about parenting and educating gifted children often have book review sections. Even newsletters of local associations for parents of gifted children may have suggestions of good books.

Browse through the education section of bookstores; there are always books to help adults encourage children to read. For discussion purposes, however, look for publications that focus on books to read rather than on the process of reading or on reading readiness. There is a partial list of these at the end of Chapter Six.

Develop the habit of reading reviews of children's books, keeping in mind the criteria in Chapter Six for books that meet emotional needs while challenging the intellectual. Good ideas come from other educators and from children, too. As discussion leaders gain experience with excellent literature, they will recognize trusted authors and good writing so they can browse effectively. Before long, by reading just a page or two they can sense whether a book is likely to justify their time to preread it for use with the children they have in mind.

After gathering lists of suggested titles, leaders need to find the books for preview. If they are not available they can be ordered. Because several copies will be needed, cost considerations may limit the choices to paperbacks. Remember that it can take four to six weeks for books to arrive.

In addition, thanks to library networking developed in the last twenty-five years, any title can be located through interlibrary loan at most public libraries. In some cases, a small charge is assessed. In my research for this book, almost every library book I requested was located in Michigan or a nearby state, and they arrived faster than I could read them.

Students may wish to buy their own copies to build personal libraries or borrow from local libraries. However, the most efficient way of making sure that each student has the book under discussion is for the school to provide multiple copies of the titles selected, keeping them in the school library for use in future years and making them available in the meantime to other students.

Try to select titles that most of the students have not read. This is a challenge that is worth the effort, especially when the titles are announced to cheers of "Oh, great! I've heard of that one!" instead of groans of "I've already read it."

An issue that always arises in assigning reading is that of free choice. Children prefer to read books of their own choosing, but obviously, unless everyone in the group has read the same book, it will be difficult to establish common ground for discussion. On the other hand, when every child reads a different book, the expense of multiple copies is saved, and children gain exposure to more good books.

Discussion of free-choice books is necessarily more open-ended, perhaps with each student answering a core question in whatever way it applies to his or her book. Or there could simply be a series of brief oral reports from the students, including an explanation of why they think the book they have chosen is or is not suited to this discussion group.

Since free-choice discussion sessions are not as focused as those based on required reading, leaders may want to establish a ratio of more required than free-choice books, saving the free-choice books for the end of the series. By then, too, children will be sufficiently familiar with the discussion process to take more responsibility for it.

Place and Time

Privacy is important when choosing a place for the discussion group. A special room or corner of the school library would be best if the library is empty at the time. A corner in the classroom is not a good place to discuss feelings the participants would not want all classmates to hear; in fact, such a spot will probably limit the effectiveness of the discussion.

The difficulty in scheduling a time will depend on whether children are coming to the group from more than one class, and on what degree of priority the school gives to the book discussion group. Until recently, the most logical time for a book discussion group seemed to be during classroom reading time, since the children participating can well afford to miss instruction in reading skills they probably already possess. With the introduction of literature-based reading programs, however, this has changed. It would be counterproductive to remove them from one book-oriented experience to join another.

It is generally not a good idea to schedule programming for gifted students at a time that requires them to miss recess, physical education, or lunch—taking them away from social opportunities and emphasizing their differences. In one school, however, these were the only options. The principal's suggestion that the students vote on the time they preferred was a happy one for all concerned.

For children in grades three to six, a series of four sessions may be adequate, spaced one week apart. Junior high students may need more time to read their books; biweekly sessions might be better for them. For high school students, book discussions could be held once a month throughout the school year.

Book discussion groups can also be offered as part of summer enrichment programs. These sessions may be spread over a period of two to three weeks, with two or three meetings a week, assuming children have more time in the summer. These groups can incorporate students from different schools, granting them an anonymity that may make it easier to talk.

Bibliotherapy at Home

When parents use book discussion with their children at home, the question of which children to involve is not an issue. Still, like teachers and librarians planning a discussion group at school, parents must solve the problems of finding good books and a suitable place and time for discussion. In addition, they must consider different ways to motivate their child to participate, and slightly different techniques of talking with an individual instead of a group.

Finding Good Books

The bibliography in Chapter Eight is designed to help parents as well as teachers find books that are well-written, challenging (as they must be to hold the interest of discriminating readers), and suitable as discussion starters.

In addition, parents will find both help and inspiration in *From Wonder to Wisdom: Using Stories to Help Children Grow* (Smith, 1989). A specialist in human development at Kansas State University, Dr. Smith highlights books for children from two to eight years old, relating the stories to challenges similar to the five developmental tasks outlined in Chapters One and Two of this book. Parents will find much understanding of their young child's emotional development woven into Smith's discussion of appropriate books.

Suitable Place and Time

Where and when are good opportunities for you to read and talk about books with your children? In a more leisurely era, a book like this might have suggested firmly establishing a family book discussion at the same time every week. Some modern families may be able to manage that, and we applaud them—even while we acknowledge that for most, hectic schedules require imaginative solutions.

Busy working parents can make use of snippets of time throughout the day. If books are a priority, they will be in the car, carried into the dentist's waiting room, in a back pocket or a purse to be pulled out while waiting for a ride or a rider. Conversations take place in the car, over dishes, after the homework is done, on a walk.

One family's tradition of "talk-talk time" available to each child after the lights go out provides a satisfying place and time to talk about books. Another family might designate a routine chore, such as a Saturday run to the recycling plant, for book talk time. Once the importance of finding time to read and talk about books is established, every member of the family can get into the act of finding time to do it—and meeting the challenge tells children how important it really is.

Motivation

Motivation is usually more subtle and relaxed at home than at school. With an avid reader, a parent may need do no more than mention that she would like to read a book he is reading; when both have finished the book, they can talk about it over dishes or while driving home—whenever there are fifteen or twenty uninterrupted minutes. Once a pattern of discussing books is established, the parent can reciprocate by recommending a book to him, and they will be on their way.

With a resistant reader, parents may have to be more assertive. It will help if reading time has been built into the daily schedule from the early years, and it will certainly help if the parents are readers. Some parents find that they can strike a deal with their child: they will read what the child recommends to them, and she will read what they recommend to her—some of the time.

Discussion with an Individual Child

What a parent does in bibliotherapy will be much the same as what a teacher or librarian would do, except he will usually be talking with an individual instead of a group. He can use the same procedures for planning and leading a discussion that are outlined later in this chapter for use with a group, modifying them to suit the home situation and the child.

The discussion itself will be slightly different from one with a group. If one child is doing all of the responding, she is more likely to become involved in the discussion than if she could leave some of the work to others. On the other hand, she will miss the reinforcement of ideas from peers; the parent may need to compensate for that by bringing up the points of view that other children might mention if they were there.

Just as motivation is likely to be less structured at home than at school, so do discussions tend to be more relaxed. Parents should capitalize on the advantages of this difference rather than worrying about following a plan too closely.

In a less structured home setting, parents may accomplish less in a given amount of time, but they have the advantage of being able to continue over a period of several years. In addition, they will bring such a wealth of family experience to the conversations that in the long run they may well be able to accomplish much more. Imagine the following scenario:

> *The Miller family began reading to their children in the nursery, and both Jon and Laurie began reading early. When they were three and four Dad would push back his chair from the dining table in the evening and say, "I feel a little Pooh coming on," and they would pile into his lap for a chapter*

100

or two of Winnie-the-Pooh. *The family read aloud on vacations and camping trips, and it was a natural step to begin talking about the books the children were reading.*

Usually, Mother had read the books they read, and when she asked Laurie what she thought of The Wolfling *the discussion expanded to include Dad's and Jon's thoughts on why higher education is important for someone like Robbie Trent—and Jon and Laurie. Laurie's excitement over* Anno's Medieval World *led to a family discussion that helped Jon understand superstition and scientific thought in a new light, an understanding that he tucked away for further attention as he pondered budding career ideas. When Laurie showed evidence of feeling uncomfortably different and out of place in her new junior high school, Mother reminded her of Jess in* A Bridge to Terebithia, *who did not fit in his family or his school but who did have one friend and one teacher who understood. Over the years, their love of books led to productive conversations and mutual understanding for the entire family.*

Planning

Whether working informally with a child at home or setting up a series at school, some planning is necessary before discussing a book with a child. Prior to a discussion the leader must choose a book, read it, prepare discussion questions, and motivate the children to read the book.

Choosing the Book

Chapter Six is devoted to selecting appropriate literature for gifted students and eager readers. Briefly, we can follow the suggestions of Robinson (1989): look for situations that evoke emotions, situations that offer alternatives, and characters with whom the reader can identify.

For a good discussion, the book must deal with a range of human emotions, not only the fear or excitement engendered by adventure stories. When characters are faced with alternatives, readers are led to consider the options, too—a focal point for discussion. And the reader must be able to identify with a character for the first step in bibliotherapy.

Reading the Book

The first step is to read the book. For those not familiar with children's literature, this may at first sound like a tedious task, but good children's literature will hold adults' interest too. In fact, a book that does *not* hold the leader's interest should be reconsidered before being recommended for gifted students. One way to test for good writing is to read a passage aloud: If the tongue feels stiff and stumbles over the words, the book simply may not be well written. Look for books that glide along, flowing from word to word and from thought to thought when read aloud. But above all, read the book!

The leader must plan discussion questions related to the book; this will be easiest if she thinks about them as she is reading. She must also keep in mind the child or children with whom the book will be discussed, and the purpose in discussing it with them. She can use as a bookmark a three-by-five slip of paper on which she jots down page numbers and key phrases that strike her as potential discussion material. When she goes back later to write questions, she will have an overview of themes in the book that will be useful for discussion.

It is a good idea to allow a day or two after finishing a book to let it "settle in" before writing questions. During this incubation period, the leader will be subconsciously working on the book, and when she does sit down to write, the questions that come will be a distillation, probably of better quality and drawn more from the true heart of the book than if she had begun to write immediately. What she is doing in that dormant period is allowing the book to sift down into deeper levels of her own understanding, so that her responses will contain some measure of wisdom as well as intellectual analysis. Some people find that certain "pump-priming" activities, such as walking, drawing, or playing a musical instrument are helpful during this period.

Busy students will probably not have the time for a similar incubation period before they come to the book discussion. It can't hurt, however, to suggest it to them.

Adults may find that their immediate response to a book is that it can't possibly be used with gifted children. When they sit down with pencil and paper they may still think the book has nothing to offer. But if they go on with the physical act of writing, beginning with a summary of the plot, the potential of the book begins to unfold and usually questions will occur as quickly as one can write them down. Sometimes, of course, this does not happen; the book truly is unsuitable for this purpose. In this case it is worth taking the time to clarify exactly why

102

it is unsuitable; this bit of discipline helps in the ongoing definition of what the leader *is* looking for in books to use for bibliotherapy with gifted students.

Preparing the Questions

Bibliotherapy differs from intellectually-oriented book discussion in that it is based on the readers' emotional responses to the book rather than on questions of plot and character or writing quality and style. Chapter Five analyzes these issues; a comparison of this chapter and the next should clarify the differences in the two types of discussion.

For either type, the leader must know the difference between fact questions and interpretive ones, and use each intentionally. Fact questions are those to which the answer can be found in the book; the leader knows what answer he wants when he asks the question, and he will use the answer to judge how well the student read the book. Interpretive questions are those whose answers are open to interpretation. They are "honest" questions in that the leader does not know the answer—that is, he does not know what the student thinks. Having had time to think about it, the leader may know what his own answer is, but the student may well give an equally valid different answer. Interpretive questions are appropriate when the leader (1) assumes the youngster has read the book, and (2) is interested in the student's response.

It is best to begin a discussion with a few fact questions to ascertain the general level of understanding and response to the book. These introductory questions also provide a warm-up period, a chance for readers to recall the impact of the book and to build to the emotional level called for by the interpretive questions.

The annotations of the books listed in Chapter Eight include a few suggested interpretive questions for each book. Here is a list of general interpretive questions that can be adapted to specific books:

1. What is the central character's biggest problem?
2. How do you think (he) (she) feels?
3. What strengths does (he) (she) have that help (him) (her) cope?
4. Do you know anyone who has ever been in the same situation?
5. What would you have done?
6. If you were (his) (her) best friend, what advice would you give?

7. How would that help the situation?

8. What effect do the people in the book have on one another?

For writing interpretive questions, the stages of bibliotherapy—identification, catharsis, and insight—are more easily understood as actions: recognizing, feeling, and thinking. In planning bibliotherapy sessions, structure the questions so that they lead students from one mental activity to the next.

For example, here are discussion questions for Constance C. Greene's *A Girl Called Al*, which can be used with gifted third or fourth graders. The questions progress from encouraging identification with Al to generating insight into the reader's own life.

Identification (Recognizing)	Describe Al; describe the narrator (who is never named in the book).
	Whom are you most like, Al or the narrator?
	Why? (Al is a leader; the narrator, a follower.)
	In what ways does Al have extra trouble because she is bright? How are things easier for her because she is bright?
Catharsis (Feeling)	How do you know Al is lonely, even though she never says so?
	What happens in the book to help Al overcome her loneliness?
	What effect does Mr. Richards have on Al? Do you know anyone who is as important to you or to someone else as Mr. Richards is to Al? What effect will his death have on Al? On what do you base your answer?
	How does Al feel when Mr. Richards dies? How do you know? Do you know anyone who has trouble showing feelings as Al does?

Insight (Thinking)	When do you hide your real feelings? What are the advantages of doing so? Why is it hard to show real feelings?
	Why does showing real feelings make people feel less lonely?

These questions pursue just one of the themes in the book: loneliness. An equally productive theme is Al's defiant nonconformity. To follow that theme, a discussion leader might use the same identification questions, and then continue with these:

Catharsis (Feeling)	Why has Al chosen to be a nonconformist? How (Feeling) do you think she feels about it?
	Think of nonconformists you know, or even of yourself, if you are one. What feelings (good or bad) do you think compel people to be nonconformists?
	How do you imagine nonconformists feel about themselves generally?
Insight (Thinking)	When do you choose not to conform? Why?
	What are different ways to be a nonconformist?
	When is nonconformity destructive? When is it productive?

These questions assume identification with Al more than with the narrator. If a child in the group is more likely to identify with the narrator, the leader may want to develop different questions, perhaps with the purpose of encouraging understanding of what the follower brings to a leader/follower relationship, or of developing empathy for nonconformists from the point of view of those who find it easier to conform.

For a thirty-minute discussion with middle or late elementary children, a list of twenty questions is more than enough. Each interpretive question can carry the entire discussion, if it catches the imagination of the students. Having more questions than needed gives flexibility, preparing the leader to go in any of several directions when student interests become apparent. And for beginning discussion leaders, it builds confidence to know there is more than enough material to fill the time.

These questions are only suggestions to get started. As leaders gain experience, they will want to use their own insights and questions. As students gain experience, they also will be able to generate their own questions. When they can do this, they are learning enough of bibliotherapy to be able to use it independently. It could become a skill they will be able to use even in adulthood.

Motivating the Children

Of course, book discussion can't proceed until the student has read the book. This may be no problem at all, or it may be a matter of some difficulty, depending on the level of interest the student already has in reading and on how the whole idea is presented.

It is clearly better to pique students' interest in the book itself, as well as in the discussion of it, than to present reading and discussing as a way of "working on gifted people's problems." (That motivation may come up later, as a natural result of conversation, and will be more authentic as a result. Or such problems may never be mentioned directly, but left unspoken, to be addressed by the child's internal processing.) The best aid in motivating children to read specific books is the leader's enthusiasm and his ability to convey it.

For the teacher or librarian planning a discussion series at school with a group of children, motivation is done according to good teaching practices. The leader gathers the group for an initial meeting and outlines his plans: duration of series, meeting time and place, how many books are to be read, how this group will fit into their reading program, their responsibility to read the books on time and be prepared for discussion, etc.

Agreeing to participate in the group should constitute agreement to read the books on schedule. This seems to be a bit more difficult, and the leader should know ahead of time how he will deal with those who have not finished a book by discussion time. May they participate or not? One solution is to allow participation, but to try to change the parameters of the group to prevent recurrences. Allowing more time between sessions may help; so may providing more classroom reading time, as well as counting the reading done for this group toward required book reports, to provide a deadline external to the book discussion group.

With the logistics out of the way, it is time to present the first book to be read. This can be done in a brief book talk, in which the leader

- hints at the plot or conflict in the book: "In *Jacob Have I Loved*, Louise's abilities are unrecognized, and all the family's meager resources go for voice lessons for her musically gifted twin, Caroline;"

- mentions ways in which the conflict might relate to students' own experience: "Louise grows up believing that her family loves Caroline more than they love her;"

- tells enough about the characters to initiate the reader's identification with them: "Louise is hard-working and resourceful, but not much interested in schoolwork or in her own future until circumstances force her to make a decision;"

- tells why he likes the book enough to think they would like to read it too: "I like this book especially because I like each of the characters—even Caroline—by the end of the book."

Any difficulties in the book might be mentioned, also: the structure of Konigsburg's *Father's Arcane Daughter*, for instance, may be discouraging to some readers unless it is pointed out that the book has flashbacks that will become clearer as they read. *Across Five Aprils* will start slowly for some; the leader might pass along the judgment of one sixth grader, that the book does not get interesting until page 64!

It is probably best to introduce just one book at a time, rather than giving a reading list for the whole series. Avid readers may read all the books immediately, and then the stories will not be fresh in their minds for the later discussions. Closing each session with the introduction of the next book is one way to keep motivation high.

Leading the Discussion

Whether leading a group or talking about a book with a single child, there are certain techniques that will help to make the book discussion as meaningful as possible:

1. Confidentiality is important. Group members should understand that what is said in the group should not be repeated elsewhere. Even if the leader is her father, the

child will want to know that he will not talk about the discussions to others without her permission.

2. Confidentiality will be difficult for some children to maintain. Therefore it is important to help children avoid giving information they will later regret. Children may not yet have a firm sense of how much personal revelation is appropriate. Use the "capping" technique, especially in a group: be alert to those times when a child may be saying too much, and divert attention to another question and another child, effectively "capping" the overflow of emotion and self-revelation. (The leader may speak to the child later, giving him a chance to continue the discussion individually.)

3. Encourage children to share any ways they have found useful for coping with common problems. Some of the more mature children may have simply adopted attitudes that enable them to transcend difficulties, at least part of the time, and it will be helpful for others to hear about these.

4. Let the conversation flow where the group or the child wants to take it. The leader may understandably be eager to get to her prize question, the one that for her gets to the heart of the book or the problem; however, if she forces the discussion in that direction, her wonderful question may fall flat. This is not to say that she should allow the discussion to wander away from the book; rather, that the children may select another theme they are more ready and able to discuss.

5. Outline good discussion techniques with the children before beginning, and remind them of these when necessary. Some rules to establish are that everyone must have a chance to talk, that only one person will talk at a time, and that there are no right or wrong answers.

6. Remember that the leader's role should be not too intrusive. She is not there to be sure they understand her interpretation of the book, but to moderate and to facilitate their own understanding.

At first it is only natural that the leader will be concerned about pacing. With experience, she can relax about time and become more involved in the discussion herself, giving real answers to the children's comments and validating their emotional responses. In a thirty-minute session with elementary school children, it is enough if only the middle twenty minutes are spent on interpretive questions. The leader can close with a review of the major points that have been brought out, or ask the group to do this, then introduce the book to be read for the next meeting.

Goals of Bibliotherapy at Different Stages

How a child feels about being different because of giftedness or unusual intellectual curiosity is determined partly by the child's age and partly by the degree to which adults have openly discussed differences in ability. In turn, the child's level of awareness will determine the character of the book discussion.

Preschool and Early Grades

A conversation about books with preschoolers or early elementary children will be just that: a conversation, not a discussion in the sense of a series of questions and answers. Accordingly, this book does not suggest discussion questions for this age group in Chapter Eight, but merely lists concepts found in the book that would be useful as the focus of a conversation.

Reasonable goals with this age are to introduce concepts, label feelings, and develop frames of reference so that when an event in the child's life recalls a story read together, the concepts can be reinforced. This process establishes the importance of books as windows into various life experiences, builds foundations for years of discussion based on books, validates the child's feelings, and assures him that talking about feelings is not only permissable but also a positive way to release emotions.

For early elementary children, a combination of conversation and deliberate questioning can be used, still with an individual child rather than with a group. Watch for signs of fatigue or restlessness and be prepared to stop as soon as they appear. This is still a preparation time for true give-and-take discussion; the emphasis should be on the warm relationship between adult and child, with books as the catalyst for occasional conversation but not yet the focal point.

Upper Elementary

It is in the later elementary years, grades 3-5, that gifted programming typically begins. Many children hear the term *gifted* applied to them for the first time at this age; however, they may not know what it means or how they are expected to react.

When selected children are invited to join a gifted program, there is usually a larger group of children who are also very bright but did not meet the criteria established by the school. They, too, need to understand their potential, and they should have special attention at this time.

It makes sense at this stage to discuss giftedness, talent, and appropriate aspirations with both groups. Since these are also the peak reading years, it is a particularly good time to begin book discussion groups.

A realistic goal for discussion groups with gifted children in the late elementary years is to help them become aware of the word *gifted* and gain some understanding of what it means. Looking inward, they may not yet be comfortable applying the term to themselves, but they can recognize some of the problems that gifted children in books have and how they cope. Looking outward, they can also begin to recognize the importance of empathy and respect for all people who are different, in whatever way.

Problem Solving Through Literature (PSTL), developed by Beverly Scofield and Revell Allen for gifted middle school students in rural Vermont, encourages understanding of self and others through reading and book discussion. Scofield and Allen base their lesson plans on the five areas of emotional development outlined in Chapters One and Two of this book, and follow up with activities designed to promote self-understanding and community awareness. Their students talk frankly about giftedness and identity, being alone, relationships with others, using their ability, and the need to understand. (Beverly Scofield, personal communication, January, 1993)

On the other hand, students can talk about differences related to giftedness without using the term. In a program designed but not labeled for gifted students, fourth graders who had read *Mrs. Frisby and the Rats of NIMH* talked about why other rats edged away from the superintelligent ones who had escaped from NIMH. The students agreed that they have felt others pull away from them, and they

110

discussed how they respond to that: by trying to be more like other people. Later, when they evaluated the series, one gain they mentioned was "learning not to edge away until you know a person better."

Middle School

Social needs are paramount for middle school students. The major contribution of a book discussion group may lie in simply bringing bright and intellectually-oriented students together, to allow them to belong to a group of peers. They need to blend with their social group while retaining their own identity, which includes their high ability level. One goal will be to remind them from time to time of this part of their identity, so that it will be available to them to build on when they emerge from this period. Books with characters who have the same abilities or interests (whether labeled gifted or not) can help to keep them aware of their potential.

Some gifted adolescents, in middle school and senior high, become poignantly and cynically aware that adults have failed to realize the potentials that life has to offer. They may begin to question the meaning of life, and given the intensity that characterizes gifted youngsters, they may carry this questioning to the point of the existential depression mentioned earlier. Leaders should be prepared to refer to a psychologist or other mental health professional any student who shows signs of depression.

Senior High

During the senior high years, students become increasingly concerned about the decisions they must make for the future. High-potential students of this age are working on college and career choices, very often struggling with the issues raised by their multipotentiality, and the reluctant realization that they must choose from among several abilities and interests. It is important now that they recognize that their abilities are different from the norm, become comfortable with them, and acknowledge some of the responsibilities their talent may imply.

A major goal of book discussion with senior high students is to help them consider these issues. The books chosen will be mostly adult literature. And since these students want literature that deals in depth with the moral and ethical decisions they are making, their reading list will include many of the classics—books whose characters struggle with eternal issues, written in language that has stood the test of time.

An Author's View

When Stephanie Tolan, the author of *A Time to Fly Free* and other books for young adults, was asked what she would say to potential bibliotherapists, she answered that discussion leaders should realize that the purpose of writing literature is not to prescribe solutions to problems. The author is trying to create a world that is real and true, not to teach. Discussion, she said, should be open-ended, helping the child to see why things work out as they do in *this* book. The author is not saying that this is what should happen, only that this is one way it could happen. It is not the only answer.

If we look from the author's point of view, we see that stories as they are being written are organic, developing in their own ways, and that other ways are possible. There is always the question, "What if. . .?" Realizing this will help to derive the widest possible meanings from the story, and the most flexibility in relating a book to a child's own life.

In books in which characters make life-shaping decisions, such as *Shadow of a Bull* and *Jacob Have I Loved*, the possibility of other options is especially clear. Each reader can respond to these books by making the decision for himself, adding components from his life that the author did not include in the book. Thus the book continues to live in the reader, informing his future decisions. With healthy development, children as they grow create lives that are real and true, even though they differ from the world the author creates.

Bibliotherapy: An Affirmation of Strengths

To most people, giftedness doesn't sound like a source of trouble at all. Those of us who call attention to potential difficulties for persons whose very label implies they have been blessed could be accused of making up problems where there may not be any and generally holding too gloomy a view of the lives of unusually bright children. It may appear that we have forgotten that they have strengths and joys as well as vulnerabilities and loneliness.

For now, however, it is vastly important that we recognize the fact that those whose high ability and intellectual or artistic interests distin-

112

quish them from the norm have a particular set of problems. Once that recognition is commonly accepted, those who discuss the social and emotional needs of gifted children will be free to place more emphasis on their strengths and capabilities.

In the meantime, bibliotherapy can be used to affirm and develop those capabilities. The fact that it is a vehicle for discussing problems should not cloud the fact that it is also a tool for calling upon the strengths of gifted children and young people. Bibliotherapy is a process uniquely designed to do just that, as Hynes and Hynes-Berry (1986) point out:

> ... *the emphasis on strengths plays a fundamental role in the bibliotherapeutic process. In the first place, the initiative for each step of the process lies with the participant. The facilitator can guide, but it is the individual participant who must recognize, examine, juxtapose, and integrate the feeling-responses and the understandings ... Moreover, progression from the first to the final step calls increasingly on the individual's strengths ... including (1) some ability to analyze issues, (2) sufficient honesty to look at the inner self, (3) enough objectivity to view a feeling or behavior pattern from another perspective, and, finally, (4) adequate self-confidence and hope to feel that change is possible and that one is personally capable of making such a change.*
>
> *Another way of making the same point is to say again that bibliotherapy is a process of* self-actualization. *Moreover, we consider the self-actualizing process to be one that not only enhances existing strengths but also corrects discrepancies ...* (p. 58)

For gifted and talented children at home or at school, in groups or as individuals, bibliotherapy is a way of building on the strengths of their reading abilities, analytical skills, and heightened sensitivity. It uses and enhances their ability to see relationships, draw conclusions, synthesize and evaluate. And it can give direction, focus, and purpose to their introspective self-awareness. Bibliotherapy should be seen not as a remedial step but as a positive, forward thrust toward the full use of the strengths these children possess—and, eventually, toward self-actualization.

References

Adderholdt-Elliott, Miriam. (1991). Perfectionism and the gifted adolescent. In Marlene Bireley & Genshaft, Judy (Eds.), *Understanding the gifted adolescent* (pp. 65-75). New York: Teachers College Press.

Coles, Robert. (1989). *The call of stories: Teaching and the moral imagination.* Boston: Houghton Mifflin.

Cornett, Claudia E & Cornett, Charles F. (1980) *Bibliotherapy: The right book at the right time.* Bloomington, Ind.: Phi Delta Kappa Educational Foundation.

Delisle, James R. (1990) The gifted adolescent at risk: Strategies and resources for suicide prevention among gifted youth. *Journal for the Education of the Gifted, 13,* 212-226.

Hebert, Thomas P. (1991, June). Meeting the affective needs of bright boys through bibliotherapy. *Roeper Review, 13,* 207-212.

Hunter, Mollie. (1990). *Talent is not enough: Mollie Hunter on writing for children.* New York: HarperCollins Children's Books.

Hynes, Arleen McCarty & Hynes-Berry, Mary. (1986). *Bibliotherapy: The interactive process: A handbook.* Boulder: Westview Press.

Lack, Clara Richardson. (Spring, 1985). Can bibliotherapy go public? *Collection Building, 7,* 27-32.

Lerner, Arthur & Mahlendorf, Ursula R. (1992). *Life guidance through literature.* Chicago: American Library Association.

Reis, Sally M. & Dobyns, Sally McClure. (1991, April). An annotated bibliography of non-fictional books and curricular materials to encourage gifted females. *Roeper Review, 13,* 129-130.

Riordan, Richard J. & Wilson, Linda S. (1989, May). Bibliotherapy: Does it work? *Journal of Counseling and Development, 67,* 506-508.

Robinson, Doris. (1989, September/October). Bibliotherapy discussions. *Ohio Libraries, 2,* 22.

Rubin, Rhea J. (1979, Fall). Uses of bibliotherapy in response to the 1970's. *Library Trends, 28,* 239-252.

Schrank, Frederick A. (1982, February). Bibliotherapy as an elementary school counseling tool. *Elementary School Guidance & Counseling, 16,* 218-227.

Schrank, Frederick A. & Engels, Dennis W. (1981, November). Bibliotherapy as a counseling adjunct: Research findings. *Personnel and Guidance Journal, 60,* 143-147.

Slavson, S. R. (1950). *Analytic group psychotherapy with children, adolescents, and adults.* New York: Columbia University Press.

Smith, Alice G. (1989, Spring). Will the real bibliotherapist please stand up? *Journal of Youth Services in Libraries, 2,* 241-249.

Smith, Charles. (1989). *From wonder to wisdom: Using stories to help children grow.* New York: Plume.

Spache, George D. (1978). Using books to help solve children's problems. In Joyce Rhea Rubin (Ed.), *Bibliotherapy source book.* Phoenix, Oryx Press. (Original work published 1974)

Tillman, Chester E. (1984, May). Bibliotherapy for adolescents: An annotated research review. *Journal of Reading, 27,* 713-719.

Zaccaria, Joseph S., Moses, Harold A., & Hollowell, Jeff S. (1978). *Bibliotherapy in rehabilitation, educational and mental health services.* Champaign, Ill.: Stipes.

CHAPTER
FIVE

Intellectual Development Through Books

A pproaching books from the intellectual point of view is much more widespread and has a far longer history than bibliotherapy. It is more familiar and comfortable for parents and teachers who want to talk about books with curious, motivated learners, and is without doubt the easier starting point.

This chapter begins by exploring how reading and discussing books—whether at school or at home—can meet the intellectual needs outlined in Chapter Two. Next is a section on new developments in school reading programs, followed by steps for leading groups in intellectually-oriented book discussion. Suggestions for parents who wish to supplement the school programs at home come next, and the chapter concludes with information for parents who want to be certain their students are learning to seek information independently.

What Books Can Do for Intellectual Development

The needs listed in Chapter Two suggest that for optimum intellectual development, highly able children should have opportunities to do the following:

- learn to think effectively
- encounter a variety of people and ideas
- benefit from individual pacing of learning experiences
- talk with intellectual peers

Curious, eager students who read widely and well, whether identified as gifted or not, can benefit from programs designed with these goals in mind. With carefully chosen books and skilled and enthusiastic leaders, reading and book discussions accomplish all of them.

Simply reading well-chosen books challenges us to think, enables us to experience a wider range of people and ideas than we encounter in our daily lives, and permits us to move at our own pace among books of our choice.

Adding opportunities for discussions of what we have read increases the chance that we will think *effectively*, exposes us to even more people and ideas, expands our avenues of response to the reading, and provides the possibility of talking with intellectual peers.

If books are chosen for high-potential students with their age and interests in mind, using the criteria for intellectually challenging books in Chapter Six, a program of reading and book discussion—although it may seem unglamorous—can be remarkably effective in developing intellectual ability.

Thinking Effectively

Many bright children are able to move easily (not to say lazily) through the elementary grades without learning to make effective use of their intellectual abilities. They can listen with half an ear and pick up enough to stay up with the class. If this pattern continues too long, they develop neither study skills nor thinking skills.

Daniel was a very bright child in elementary school and he shone in high school, graduating near the top of his class.

118

No one was surprised when he was accepted at one of the most academically demanding eastern universities. However, he is not doing well there, although he is the same serious, purposeful student. He knows why: he has not learned to think analytically or to examine his assumptions. In grade school and high school, his answers were correct so often that few listened critically to what he was saying. Now, in a class of many other outstanding students, Daniel's lack of study and thinking skills is hampering his progress. His intellectual ability is not diminished, but he has not learned to use it effectively.

Expressing ideas freely. Children who are eager to talk about their ideas are stimulated by opportunities to talk in more depth than is possible in the usual classroom discussion or casual conversation. Using their vocabularies without restraint, sharpening their thinking in talks with knowledgeable others who can spot flaws and helpfully point to discrepancies in their reasoning, they are encouraged to develop their verbal abilities.

Children who have unusual ability to think critically, evaluate, and reason out unusual solutions to complicated situations should be able to voice opinions and ideas in an environment that respects divergent thinking, where their different approaches will be encouraged and heard, rather than ignored or openly rejected by others.

During the Vietnam era a fourth-grade class discussed sending bandages and soap to the people of South Vietnam. Jeff suggested that probably the same staple commodities were needed in North Vietnam. Could the class not send packages to both? This was so serious a departure from the norm that Jeff's father (mother would not do) was called in to discuss the situation. Obviously, this was not a safe environment in which to express divergent opinions.

The sense of safety is terribly important to children whose intellectual abilities drive them to express thoughts which others may think are strange. It is, in fact, essential to their further intellectual growth.

Various situations presented in books can provide safe focal points for in-depth discussions. Children can follow up on ideas a good book has generated, feeling safe enough to express even half-formed ideas without fear of ridicule. With an understanding adult or in a group with other insightful children, they can feel free to exchange views without toning down their vocabularies. These opportunities for regular dialogue with intellectual peers and bright adult friends are enriching and valuable.

Precise thinking. Too often, careless use of language and the lazy thinking it permits are accepted both in school and at home. Children must be free to speak the way their peers do, but adults can do children a great service by creating a milieu in which, some of the time, they can practice the exact expression of incisive, critical thought. In the process, they will be learning to think with improved precision. Just as they should learn the difference between "good" and "escape" literature, they should learn the difference between casual conversation and productive discussion of ideas so they can use each when appropriate.

In individual or small group discussions, the leader has opportunities to probe for exact statements, demanding penetrating thinking which produces greater understanding. This kind of questioning can be used in any context, but books provide an especially productive opportunity for it.

> *In a discussion of Sperry's* Call It Courage *the leader asked, "Why is someone in the book alone or lonely?" When the response was a retelling of the events of Mafatu's childhood, she said, "You are telling the whole plot. I only asked why someone in the book is alone or lonely." Nine-year-old Andy immediately answered, "Mafatu was lonely because he was afraid of the sea and everyone else was courageous," eliminating all extraneous information and zeroing in on exactly what the question asked.*

Higher levels of thinking. To develop their ability to analyze, synthesize, and evaluate (the higher levels of thinking in Bloom's Taxonomy, which is discussed in more detail later in this chapter), students should work with these processes, identifying each level of thinking as they use it. Open-ended book discussions conducted in an atmosphere that promotes respect for individual opinions can be rich training ground for higher levels of thinking.

For example, in leading a book discussion series with a group of sixth graders, the teacher might talk to the students about analysis, synthesis, and evaluation. As she asks about the books, she labels each question so the students, in answering, know that they are analyzing, synthesizing, or evaluating. For the last meeting in the series, she may ask the students to bring three questions for discussion, one of each kind. The books provide the focus and the discussion group provides the opportunity for the students to clarify the meaning of each process and learn to use those processes independently.

Encountering a Variety of People and Ideas

When trying to describe the constant need of gifted children for new information, parents and teachers often find themselves using metaphors for food. "I've never known a student so thirsty for knowledge." "She is so hungry to learn." "He is a voracious reader." These are not just cliches; they express how eager gifted students seem to observant adults. Indeed, knowledge, information, and new ideas are nourishment for their minds, and (perhaps unconsciously) they sense they are in danger of intellectual starvation without them. Book discussions can expose these receptive readers to a broad spectrum of information, alternative ways of doing things, and different kinds of people.

Information. Children who absorb information rapidly and well and then clamor for more should have access to many more subjects and concerns than typically are covered in the standard curriculum. The extensive range of nonfiction available through school libraries makes this need easy to meet.

However, fiction is useful in this regard, too. Literature introduces children to times and places they will never see, and to lives they will not be able to live. It can expand their awareness of the variety of human concerns, styles, emotions, and ways of relating to others, and do it in a way that makes them care, opening doors to topics ranging from the Holocaust (*The Upstairs Room*) to the plight of migrant workers (*Roosevelt Grady*) or the struggle for education for blacks (*The Tamarack Tree*)—subjects that might not seem real if read only in history books or newspapers.

Alternative ways of doing things. Many bright children enjoy a capacity for thought processing that includes the ability to think in alternatives, to sense consequences, and to make generalizations. To turn these abilities into skills, they must play with a variety of ideas, including some that may not be familiar to most people in their schools and neighborhoods. Opportunities to experiment with these ideas in exploratory conversations build both ability and confidence.

For example, during the reading of *The Arm of the Starfish*, a group of eighth graders might be directed to stop reading at designated points and write down whether Adam should side with Dr. O'Keefe or with

121

Kali and her father, along with reasons for and probable results of their decisions. They will then have the makings of a discussion that enables them to test their judgment and decision-making skills against the outcome of the book and against the ideas of their peers.

Books are laboratories for bright students, a proving ground where they can reason out solutions to complex problems, examine the consequences of their decisions, and then try something else. Good fiction reflects life truly and, as in life, the outcome of the story can depend on one small decision or a series of events beyond one's control. There are always turning points that lead to the question, "What if. . .?" Book discussions that consider "what if" invite the expression of divergent thought.

By suggesting books that approach an issue from several angles, adults can introduce new ways of looking at that issue, helping students toward a broader point of view. Gifted children respond readily to this expansion of vision; through their broader awareness of human potential, they will learn what is possible for themselves.

Different kinds of people. A less obvious reason why gifted children need to be exposed to a variety of people is that they can be highly critical, even intolerant, of people, including themselves, who do not measure up to their standards. They need to be aware that there are different abilities and talents, and different ways of solving problems. Exposure to a variety of people can help them develop tolerance, empathy, understanding, and acceptance of human weakness in others and perhaps also in themselves.

Literature not only provides an infinity of characters who exhibit human weaknesses and learn somehow to accept them, it introduces these characters in ways that make children care about them—and learn to accept human weakness as well as to celebrate human strength.

Individual Pacing

By encouraging voluntary reading and discussion, teachers introduce flexibility to the standard classroom format, meeting individual needs by allowing for accelerated thinking, slower processing, and willingness to delay closure—all characteristic of high-potential learners.

Accelerated thinking. When thinking processes are faster than normal, the pace of a typical classroom discussion can be agonizing. It is a welcome relief for pent-up frustration and boredom if for at least part of the time those who learn more rapidly can acquire knowledge at their own rate.

Reading is wonderful for this—it is a thoroughly self-paced activity. Skimming and rereading by turns, readers can move at whatever pace they choose. A reading program increases the amount of self-paced learning available to quicker students as soon as they become independent readers.

These youngsters should be able not only to learn at their own rate, but also to talk, at least part of the time, with others who also process at an accelerated pace. Book discussions provide this opportunity. For some gifted youngsters, it may be the only such opportunity available in this period of their lives.

> *When Aaron began sixth grade at a new school, the pace of instruction was too slow and the other children were reluctant to accept him. He took refuge in the school library, where the librarian soon learned that he loved to read and that—joy of joys!—he listened to her suggestions. She recommended books such as* Anthem *to Aaron, and he began asking questions about the books when he returned them. Throughout the year, this give and take of books and talk allowed Aaron to learn at his own accelerated rate despite the repetitive pace in the classroom.*

Slower processing. At the same time, gifted people are capable of comprehensive synthesis and can benefit from a rather long incubation period to integrate new ideas. Some gifted children process information more slowly and deeply—and thoroughly—than others. Those who tend toward introversion are especially likely to take extra time to reach a conclusion or decision.

Reading and book discussion, if properly arranged, can accommodate this slower processing better than the typical routine of classroom assignments. If an adult discusses the concepts of incubation and slower processing time with these students, they can gain useful knowledge about their own work patterns and learn to provide incubation time for themselves—for example, by planning to finish a book a day or two before meeting to discuss it.

> *Cindy is in the gifted program, but she isn't sure she belongs there. While most of her classmates are racing to be first with the right answer, she is quietly going over information in her mind, connecting new ideas with already acquired knowledge. In book discussion, however, she is ready to*

speak with the rest and her well-formed opinions are respected by the group. When the teacher mentions that Cindy makes good use of incubation time, she begins to understand and appreciate the advantages of her slower processing.

Delayed closure. Earlier than most, gifted children often show the ability to delay closure, to accept a situation for which there is no immediate solution. Therefore, questions with single, final answers are not always appropriate for them. They are more likely to want to wait until all the information is in, to spend time looking at all sides of a question.

To develop this ability, they should be allowed to pursue their ideas and integrate new ones into their thinking without being forced to make final decisions or judgments immediately. They need open-ended discussion and open-ended situations to discuss.

In a book discussion final judgments are never necessary; in fact, one result of a good book discussion will be the new insights it evokes. The process of interacting with the book may only begin with the discussion.

Further, some children's literature provides open-ended situations; such books do not come to final conclusions, in order to let readers consider possible endings. These books, which often have characters who are able to delay closure, provide excellent discussion material.

The Beethoven Medal presents such an open-ended situation. Throughout the book Pennington displays first one and then the other side of his personality: the talent and discipline of the promising professional musician and the aggression and temper that have left him with a jail record. A second unresolved theme in the book is his relationship with Ruth. Students who can accept the lack of resolution benefit from discussion of the complexities of human nature that the book presents.

Talking with Peers

We all need friends we can talk to comfortably, as equals. It is hard for unusually bright children, or those with artistic or intellectual interests, to find such friends—even harder than for gifted adults—and it is impossible to measure what a difference such a friend can make in their lives.

During the summer between seventh and eighth grades, Ben spent two weeks on a college campus at a summer program for gifted teenagers. He had never before been exposed to so many people with exciting ideas and the eagerness to talk about them. When the program ended, his parents and younger brother picked him up and took him out for dinner and then to a nearby campground to begin a family vacation. Ben was so stimulated by the campus experience that he talked about it nonstop through dinner and while they set up camp. He woke up the next morning still talking; it was late that afternoon before it was completely out of his system. Ben had discovered something momentous: There are other people like him. A new confidence began to replace Ben's long-standing sense of isolation.

One reason the summer experience had such an impact on Ben is that it included older students. When their comprehension is advanced beyond their contemporaries', children need contact with intellectual peers, regardless of age. It is essential for them to be able to talk with people who challenge and stimulate them and who respect their ideas, at least part of the time. Adults who talk about books with young people like Ben can provide intellectual challenge during the awkward years some of them experience before they attend a high school or college where they can find agemates who match their intellectual ability.

Intellectual peers offer other benefits. For one, equally-intelligent friends usually can be counted on to see through glibness and to question shaky assertions—lazy discussion techniques too easily developed by highly verbal and socially charming youngsters, who benefit when their opinions are challenged in a well-managed discussion group. Also, most gifted and bright young people are socially aware, sensitive and concerned with values and ideals at a surprisingly early age. They need to know others who can help them put these concerns into perspective so that they can develop a positive focus rather than becoming negative or cynical.

Parents, teachers, and librarians can suggest books that deal with social concerns and depict committed people taking positive action. Discussion about these books may help students to see serious issues from a problem-solving point of view rather than from one of hopelessness. Such perspective-building is especially important for sensitive, concerned adolescents.

What Schools Are Doing with Books and Reading: A Primer for Parents

"Serious reading, serious teaching of reading, and inculcation of a love of reading are the proper goals of education." This is a fair summary, according to one reviewer (Alexander, 1991), of the argument presented by Jacques Barzun (1991) in his book, *Begin Here: The Forgotten Conditions of Teaching and Learning.*

Whether or not Barzun's goals are a national educational priority, several changes are occurring that alter traditional classroom reading experiences. Teachers reading this book are well aware of these changes, and possibly involved in implementing them, but parents may need a brief explanation.

Overarching these innovations is *restructuring*, a response to the alarm sounded by the 1983 report of the National Commission on Excellence in Education, *A Nation at Risk*. Related terms parents may encounter are *outcome-based education, whole language, literature-based reading* and *literature-based curriculum.*

Restructuring

"Restructuring" is the term that replaced "reform," the educational buzzword of the 1980s, as it became clear that mere reform was too slow (Lewis, 1989). Something more sweeping—a restructuring—was needed to address the problems of America's schools. Much of the following discussion is based on Lewis's book.

To a surprising degree, the impetus for restructuring comes from the business community. Facing the challenges of competing in an international marketplace, business leaders are alarmed by the gap between qualifications needed by today's workers and the preparation high school graduates bring to the workplace. To be prepared for a lifetime in a changing job market, young people must know not particular facts so much as the following:

- how to learn
- how to work in teams
- how to direct and evaluate their own work
- how to communicate well with other workers

Furthermore, they need higher-order thinking skills: the ability to synthesize, analyze, and evaluate.

In the best schools and in many gifted programs, these skills are already being taught. Leaders in gifted education for years have been developing, researching, and evaluating various approaches to this kind of teaching. Because restructuring attempts to provide instruction in these areas for all students, the investment over the last three decades in gifted education should prove to benefit everyone—as gifted educators long have maintained it could.

Restructuring is a new idea, still in the formative stages; it means different things to different people in different school districts across the country. Since it follows no single model, its features may include a variety of innovations in organization, curriculum, and classroom strategies.

Organizational changes include increased transference of decision making from the central administrative office to the principal's office—and the faculty meetings—of individual schools. This "site-based management" began with the finding that neighborhood schools are where real change takes place, and that changes do not last unless teachers are active participants in planning for them.

In *curriculum* change, the goal is to shift away from building a knowledge base toward promoting a deeper understanding of that knowledge, problem solving, and creative and analytical thinking—so that students learn to apply their knowledge to solve complex problems. Two programs designed to effect these changes are Mortimer Adler's Paideia Proposal (Adler, 1982), based on the assumption that all children are educable and should be exposed to a demanding curriculum; and Theodore Sizer's Coalition of Essential Schools (Sizer, 1984), the philosophy of which includes, in addition to the idea mentioned above, the proposal that a secondary teacher's class load not exceed 80 students—and contends that this can be done with only a 10% increase in per-pupil cost. (For comparison, a teacher responsible for five classes of twenty-eight students each has a class load of 140—a serious deterrent to writing assignments.)

New *classroom strategies* which may adversely affect gifted students are untracking and cooperative learning. "Untracking" is a move away from assigning students to full-time instructional groups which may persist from one year to the next. But untracking often translates into the elimination of ability grouping as well. Ability grouping enables teachers to provide specific instruction aimed at a common level, as in the familiar homogeneous reading or math groups in a heterogeneous elementary school classroom. Such groups do not permanently lock students out of settings where they may be appropriately challenged (the charge against tracking); rather, these groups place students with similar learning needs together for the length of time needed for instruction (Fiedler, Lange, and Winebrenner, 1993).

Untracking is increasingly accomplished by eliminating gifted programs. If the educational needs of gifted students are to be met, then, alternative methods of working with them in a heterogeneous classroom must be developed. This may happen naturally in schools that adapt techniques from gifted education—and the rigorous intellectual content recommended by the Paideia Program and the Coalition for Essential Schools—for general classroom use. Parents of bright and gifted children should watch to make sure, if the gifted program in their school is diminished, that compensating programs are put into place that will continue to challenge their students.

Parents should also monitor the effect on their gifted children of "cooperative learning," a popular method of teaching children to work in heterogeneous groups. For various activities cooperative learning places children in different groups which include students of all ability levels; the group is responsible for the learning of all its members. Research indicates, however, that cooperative learning cannot be shown to be academically beneficial to gifted and talented students (Robinson, 1990). In fact, if used excessively, it may be resented by gifted students who prefer to work individually and to be responsible for their own learning.

In a column on the needs of highly gifted children, Kearney (1993) states, "certain popular educational strategies, such as cooperative learning, can exploit these children, especially if they are permitted no time with intellectual peers and no regular, daily access to curriculum at an appropriate level of difficulty." Her concern offers guidance to parents in evaluating their children's schools: Is there a balance between cooperative programs and time allowed with intellectual peers, studying appropriately difficult material?

The advent of restructuring proceeds at an uneven pace across the country. Parents who are not well-versed in educational change may have to become active investigators to learn what has happened or is planned in their home community—if, indeed, any local restructuring is occurring. Those who wish to advocate for their children would do well to look behind the plans for the funding, and to inquire gently and politely—but persistently—about provisions for students of high ability.

Outcome-Based Education

The main idea behind one form of restructuring, outcome-based education, is that student performance should replace "seat time" as a criterion for accomplishment—that is, a student's achievement should be judged on what he shows he understands and can do rather than how many semesters he has been enrolled in a particular course of study.

Springing from a 1988 study ("Rethinking Curriculum: A Call for Fundamental Reform," released by the National Association of State Boards of Education), outcome-based education is built on the assumption that states will establish a core curriculum and define goals in the form of "student outcomes"—abilities or competencies students will be expected to have when they graduate. States will hold school districts accountable for student outcomes, but will give districts and schools latitude in determining the methods they will use to meet the goals.

In outcome-based education the acquisition of academic knowledge, rather than being regarded as an end in itself, is woven into activities designed to produce competent future citizens. Instructional methods include hands-on experience, cooperative learning, and a greater use of technology and supplemental resources rather than reliance on textbooks or workbooks. Although it is assumed that the methods and materials now used in gifted programs will be made available to all students, some schools do so in ways that emphasize minimal outcome standards, rather than the high standards of excellence appropriate for the brightest students.

Regardless of shifts in the educational winds, gifted and intellectually curious students are still the people described in Chapters One and Two, with the same emotional and intellectual characteristics and needs. There will always be some who learn faster than others, and some for whom knowledge in academic content areas, the sheer joy of learning about the arts and sciences, *is* an end in itself. Parents and teachers concerned with meeting such students' special needs must continue to be vigilant to ensure that provisions are made for them.

Whole Language

The innovation of the last few years that has had most impact on reading is the whole language movement. Confusion can arise when the terms *whole language*, *literature-based reading*, and *literature-based curriculum* are used interchangeably. They are related, but not identical, innovations in reading: the latter two are curricular initiatives developed within the whole language movement.

In *whole language* classrooms, reading is taught by integrating all language areas—reading, writing, listening and speaking—rather than treating them as separate subjects. Whole language instruction is based on new perceptions of how children naturally learn language (Healy, 1990). Since it is more an attitude toward the learning process than a set program, implementation of the whole language philosophy varies from one school to another. In some cases it replaces the basal textbook; in others it is used supplementally.

Literature-based reading is an aspect of whole language which places less emphasis on basal readers and more on the reading of real books or story collections. It began with the desire to correct a problem: basal readers often used selections of children's books which sometimes were so simplified they no longer resembled literature and could not attract and hold the child's interest. In literature-based programs, whole books or anthologies are used in place of (or in addition to) the contrived selections found in reading textbooks.

Librarians and others interested in reading have hailed the move to real literature as a long-awaited positive step. However, it is not without problems, which have to do not with the idea itself, but with its implementation: the basalization of literature and inadequate funding.

Basalization means using whole books for reading classes, but treating them like basal textbooks—following up the reading with worksheets which emphasize isolated reading skills. This practice reveals a misunderstanding of the whole language theory, and it is fed by a proliferation of commercial study guides offering prepackaged questions. Too often, these are fact questions guaranteed to deaden interest in the art of literature.

Difficulties occur, too, if funding is inadequate to supply quantities of books, and when elementary schools do not have trained librarians who can guide teachers and students to appropriate books. Bernice Cullinan (1989) has interviewed teachers who tell her they have difficulty getting books: "Even those who have money to spend and know which books they want have trouble ordering from book distributors. They assure me that it takes up to two years to get a new book into their hands. Somehow, their enthusiasm has waned by the time they get the book" (p. 31).

Parents and teachers evaluating a literature-based reading program can use criteria proposed by Spiegel (1990). Here are some of the questions she suggests:

130

- Is the literature of high quality?

- Is the language rich?

- Does it include a wide variety of genres, themes, and authors?

- Does it provide a good model for children's own writing?

- Do the activities focus primarily on meaning rather than on isolated decoding strategies?

- Do they promote a love of reading, writing, and literature?

- Can they be generalized beyond a particular piece of literature or a particular genre?

- Are enough experiences offered with the same types of activities for children to learn a particular strategy or approach?

A *literature-based curriculum* extends the use of literature to other areas, usually social studies or science, for example using historical fiction to introduce a unit of American history. Students need not be limited to fiction, as Haycock (1989) points out: "The range of resources available to the teacher and student must . . . extend far beyond fiction books . . . The underlying philosophy and precepts are applicable to the social studies and sciences as much as to the language arts. The resources required include information books and nonbook media as well as fiction books" (p. 22-23).

Reading Programs for Gifted Students

"The frustration faced by a precocious reader entering kindergarten or first grade may be impossible for most adults to understand. When a six year old who loves to read and is accustomed to reading several books a day encounters the typical basal reading system, the beginning of the end of a love affair with reading may result. As Brown and Rogan (1983) have stated, 'For primary level gifted children who have already begun to read, modification toward the mean represents a serious regression'" (p. 92). Reis and Renzulli (1989) so begin an article on reading programs for gifted students. While the authors point out that early reading and giftedness are not synonymous, they suggest that early readers need an appropriate reading program whether or not they are identified as gifted.

What elements distinguish a reading program specifically designed for gifted students and precocious readers? Reis and Renzulli propose a list from a study by Dole and Adams (1983):

- independent research projects
- opportunities to pursue these projects over a long period of time
- development of research skills
- self-selected reading experiences
- guided study of literary genres
- involvement with the Great Books Program

To the last item I would add "or other structured book discussions," for which several models follow.

Discussing Books for Intellectual Growth

When I was in high school, one English teacher invited six of us to form a small reading group. We met above the study hall in a loft used mostly for storage. At that time, the senior high did not even have a library; we stopped by the public library on our walk home to borrow the books we read as a group.

We met for just a few months, and I have only two specific memories: one girl said that her mother had told her that *Gone with the Wind* is not great literature (this was news to me), and we had to ask our parents' permission before we could read *Grapes of Wrath*. All the parents consented.

Despite my sparse memories, I am sure that good things happened in that group. No one called it a group for gifted students; no one identified gifted students then, just before Sputnik. It stands out in my high school experience because in that group, students truly were a part of excellence—trying to match the thinking of great authors with our own best thinking. Even under fine teachers, that did not happen in English class.

This group was an experiment in my high school; I don't know whether it was considered a success, or even whether it was repeated the following year. It may be that if I could listen now to one of the sessions, I would be disappointed in the quality of the discussion; but the sense of touching excellence has remained with me. Book discussion groups have the power to convey that sense, and they have that power even when they may seem not as successful as the leader would like.

Even with the new flexibility in whole language instruction, pulling a group of students together for a book discussion can present logistical problems. Teachers and librarians who attempt it and administrators who must approve the use of time will want to know that it is worth the effort.

It is, according to conclusions reached by Clark (1992). After charting intellectual characteristics of gifted children, the needs those characteristics imply, and possible related problems, she offers organizational patterns and strategies. She emphasizes that gifted students need educational programs that offer:

- small group discussion
- flexibility
- respect for ideas
- time for reflection
- opportunity to compare communication and decision-making processes with academic peers

Students discussing literature in small groups are meeting all of the above requirements. That should be good news to parents, teachers and administrators who are concerned about efficient use of valuable school time.

Logistics

Arrangements for an intellectually-oriented discussion group differ only slightly from those offered in Chapter Four for bibliotherapy groups.

Even for groups designed for intellectual rather than bibliotherapeutic discussions, children's selection should be based on their emotional development as well as on reading ability. For younger children accelerated into older reading groups, it is especially important that their emotional level be weighed against the material to be read.

If children are pulled out of a regular classroom for a book discussion group, the leader may need to help them explain the group to their friends. The necessity for explanation depends on attitudes in the school about gifted children and specialized groups.

Other questions—group size and whether participation should be required or optional—are the same for these groups as for bibliotherapy groups.

The books, however, are not the same. Unconstrained by the goals of bibliotherapy, the leader of intellectually-oriented discussion groups can choose from an array of books, limited only by the desire to present books of the highest quality and intellectual challenge. The usual requirements for finding appropriate books apply: knowing children's literature and what makes a book especially appealing to gifted children, examining reviews, and prereading all books before recommending them.

The problems of having enough copies available at the right time remain the same, as does the question of free choice of reading for group members.

Place and time must also be considered. Privacy is not as important as in a bibliotherapy group, but quiet is necessary. The discussion should be in a place where students feel free to become thoroughly involved and to voice opinions with passion.

Timing the discussion is the same as with a bibliotherapy group, especially planning so students will not miss lunch, recess, or physical education.

The discussion can incorporate drama, art, music, guest speakers, and projects. The leader may develop lesson plans to introduce the children to criteria for good literature, so they can move toward making their own informed judgments about books.

Discussion Techniques

In bibliotherapy, discussion is based on the reader's emotional response to the *story*. Questions, designed to clarify that response, often focus on the motives of the characters: Why do they act as they do? What personal characteristics lead to success or failure? What are their relationships to others in the story? What are their feelings, their attitudes? How and why do these change?

An intellectual discussion, by contrast, aims to develop the reader's understanding of the *literature*. While the leader may ask all of the questions given above, he may also inquire into the motives of the author: Why did she decide to have this or that happen? What response did she hope to elicit from readers, and how did she plan to accomplish her aims? An example would be these two questions from *A Bridge to Terebithia*:

> Why did Jess and Leslie spend so much time in Terebithia? (characters' motive)

> Why did Paterson have Jess and Leslie spend so much time in Terebithia? (author's motive)

In forming an answer to these two questions we can almost feel an interior shift in focus take place. To answer the first we try to feel our way into the minds and hearts of Jess and Leslie, while the second question moves us some distance from the story, to stand outside it and look at it analytically, to consider the author's carefully planned use of symbolism.

Another line of questioning in an intellectual discussion, evaluating the author's techniques and skill, helps to avoid limiting the discussion to the plot. Are the characters believable? How does the setting contribute to the development of the plot? To the mood? How effective is the author's use of language? In answering these questions we gain an understanding of literature as an art form having specific methods that, if employed well, convey much more than the mere progression of words on the page can do.

Children's Responses. In *The Child's Developing Sense of Theme: Responses to Literature*, Lahr (1991) outlines the stages of a child's ability to perceive theme in a story. She bases her comments on Applebee's (1978) use of Piaget's study of the gradual development of the child's ability to symbolize events.

Preschool and early elementary children—up to about the age of six—are in the preoperational stage, characterized by egocentric and magical thinking. Visual perception is all: a child at this stage believes that a taller glass has more water in it, even if he has watched the water poured from a shorter, fatter glass. The focus on self, magical thinking, and reliance on appearances affects the child's experience of a book and his conversation about it. Very young children can understand the meaning of a story but cannot put it in their own words, while most five-year-olds can give a brief narrative.

Children from around ages seven to eleven, in the concrete operational stage, begin to use logic to explain events. A discussion leader will find these children able to summarize a story, and she can use to advantage their strong interest in understanding and analyzing experience and relationships.

135

Adolescents, at the formal operations stage, are able to think more abstractly and hypothetically, to organize facts and events by manipulating symbols in their minds. Capable of viewing problems from several different vantage points, they can resolve conflicts through mental effort alone. Young adolescents are able to analyze the structure of a plot or the motives of the characters in a book; older students can make generalizations as they consider the theme or author's point of view. Not everyone, even among adults, functions at the formal operational level—but apparently most gifted people do (Newman and Newman, 1983).

Thus, children see different themes in books than adults do, and respond to them differently—a point for discussion leaders to remember. Furthermore, the construction of meaning is individual, based on the background and experience of the reader, accounting for differences in responses to reading. A factually inaccurate answer, however, should be addressed. Lahr (1991) suggests doing so not with a correction but with another question—"Does that seem right?" "Are you sure?"—that will cause the child to reexamine her response.

Questions. VanTassel-Baska (1989) recommends that leaders plan questions that serve specific purposes. She suggests the following:

- factual questions to determine the students' comprehension
- interpretive questions to develop a deeper understanding
- divergent questions to encourage the reader to think outside the story
- evaluative questions to challenge the student to make judgments about the story

Her question types may be more easily used if the leader thinks in terms of the following opening words:

- factual: What happened?
- interpretive: Why did it happen?
- divergent: What if something else had happened?
- evaluative: What did you think about what happened? Why do you think so?

These openings provide only a skeletal framework to start the leader's thinking. A good discussion leader will build a structure based on them to suit the story at hand.

Questioning. Techniques of questioning include observing *wait time* after a question and also after a response. This pause for reflection causes anxiety for leaders but encourages more achievement for students. It also allows for the fact that while we value quick responses, we know that some gifted people process slowly. Castiglione (1987) says the average wait time is 0.2 - 0.9 seconds; if a discussion leader increases it to 3 seconds, major changes occur in the quality of the discussion. Others recommend ten to twenty seconds after a "higher level thinking" question.

Castiglione suggests asking divergent questions to increase participation in the discussion. And if a child's answer is unclear, he suggests that the leader not say, "Your answer is unclear," but rather, "I'm not sure what you mean," so the burden of responsibility is on the adult, not the child.

Another questioning technique is "think-pair-share." After asking a question, the leader allows two minutes of individual thinking time and two minutes for students to discuss it with a partner before beginning group discussion.

Asking follow-up questions, requiring students to defend their responses against other points of view, inviting one student to summarize the response of another, asking participants to describe how they arrived at an answer, and letting students develop their own questions are other techniques of successful discussion leaders.

What follows next is a summary of a structured approach to discussion that is well-known to teachers—an approach so commonly used that it is described here primarily for the benefit of parents.

Bloom's Taxonomy. Benjamin Bloom's *Taxonomy of Educational Objectives* (1956) lists the higher levels of thinking: analysis, synthesis, and evaluation. One way to approach book discussion with gifted children is to focus on questions that call forth these kinds of thought.

Analyzing a book involves questioning some of the author's decisions. Why did he choose that form, setting, or organization? Are there inconsistencies or inaccuracies? How does he make the characters seem like real people? Analysis questions might begin with phrases such as the following:

What are the parts of ...

Which steps are important in the process of ...

If ..., then ...

The difference between ... and ... is ...

The solution would be to ...

What is the relationship between ... and ...

How would you have ...

Synthesis means connecting elements from a book to each other or to knowledge the students have acquired, to create a new way of looking at the issues. Some examples of synthesis questions:

Can you retell this story from the point of view of

. . .

How is a character from this book like ... in ...

Can you write a similar story that would ...

Change ... so that ...

Develop an original plan for ...

Good background music for a tape of the story would be ...

Evaluating a book or a decision of a character in a book requires making a judgment based on established criteria. The criteria can be developed in group discussion before the children are asked evaluative questions. Such questions could include:

Which characters are best developed?

Which character would you like to be?

Which of these stories is the most believable?

Rank these books on the basis of quality of language.

Which situation required the most courage?

Junior Great Books. A program that offers training in both forming questions and in the techniques of leading a discussion is Junior Great Books. Although it was not originally developed for gifted students, it is often used as the first offering when a school initiates services for high-potential youngsters. Inexpensive and highly regarded, Junior Great Books is easily accepted as a gifted program. Furthermore, it develops a seriousness of purpose in reading and offers a structured discussion format that makes it an excellent introduction to intellectual book discussion.

Junior Great Books discussions are offered either as an extracurricular activity or as part of the language arts curriculum, and are led by parent volunteers or by teachers. A two-day training course, offered in many locations around the country, prepares leaders to create the reflective, interpretive questions on which the discussions are based. Trained teachers and parents are certified as Junior Great Books leaders and may order the collections of books used for the discussions.

The program offers readings for each grade from kindergarten through twelve. For kindergarten and first grade, four read-aloud series are available, with nine readings in each series. The series offered for grades two through nine include twelve readings and last for one semester, with two series available for grades two through six—a full year's program for this peak reading period.

Traditionally, Junior Great Books has been offered to a small group of students who meet once a week for a pull-out or extracurricular program. As a new alternative, the Great Books Foundation has developed an expanded curriculum that can be used as the reading program for a full class, for one to four days a week for twelve weeks.

Trained parents can volunteer to offer the program through the school or independently. More information is available from The Great Books Foundation, 35 E. Wacker Drive, Suite 2300, Chicago, Illinois, 60611-2298.

Other models. Creative teachers may develop their own methods of leading discussions, based on preferred elements from Bloom's Taxonomy, Junior Great Books, and other formats such as the reading workshop proposed by Nancie Atwell (1987).

Because "The basis of instruction for gifted readers is the choosing and reading of books" (p. 15), Howe-Cousar (1990) suggests a reading program based on Atwell's work that allows students to select their own books from a classroom collection, receive a few minutes of instruction, and spend much of the time in silent reading—then recording their responses in a reading journal.

She describes the discussions she leads with her middle school students, beginning with a group sharing of responses to what they have read. She follows Probst's (1988) ground rules: be receptive of each other's ideas, tentative about initial reactions, rigorous in intellectual standards, and cooperative in the search for meaning. Howe-Cousar serves as both guide and colleague, adding her own responses to the group (but never first). In her role as teacher and guide she introduces material related to the reading; speaking from her role as colleague she says, "We ask each other questions" (p. 18).

Authors' comments. Laudable though it may be to read books and discuss them, the sudden widespread use of this procedure has led to some concerns that books are being "used," in a negative sense, so zealously that we are overlooking the fragile nature of the art of literature. Authors, of course, are particularly sensitive to this, and some of them have written quiet protests that deserve our attention.

The poet Lee Bennett Hopkins raises objections to the use of discussion guides so extensive they overwhelm the poetic experience. Describing a teaching guide for the poem "City" by Langston Hughes, he concludes, "In the time—the meaningless time—students might spend doing all this, they could relish an entire volume of poetry, coming away with so much more...!" (1991, p. xiv). Some poems, like some books—see Bauer's suggestions below—are best pondered over as a whole rather than analyzed.

In an open letter to teachers, Marion Dane Bauer (1991) offers several points arising from letters received from students as class assignments:

- Books selected for children should be appopriate for their emotional age. "There is a difference between the ability to absorb facts and the readiness to deal with issues" (p. 112).
- Not all books are meant for group discussion. Some need to be a private experience, "a kind of personal letter between author and reader" (p. 113).
- A book is more than a summary of its plot.
- Books should not be used to teach lessons. "Fiction is about questions, not answers" (p. 115).

Bauer's last point, especially, should be taken to heart, not only out of respect for literature but also because it is with an openness to questions and questioning that we can offer the most benefit to sensitive, intelligent children through book discussion.

Especially for Parents: What You Can Do to Meet Intellectual Needs at Home through Books

Although a group discussion is often not possible at home, you can meet many of the same needs through a loosely structured plan for family reading and conversation. Moreover, by providing a favorable environment at home, you can offer a haven to your children, a place where they can know they are safe to express their thoughts, ideas, and opinions without risk of censure. As parents, you can offer the psychological security that schools cannot guarantee.

Several books offer suggestions to parents who want to provide various forms of enrichment for highly able children at home (Alvino, 1985; Graue, 1982; Moore, 1981; Saunders, 1986). However, although these publications mention the value of reading, not much is said about book *discussion*. By adding discussion to the reading, you can use books not only for the pleasure which is their primary reason for being, but also to respond to your gifted children's intellectual needs and as a focus for thoughtful family conversation.

When you encourage reading and promote book discussions at home, you are doing your part to meet the intellectual needs discussed in detail in the first section of this chapter. Your unique contribution can supplement a school reading program or compensate your child's loss if the school does not provide an appropriate reading program.

Early in this chapter, the intellectual needs of gifted children are discussed in detail. As a parent, you can meet some of these needs in ways which may not be possible at school.

Using Intellect Effectively

At home your child should feel free to use the full range of her growing vocabulary, trying out new connotations as she tests the full meaning of words she has read. If she makes a mistake in pronunciation (common for children who pick up new words by reading as well as by hearing them), you can correct her gently.

You can allow divergent thinking, recognizing that children need to try out ideas by talking about them. In this trying-out period, children may sound more convinced than they really are, and your role is to listen calmly, ask thoughtful questions, and offer your own opinions as something the child might want to consider.

You can provide enough time to consider ideas in depth. By asking follow-up questions ("What do you mean by that?") and identifying meaningless slang expressions when your child uses them, you can help your children think carefully and use language more precisely. By asking questions that require analysis, synthesis, and evaluation, you can challenge your child to deeper thinking.

Encountering a Variety of People and Ideas

When you routinely take your child to the library and help him select books, you have an opportunity to expose him to new worlds of people and ideas. You can suggest books that open up new topics and points of view. When discussing these books, you can guide your child to think of alternatives, and to predict and examine the consequences.

If your child is hypercritical of others, you may make a special effort to find books that promote sympathy for people in difficult situations. Librarians are always glad to make suggestions.

Individual Pacing

Simply by helping your child find books that interest and challenge her, you are individualizing her reading. You will find suggestions and criteria for choosing books in Chapters Three, Six, and Seven, and in the bibliography.

You can introduce your child to the idea of an incubation period, and help him learn to recognize his own patterns of processing information. This self-knowledge will be useful in scheduling book discussions at home, and can be transferred to the scheduling of school assignments and social relationships.

By allowing open-ended discussion and not expecting a conclusive answer, you can give your child experience in considering diverse approaches to problems. Your acceptance will confirm the value of different responses and encourage individuality.

Talking with Intellectual Peers

In a discussion of a book that both participants have read, the importance of age differences tends to diminish. If you have a genuine desire to know what your child thinks rather than an overriding need to give your own opinion, then you and your child are starting the discussion as peers.

Parents who lack time for or interest in book discussion may find a relative or friend who can act as reading partner for their children. Although this means the loss of family interaction, it could be a mutually enriching relationship and a very satisfactory solution.

In a book discussion, whether group or individual, there is always a triad: the leader, the child(ren), and the author. As gifted children grow older, they will find authors who can play the role of intellectual peers. Thus, when you foster book discussion at home you are setting the stage for continually introducing your child to potential peers.

If book discussions are offered at school, you can reinforce them at home with your unique knowledge of your children. If not, home may be the only place where intellectually curious children have the advantages of reading and talking about books.

Discussing Books with Your Children

The first step, if you are not sure how to begin talking about books with your children, is to read the earlier section called Discussion Techniques (p. 134) carefully, and perhaps look into some of the references listed at the end of this chapter. Many questioning techniques, as well as the programs mentioned, can be adapted from group to individual discussion.

With this information in your background, you are ready to begin. For a good starting point, try these tips from a booklet called *Communicating through Young Adult Books*, by Pat Scales:

- Make available as many books as your teen wants.
- Ask your teen for recommendations for books he would like you to read.
- Read the book and focus your thoughts on the adolescent main character.
- Discuss the book with your teenager.
- Encourage the exchange of ideas and opinions without being judgmental.

- Find a special family time to talk about books and encourage each family member (even the youngest) to join.

In addition to asking your child for book recommendations, you may wish to suggest books for him to read. You can arrange with your child to trade book recommendations, so that both parents and child have an opportunity to ask the other to read a favorite book.

How to begin a discussion? Plan ahead, thinking about your conversation as you read the book. You will probably find the plot and the characters to be the best sources of questions, although you may want to go beyond these to questions about the setting or the author's writing style.

Plot.	Think about the points of *conflict* and *decision*. How did they affect the outcome of the story? What would have happened if...? Would that have been better or worse than...?
Characters.	Consider their *motivation*. Why did X do as he/she did? What would you have done? How did relationships among the characters affect their choices?
Setting.	In some books the setting is enough of a factor to warrant discussion. How does the environment (social, political, natural, family) affect the plot (decisions)? How does it affect the characters (motivation)?
Writing style.	Pay attention to the author's choice of words, symbolism, and figurative language—imagery, metaphors, similes. Note elements of style you relish, mark sentences you find especially apt or beautiful.

Have two or three questions in mind as you begin talking with your child. Be certain they are real questions. Having thought about them, you may have your answers ready, but that does not make them the right answers. You must truly want to know *what your child thinks* about the question, in order to have a real discussion. The less you talk, the more you listen, the more you will learn about your child. Listen to her first, and share your thoughts with her later.

If your child is not in a school reading program that includes the use of a reading log, you may want to encourage him to begin one at home. Different from a mere list of books he has read, the reading log is a record of the date of the entry and the book read, followed by his responses or reactions to the book. He can write his thoughts and questions about the characters, plot, ideas, symbols, theme, or any other aspect of the story after each reading session, not waiting until he has finished the book. Also appropriate are comments about what he does or doesn't like or doesn't understand, and personal experiences that relate to the story. What he should not write—because it is not really helpful—is a simple summary of the plot.

Whether he shares his journal or parts of it in discussion with you should be his choice. In any case, the thinking and analysis that have gone into the reading log will become evident in your discussions.

Using the Library

If children are to learn how to use books, as well as other media, to satisfy their craving for knowledge, they must be able to use libraries effectively. Since good school library services are not available every-where, parents should know what resources and library staffing students ideally would have available to them, and what information-gathering skills they should acquire at each step of the way. This section is designed to help parents evaluate the school library services available to their child. If the school library program is not ideal, it may be possible to find a nearby public library with more resources and a staff willing to help an eager learner.

Resources

Just a few years ago, "library resources" referred to print (fiction, non-fiction and reference books, and magazines) and audio-visual media (films, filmstrips, tape recordings). These familiar resources are now overshadowed by electronic media and the networking capabilities of computers.

Secondary school libraries are usually equipped with computers first; elementary libraries follow, and many elementary students are still using print resources entirely. Your child's library books may be checked out on a computerized circulation system, the only terminal in the library, inaccessible by students. Or he may be able to use a computer to search the library's public access catalog (a new, more inclusive term for the old card catalog, which now may be on a screen instead of cards). In the most sophisticated libraries, he is also learning to use computer terminals to consult an encyclopedia on a CD-ROM, or to search for magazine or newspaper articles.

Parents who are evaluating library services should welcome any opportunity for their children to master the tricks of using computers, of searching for information from electronic as well as print sources. However, computers in themselves do not provide a fine library program. In research, they can actually limit the resources available. One encyclopedia in print form provides access to many students, whereas an encyclopedia on a CD-ROM is available to only one student at a time (unless an expensive network system is in place, which is still very rare). Sometimes too much money goes toward the CD-ROM, leaving inadequate funding for timely updating of the print encyclopedias. And one CD-ROM, featuring one encyclopedia, is not adequate for teaching students to consult a variety of authorities as they learn to reach their own conclusions.

While our nation's schools upgrade their technological capacity, the temptation will be to emphasize the purchase of computers over books. Encourage the addition of computers in your school libraries, but remember that books, too, are needed for the optimal emotional and intellectual growth of your student.

Staffing

The quality of a library program always depends on the energy, training, and commitment of the person in charge. At the secondary level, where accreditation standards apply, you will probably find professionally-trained librarians.

Unfortunately, elementary libraries sometimes lack adequate staffing. Too often a single professional librarian oversees the libraries in several elementary schools, acting as consultant to the parent volunteers or library assistants who are there to assist when children come in.

If your children attend a school without a librarian, learn how much they are being taught about library skills and ask for help at the public library if necessary. Redouble your efforts to learn about children's literature and encourage your children to read good fiction. And if possible, become a library volunteer, support the library assistant, and work for the hiring of more professional librarians in your community's schools.

Information-Gathering Skills

As electronic technology is introduced into school libraries, old research methods—and ways of teaching them—become obsolete. At the same time, new teaching programs blend age groupings of students for units of study, altering the old schedules for teaching library skills.

While these trends create a patchwork, making it difficult to say just what a student in a given grade should be expected to know about using a library, they vastly improve opportunities for students to learn. When innovative educational practices are implemented in their ideal form, with a trained librarian available to plan with teachers and guide students, they offer a major advantage over traditional approaches: the opportunity to teach library and research skills *at the right time*, when the student needs the resources of the library to proceed with a study for which a skilled teacher has already sparked interest. Then the library materials are important tools and the librarian a valued resource, while the focus is on the knowledge the student wants.

What They Need to Know and When

The ideal time to teach children to use the library is during the elementary years, when they regard the library system as both a code which they can break and an exciting challenge. For middle schoolers, the system appears just easy enough to be boring and if introduced for the first time at that age, few students pay enough attention to master it.

Lower elementary grades. In the early years, children should learn the basics: what resources are in the library and how to find them.

Primary children begin by learning (if they do not already know from public library experience) that books are on the shelves according to the author's last name, making the connection between the letter on the spine of the book and the label on the shelf. Soon they differentiate between fiction and nonfiction, and learn where these sections are in the library. They also identify the parts of the book (author, title, illustrator)—actually the preparation for later bibliographic work.

Later, learning that nonfiction is in order numerically by subject, and that fiction is arranged alphabetically by the author's last name, they begin to search purposefully for both.

Using the public access catalog, they learn to locate information about a book whether they know the author, the title, or the subject. They learn the major classes of the Dewey Decimal system and how to decode the call number to find the book on the shelf.

Beginning research, they learn how to use long encyclopedia articles effectively, and discover various reference books in addition to encyclopedias. They can also use indexes in books and the vertical file.

Upper elementary grades. Older students need more sophisticated techniques for gaining access to information. Whether they learn through print indexes to magazines (for instance, the *Readers' Guide*) or through one of the electronic programs that are replacing print searches, they need instruction in the use of indexes to locate information hidden in magazines or beyond the reach of the catalog of their local media center.

Where computers are available, students become familiar with various data bases and supporting microfiche. Using computer terminals and modems to search local and distant data bases, they must master the techniques of keyword searching. Encyclopedia articles on CD-ROMs provide key words and phrases, as well as outlines that help organize information from several sources.

Middle school and senior high. If the basics of library use—the location of materials and the means of access to information, whether print or electronic—are taught in the elementary years, secondary students can focus on using more sophisticated reference sources and learning correct bibliographic form. Middle school students can learn the tricks of using the subheadings of subjects, looking up geographical and historical information in the public access catalog. If they have not already done so, they should begin to use the public library as well as the school library.

High school students who have newfound mobility and may begin using larger libraries should be introduced to the Library of Congress Classification system, as well as to the value of Sears and Library of Congress subject headings lists for research. They can branch out to specialized indexes for art, biography, science and technology, education, and the humanities. They are able to recognize and use more sophisticated access points than the familiar author, title and subject, and they can write correct and complete bibliographies for books, encyclopedias, and magazine articles.

If it is possible for them to use a large college or university library for some of the research, that would be a fitting culmination of the process that began in kindergarten. This will be easier if they go armed with a few key questions: What magazine indexes are available? Where are the newspaper indexes? Is any source of information available beyond books, magazines, and newspapers—such as an online data base? They are ready to use any library in the country to satisfy a lifelong need to continue learning.

That is the real goal of teaching library use: to enable students to enter any library with confidence, free to concentrate on the information they are seeking rather than on the process by which they get it.

References

Adler, Mortimer J. (1982). *The Paideia Proposal: An educational manifesto*. New York: Macmillan.

Alexander, David. (1991, April 21). He told us so. *New York Times Book Review*, p. 16.

Alvino, James. (1985). *Parents' guide to raising a gifted child: Recognizing and developing your child's potential*. Boston: Little, Brown.

Applebee, A. (1978). *The child's concept of story: Ages two to seventeen*. Chicago: University of Chicago Press.

Atwell, Nancie. (1987). *In the middle: Writing, reading, and learning with adolescents*. Upper Montclair, NJ: Boynton/Cook.

Barzun, Jacques. (1991). *Begin here: The forgotten conditions of teaching and learning*. Chicago: University of Chicago Press.

Bauer, Marion Dane. (1991, January/February). An author's letter to teachers. *Horn Book*, *67*, 111-116.

Bloom, Benjamin, Ed. (1956). *Taxonomy of educational objectives*. New York: David McKay.

Brown, W. & Rogan, J. (1983). Reading and young gifted children. *Roeper Review*, *5*, 6-9.

Castiglione, Lawrence V. (1987). *Questioning methods for gifted students*. East Aurora, NY: DOK.

Clark, Barbara. (1992). *Growing up gifted: Developing the potential of children at home and at school*. 4th ed. New York: Macmillan.

Cullinan, Bernice E. (1989, April). Latching on to literature: Reading initiatives take hold. *School Library Journal*, *35*, 27-31.

Dole, J. A. & Adams, P. J. (1983). Reading curriculum for gifted readers: A survey. *Gifted Child Quarterly*, *27*, 64-77.

Fiedler, Ellen D., Lange, Richard E., & Winebrenner, Susan. (1993, September). In search of reality: Unraveling the myths about tracking, ability grouping and the gifted. *Roeper Review*, *16*, 4-7.

Graue, Eliza Brownrigg. (1982). *Is your child gifted? A handbook for parents of gifted preschoolers*. San Diego: Oak Tree Publications.

Haycock, Ken. (1989, November/December). Whole language issues and implications. *Emergency Librarian*, *17*, 22-26.

Healy, Jane M. (1990). *Endangered minds: Why our children don't think*. New York: Simon and Schuster.

Hopkins, Lee Bennett. (1991). Leave me alone! Cries the poem. *Perspectives*, *7*(3), xiii-xv.

Howe-Cousar, Christine. (1990). *Instructing gifted middle-school readers*. Rowley, MA: New England League of Middle Schools.

Kearney, Kathi. (1993, November/December). Discrimination against excellence. *Understanding Our Gifted*, *6*(2), 16.

Lahr, Susan S. (1991). *The child's developing sense of theme: Responses to literature*. New York: Teachers College Press.

Lewis, Anne. (1989). *Restructuring America's schools*. Arlington, VA: American Association of School Administrators.

Moore, Linda Perigo. (1981). *Does this mean my kid's a genius?* New York: New American Library.

Newman, Philip R. & Newman, Barbara M. (1983). *Principles of psychology.* Homewood, IL: Dorsey.

Probst, R. (1988). *Teaching literature in junior and senior high.* Portsmouth, NH: Heineman.

Reis, Sally M. & Renzulli, Joseph S. (1989, December). Providing challenging programs for gifted readers. *Roeper Review, 12*, 92-97.

Robinson, A. (1990). Point-counterpoint: Cooperation or exploitation? The argument against cooperative learning for talented students. *Journal for the Education of the Gifted, 14*, 9-27.

Saunders, Jacqulyn. (1986). *Bringing out the best: A resource guide for parents of young gifted children.* Minneapolis: Free Spirit.

Scales, Pat. n.d. *Communicating through young adult books.* New York: Bantam.

Sizer, Theodore R. (1984). *Horace's compromise: The dilemma of the American high school.* Boston: Houghton Mifflin.

Spiegel, Dixie Lee. (1990, December). Literature resource materials revisited. *The Reading Teacher, 44*, 336-339.

VanTassel-Baska, Joyce. (1989, November/December). The fine art of discussion (Part I). *Understanding Our Gifted, 2*(2), 5.

PART
THREE

The Books

CHAPTER
SIX

Choosing Books That Challenge

Nearly everywhere children go, they can easily pick up inexpensive books. While many of these are excellent, books of poor quality—but with enticing covers—are everywhere. How can children learn to make good choices?

Selecting books for children, and helping them select their own reading, requires thought and effort. Yet parents who carefully monitor their children's television may pay no attention to what the children are reading; they may not know what is good and what is not. (Monitoring reading, incidently, is much more fun than monitoring television, because there are many more alternatives to bad books than there are to bad television programs.)

For teachers and librarians, too, a perennial issue is the quality of children's reading. Some say, "It doesn't matter what they read, just so they're reading." But if we apply this attitude to children who have the potential to become serious readers, acquainted with books of substance and literary value, we do our children a disservice.

We who guide the development of children have the responsibility—and the pleasure—of supplying them with the most meaningful material available. Part of the pleasure is that there is a wealth of children's literature. But what makes certain books especially appropriate for gifted children?

Like the children themselves, the books they cherish have a special spark. This spark has been analyzed and codified so that it is possible to list the characteristics that make some books particularly good choices—not exclusively for children of high potential, but especially for them.

This chapter brings together ways to identify books that not only are good literature, but also appeal to gifted readers.

For Emotional Development

Finding literature that speaks to the emotional world of the bright or intellectually curious child requires knowledge of that world, reflected in the categories in Chapters One and Two (establishing an identity, being alone, relationships with others, using one's ability and the drive to understand) and in the longer list of categories in the index to Chapter Eight, the Bibliography. It also requires wide-ranging knowledge of books that depict that world.

To meet these two requirements takes time and sensitivity, but it can be done. Children's author Katherine Paterson (1989) relates that she declined an invitation to serve on a panel on using books with troubled children, because she wants a reader to "come to a book from his own experience and take from the book what he can and will. I don't want anyone telling a child what he should get out of one of my books." But she attended the panel discussion, where she heard "three highly competent, obviously compassionate people tell about the healing power of the imagination. They never diagnosed a child and then prescribed a particular book. They read widely themselves and had available in their offices many books. 'When I get to know a child,' one of them said, 'I also know four or five books that I think he might like and that might mean something to him'" (p. 68-69).

To build toward that kind of intuitive response, most of us must begin with concrete criteria. Here are some components of the spark that gives a book emotional appeal for gifted readers:

1. The characters are coping with one or more of the same problems the readers are facing, such as establishing an identity—learning how to be human in their own

156

particular way. While few children are in exactly the situation of Laura, who learns that she is psychic in *And This Is Laura*, they can recognize her growing sense of who she is and what it means for her relationships with others.

Characters may be in the process of accepting themselves as people who enjoy being alone, like Arvid, the introspective young king in *In the Time of the Bells*; or Jamie, the quiet boy who doesn't mind being different in *Part-Time Boy*.

They may be learning to find friends as in *Jennifer, Hecate, Macbeth, William McKinley and Me, Elizabeth*, where Jennifer displays her own rather unusual method of making a friend when she needs one. Or to keep friends like Stephanie and Rachel in *Just As Long As We're Together*, who discover that there are times when it is best to tell secrets.

The issue may be choices about commitment to school work, practice time, or to one's own talent—a theme which is especially well-developed in stories set in a time when school conflicted with farm labor, as in *Across Five Aprils* and *The Wolfling*.

2. The characters are not necessarily gifted themselves, or at least not labeled as such, but they stand alone or in a small group for their convictions. In *The Cat Ate My Gymsuit*, Marcy takes a stand against an administrative decision at school and then finds herself for the first time part of a group, as students who agree with her speak out.

3. A character may be different from his peers and learning to cope with the difference, which could be an interest, a family situation, a handicap or anything that sets that person apart. For Joshua Taylor in *A Time to Fly Free*, the difference is his extreme sensitivity to his classmates' cruelty toward living creatures. Through the understanding and support of his parents, he is able to work with an older man who helps Josh learn to use his sensitivity and to temper it with realism.

4. The characters may be learning to accept someone else who is different, as in *Summer of the Swans*. This is the

story of a sister's affection for a mentally handicapped younger brother, affection not always shared by neighborhood children.

5. Adult characters should be present and supportive in at least some of the books. Much contemporary literature for adolescents depicts adults who are weak or absent, giving the young people more control over their own lives. They still need adult concern, however, and it is comfortingly present in books such as Garner's *The Stone Book*, when Mary's father introduces her to her family's heritage, recorded in a cave she must enter alone. In *Two Piano Tuners*, Debbie's grandfather and his old friend, a famous pianist, are available to encourage her to find her own path.

6. Some characters should be gifted adults who lead productive and enjoyable lives, and in general function well as gifted people in the adult world. Tom Curtis in *Jazz Country* finds such people, jazz musicians as well as his father, who act as mentors while he works toward a decision for his own life.

7. Some of the child characters should clearly be gifted themselves, so that the reader can say, "He's like me. I feel that way, too. Maybe I'm not the only one who thinks this way!" Several books in the annotated bibliography meet this criterion. A good example is *Willaby*: Willaby is so engrossed in her drawing that she forgets the assignment. She is not called gifted in the book, but her intensity can be recognized by readers who understand what it is to be lost in their own projects. Young readers can see themselves in stories told as myths, too, like Jane Yolen's *The Boy Who Had Wings*, and can discuss the nature of their own "wings."

8. Giftedness need not necessarily be labeled, but may be implicit, that is, comfortably accepted, and life goes on from there. It is clear enough in such stories of warm, lively, and supportive families as *Cheaper By the Dozen* and *May I Cross Your Golden River?*

9. Characters should be people to whom the reader can relate: open-minded, questioning, with a passion for learning everything or devoted to one subject of in-

tense interest. Junior high boys with a strong interest in science and nature can easily understand why Mike Harrington, the amateur biologist in *A Heart to the Hawks*, cares so much for the pond near his home that he tries to fight the construction that threatens it. Readers can also identify strongly with Raisha's passion for freedom in *My Name is Not Angelica*, Scott O'Dell's novel based on a slave revolt in 1733.

10.	Some books for gifted readers should depict characters struggling with issues of personal or moral courage, personal values, and moral and ethical choices. In *The Witch of Blackbird Pond*, Kit Tyler, newly arrived from Barbados, befriends an old woman who is thought by the people of her village to be a witch; evident in the story are Kit's courage and also the greater moral struggle of her Puritan uncle. Also about inner courage, but in a lighter vein, *The Magic of Myrna C. Wax-weather* depicts Bertha's struggle to be herself despite the unpopularity of her role as teacher's pet.

11.	Some books should have humor of a high level: spontaneously arising from a situation, springing from a character's way of looking at the world, based on intelligent use of language. An example is *A Day No Pigs Would Die*. The character Rob's humorous use of language is unconscious, but the author Robert Newton Peck clearly knows what he is doing. In her books about the Bagthorpes, a family of British eccentrics (*Ordinary Jack* and others), Helen Cresswell uses every opportunity to add a zany twist. Picture books, too, can provide sophisticated humor—for example, *Sir Cedric*, where humor is based on impossible proportions in the illustrations and on elevated language of mock seriousness.

Of course, no one book can be expected to meet every item on this checklist, but a collection can. The goal is to keep the criteria in mind while gathering as many books as eager readers have time to read. With the list as a guide, and experience and exposure to a number of excellent books, it is possible for adults to develop an instinctive sense for books that will catch and hold readers' interest and give them something to think about long after the books have been read.

For Intellectual Development

For optimal intellectual development, very bright children must learn to acknowledge and satisfy their need to know. Books that will help them achieve this goal must both satisfy and whet their curiosity, and be intellectually challenging. But just what does make a book intellectually challenging?

Three valuable books on this topic are Polette's *Picture Books for Gifted Programs* (1981) for young children, Baskin and Harris's *Books for the Gifted Child* (1980), and Hauser and Nelson's *Books for the Gifted Child, Volume 2* (1988). The last two titles are about books for readers from beginning levels to late middle school or early senior high.

Picture Books

Writing about requirements for successful picture books, Rosemary Wells (1990) begins with feelings: "First of all, a good picture book must ring with emotional content, so that children care about what's going on. William Steig's *Amos and Boris* and *Sylvester and the Magic Pebble* never fail to overwhelm a reader with both worry and love . . . What is in them is in all of us: guilt, fear, devotion. As a writer you have little time and few pages to achieve this. The characters in a children's book must reach into the heart of the reader on page one" (129-130). Moving on to more practical criteria, Wells says picture books must be short. "A picture book is in trouble if it's longer than eight double-spaced typewritten pages. It's also in trouble if it's bland, or if the tone is false and hysterical. It must never be cute or it will insult children. It's in trouble if it uses television characters, or if it's written by anybody with a degree in child psychology" (p. 131).

Picture books are a unique blend of visual art and language. Looking for the best among them means assessing the illustrations, the text, and the fit between the two. If a book passes muster in these three ways, what further characteristics make it intellectually challenging?

Polette (1981) calls for books that develop visual, language, and thinking skills, and promote both productive thinking (fluency, flexibility, originality, elaboration, and evaluation) and critical thinking (planning, forecasting, decision making, and problem solving). Mockett and Welton (1990) present a list of picture books that demand higher-level thinking skills in the pictures, the text, or both. They also mention the importance of books that promote creative and divergent thinking, and provide humor and wordplay.

At first these expectations may seem unrealistically high for a picture book, but the best of them have much to offer, and a rich assortment will contain all of these elements. Picture books for gifted children should have the following characteristics:

1. Illustrations should be vibrant and original rather than stereotyped. This is what Wells means when she says a picture book is in trouble if it uses television characters—and she might have added comic book characters, as well. For example, consider a book with Disney characters, or with pictures like those in the grade-school reading textbooks of the past. Then see the illustrations by Marcia Brown for Cendrars' *Shadow*—art work that evokes in color and shape the sense of awe and mystery that is conveyed by the words of the poem.

2. Illustrations should not merely accompany the story line but complement and enhance it. Good examples are the books by Maurice Sendak, in which the expressions on the characters' faces tell the story from their own points of view. In *Where the Forest Meets the Sea*, the illustrations show the boy's sense of the faded presence of ancient life as he explores the rainforest, adding emotional overtones not found in the text.

3. Details of the illustrations should be so fascinating that a child can look repeatedly, and always find more: a surprise or a bit of humor, a private joke between the illustrator and the attentive child. Books by Anno and by Scarry are prime examples. *Anno's Alphabet* invites adults to join the game, challenging them to identify the plants and animals woven into the borders of each page.

4. Some books should be provided that offer abstract illustrations which, while recognizable, still require mental exercise to be understood. Arnold Lobel's *The Turnaround Wind* can—and should—be read both right side up and upside down, inviting the child to see the pictures both ways at once.

5. Illustrations should not supply all the details or information, so that some imaginative effort on the part of the child is needed to complete the picture. *The Look Again...and Again, and Again, and Again Book* supplies four challenges to the imagination on each page, as the child turns the book and rearranges the picture in her mind. *Fire Engine Shapes* focuses on geometrical shapes that are part of a fire engine—with close-up illustrations that challenge the reader to discern where on the fire engine each shape would be.

6 Books should introduce new and fascinating words, satisfying to the tongue as the child learns to say them, mixed in plentiful measure among the familiar words. Cuteness and condescension to the child's verbal level are neither necessary nor welcome; what is needed is respect for the child as an intelligent, learning person. Authors of good children's books about dinosaurs, for example, make the correct assumption that four-year-olds can pronounce Ichthyosaurus and Tyrannosaurus Rex.

7. Authors who obviously take delight in the use of language, whose books demonstrate a playful, joyful sense of fun with words, appeal to gifted children. Dr. Seuss books encourage children to experiment with words, making them up as necessary and bending them slightly to create a rhyme.

    Some picture books offer play with languages other than English. The text of *Abuela* includes Spanish, tantalizing an English-speaking child with the possibility of learning bits of another language. *Who's In Rabbit's House?* and other African folk tales are told with the soothing repetition of African sounds.

8. Books should depict characters, whether animal or human, who display real emotions, feelings, and relationships the child will recognize. In *Alexander and the Terrible, Horrible, No Good, Very Bad Day*, for instance, Alexander displays frustration, anger, and finally resignation toward the kind of day he is having—a day in which ordinary, everyday disasters happen to him all day long, as they sometimes do to

everyone. A similar example is *The Sorely Trying Day*—a title one earnest child turned into what seemed to him more appropriate: *The Trying-Hard Day*.

9. Plots that are not completely predictable allow for conjecturing and discussion between adult and child as the book is read. *Time to Get out of the Bath, Shirley* presents two plots, one about Mother and one about Shirley. Shirley's story is much more interesting, full of surprises to anticipate.

10. Even picture books can raise moral questions, helping young children who are already concerned about the environment, for example. These books can too easily be cloying and "preachy," but if well done they can offer reassurance that a child is not alone in her concerns. In *Harald and the Great Stag*, set in medieval England, Harald learns that one of the Baron's huntsmen shares his respect for the stag and his wish to help it evade the hunters.

11. Stories, pictures, and characters that are outside of the daily experience of the child can help to expand his world view. Ceserani's *Marco Polo* tells the story of Polo's journey supported by illustrations that are filled with detail and interest, presenting not only other countries but another time. *Eyes of the Dragon*, Margaret Leaf's retelling of a Chinese legend accompanied by Ed Young's dramatic artwork, offers an intellectually and emotionally appealing glimpse of China.

Books for Older Children

Books for older readers can be judged according to language, style, plot, and setting; the following list is categorized by these terms. In all of these areas, books appropriate for gifted readers are complex rather than simple; rich and varied rather than predictable; and open-ended and thought-provoking rather than neatly contained.

Look for the following characteristics in books that provide intellectual stimulation for gifted readers:

Language:

1. Language should be on a high level, making strong demands on the reader's vocabulary. Hermann Hesse's *Demian*, first published in 1925 in Europe, assumes an extremely well-educated reader, and rewards good readers with a rich and unrestricted vocabulary.

2. Like illustrations in a picture book, language in a book for older readers should reflect and enhance the plot. In Garfield and Blishen's retelling of Greek myths, *The God Beneath the Sea*, the level of language serves to ennoble the text. In *The Phantom Tollbooth*, humorous, pun-filled language is part of the message of the book: that language itself is a source of delight and challenge. In both cases, the language does more than present the story; it becomes an essential part of the reading experience.

3. Pronunciation guides are helpful for gifted readers (though they are rare, and a pleasant surprise when found) since so many avid readers know words only from reading and therefore mispronounce them. One excellent teacher of gifted high school students calls this "The Calley-ope (calliope) Syndrome."

4. Look for masterfully-chosen descriptive words that stimulate strong visual imagery. For example, in *A String in the Harp*, Bond's descriptions encourage the reader to picture the modern Wales that Peter knows in daily life—and later, to superimpose onto that picture the Wales of Taliesin's time, which Peter envisions.

5. As with picture books, books for gifted readers should be written by authors who delight in language and who skillfully express nuances of thought and feeling. Joyce Carol Thomas's *Marked by Fire* is remarkable for the way in which language—prose and poetry— evokes place and mood, moving the story along on an emotional level.

6. Language patterns and vocabularies from other times and places, used without apology or explanation, encourage the reader to glean the meaning from the context. Examples abound: Garfield's *Smith*, which

164

evokes 18th Century England; the language of remote corners of modern Wales, as in Mayne's time-warp fantasy, *Earthfasts*; a language of the future as imagined by Ayn Rand in *Anthem*; or even a supposed language system of the past, as in *The Clan of the Cave Bear*.

Style:

7. Books for gifted readers can display the full complement of literary devices that enrich the fabric of literature and the reader (whether he recognizes them by name or not): metaphor, simile, paradox, symbol, allusion. Poetry does this by nature; one example in prose is *The Bat-poet* by the poet Randall Jarrell.

Plot:

8. In book selection as in curriculum, it is helpful to remember Maurice Freehill's (1961) insight that gifted children are "challenged by the unfinished and the misunderstood." If this is true, at least some of the books they read should present problems that are unresolved, even at the end of the book.

   Plots should cause the reader to look at a situation from different perspectives, and then reach some conclusion. At the end of *The Beethoven Medal*, for instance, it is still unclear whether Pennington will be able to control his self-destructive impulses and become a successful pianist, and the future of his relationship with Ruth remains in doubt. The reader is left to ponder what desirable or likely options are available. Likewise, at the end of *Izzy, Willy-Nilly*, we know that Izzy is forever changed—but we are left to conjecture about how the changes in her will affect her relationships with friends and family.

9. Good readers should be developing the ability to hold different levels of meaning in their minds simultaneously, and some of the books they read should give them experience in doing so. Books like *The Village by the Sea* and *The Tempered Wind* require the reader to look below the story line to understand the universal

motivations that are being played out in these instances.

10. The structure of a plot can put the mind to work—flashbacks, narration that shifts from one person to another, or the use of journal format. A good example is Konigsburg's *Father's Arcane Daughter*, in which each chapter is introduced by a dialogue between unidentified characters, adding to the mystery while simultaneously supplying clues for the surprise ending. More complex and demanding is the structure of Vonnegut's *Slaughterhouse Five*, which presents a fluid view of time through Billy Pilgrim.

Setting:

11. The settings of some books allow children to experience vicariously lifestyles that are not their own; an example is the vivid description of traditional living patterns on Mafatu's Pacific island in *Call It Courage*. Children growing up in small towns or rural areas can learn something of great art museums and of life in New York City by reading *From the Mixed-up Files of Mrs. Basil E. Frankweiler*, or can see a darker view of New York street life in *Slake's Limbo*. Pearl Buck's books on China, including *The Exile*, help the reader to create a clear picture of a different time and a foreign place.

Finally, to challenge intellectually, books should be written with the assumption that readers possess some background either in experience or in reading. With this in mind, one quick way of finding books that are intellectually demanding is to look for books from England or in translation from a foreign language—because authors of children's books in other countries generally assume more background and education on the part of the reader than many American children's authors do. Such books will probably contain some colloquial terms unfamiliar to American readers, but the meaning of most can be determined from the context, and they add both to the challenge of the book and to its power to expand the reader's knowledge of other cultures.

Bloom's (1956) terminology helps to form a neat statement of the characteristics of books that offer intellectual challenge to gifted students: Such books invite *analysis* of characters and events; *synthesis* of ideas from the book under discussion and from anywhere else in the reader's experience; and *evaluation* of the relationships, actions, consequences, alternatives, and possibilities found in the book and in the reader's interpretation of it.

Again, it is obvious that no book will contain *all* characteristics listed for intellectually stimulating reading. However, if adults will keep the characteristics in mind while they read reviews and browse the shelves of young people's literature, they will gradually be able to gather a collection that will include these criteria in abundance—a collection that will be invaluable for the gifted children and young people who have access to it.

Suggested Book Lists

Several good selection guides are available for parents and teachers looking for books to recommend.

Baskin, Barbara H and Karen H. Harris. *Books for the Gifted Child.* New York: Bowker, 1980.

Hauser, Paula and Gail A. Nelson. *Books for the Gifted Child, Volume 2.* New York: Bowker, 1988.

Hearne, Betsy. *Choosing Books for Children: A Commonsense Guide.* Rev. ed. New York: Delacorte, 1990.

Larrick, Nancy. *A Parent's Guide to Children's Reading.* 5th rev. ed. New York: Bantam, 1983.

Polette, Nancy. *Picture Books for Gifted Programs.* Metuchen, N.J.: Scarecrow, 1981.

Waldhorn, Arthur, Olga S. Weber, and Arthur Zeiger. *Good Reading: A Guide for Serious Readers.* 23rd ed. New York: Bowker, 1990. (For senior high and older.)

References

Baskin, Barbara H. & Harris, Karen H. (1980). *Books for the gifted child.* New York: Bowker.

Bloom, Benjamin S., Ed. (1956). *Taxonomy of educational objectives.* New York: David McKay.

Freehill, Maurice. (1961). *Gifted children: Their psychology and education.* New York: Macmillan.

Hauser, Paula & Nelson, Gail A. (1988). *Books for the gifted child, Volume 2.* New York: Bowker.

Mockett, Sara & Welton, Ann. (1990, September 1). Picture books for the gifted. *Booklist, 87,* 63-66.

Paterson, Katherine. (1989). *The spying heart: More thoughts on reading and writing books for children.* New York: Dutton.

Polette, Nancy. (1981). *Picture books for gifted programs.* Metuchen, N.J.: Scarecrow.

Wells, Rosemary. (1990). The well-tempered children's book. In Zinsser, Paul (Ed.), *Worlds of childhood: The art and craft of writing for children.* Boston: Houghton Mifflin.

CHAPTER SEVEN

All the Wealth: Kinds of Literature

"Literature is the dominant art," says our son David, who holds a doctoral degree in comparative literature. In order to know music, sculpture, or painting, he points out, we have to know literature. Through most of history, composers have assumed listeners have read classic literature, but a writer does not normally assume his readers have heard a certain body of music. As far back as Homer, makers of literature were recognized as artists, but 2300 years later sculptors were still considered stonecutters. In his lifetime, Michelangelo was recognized as a great craftsman, not an artist.

Historically, painters, sculptors, and musicians sought inspiration in literary themes to legitimize their work as art. Even now, the modern critic of other arts uses the history of literature as a frame of reference, while a literary critic—perhaps mistakenly—finds the history of his own field sufficient. (David G. Halsted, personal communication, September 5, 1992)

If our children are to be truly educated, they must have a rich background in literature. They won't acquire all they need before the age of eighteen, but if we enthusiastically introduce them to all kinds of literature, they'll have a chance to become discriminating, mature readers who continue reading literature for pleasure throughout a lifetime. This chapter is designed to remind parents and teachers of the wealth of good books available to children.

The comfortable phrase, "curling up with a good book," brings to mind the prospect of spending an evening with a thick novel—a romance or a mystery, perhaps an historical novel, but certainly fiction. Although we tend to think of fiction first, there is much more to reading than that.

Within fiction there are several different types; there are also various categories of nonfiction. All of these are available to the child who wants to curl up with a good book—but only if she knows about them.

Here are four points to remember in using books to guide and enrich bright children:

1. Some children, especially as they grow older, resist reading fiction.

2. A lack of interest in this genre does not mean they must stop reading. There are many kinds of literature: *fiction, nonfiction, biography, traditional literature, fantasy and science fiction,* and *poetry* are all discussed in this chapter.

3. Gifted and talented youngsters, like other children, must be introduced to the best in literature. They will not automatically find it on their own.

4. The different types of literature vary in their power to meet emotional and intellectual needs for gifted children, and their effect varies from one child to another. It is important that children be introduced to all kinds of literature, with enough exposure so that each child can decide which is most valuable for him or her.

Fiction will fall naturally into the hands of good readers in elementary school, but unless a planned effort is made to introduce them to other branches of literature, especially traditional literature and poetry, children may miss them altogether. Middle school and senior high students need guidance, too, to become aware of the wealth of literature as they develop into adult readers. Any kind of literature can be an important part of education—a key to histories, arts, and cultures, particularly for these youngsters who are more likely to draw information from many sources and integrate it in new ways.

Guiding the reading of intellectually curious children, therefore, includes making them aware of the varieties of literature and helping them learn which kinds have most appeal for them. The resulting knowledge of books and of their own preferences is part of what makes a mature reader.

In elementary schools, the logical person to coordinate the introduction of literature through the grades is the librarian. Not every elementary school, however, boasts a professional who has time to plan and implement a program for introducing various types of literature at appropriate grade levels. For teachers in such schools, the chart on page 172 outlines a sample literature curriculum. Parents whose children have no school librarian will find that the children's staff at a nearby public library can suggest good books in each literary category.

This chapter offers background information on each literary type, criteria for excellence, and some answers to these questions:

1. What are the implications for work with especially bright children?

2. How should the literature be presented developmentally, as children grow from one stage to the next?

3. How can adults who are not yet familiar with children's literature most easily find the best?

Fiction

Fiction (called "realistic fiction" when fantasy is considered as a separate category) is the broadest body of literature, the earliest found by children exploring on their own, and the most easily judged by the traits given in the previous chapter. It comprises the bulk of the titles listed in the annotated bibliography in Chapter Eight.

Since authors write about what they know, and many authors were gifted children, the characters in juvenile fiction are often gifted. However, rarely is the giftedness pointed out; it is simply there to be recognized by child readers who see something of themselves in the story.

Table 7-1. K-6 Literature Curriculum

	Picture Books	Poetry	Traditional	Nonfiction	Fiction
Kindergarten	x	x	Folktales Fairytales	x	Each genre is presented at the grade levels indicated by x or by the name of a type of literature
First Grade	x	x	Folktales Fairytales	x	
Second Grade	x	x	Folktales Fairytales	x	Realistic Fantasy
Third Grade	x	x	Folktales Fairytales Fables	x Biography	Realistic Fantasy
Fourth Grade		x	Folktales Legends	x Biography	Realistic Fantasy High Fantasy
Fifth Grade		x	Legends Myths	x Biography	Realistic Fantasy High Fantasy Historical
Sixth Grade		x	Myths Epics	x Biography	Realistic Fantasy High Fantasy Historical Science Fiction
	These are read aloud when classes come to the library.			These are introduced in the library through excerpts or booktalks.	

Types of Fiction

Realistic fiction can be divided into a number of subtypes: adventure, animal stories, mystery, sports stories, humor, romance, historical fiction, etc. Most of these can be thought of as one group, although historical fiction deserves special consideration, as do series books.

How well each type suits the emotional or intellectual needs of especially talented children depends largely on the author's point of view and on how well the books are written. Each kind, but some more than others, can be treated in ways that offer intellectual challenge or provide insights into emotional development.

Recognizing Good Fiction

In order to continue to appeal to new generations of young readers, fiction must speak to their universal concerns, help them explore themselves through the characters in books, and introduce them to life in other places and times. It does this by dealing honestly with the material and with its readers.

Honesty and accuracy are the two most important criteria for children's fiction. Settings must be described so that the reader can imagine them. Plots must relate something that could plausibly happen. Above all, people must react with understandable emotions and behavior; their speech must be true to their ages and experience and to the environment established for them in the story.

Beyond that, for fiction that has enough depth to engage the imagination of sensitive readers, something should happen *within* the characters during the course of the book. Even fiction for young children offers this: *Evan's Corner*, for example, is not just a story about a boy who needs a little privacy and is allowed to turn a corner of a room into his own space. It is also about Evan's getting everything he thought he wanted, and then *realizing* (the internal event) that it is not enough. He wants to share it, too.

Historical fiction. Writers of historical fiction must walk a line between overburdening the plot with too much historical detail, and using so little historical background that the book amounts to a novel placed in an historical setting. The best writers base their books on serious research, and weave realistic details into the narrative to lend authenticity to plot and characterization.

For alert and questioning readers, historical fiction should show not only the culture and daily life of the period, but also should deal with some of the political and personal issues encountered by people of the era. An example is Esther Forbes's *Johnny Tremain*, in which Johnny, initially concerned with his burned hand, is gradually caught up in the political and military turmoil around him as the Revolutionary War begins.

Series books. Series such as Sweet Valley High and the Baby Sitters Club, with 88 and 107 titles respectively in 1992, enthrall girls in the eight-to-twelve age range. Why? And is there anything wrong with that?

They appeal because they are safe and predictable, according to Cooper (1992). Although critics charge that "the characters are stock, the situations redundant and the settings hopelessly middle-class sub-urban," Cooper points out that even in idealized settings, the plots allow real issues—divorce, sexuality, racism—to creep in. "In an uncertain world, there is security in knowing that somewhere the nice kids win out, the others get their comeuppance and the story will end with expectations met."

Like television, series books become a matter of concern when they are overused, blocking out more challenging reading. Ferraro (1992) quotes a mother's worry: "The books can keep kids at a fourth-grade reading level too long. I find a reluctance to move to other books with a little more complex sentence structure and vocabulary."

Girls who are immersed in series books could benefit from intelligent reading guidance (see Chapter Three), with a quiet acceptance of their present reading combined with the expectation that they will soon—or simultaneously—read books that offer more rounded characters, a variety of settings, and more artful use of language.

Finding Good Fiction

Young children find a "good book" mostly by watching what their friends are reading. They may also be given recommendations by the school librarian or get ideas from what their teacher reads aloud. However, unless someone guides them to good books, their progress is haphazard at best.

Those who want to recommend good literature to children can follow a more systematic procedure. See the sources listed on page 167 and at the end of this chapter.

Another rich source of information is the librarian's own reference collection. Here are reference books and periodicals which list children's books by categories, often providing annotations or reviews for each. For most of these, inclusion equals recommendation; that is, they list only books that by some established standard merit recommendation to children. The public is usually welcome to use these references, though probably they cannot be checked out of the library. A list of some of the most useful sources is provided at the end of this chapter.

Nonfiction

It may surprise some to know that at the end of a library story hour for primary-grade children, when the children are free to find a book to check out, they are more likely to swarm to the nonfiction shelves than to the picture books. No matter how attentively they have just listened to fiction or folklore, they appear to be hungry for fact as they explore on their own. It may be that as nonreaders, they feel they can gather more information from the pictures of a fact book than they can from those in a picture book whose story they do not know.

Whatever the reason, it is obvious that even at that early age, nonfiction or "information" books are important to children, and this continues to be true as they grow older. With the introduction of new methods of teaching that require students to search for information beyond their textbooks, the number and quality of nonfiction books for young people have increased dramatically over the last three decades— a bonus of the educational reforms inspired by Sputnik. Gifted students in particular benefit from exploring the views of different authors, in books that offer more information at a more challenging reading level than graded textbooks can.

For readers of any age, nonfiction written for children is a good introduction to a new field. For a report on any topic only vaguely familiar to them—examples might be continental drift, the human brain, astronomy or economics—older students can begin with books written for younger children to gain a quick overview of basic concepts, essential vocabulary, and an organizational framework. All of this will help them make better use of information they find later in more advanced books and articles.

Recognizing Good Nonfiction

It is not easy to write good nonfiction. Lacking a plot to maintain interest, the author must write with both a lucid style and a clear purpose. The author's attitude toward his audience and his reason for choosing to write about his topic for young people help determine the success of his book, providing a framework that may be nearly invisible but nevertheless gives shape to the contents.

The physical appearance of the book, the size, the format and the organization of the material, aesthetic qualities such as the appeal of illustrations and the print type—all add to the book's ability to attract and hold readers.

Beyond these essential considerations are the characteristics of good nonfiction: accuracy, readability, and for especially bright readers, open-endedness and the potential for stimulating as well as satisfying curiosity.

Accuracy. Accuracy is absolutely essential in nonfiction. The copyright date should be recent, especially if the book is in a field that is changing rapidly. The dust jacket or endpapers may provide biographical material on the author indicating his or her level of expertise. If possible, check the accuracy of a section of text that covers an area of knowledge that is familiar to you, or ask an expert to check it. Try to determine whether the author is writing from a biased point of view, keeping in mind that young children in particular are vulnerable: they are likely to believe what they read simply because it is in print.

Look for accuracy in the graphic material, also. For illustrations in science books, a clear and precise line with correct labeling is needed. Photographs may be best for some social studies books, but they should be updated when the books are revised. Graphs and charts must be clear and current.

Readability. Since the appeal in nonfiction is to the intellect rather than to an emotional response, the author must be skilled in techniques that hold the reader's interest. Readability, the way in which the material is presented, is of paramount importance. Like a good teacher introducing a new subject by referring to what the children already know, the author of a good nonfiction book will begin with an image or a setting that is familiar, then take the readers into new territory. A book for primary children on building barns, for example, might demonstrate stress factors with illustrations and text showing structures made of building blocks.

Nonfiction requires clear writing, logically and sequentially presented. In addition, writing for children requires some special techniques.

Because young children cannot yet think in abstractions, abstract concepts should be supported by concrete images, either in illustrations or by giving clear examples. A description of the structure of a bridge, for instance, should be accompanied by a drawing, preferably with the parts labeled. General statements must be followed by specific examples. Repetition is important—authors should repeat key words throughout the book, and provide a summary at the end. The vocabulary should be accurate, reflecting the terms used by workers in the field discussed in the book. A glossary in books about specialized topics is always welcome. The writing style should flow comfortably, drawing the reader along.

Readability can be enhanced by the organization of the book. Maps, charts, graphs, drawings, and photographs increase readability and should be placed near the text they illustrate. An index helps readers to find their way around the book. Intellectually-oriented readers should also use some books that include bibliographies—so they can learn where they can read more, and become familiar with the researcher's practice of documenting sources of information.

Reading level should also be considered, since a book can be readable, or not, at any reading level. Often an assumed reading level is indicated either on the book or by its placement in a library or bookstore. However, gifted children with a strong interest in a topic will read beyond their grade level or even their measured reading level to learn as much as they can from a book that might otherwise be considered too advanced for them. They should, of course, have the freedom to select books for older readers along with those that are at a comfortable reading level.

Open-endedness. Finally, nonfiction for gifted readers should be open-ended. This may sound like a contradiction in terms for a fact book, but consider: Is the author clear about which statements are accepted facts and which are theories? Does she use an interdisciplinary approach, indicating points at which this subject leads into other, related topics? Is there some mention of the ethical questions that are being raised by new knowledge in the field?

Much of what we memorized as children—about space, genetics, paleontology—has been modified by newer discoveries. With their ability to delay closure, gifted children are receptive to uncertainty and they are challenged by the unknown. They should be informed of the unanswered questions and methods used in current research and they should be stimulated to examine more deeply themselves. Challenging nonfiction gives satisfactory answers to some questions, but it also raises more, and invites readers to continue the search for information at a new level.

Nonfiction and Gifted Readers

Intellectually-oriented youngsters can and should learn to select nonfiction well, to pursue their own interests through reading. It is helpful to discuss with them the characteristics of good nonfiction books, so they can make judgments for themselves.

Sometimes, gifted children run into barriers as they look for new books that match their interests. Adults who can't believe their children can read far beyond their age level may be reluctant to allow them to use expensive books. Paul, for example, discovered at the age of eight that the library in his K-through-twelve school had purchased a new astronomical atlas. More than anything, Paul wanted to take that atlas home, even though he could hardly carry it. In addition to the question of a third-grader's reliability with a costly new book, the librarian had to consider that it was a reference book and could circulate only overnight. However, she knew Paul and understood his passion for science; arrangements were made. For months, he came to the library every Friday afternoon and checked the book out for the weekend, always returning it early Monday morning, in perfect condition in spite of the winter weather. Paul certainly gained more from the atlas than the seniors for whom it had been ordered.

When librarians are not acquainted with children like Paul, parents or teachers may have to run interference, explaining why a child may need and merit special consideration. They may also help by coaching the child in how to respond effectively to restricting rules.

Finding Good Nonfiction

Even armed with a list of characteristics to help select the best, a reader approaching the nonfiction section of a school or public library is likely to be overwhelmed by the sheer volume of material. It is worth the time to make a list of recommended books, using reviews or booklists, before turning to the public catalog.

Reviews of nonfiction may be difficult to uncover because reviewing children's nonfiction is especially demanding—reviewers must be knowledgeable about the topic of the book as well as about good children's writing. Reviews of newly-published books appear in periodicals first; it is usually at least a year before they appear in book form. The periodical *Booklist* divides reviews of books for young people into several sections, placing reviews of nonfiction books first in each case. In addition, journals for teachers often list a few new books for students among the book reviews. And newsletters for parents of children enrolled in gifted programs sometimes offer recommendations for good reading.

Finding a review of a book that sounds ideal does not assure that the book will be at the library. But readers are not limited to books in the local school library or bookstore, since most titles can be ordered. With so much nonfiction available, some of it highly specialized, it is unreasonable to expect bookstores and libraries to stock enough for the varied needs of curious, avid readers—underscoring the importance of finding and reading reviews, so you can make specific requests when ordering.

Reference books suggested at the end of this chapter provide lists of recommended books, often without reviews. Some have nonfiction sections; others are entirely about nonfiction books.

Biography

Biography often becomes a favorite with young people who prefer more difficult reading. Since life stories of individuals who realized their high potential can offer intellectually and emotionally rewarding reading for gifted adults, it's important that bright children have a good introduction to this genre. Like other forms of nonfiction, biography is often assigned as part of a study unit, so most children are aware of it as a separate kind of literature by the time they are in the upper elementary grades.

Types of Biographies

Biographies can be classified on a continuum, with nonfiction at one end and fiction at the other. At the nonfiction end, *definitive* biography relies on historical evidence, containing nothing that cannot be documented. *Fictionalized biography*, in the middle, is a blend—the author conducts extensive research and then invents dialogue or events based on the historical record. And at the other end of the continuum, *biographical fiction* is frankly fiction, with a historical person as the main character.

The characteristic that establishes biography most reliably on the continuum is dialogue. In a scholarly biography, dialogue is rare, and occurs only when there is a written record of the discussion. For the most part, the characters "speak" only through their letters.

In fictionalized biography, the author is free to blend fact and fiction by creating scenes in which an imagined conversation furthers or dramatizes the historical account. For a cataloging class, one of my library school professors described fictionalized biography with a memorable example: "If there is a line like, 'After the last guest had left, Victoria dismissed the servants, retired to the royal suite, closed the door, turned to Albert, and said, ". . . .",' then you know you have a fictionalized biography."

In biographical fiction, on the other hand, conversation flows as freely as in any other kind of fiction, even between bit players for whose very existence there is no historical record.

The type of biography children enjoy depends in large part on their age. For young children whose sense of history is not developed, biographies are stories that familiarize them with names such as Washington, Lincoln, or Martin Luther King. Older children enjoy both biographical fiction and fictionalized biography, and talented senior high students should be encouraged to read some of the classic biographies such as Lytton Strachey's *Queen Victoria*, Marchette Chute's *Shakespeare of London*, or selections from Plutarch's *Lives of the Noble Greeks and Romans*.

Recognizing Good Biography

At one time, biography was a weak link in children's literature. Much of it was didactic, written to teach a lesson, as young readers could clearly see. However, in recent years there have been three significant changes (Flack, 1992): more biographies about women and members of minority groups have appeared, biographees are presented as real human beings rather than impossible paragons, and authors model good scholarship for their readers through the biographies they write.

Running the gamut from nonfiction to fiction, biography can be judged by some of the criteria used for each. As nonfiction, it must be accurate, readable, and objective.

Historical accuracy depends on which type of biography the author has written. Even in biographical fiction, however, historical details should be authentic, as they should be in any good historical fiction.

A readable biography must bring a historical person to life, presenting characters as real people with human problems and responses. Small, intimate details make the biographee seem like a contemporary friend. Dialogue should flow as naturally as it does in a novel.

All nonfiction writers should approach their subjects with objectivity, but it is perhaps more difficult to be objective about people.

Objectivity requires authors to maintain a balance between admiration and criticism for the biographee. Objective authors leave readers free to draw their own conclusions based on the facts; they do not suppress relevant but negative aspects of the principal character's life and place in history. Biography for children should show restraint and sensitivity in discussing character weaknesses, particularly when they are unrelated to the person's historical importance.

Finding Biographies

In libraries, biographies are usually shelved together in the nonfiction section, at the point where the number 921 would occur in the Dewey Decimal system. However, the call "number" is often a B followed by the last name of the biographee, so the books appear in alphabetical order by the person whose life they tell, not by the author.

The biography section may be astonishingly large in proportion to the rest of nonfiction. How to find the best? The sources suggested at the end of the chapter include sections on biography. Ask for the librarian's help, if necessary, to locate the biography sections in these listings.

Biography in Bibliotherapy with Gifted Students

The role of biography in bibliotherapy is a matter of some controversy. There are those who would recommend it as a way of presenting role models for young people. Others say that children cannot identify with adults until they reach adolescence; hence, biography could not be useful for bibliotherapy. There is the further objection that biography, like mythology, presents heroes of such dimensions that most readers are overwhelmed and left with no hope of emulating such a successful life (Groff, 1980).

While these arguments may be valid for young children, and perhaps for most children of any age, there are other considerations for highly talented junior and senior high students. Biographies can be used with them with certain purposes in mind, which may outweigh any other objections.

One purpose is to demonstrate that many trials and failures often precede success. The biographies of scientists in deKruif's *The Microbe Hunters*, for example, provide evidence of the hours of preparation and even drudgery that must pay for the moment of discovery—and it is obvious that deKruif's scientists paid the price gladly, with lasting enthusiasm for their work. It is not difficult to imagine that this book might be informative, perhaps even inspiring reading for a gifted child who resists routine work.

Another purpose is to show the role of personal characteristics in achievement, characteristics which could be either evident or latent in the gifted child reading the book. *Carry On, Mr. Bowditch* is a good example, illustrating how Nathaniel Bowditch's inner drive, his energetic curiosity and thoroughness in inquiry, helped him achieve far more than usual for those with his scant opportunity for formal education.

In searching for appropriate biographies for gifted readers, look for this emphasis on the internal drives that propelled the individuals to become subjects of biographies. What is revealed about their motivation, moral imperative, intellectual curiosity, impulse to inquiry? What advantages did giftedness bring to them, and what problems? How did they turn their talents to their own advantage in coping with the problems? What evidence is there, if any, that they recognized their own gifts and consciously made use of them? What role did a sense of commitment, mission, or responsibility play in their achievements?

A third use of biographies with gifted adolescents is to provide them with examples of gifted people who experienced feelings of isolation and loneliness that readers can recognize. Gifted young people, especially if they sense their own giftedness, are quite likely to be able to identify with the aspirations and struggles of gifted adults—like Marie Curie, studying alone in a Paris apartment so cold that one night she piled everything she could, including a chair, on top of her bed for warmth. Some gifted teenagers can understand that to Marie, the cold and the loneliness were incidental nuisances compared to the privilege of studying science at the Sorbonne. Rather than feeling overwhelmed, they can use such people as models without necessarily expecting themselves to achieve to the same degree.

Contemplating the potential grandeur of the wondering, reaching, striving human spirit is now rather out of fashion, but it is still necessary, especially for people so talented that the highest aspirations are appropriate for them. Biography can be one of the most intellectually demanding forms of literature, but it can also be among the most inspiring. On both counts, it should be part of the reading program for gifted young people.

Traditional Literature

The literatures that have been passed from generation to generation since the beginning of human culture include folk and fairy tales, fables, myths, legends, and epics. This rich heritage, once oral, is now collected in many written versions, available now to children in greater variety and from more different cultures than ever before. It is a vital part of the background of anyone who would hope to be truly educated.

Most children will not find traditional literature on their own. When they swarm to the nonfiction shelves after the story hour, it is to science, technology, and craft books, not the mythology or folklore sections (which are also classified as nonfiction, strange as it may seem, because they are a way to learn about the cultures from which they come). Rare is the child who will ask where to find fairy tales or King Arthur stories, although they enjoy these stories when they are read to them. Traditional literature, therefore, must be actively introduced, or most children will grow up without adequate knowledge of it.

Mythology. In particular, a knowledge of the Greek, Roman, and Norse myths will go far toward making young people feel at home with European and American art, literature, and history—but our children are less and less likely to become acquainted with them at school. Parents who want to be sure their children are acquainted with this literature may have to make an extra effort at home.

When we say "myths" we mean "untruths" more often than we mean the stories human beings have used through most of history to express ultimate truths and values. The psychoanalyst Rollo May (1991) regrets our failure in recent years to take myths seriously as givers of meaning. "Western society has all but lost its myths," he states, and "many of the problems of our society, including cults and drug addiction, can be traced to the lack of myths," (p. 9). Perhaps the loss is not only our knowledge of myths but also our capacity to think mythologically, to use symbols to make or discover meaning in our lives.

Introducing Traditional Literature at the Best Time

Presenting folklore, myths and epics effectively requires a knowledge of the ages when children are most likely to respond to them. Parents and nursery school teachers should begin by reading folklore, simple tales of the wisdom and foolishness of common people, to their three- and four-year-olds. Preschoolers love cumulative tales like *The Three Little Pigs*, *The Gingerbread Boy*, and *The Little Red Hen.*

Fairy tales come next, appealing to children from about five to eight years old. Although the Grimm tales are the most familiar, there are many others in collections from different countries. Any concerns adults may have about violence in fairy tales can be allayed by reviewing the wide variety available—remembering Bettelheim's (1976) view that in their eagerness to see justice served and with their black-and-white view of the world, children are not nearly as alarmed by the violence as are adults.

By the time they are in fourth grade, students should be introduced to some of the Greek and Roman myths. It may be difficult to believe that children can grow up without knowing these essential stories, but unless adults plan to prevent it, this can happen. The American Jack tales and other American folklore—Paul Bunyan, John Henry—are appropriate at this age, too.

Fifth and sixth graders are ready for Robin Hood and the Arthurian legends, as well as more Greek and Roman myths. Norse mythology can also be introduced at this age. Some sixth graders enjoy versions of the Odyssey and the Iliad, as well as legends from other countries like Kate Seredy's *The White Stag*, the legend of the founding of Hungary—any of which could be read aloud in a classroom to enrich a history or social studies unit. These stories continue to interest some students through the early junior high years.

As American society continues to diversify, it becomes increasingly important to offer more than the familiar Greek and Roman myths. Folktales reveal the values and wisdom of a culture, and they appeal to children regardless of their origin (Dailey, 1991). Norse mythology, Celtic legend, African tales, and Eastern European stories hold the cultural heritage of many children, some of it from so long ago that it is nearly forgotten. Books can keep it alive. Middle Eastern and Oriental traditional literatures represent the heritage of a growing number of children in American schools. A knowledge of these stories and others that appear in similar versions from different parts of the world help children understand their common humanity. In encouraging students to think of themselves as citizens of the world rather than having a provincial outlook, traditional literature is a valuable tool.

Recognizing Good Traditional Literature

Imagine, of all that is written today, what will have survived in 500 or 1,000 years. Even with many details lost, that distillation will provide a better picture of the essence of our time than any of us could perceive by browsing in a library today, or glancing through the daily newspapers. It will have become traditional literature.

By definition, traditional literature is the best of the ancient stories, those that have survived. In many tellings over the years, folk and fairy tales been shaped and polished; in the last century and this, they have been gathered and put into print. Myths and epics represent the highest literary achievements of the cultures that produced them. In a sense, the term "good traditional literature" is redundant.

But this does not mean that every book on the shelves is a masterpiece. How to choose, especially for gifted children? What's best is not one specific story or genre over another, but *versions* written in demanding language, perceptive in delving into human character—and into relationships among people and between human beings and their fate or their gods. The only way to judge is to read as widely as possible.

Look first at the quality of the language when choosing versions to share. These tales, after all, represent the beginnings of our literary heritage, and the language should both respect and reflect the long history of refining that the stories have undergone. Modern versions do not always serve them well; some of the wonder they stirred in their listeners centuries ago should linger in the present telling. Leon Garfield and Edward Blishen achieve this in *The God Beneath the Sea*; so do Rosemary Sutcliff in her version of *Beowulf* and Padraic Colum in his compilation of stories of the heroes who lived before the Trojan War, *The Golden Fleece*.

Illustrations, too, should convey a sense of the simple and eternal truths with which the stories are concerned. Banality and cuteness are too often found in children's books of fairy tales, but a little searching will yield books whose illustrations shine with dignity and grace. Examples of artists who illustrate traditional literature well are Kate Greenaway, Arthur Rackham, Barbara Cooney, and Adrienne Adams.

Finding Good Traditional Literature

Information about fine versions of traditional literature can be found in textbooks and reference books on children's literature. See "Textbooks in Children's Literature" and "Reference Books about Children's Literature" at the end of this chapter.

As with other "nonfiction," libraries usually carry much larger collections of traditional stories than bookstores do. In the nonfiction section of the children's collection, folk and fairy tales are found under sociology, Dewey Decimal number 398. Mythology may be shelved with religion in the 200s, since it was the religious literature of its culture, and epics in the 800s, with the literature of the country of origin. Each library may interpret the Dewey system slightly differently, however, and your library may be cataloged by the Library of Congress system instead of Dewey, so ask for help if necessary.

Many, many versions of the different tales are available. Here are a few examples that will appeal to good readers:

African

Aardema, Verna. *Tales from the Story Hat*. New York: Coward, 1960.

American

Caduto, Michael J. and Joseph Bruchac. *Keepers of the Earth: Native American Stories and Environmental Activities for Children*. Golden, CO: Fulcrum, 1988.

Chase, Richard. *The Jack Tales*. Boston: Houghton Mifflin, 1943.

Sanfield, Steve. *The Adventures of High John the Conqueror*. New York: Orchard, 1989.

Celtic

Sutcliff, Rosemary. *The Hound of Ulster*. New York: Dutton, 1963.

English

Picard, Barbara Leonie. *Stories of King Arthur and His Knights*. np: Walck, 1966.

Pyle, Howard. *The Story of King Arthur and His Knights*. New York: Sharon, 1981.

_____. *The Merry Adventures of Robin Hood*. New York: Dover, 1968.

Sutcliff, Rosemary. *Beowulf*. Magnolia, Mass.: Peter Smith, 1984.

Far East

Courlander, Harold. *The Tiger's Whisker and Other Tales and Legends from Asia and the Pacific*. New York: Harcourt, 1959.

Yep, Laurence. *The Rainbow People*. New York: Harper and Row, 1989.

Greek and Roman

Colum, Padraic. *The Golden Fleece*. New York: Macmillan, 1983.

_____. *The Children's Homer*. New York: Macmillan, 1982.

Coolidge, Olivia. *Greek Myths*. Boston: Houghton Mifflin, 1949.

Garfield, Leon and Edward Blishen. *The God Beneath the Sea*. New York: Pantheon, 1971.

Picard, Barbara Leonie. *The Iliad of Homer*. New York: Oxford, 1960.

Norse

Colum, Padraic. *The Children of Odin*. Havertown, Pa.: Havertown Books, 1920.

Coolidge, Olivia. *Legends of the North*. Boston: Houghton Mifflin, 1951.

D'Aulaire, Ingri and Edgar Parin. *Norse Gods and Giants*. New York: Doubleday, 1967.

Russian

Ginsburg, Mirra. *Twelve Clever Brothers and Other Fools*. New York: Lippincott Junior Books, 1979.

This list is a mere beginning. There are many more collections and individual stories on the library shelves, evidence of the stature of traditional literature in the human story. For some, it is the literary form most likely to move the spirit in the same mysterious way that art and music can do. Elizabeth Cook expressed this in *The Ordinary and the Fabulous* (1969, p. 5):

> There is another door that can be opened by reading legends and fairy tales, and for some children, at the present time, there may be no other key to it. *Religio*, in one Latin sense of the word, implies a sense of the strange, the numinous, the totally Other, of what lies quite beyond human personality and cannot be found in any human relationships. This kind of "religion" is an indestructible part of the experience of many human minds, even though the temper of a secular society does not encourage it . . . it may very well be in reading about a vision of the flashing-eyed Athene or the rosy-fingered Aphrodite that children first find a satisfying formulation of those queer prickings of delight, excitement and terror that they feel when they first walk by moonlight, or when it snows in May, or when, like the young Wordsworth, they have to touch a wall to make sure that it is really there. Magic is not the same as mysticism, but it may lead towards it; it is mystery "told to the children."

Fantasy and Science Fiction

For our older son's ninth birthday I went shopping, as usual, for a book. Browsing through the juvenile shelves of a favorite bookstore, I came upon a title that was then new to me: *The Book of Three.* Something about that title, something about the very feel of the book in my hand, told me that this was the book for David at this time and that there was something there for me, too, although just what wasn't so clear.

The book was David's introduction to fantasy, and he could not have had a better one. Later I learned that the story was based on Lloyd Alexander's extensive knowledge of Welsh legend, part of my unknown heritage, and David's. Later still, after reading much more fantasy, mythology, and modern literature, David spent a summer studying Welsh at the University of Aberystwyth. His personal library now includes several titles in Welsh, and it will not surprise me if he returns to the study of that language in the future. All this might have happened in any case, but it is clear that *The Book of Three* reached David at just the right moment to catch his imagination, give it focus, and send it soaring.

Fantasy and science fiction can do this for some children. They discover it—and there is much of it for them—at just the age when they are entering their own personal quests for identity and beginning consciously to establish their personal values. The quest, and the attempt (sometimes failed) to live up to lofty ideals, are hallmarks of high fantasy. To judge from the devotion with which many young people read fantasy, it must be exactly what they need in the late elementary and middle school years.

Fantasy, Science Fiction, and Gifted Readers

Gifted readers are likely to read more fantasy and science fiction than average students; some children go through a stage lasting for several years, from the late elementary grades through middle school, when they read fantasy and science fiction almost entirely.

This becomes a source of concern for those parents and teachers who see it as escape literature and wonder whether the child will ever read "serious" literature again. It is an unnecessary worry; young people do move through this stage, and if they know how to distinguish good literature, they will continue with excellent choices in other areas. This is even more likely if they are reading *good* fantasy and science fiction.

Adults sometimes have more serious concerns that gifted children can become too engrossed in science fiction and live too much in a fantasy world. If a child is able to relate to others *only* through fantasy (only through games based on fantasy, for example), there is cause for concern. However, if this is only a part of his life and he has other ways of relating to friends, it should not be a serious worry.

The interest in fantasy should not be seen merely as a stage to be endured. What we are beginning to learn about right and left brain functioning may have intriguing implications here. It is too simplistic to say that rational, analytical, logical thinking is the function of the left brain, while intuitive, imaginative, mystical thinking originates in the right brain, but certainly there are unique learning styles. This description of the brain at least provides a framework within which to consider how imaginative literature may promote intellectual development.

It appears that creativity requires using both hemispheres of the brain, with a flow of information from one to the other (Clark, 1992). Furthermore, the productive use of acquired knowledge (left brain) apparently can be enhanced by the ability to be imaginative (right brain). Undoubtedly, creativity is a product of integrating imagination and knowledge.

Thus it is important that children have the chance to be imaginative as they progress through the grades, spending more and more time gaining factual knowledge. Fantasy and science fiction provide such an opportunity. Perhaps this need to keep their imaginations alive is behind the voracious appetitite of some gifted young people for this type of literature.

Introducing Fantasy and Science Fiction at the Best Time

For young children who have had a rich background in traditional literature in their preschool years, the introduction of fantasy may be barely noticeable. For adults who guide their reading, however, it is helpful to mark the inexact line between folklore and modern fantasy.

One way to clarify the difference is authorship. Traditional literature, true folklore, began as oral tradition and has no known author. The Grimm brothers did not write their tales; they collected them from those who were still telling them, in the oral tradition. Hans Christian Andersen, on the other hand, created his stories, which incorporate many elements of folklore but are modern fantasy. Many authors since, such as MacDonald, Tolkien, Lewis, Alexander, Cooper, and LeGuin, whose works are mentioned below, have done the same, building a rich body of modern imaginative literature.

Fantasy. Elements of traditional literature linger in modern fantasy. Familiar characteristics of folklore and fairy tales blend over into fantasy in books like A. A. Milne's *Winnie- the-Pooh*, in which animals talk, and P. L. Travers' *Mary Poppins*, in which the source of magic is not fairies but Mary Poppins herself. A child can move in easy stages from these early fantasies to modern fairy tales, fantasy based on time warps, high fantasy, and science fiction. With care, she can read excellent literature every step of the way.

For middle grade children, animal characters continue to appear in classic fantasies like *The Wind in the Willows* and *Charlotte's Web*,

190

echoing the talking animals of folklore. In George MacDonald's late nineteenth-century story, *At the Back of the North Wind*, the North Wind is a lady remarkably like a fairy godmother. Some fantasies written for this age group, like Mary Norton's *The Borrowers*, feature characters who are miniature people, reminiscent of the elves and dwarfs of folklore.

The element of the time warp appears in Lucy M. Boston's *The Children of Green Knowe* and its sequels, and in Philippa Pearce's *Tom's Midnight Garden*. In these books, a contemporary child meets and plays or struggles with a child or children from the past.

There is much more fantasy for middle and upper elementary children than can be mentioned here. A few more titles will suggest the range: talking animals appear in Kipling's *Jungle Books*, Lawson's *Rabbit Hill*, O'Brien's *The Rats of NIMH* (which might also be classified as science fiction), and in Adams' *Watership Down*, an adult book which gifted children of this age enjoy hearing read aloud. Although these books are very different from fairy tales or magic, they are all fantasies.

For older readers another author worth knowing is Robin McKinley, whose retelling for older readers of "The Beauty and the Beast," called simply *Beauty*, is completely credible and compelling. The British authors Alan Garner (*The Owl Service*) and William Mayne (*Earthfasts*) also write fine fantasy for older readers.

High fantasy. By the fourth grade, many children have discovered C. S. Lewis' Narnia series, beginning with *The Lion, the Witch, and the Wardrobe*. There are seven books in this series, and as in most fantasy series, any one can be read independently of the others, although some children will want to read them in order. Written for middle-grade children, the Narnia series is the first experience with high fantasy for most.

It is in high fantasy that the protagonists are usually involved in a quest, drawn into it by forces beyond their control. They go willingly, but there is often some sacrifice involved and much learning; they grow up in the process of the quest. The theme is often no less than the epic and never-ending struggle between good and evil, the relationship between human beings and the gods, with ordinary human beings risking all, often alone, in their attempts to perform seemingly impossible tasks and to live up to high ideals. Authors of high fantasy typically spin out their tales in a series of books instead of a single volume because the theme and plot are so involved.

High fantasy is frequently based on mythology and legend—in particular Germanic and Norse mythology, the Welsh *Mabinogion*, and the Arthurian legends (which are Welsh in origin). This background gives it a mythical quality which heightens the effect of the quest theme and strengthens the potential for nobility and a kind of grandeur, even when humor is also present.

Both grandeur and humor are certainly present in the second example of high fantasy children are likely to meet: Lloyd Alexander's Prydain series, five titles beginning with *The Book of Three*. Although he tells his stories with a light touch, Alexander's purposes are serious. To achieve them, he departs from Lady Charlotte Guest's edition of the *Mabinogion*, the basis for his fantasy series. When Eilonwy declares her independence in favor of Taran, she breaks from the Celtic legend, and Alexander's story becomes an American fantasy, protesting the monarchy (May, 1991).

Children may also discover in the late elementary grades Ursula LeGuin's Earthsea Trilogy (*A Wizard of Earthsea, The Tombs of Atuan*, and *The Farthest Shore*), and the Dragon books of Anne McCaffrey.

Middle school readers enjoy Susan Cooper's series, which begins with *Over Sea, Under Stone*. They have probably already found Tolkien's *The Hobbit*, and some may attempt the trilogy which follows, *The Lord of the Rings*, although it is more difficult. McKinley's *The Blue Sword* and its prequel, *The Hero and the Crown*, for readers of middle school age and older, are also in the tradition of high fantasy.

Science fiction. At some time during the middle school years, students may shift from fantasy to science fiction. Or they may read science fiction without ever having read much fantasy. The line between the two is blurred.

One way to distinguish them is to remember that fantasy could not happen in the future because it includes imaginary creatures (and often magic), while science fiction tells what conceivably could happen based on current scientific knowledge. A further distinction may also be that fantasy is concerned with the development of the internal, intrapersonal world, and science fiction with that of the external, interpersonal world.

Science fiction, however, includes an emphasis on technological expertise and comments on what future societies might be like, based on present predictions regarding the environment, population density, and the likelihood of catastrophic war. Or as Rosenberg (1986) puts it, science fiction is "speculative about the potential uses of science and speculative about the potential future of mankind on this world and within the universe" (p. 182).

Rosenberg goes on to identify several types or themes in science fiction. Here are some of her types, with examples:

Hard science	Asimov, Isaac	*I, Robot*
New wave	Burgess, Anthony.	A Clockwork Orange
Dystopia/ Utopia	Bradbury, Ray	*Fahrenheit 451*
Messianic/ religious	Herbert, Frank	*Dune*
Ecology	Anthony, Piers	*Omnivore*

Interestingly, children's science fiction often differs from that written for adults (Nodelman, 1992): in many science fiction novels for children, the view of technology is strongly negative, and the path to a better future lies in returning to a pre-technological age.

Science fiction is not often written for very young children because the content is so complex. It is in fifth or sixth grade that students may begin reading John Christopher's trilogy, *The White Mountains*, and Madeleine L'Engle's *A Wrinkle in Time* and its sequels.

By junior high, students are reading the science fiction of William Sleator, and also beginning to read adult science fiction. Frank Herbert's Dune series, Michael Crichton's *Andromeda Strain* and *Jurassic Park*, Ray Bradbury's *Fahrenheit 451*, and many of Madeleine L'Engle's books are titles junior and senior high students enjoy.

Intensified concern for the quality of life will often prompt senior high gifted students more than others to become interested in reading utopian literature and also dystopian books, which are not about ideal societies but about society gone wrong. Aldous Huxley's *Brave New World* and George Orwell's *Animal Farm* and *1984* are examples of good literature in this category.

Recognizing Good Fantasy and Science Fiction

Good fantasy and science fiction are judged much like good fiction of other types. Plot, setting, literary style, and convincing characters are just as important here as elsewhere. The criteria for literature that meets emotional and intellectual needs listed in Chapter Six apply here, too.

Science fiction lends itself to one particular flaw: it often relies too much on adventure, and provides too little in characterization or plot complexity. Plenty of action is an initial draw, but good science fiction also has characters who seem real and a plot that retains interest. Action alone quickly becomes boring to discriminating older readers.

One additional criterion, which may sound paradoxical, is that good fantasy and science fiction must be believable. The reader must be drawn into whatever world the author has created, and must believe in it; the created world must be consistent within itself. And the theme, the underlying thread which reveals the author's attitude toward the intrapersonal or the interpersonal world, must be based in truth.

Finding Good Fantasy and Science Fiction

There are excellent, prolific authors in both fields, and one way to find good fantasy or science fiction is to look for these and other books by the authors named above. But we have certainly not mentioned all the authors worth knowing. To learn more, consult the booklists suggested at the end of this chapter. Not all of these references list fantasy and science fiction separately, so you may need to search in the fiction section of the reference book.

Usually, fantasy and science fiction are shelved with fiction on library shelves, but some libraries either shelve them in a special section or place stickers on the book spines with symbols identifying specific types of fiction.

Mythology, Fantasy, and Gifted Children

If I have overemphasized traditional literature and fantasy in this chapter, it is because I believe that the one is neglected and the other unfairly maligned, and that together they offer a vital mixture for the balanced development of gifted children.

Mythology and high fantasy in particular validate the inner drive to cherish high ideals, to make commitments that cannot be justified on rational grounds, to find meaning outside of oneself. In our harsh world, it may be only in literature that some adolescents can find such affirmation. For especially bright and talented children, with their emerging sense of the potential in themselves and the accompanying confusion about how or whether to reveal it and use it, every possible source of affirmation must be recognized and encouraged.

Poetry

It is not difficult to introduce poetry to children, and the rewards are great—but it does require a special approach. No matter how effectively they encourage children to explore other forms of literature, many people lose their enthusiasm when they consider introducing poetry. The result is that children also may grow up feeling vaguely uneasy with poetry, not understanding it and not knowing how to approach it.

This is a regrettable loss. For the very young child who is experimenting with sound and language, the rhythm and nonsense syllables of nursery rhymes provide invaluable enrichment. Nursery rhymes may sound light and frivolous to adults, but they appeal to young children at a critical point, as they master one of the most important tasks of early childhood: the acquisition of language.

The elastic mind of a child of four or five shows an agility for learning foreign languages that the more rigid mind of the adult has lost. Parents who grow impatient with the repetition of Mother Goose rhymes need to understand that their child's language ability is greater than their own, and that his fascination with the sounds reflects his intelligence as he works at learning language.

In addition, poetry is one way to encourage intuition and imagery while the child learns also to think more scientifically and literally. Music is another way, but children will be exposed to music in at least some forms whether or not adults make a conscious effort to introduce it. Unless someone deliberately shares poetry throughout the elementary years, most children will be left with a nursery school level of awareness of poetry—as serious a handicap, in its way, as it would be to enter junior high with "Three Blind Mice" as their highest musical attainment.

Many children are offered nursery rhymes when they are preschoolers. From then on, however, their exposure to poetry may be limited to a few poems in elementary school reading texts, or taught as part of secondary school literature courses. They need more guidance than this, if they are to learn to love poetry—more guidance than other forms of literature require. They will surely discover books by Beverly Cleary, for example, in the second or third grade simply because Beverly Cleary is part of the culture of children of that age, but they are not likely to discover each new step in poetry for themselves.

Preparing to Introduce Poetry

For poetry more than for any other form of literature, adults must love it themselves—or learn to love it—in order to give it to children. Teachers know that they have to make an effort to find time in the day for poetry if it is important to them. It may be up to parents to keep poetry alive in their children if teachers cannot.

How can you as a teacher or parent achieve this, if poetry has not previously been part of your own life? You can go to the public or school library for books of poetry for children and books about children's literature. If children's poetry has never held much appeal for you, it is a good idea to read the poetry sections in the children's literature books first. One especially good book is *Literature for Thursday's Child* by Sam Leaton Sebesta and William J. Iverson (1975)—out of print, but worth looking up for the poetry section alone. Designed for teachers but adaptable by parents, it will surely send you on to the poetry shelves with energy and enthusiasm.

More background reading may help. *Climb into the Bell Tower* (1990) by the poet Myra Cohn Livingston is a collection of writings and speeches spanning her career, from 1967 to 1986. Admittedly based on her personal point of view, this book nevertheless offers helpful touchstones for evaluating children's poetry.

For example, Livingston summarizes the contributions of several well-known poets: William Blake leading the way from the older didactic poetry (verses designed to teach moral lessons) by insisting on the need for "joy, dreaming, and play," Lewis Carroll and Edward Lear adding nonsense and wordplay, Robert Louis Stevenson focusing on a child's everyday experiences, Shel Silverstein reviving didactic poetry but using humor so skilfully that readers may not realize that he is teaching as well as providing entertainment.

Livingston makes a distinction between comprehending and apprehending poetry. Comprehension, she says, is complete understanding, while apprehension is "the almost unconscious awareness of what is rumbling beneath the words, the intuitive understanding ... I tend to view literature and art in terms of apprehension, and I suspect children do too" (p. 208).

And Livingston speaks of image and symbol. Image is necessary, but it is not enough. "[T]o pretend that poetry is sugar-coated rhythm and rhyme and image is to rob [children] of the ability to deal with more serious aspects of life that they will surely meet, in ways we do not even suspect" (p. 131). To convey adequately the more serious, darker side of life, poetry must transcend image and offer symbol, must lead from a picture to a universal response which the reader can remember and adapt when in need. Symbol offers "the opportunity to respond beyond stereotype, beyond despair, with new insights and meaningful action. Symbol helps us learn that change is possible, that action is possible, and that each of us has the creativity to effect that change and action in a unique way... [S]ymbols ... sustain and strengthen us when times are out of joint" (p. 132).

After reading and reflecting on such background material, you can examine poetry anthologies, both traditional and modern. Begin a pattern of reading a poem or two aloud, along with prose, at story time. A representative stack of anthologies might include Walter de la Mare's *Come Hither*, Padraic Colum's *Roofs of Gold*, Nancy Larrick's *Crazy to Be Alive in Such a Strange World* and John Rowe Townsend's *Modern Poetry*. Inevitably you will develop favorites, and so will the children. When you find yourself or the children reciting lines spontaneously at appropriate moments, you will know that poetry is alive in your home or classroom.

Introducing Poetry

Poetry requires a unique approach. With other kinds of literature, teachers introduce examples to children as soon as they can read well enough to decode the language, and the children generally continue independently to find other examples if they are interested. However, until early adolescence, poetry is more accessible to children if they can hear it rather than read it silently, and they will need adult suggestions of poetry that will appeal to them. The different approach is to be more active in finding poetry to present, and to plan for time to read it aloud.

The teaching of poetry should begin with plenty of reading aloud until children have effortlessly learned a few poems "by heart." Gradually, discussion can then begin about the power of poetry. Rhythm, for instance, can be felt by the children when they are encouraged to sway with the lines of Stevenson's "The Swing," and they can hear how the words of David McCord's "The Pickety Fence" reproduce the stacatto sound of a stick being pulled along the top of a picket fence.

Generally it is thought that the best way to teach poetry to young students is to draw on their imagination, reading a poem aloud and then inviting children to respond to it through another medium, such as movement or drawing. Analysis—discussing elements of poetry like meter and imagery—is usually considered best left for secondary students. Sebasta and Iverson (1975), however, give arguments and methods for some analytical teaching of poetry to younger children. Other children's literature books also suggest creative ways to introduce poetry.

Parents may have more fun simply reading poetry aloud, rather than teaching it, and teachers as well may wish to introduce poetry by reading a poem each day. To choose well, parents and teachers need to know what kinds of poetry will hold the interest of children of different ages.

From Mother Goose rhymes in the preschool years, children in the primary grades grow to love humor and nonsense verses that play on words. Middle elementary children begin to enjoy ballads and other narrative poetry, and they prefer modern children's poems with ordinary, everyday language and content to traditional poetry. At all ages, humorous poetry is a great favorite—Shel Silverstein is always welcome. In order to explore the potential for emotional depth in poetry, some lyric poetry should be presented as well, to older students. Junior and senior high students should take literature courses that introduce them to a variety of poets and types of poetry, including modern poets like Maya Angelou and John Updike—poets whose allusions are more familiar to contemporary readers than the references found in the poems of historical writers.

Recognizing Good Poetry

As the title of one book of children's poetry tells us, "It doesn't always have to rhyme." Poetry is not necessarily about rhyme; it *is* about rhythm, words, and the concise, even startling expression of thoughts and feelings.

Poetry's *rhythm* appeals to young children: they clap their hands or bend their bodies to the beat of the lines. They should experience a variety of poetic meters and poetry with lines of varying length.

Words used in good poetry are vivid, evoking strong, clear images, like the opening line of Irene Rutherford McLeod's "Lone Dog:"

I'm a lean dog, a keen dog, a wild dog, and lone.

198

They are also imaginative, perhaps made up for the occasion or used in a new context, like E. E. Cummings' words "Just-spring" and "mud-luscious" for his poem, "In Just-." For young children, Dr. Seuss books offer imaginative and creative uses of words.

Children, especially highly verbal children, respond well to poetry with unfamiliar words. There is no need to worry about a controlled vocabulary—the rhythm and the content of the poem carry the listener along.

The *expression of thoughts and feelings*—the humor, the narrative, the moods expressed in lyric poetry—should use subject matter of interest to children: animals, friends, heroes, the stuff of their lives.

There is a difference between poetry and verse. Verse usually rhymes, as does some poetry, and both typically have meter. But poetry incorporates other, more sophisticated poetic elements as well, such as onomatopoeia, word play, alliteration, and literary techniques used in prose: imagery, metaphor, symbolism. Verse, like poorly written prose, *tells* too much ("John was sad.") Poetry, like good literature, *shows* an image ("John walked slowly, his hands in his pockets and his head down") and leaves the reader to interpret as he will. Verse explains all; poetry leaves something out for the reader to add—to apprehend, in Myra Cohn Livingston's word.

What is considered acceptable content for children's poetry has undergone a change in recent years, along with the change in fiction for young people. Contemporary poets write about the harsh realities of modern life—hence modern poetry provides a vehicle of expression for the outraged idealism that is one characteristic of gifted children and adolescents. Such poerty assures gifted students that others share their moral concerns, and it can prompt discussions that allow them to voice their own feelings.

Finding Good Poetry

As with every other type of literature mentioned here, recommendations for children's poetry books are found in the reference sources listed at the end of this chapter.

In the library, poetry is shelved in the Dewey Decimal 800s, the literature section; the 800s are subdivided by country, so that American poetry is 811, British poetry is 821, and so on. As with other types of literature, recommended books of poetry are listed in the booklists mentioned at the end of this chapter.

Many excellent anthologies and books by individual poets are available for children. Only a few are listed here:

Adoff, Arnold, compiler. *I Am the Darker Brother*. New York: Macmillan, 1968.

De Paola, Tomie. *Tomie dePaolo's Book of Poems*. New York: Putnam, 1988.

Janeczko. Paul B., compiler. *The Place My Words Are Looking For: What Poets Say About and Through Their Work*. New York: Bradbury, 1990.

Jones, Hettie, ed. *The Trees Stand Shining: Poetry of the North American Indians*. New York: Dial, 1971.

Livingston, Myra Cohn, compiler. *If the Owl Calls Again: A Collection of Owl Poems*. New York: Macmillan, 1990.

Merriam, Eve. *It Doesn't Always Have to Rhyme*. New York: Atheneum, 1964.

Silverstein, Shel. *Where the Sidewalk Ends: The Poems and Drawings of Shel Silverstein*. New York: Harper & Row Junior Books, 1974.

Untermeyer, Louis, compiler. *A Golden Treasury of Poetry*. Racine, Wis.: Western, 1975.

Books about Children's Literature

The preceding is only the briefest introduction to the wealth of literature for children. As with the literature itself, there is plenty to read *about* children's literature.

Textbooks in Children's Literature

For parents who have never studied children's literature, for teachers who wish to refresh memories of their children's literature course, and for the many people who assist children in school libraries without the benefit of professional training, textbooks written for college courses in children's literature provide excellent background reading.

Textbooks offer much more information than is given here on the various kinds of literature, including plot summaries of hundreds of books and critical commentary. Many of them suggest activities for introducing literature to children in the classroom. Creative parents can adapt the ideas to home use.

Look for texts in the school or public library, or in the education library of a college if possible. Parents may wish to select a favorite for purchase, since these are really reference books, containing too much to absorb in one reading. The following texts provide a good introduction:

Nilsen, Alleen P. and Kenneth L. Donelson. *Literature for Today's Young Adults*. 3rd ed. Glenview, Ill.: Scott Foresman, 1989.
> As the title implies, this book focuses on literature for young people "between the ages of 12 and 20."

Norton, Donna E. *Through the Eyes of a Child: An Introduction to Children's Literature*. 3rd ed. New York: Macmillan, 1990.
> Including criteria for evaluating and selecting books using the principles of child development, this text provides strategies for involving children in literature as well as comprehensive lists of books for children.

Sutherland, Zena, and May Hill Arbuthnot. *Children and Books*. 8th ed. New York: Harper-Collins, 1991.
> This title has long been a classic in children's literature.

Essays on Children's Literature

Purely for inspirational reading, books written about children's literature are a delight. They give insight into the work of writing for children, heighten appreciation of the literature, and leave no doubt that creating literature for children is much more than child's play. Again, just a few titles:

Cott, Jonathan. *Pipers at the Gates of Dawn: The Wisdom of Children's Literature*. New York: McGraw-Hill, 1985.

Egoff, Sheila, G. T. Stubbs, and L. F. Ashley. *Only Connect: Readings in Children's Literature*. Toronto: Oxford University Press, 1980.

Hunter, Mollie. *Talent Is Not Enough: Mollie Hunter on Writing for Children*. New York: HarperCollins Children's Books, 1990.

Paterson, Katherine. *Gates of Excellence*. New York: Lodestar, 1988 (c. 1981).

Paterson, Katherine. *The Spying Heart: More Thoughts on Reading and Writing Books for Children*. New York: Lodestar, 1989.

Reference Books about Children's Literature

Here, at last, is the promised list of reference books about children's literature:

Adventuring with Books: A booklist for Pre-K—Grade 6. 9th ed. Urbana, Ill., National Council of Teachers of English, 1989.
A list of both fiction and nonfiction, this book gives annotations without reviews. Although it is published by the NCTE, it covers more than English or the humanities, with sections on social studies, biographies, the sciences, the arts, and recreational activities.

Books for You: A Booklist for Senior High Students. New ed. Urbana, IL: National Council of Teachers of English, 1985.
A companion to *Adventuring with Books*, this reference lists fiction and nonfiction by subject. The books listed are not specifically selected for challenging reading.

Children's Literature Review. Gerard J. Senick, ed. Detroit: Gale Research Co., 1976 - .
Now in 26 volumes, this reference offers excerpts from reviews, criticism, and commentary on books from preschool through high school. Each volume covers from 15 to 40 authors from all eras. Articles are long and include comments by the authors on their writing.

Cianciolo, Patricia Jean. *Picture Books for Children*.
3rd ed. Chicago: American Library Association, 1990.

Covering nursery school through junior high, this annotated list includes fiction, nonfiction, and poetry. There is also an essay on illustrations in children's books.

Estell, Doug, Michele L. Satchwell and Patricia S. Wright. *Reading Lists for College-Bound Students.* New York: Prentice Hall, 1990.

Except for brief annotations for "The 100 Most-Often-Recommended Works," this book consists simply of suggested reading lists from 103 colleges. It makes very interesting reading for college-bound high school students who want an idea of what's ahead for them.

Gillespie, John T. and Corinne J. Naden, eds. *Best Books for Children: Preschool through Grade 6.* 4th ed. New York: Bowker, 1990.

This listing of books that have been recommended in at least two respected sources of reviews of children's literature covers fiction and nonfiction for elementary students. Biographies are especially easy to find here, with a separate section and an index.

Gillespie, John T. *Best Books for Junior High Readers.* New York: Bowker, 1991.

This addition to Gillespie's "best books" series includes books that may be of interest to advanced fifth and sixth graders, as well as students in grades seven through nine. Both subject and grade-level indexes are provided.

Gillespie, John T. *Best Books for Senior High Readers.* New York, Bowker, 1991.

This third volume rounds out Gillespie's series.

Kobrin, Beverly. *Eyeopeners! How to Choose and Use Children's Books about Real People, Places, and Things.* New York, Penguin, 1988.

Kobrin's book is enthusiastically and entirely devoted to nonfiction.

Kohn, Rita. *Mythology for Young People: A Reference Guide.* New York: Garland, 1986.

The table of contents for this reference book begins with African, (Native) American, Assyro-Babylonian,

Australian, British, Celtic—and so forth, to give an idea of the range of material included.

Malinowsky, H. Robert. *Best Science and Technology Reference Boks for Young People*. Phoenix: Oryx, 1991.

This guide to 669 science and technology books for third grade through high school is primarily for libraries, but is also useful for parents of children whose interests merit a home reference library. Annotations with suggested grade levels are provided.

Pflieger, Pat. *A Reference Guide to Modern Fantasy for Children*. Westport, CN: Greenwood, 1984.

The author includes a helpful discussion on categories of fantasy.

Wilson, George and Joyce Moss. *Books for Children to Read Alone: A Guide for Parents and Librarians*. New York: Bowker, 1988.

With a useful list of criteria for choosing books for children to read alone, this reference is helpful for finding books to recommend for a child's independent reading—although not all of the books listed are distinguished.

Your Reading: A Booklist for Junior High and Middle School Students. New ed. Urbana, IL: National Council of Teachers of English, 1988.

Unusual in that the annotations are written for and to students, this listing includes fiction and nonfiction, with separate sections for humor, poetry, and other categories.

References

Clark, Barbara. (1992). *Growing up gifted: Developing the potential of children at home and at school.* 4th. ed. New York: Macmillan.

Cook, Elizabeth. (1969). *The ordinary and the fabulous.* London: Cambridge UP.

Cooper, Ilene. (1992, November 8). Sweet are the uses of predictability. *New York Times Book Review,* p. 52.

Dailey, Sheila. (1991). Folktales—The rainbow bridge between cultures. *Media Spectrum, 18*(4), 3-5.

Ferraro, Susan. (1992, December 6). Girl talk. *New York Times Magazine,* pp. 62, 63, 86, 98.

Flack, Jerry. (1992). Biography (Part I). *Understanding Our Gifted, 4*(4), 17-18.

Groff, Patrick. (1980). Biography: A tool for bibliotherapy? *Top of the News,* 36, 269-273.

Livingston, Myra Cohn. (1990). *Climb into the bell tower: Essays on poetry.* New York: Harper and Row.

May, Jill P. (1991). *Lloyd Alexander.* Boston: Twayne.

May, Rollo. (1991). *The cry for myth.* New York: Norton.

Nodelman, Perry. (1992). *The pleasures of children's literature.* New York: Longman.

Rosenberg, Betty. (1986). *Genreflecting: A guide to reading interests in genre fiction.* 2d ed. Littleton, CO: Libraries Unlimited.

Sebasta, Sam Leason & Iverson, William J. (1975). *Literature for Thursday's child.* Chicago: Science Research Associates.

CHAPTER
EIGHT

Annotated Bibliography

The information in this bibliography is presented according to age group: Preschool, Early Elementary (Kindergarten — Grade Two), Upper Elementary (Grades Three — Five), Middle School (Grades Six — Eight), and Senior High (Grades Nine — Twelve).

Under each age grouping, books are arranged in alphabetical order by the authors' last names. Each listing is followed by an annotation which includes a brief plot summary, a few comments about the strengths and weaknesses and potential value of the book, and, in most cases, discussion aids. Discussion aids for preschoolers and for children in the early grades are often merely suggested themes which an adult will want to have in mind when talking casually about the book. For older children, specific questions are suggested to stimulate thinking.

These questions are offered only as a starting point. Each leader will learn to develop questions based on her own interpretation of the book and knowledge of the children who will discuss it.

The questions suggested are the core or interpretive questions to be asked after children have warmed to discussion with some introductory questions. In planning a discussion, the leader can choose core questions that look promising and then plan appropriate introductory questions.

Categories

Suggestions for discussion of each book are based on the *characteristics* of intellectually and artistically talented children and the *issues* they face—which were presented in the first two chapters. Because they are related to the emotional and intellectual development of highly able children, these characteristics and issues mark ways in which books and book discussion can be most useful. Following are brief explanations of how books were chosen for each category.

Achievement: plots that question whether or not a bright child will achieve.

Aloneness: books which can help bright youngsters explore feelings of isolation. These books offer opportunities to assure them that requirements for time alone vary from one person to another, and that time alone can be both productive and necessary.

Arrogance: characters who display arrogance to cope with feelings that they do not fit in.

Creativity: characters whose creative impulses set them apart.

Developing imagination: books that will stimulate thinking, observing, and questioning, keeping children in touch with the joy and power of using their imaginations.

Differentness: stories dealing with people who are different because of characteristics like ability, insight, and sensitivity.

Drive to understand: the most wide-ranging category, listing books that will challenge children intellectually and present them with ideas they may not otherwise encounter. The goal has been to suggest books that will both satisfy and whet the heightened curiosity these children experience. In some cases, no questions are suggested for discussion of these books, since topics for discussion should suit the child's interest.

Identity: books that can help highly able children work toward a strong self-concept, accepting talent as positive. Remembering that such children often feel different and somehow wrong, adults can discuss these books to help them be comfortable with their difference. Giftedness is not necessarily explicit or even represented in a character in the book.

Intensity: characters who are unusually focused on an interest, ability, or cause with a single-mindedness not shared by most children their age.

Introversion: people who prefer to spend most of their time alone, and who use that time creatively.

Moral concerns: personal or community issues that require difficult decisions.

Perfectionism: examples of what happens when a character puts too much emphasis on a perfect product.

Relationships with others: books that facilitate discussion of interdependence, empathy, and respect for others with different or lesser abilities. In addition, some of these books promote an understanding of friendships and how they are formed.

Sensitivity: characters who are intensely aware, introspective, easily hurt themselves or unusually alert to the hurts of others.

Using ability: books that raise questions about decision-making, the responsibility gifted people have for their own talents, and the rewards that can follow the best use of those talents.

Using the above headings, the Index of Categories is a guide to the books that are annotated in this chapter. Characteristics and issues change with age, and each category will be found only in the appropriate age groups. Most index entries are matched by questions in the bibliography, but in some cases the index entry acts as a reference to a related category. For example, questions suggested for Aloneness may be easily adapted to a discussion of Introversion. A book may be listed under both headings, but questions may be given under only one—since this bibliography is intended only to indicate possibilities, with parents and teachers developing their own approaches based on suggestions given here.

In the booklists that follow, nearly all of the books for preschoolers through second graders are picture books. Illustrators are named only when they are different from the author.

This bibliography includes many books published in the last five years, as well as a number of older titles—because children's books don't have to be new to be better. The life span of the adult as reader may be decades, so most adult books enjoy a period of popularity and then fade as interest turns elsewhere. But a new generation of young readers comes along about every four years, keeping much-loved older books in print as long as children find them meaningful. And older books often provide challenging reading, with long, complex sentences, wide-ranging vocabulary, and a glimpse of values and patterns of thought from an earlier time.

Finally, the decision whether a book is fit for eight-year-olds or ten-year-olds is always somewhat arbitrary. Many of these books can be enjoyed by children older and younger than the ages given. In some cases, picture books provide a quick introduction to a personal or moral issue, useful as discussion starters with middle school or senior high students. The Index for All Ages identifies books suggested for this purpose.

Preschool

The preschool years, the time of greatest intellectual growth in human development, cover a wide age span. Books for infants are decidedly different from books for four-year-olds. Accordingly, this preschool bibliography is divided into three sections: For the Very Young, for the first two years; Two and Three Years Old and Four Years Old.

For the Very Young

Books for infants and toddlers come in specialized sizes and shapes. Some are chunky, roughly three inches square and an inch thick. Most are "board books," with pages made of thick cardboard; others are made of fabric. The board books are so popular that a few classic titles are now being re-issued in this baby-proof format. Since most children are about two years old before they can reliably turn paper pages one at a time, the new materials are a boon to parents who want to read to their children in the first two years. Illustrations are often photographs, since their realism helps children relate the picture to three-dimensional objects in their surroundings.

Reading aloud to the very young child is best done by parents who are highly attuned to their child—sensitive to and accepting of her unique responses—rather than approaching reading with preconceived ideas of how she "should" react to a book. The child may be fascinated for the first three pages, and then lose interest. A book that is a favorite one week may be supplanted by another the next. One particular picture may hold the child's interest, while the rest of the book is ignored. All of this signals the child's readiness to learn according to her own schedule. Parents who enjoy *observing* the child's interest without trying to manipulate it will be most successful at reading to the very young.

Here is a small sample of books for these children. Parents are urged to browse in the preschool section of a good bookstore for a better idea of all that is available to them.

Bridwell, Norman. *Clifford's Bathtime.* New York: Cartwheel, 1991.

Clifford the puppy does not want a bath, but he enjoys it when he gets one anyway. He climbs onto the floating soap, and when he falls off, the rubber duck rescues him. The humor is not missed by one-year-olds, as parents can tell by the giggling when Clifford falls off the soap.

There are many other Clifford books, some for older children.

Brown, Margaret Wise. *Goodnight, Moon.* Illustrated by Clement Hurd. New York: Harper and Row, 1947.

This is a wonderful sleepytime book, with illustrations growing softer and dimmer as the little rabbit, tucked into bed, says goodnight to the beloved objects in his room. A favorite for generations, it is now available as a board book.

Eastman, P. D. *Are You My Mother?* New York: Random House, 1960.

A young bird who has lost track of its mother asks various unlikely creatures if they are his mother, until his mother predictably returns.

The mother of a curious and active one-year-old says that this is the first "plot" book her son sat through, and that it is a good bedtime book at this age.

Falwell, Cathryn. *Nicky Loves Daddy*. New York: Clarion, 1992.

Daddy and Nicky set off on a simple visit to the bakery, taking along Nicky's blue bunny, which appears on every page, inviting the question, "Where's the blue bunny?" I know of one toddler who gathers all his stuffed bunnies, including his blue one, when it is time for this story, and then settles down among them to listen.

Daddies appear rarely in books for this age, another reason to recommend this book.

Foord, Jo. *The Book of Babies: A First Picture Book of All the Things that Babies Do*. New York: Random House, 1991.

Clear, colorful photographs show babies in motion, while the text describes the action in verse. Babies are fascinated by pictures of babies, and the interest generated by these lively pictures will make this book a favorite to return to again and again.

Hill, Eric. *Spot in the Garden*. New York: Putnam, 1991.

This board book features the well-loved puppy, Spot, as he enjoys a morning in the garden. After greeting the birds, and helping his father work among the plants, Spot picks some flowers for his mom and returns to the house, where he waters the plants in his own window box.

Many other Little Spot Board Books are available.

Hill, Eric. *Where's Spot?* New York: Putnam, 1980.

Spot's mother looks for her puppy all over the house—in the grandfather clock, the piano, the closet. She finds an unexpected creature in each location, but no Spot, until the turtle under the rug suggests she try the basket.

Not a board book, this flap book has moveable tabs the child lifts to discover the hidden animals, which some children enjoy doing by the age of eight or nine months.

Hoban, Tana. *Black on White*. New York: Greenwillow, 1993.

This board book offers pictures of various shapes—a fork, a spoon, an elephant, glasses, keys—in stark black outlined against a white background. A companion book is *White on Black*. Both books are designed for infants, who are thought to see the high contrast of black and white before they discern colors.

Hoban, Tana. *Red Blue Yellow Shoe*. New York: Greenwillow, 1986.
These clear color photographs display objects in the baby's world—shoes, a block, a ball, a stuffed bear—in bright colors, introducing the child to names for the colors as well as labels for the objects.

Oxenbury, Helen. *Good Night, Good Morning*. New York: Dial, 1982.
The evening and morning activities of a typical family are shown in this wordless book. Included are baby's bath and story hour, watching Daddy shave in the morning—a stimulus for conversation about familiar routines in the child's home.

Ricklen, Neil. *Daddy and Me*. New York: Simon and Schuster, 1988.
This board book offers photographs of daddies playing with babies in various ways, with just one word per page to label the activities—a comforting book for the first year.

Ross, Katharine. *The Little Quiet Book*. Illustrated by Jean Hirashima. New York: Random House, 1989.
This small board book with pleasing illustrations tells us that "quiet" is a spider, the fireplace, and a chipmunk, among other examples. In the companion, *The Little Noisy Book*, "noisy" is a hammer, a brook, wet sneakers . . . Each book presents both familiar and new sources of quiet or sound.

Seuss, Dr. *The Foot Book*. New York: Random House, 1968.
A good beginning Seuss book, this one shows one foot and then two feet in various positions, with the rhyming text so typical of Dr. Seuss.

Shaw, Charles G. *It Looked Like Spilt Milk*. New York: Harper, 1947.
In white silhouettes on a blue background, we see shapes that look like a tree, a squirrel, or spilt milk. They turn out to be—a cloud.
A good stimulus for imaginative looking, this is now available as a board book.

Slier, Debby. *Hello Baby*. New York: Macmillan, 1988.
Babies here are talking, clapping, drinking—even crying, all familiar activities to children under one year old, although they may not yet have labels for them. The clear photographs

encourage babies to develop preferences for their favorite pages, which they quickly turn to whenever this book appears.

Stone, Erika. *Baby Talk*. New York: Grossett and Dunlap, 1992.
    Here are pictures of babies being tickled, cuddling with a dog, playing peek-a-boo—with a text of universal phrases we say repetitively to children. Flaps for the child to open add to the interest.

Szekeres, Cyndy. *Hugs*. New York: Golden Books, 1984.
    The illustrations of various animals receiving hugs draw giggles of delight from a child who has a treasured collection of stuffed animals and is accustomed to hugging them.

What Can You Find Around the House? New York: Dorling Kindersley, 1993.
    In board book format, photographs present items—toys, food, pets, tools—a child sees daily around the house, inviting him to find and name familiar objects. Others in the What Can You Find? series are *On the Farm*, *On the Beach*, and *In the Yard*.

Two and Three Years Old

Children of two and three, with their rapidly growing skills of comprehension, are attentive read-aloud companions. They are ready to follow a simple plot, and they enjoy humor in text and illustrations. After hearing a story outlined while viewing a wordless picture book, they can tell it themselves. They enjoy the rhythms of more complex language, and they linger over pictures as they strive for understanding. By now, reading aloud and trips to the library should be an established part of family life, and the child's home library should be growing.

Brown, Margaret Wise. *The Runaway Bunny*. Illustrated by Clement Hurd. New York: Harper and Row, 1942.
    In this conversation between a bunny and his mother, he suggests he might run away and she gently tells him what she would do to find him if he did. Clearly no action of this little bunny will separate him from his mother and her love for him.
    This classic is now available as a board book.

Charlip, Remy and Lilian Moore. *Hooray for Me!* Illustrated by Vera B. Williams. New York: Four Winds, 1975.

> Here is a joyful picture book celebrating the individual. The section on relationships with others can lead to conversation about how the child fits into his family and neighborhood. The section on identifying with things the child does ("I'm my dog's walker") is good for expanding from the book into the child's own life. Wise use of this book can enhance the child's self-concept. Personalize the book, talking about your own family, your own neighborhood, and your child's place in it.

Crews, Donald. *Carousel.* New York: Greenwillow, 1982.

> With pictures of a carousel and a calliope created as collages and then photographed by a moving camera, Crews gives the impression of the movement and sound of a carousel in this brief but memorable book.
>
> The book invites children to relate their memories of riding or seeing a carousel to the feelings triggered by pictures, a synthesis of visual imagery and physical experience.

Crews, Donald. *Freight Train.* New York: Greenwillow, 1978.

> The only words in this book identify the kinds of cars in a freight train and their colors, and then where the train goes. The impact is produced visually by means of the illustrations, and the effect is amazingly emotional for such an austere format. The illustrations give the sense of a train slowly gathering speed and then racing through tunnels, past cities, and over trestles until it is gone.
>
> Reading it aloud, an adult will hear speed and volume increasing in her voice, and will almost hear the whistle. The child will have an experience in visual and sensory imagery.

Emberley, Rebecca. *Jungle Sounds.* Boston: Little, Brown, 1989.

> Brightly colored paper cutouts illustrate this book, simply presenting a variety of jungle animals; the text is the spelled-out versions of the sounds made by each. Reading this book with a child is a matter of identifying the birds and animals by name and imitating their sounds. A glossary helps to differentiate similar jungle creatures such as gibbon and mandrel, Mexican tree frog and poison arrow frog.

The challenge presented by *Jungle Sounds* is to increase the child's awareness of animals beyond the familiar barnyard animals and pets. To follow up on this informative book, look through other books picturing other animals (or visit the zoo), and learn to imitate their sounds, too.

Hoff, Syd. *Who Will Be My Friends?* New York: Harper & Row, 1960.

Looking for friends in his new neighborhood, Freddy finds that the adults are friendly but busy, and the children ignore him. Undiscouraged, Freddy plays alone, throwing and catching a ball in full view of the other children. When they notice how well he handles it, they ask him to join them.

The obvious messages in this book are that it is easier to be accepted if we have something to offer to others, and that it is sometimes necessary to take the initiative in order to find friends. There are more subtle messages, however: Freddy does not force himself into the children's game; rather he quietly lets them see what his skills are. He seems to understand their reluctance to accept him immediately without being hurt by it.

For a young gifted child who feels rebuffed, this book can demonstrate that if we offer ourselves and our skills to others without being presumptuous, it is easier for them to accept us. Conversation about this will require a light approach, just a suggestion by the adult and then listening for response from the child, which will guide the duration and direction of any further dialogue.

Hutchins, Pat. *Rosie's Walk.* New York: Macmillan, 1968.

"Rosie the hen went for a walk . . . and got back in time for dinner." The text is deliberately commonplace; the real story is told in the illustrations. The child watches in suspense as the fox nearly catches Rosie over and over again, landing in positions of ever greater indignity as the story goes on. The fact that Rosie is blissfully unaware of the fox gives the child the opportunity to be in on a secret as she tells the full story to an adult.

Although this is not a wordless book, it offers the advantages of one by encouraging children to "read" the pictures and tell the story in their own words, and to laugh at the understated humor of it all.

Johnson, Jane. *A Book of Nursery Riddles*. Boston: Houghton Mifflin, 1985.

Jane Johnson has collected a group of traditional English rhyming riddles and has illustrated them with luminous paintings that provide clues. The illustrations are full of detail, beautifully depicting daily life over several centuries of English history. The challenge of the riddles, along with the aesthetic appeal of the illustrations, creates a book especially suitable for curious, sensitive readers.

Krauss, Ruth. *The Carrot Seed*. Illustrated by Crockett Johnson. New York: Harper and Row, 1945.

A little boy plants a carrot seed, and despite everyone's warnings that the seed won't grow, he weeds and waters faithfully. The reward for his labors is one very large carrot.

McMillan, Bruce. *Fire Engine Shapes*. New York: Lothrop, Lee and Shepard, 1988.

This wordless book of photography offers closeup color pictures of squares, triangles, rectangles, diamonds, hexagons, ovals and circles—all as they appear on the door, wheel, fender, cab, ladder and elsewhere on an Emergency One fire engine at Engine 5 Station in South Portland, Maine.

By implication, the child is invited to find shapes, to identify where they are on a fire engine, to visit a fire station to look for the shapes there, and to see shapes everywhere. A final page labels and defines each of the seven universal shapes.

Oxenbury, Helen. *Tom and Pippo Make a Friend*. New York: Aladdin, 1989.

This book in Oxenbury's Pippo series tells of the day Tom finds a pail in the sand box in the park. He is happily playing with it when a little girl returns to claim it. Her mother suggests they share their toys, but that would mean sharing Pippo—Tom hugs his stuffed monkey and walks away, thinking, "Pippo is mine." In the end, since both Tom and Pippo want to play with the bucket, they return; and the girl proves to be a good playmate for both of them. Today, Tom tells us, he and his mother are going to the park again. He hopes the little girl and her bucket are there.

Appealing facial expressions tell the story in their own way, especially in the picture of Tom thinking about returning to the sandbox and sharing Pippo. By being willing to trust the little girl with Pippo, Tom gains a friend.

Piper, Watty. *The Little Engine that Could.* Illustrated by George and Doris Hauman. New York: Platt and Munk, 1930.

On her way over a mountain with good things for girls and boys on the other side, a little engine stops, unable to go farther. Several large, proud engines refuse to help, but finally the Little Blue Engine says she is willing to try, although she has never been over the mountain. With the classic line, "I think I can, I think I can, I think I can...I thought I could. I thought I could. I thought I could," she succeeds.

Some children carry with them into adulthood the lesson about perseverance so gently taught in this book.

Scarry, Richard. *Richard Scarry's Best First Book Ever.* New York: Random, 1979.

Each page of Scarry's book is filled with pictures for discussion with labels to promote vocabulary building. A very slight story line carries the Cat family through a day that allows Scarry to touch on colors, counting, letters, and shapes as well as everyday events such as housework, school, shopping, trips to the doctor's office and a farm, and more. The book presents a wide range of information for discussion and plenty of detail for sharp eyes to search out, with an adult asking questions to guide the search. Children can then spend time alone with the book, looking for more.

Spier, Peter. *Gobble, Growl, Grunt: A Book of Animal Sounds.* China: 1988.

The pages of this book abound with farm animals, zoo animals, aquatic animals and birds—along with their sounds, several per creature in some cases. It promises some hilarious sessions between parent and child as they identify animals and reconstruct sounds.

Tresselt, Alvin. *Hide and Seek Fog.* Illustrated by Roger Duvoisin. New York: Lathrop, Lee and Shepard, 1965.

The fog approaches from the ocean and stays for three days, keeping the lobstermen and sailors off the water, and children inside by the driftwood fire.

The text and the illustrations by Roger Duvoisin blend beautifully to evoke the calmed, quiet, introspective mood induced by a heavy fog. If the book is read slowly, thoughtfully, liltingly, both child and adult will pick up the mood of cozy settledness.

Conversation about this book can focus on the warm inside feel of a rainy or foggy day, the quiet pleasure of working alone on a favorite project, the contentment of playing alone but knowing there are people in the next room or coming home soon. The child who can appreciate such experiences is on the way to becoming a self-reliant person, capable of being at peace with himself.

Four Years Old

The eager, expansive four-year-old of high ability probably already experiences some sense of being different from playmates. Books that help him understand that he is an individual with differences to be enjoyed and celebrated, help him gain skills in getting along with other children, encourage his lively imagination and add to his rapidly growing knowledge base—such books can build his confidence and pleasure as he learns to know himself. Because he is ready to conceptualize some self-understanding and social skills, the following annotations include pointers—and in some cases, suggested questions—for casual conversations about issues that may concern the bright four-year-old.

Alexander, Martha. *Bobo's Dream*. New York: Dial, 1970.

A wordless book in which Bobo the dachshund loses a bone to a larger dog. After the bone is retrieved by his master, a grateful Bobo dreams that he grows big enough to retrieve his master's football from a larger boy. When Bobo wakes up, the big dog returns. This time, bolstered by the new self-concept generated by his dream, Bobo stands up for his rights and the big dog shrinks away.

The child, not the adult, should tell the story from the pictures. This is a good book for a timid child (it is acceptable to stand up for one's rights) and for an aggressive one (a quiet assurance based on being in the right is enough).

219

Identity. You might talk about how and why Bobo is different the second time the big dog comes, and why he doesn't have to fight to keep his bone. Has the child ever had an experience like this?

Anno, Mitsumasa. *Anno's Alphabet: An Adventure in Imagination.* New York: Crowell, 1974.

A wordless alphabet book that invites looking and looking again, like all of Anno's books. Each left-hand page has a letter of the alphabet, painted as if cut out of wood, often with a twist that catches the mind and requires analysis. The right-hand pages show pictures of objects that can be named, discussed, and observed. The borders offer insects, birds, and plants whose names also begin with the letter being considered.

Developing imagination; Drive to understand. The back of the book offers a guide identifying some of the objects in the borders, which will challenge adult readers to find them. Invite the child to join you in the search.

Anno, Mitsumasa. *Anno's Counting Book.* New York: Crowell, 1977.

This wordless book begins with a snowy landscape for zero. The "one" page shows one adult, one child, one tree, one building, then two of each, progressing to 12. In the meantime the seasons change, the clock tower shows the time for each number, a tower of blocks increases by tens, and the trees, buildings, and people offer enough variety for many discussions with much observing, identifying, and counting.

Drive to understand. There is always something more to see in Anno's illustrations, and the child will enjoy looking with an adult and then alone.

Blegvad, Lenore. *Rainy Day Kate.* Illustrated by Erik Blegvad. New York: McElderry, 1987.

Plans for Kate to come to play are cancelled when it rains. Kate's unnamed friend tells us, "I am all alone. Alone with *me*"—but then he develops a new plan, depending on his imagination for a day of fun with "Kate" and finding that being alone with himself is not so bad after all.

This book about a child learning to use his own resources can be used to encourage others to do the same—or to reassure children who enjoy being alone that it is a valuable skill.

Aloneness. What are *your* favorite things to do when you are alone?

Base, Graeme. *My Grandma Lived in Gooligulch*. Davis, Calif.: The Australian Book Source, 1988.

When Grandma lived in Gooligulch she made a practice of taming wild animals—Australian animals with strong rhythmical names that carry Base's rollicking verse along. A wombat pulled Grandma's gig (cart) while a bandicoot rode beside her. The night the emus came to dine, a great fuss ensued when a frill-necked lizard appeared. Finally Grandma sails off to sea (by then it seemes her only option), but the author suggests that Grandma is probably back in Gooligulch by now.

He depicts 21 animals and Grandma, on the fly leaf, with a chart to help the child identify each. Interspersed among text pages are gorgeous colored double spreads, to give us a better view of the animals. Enticing as the pictures are, the text is equally memorable and challenging, full of names of Australian birds, animals, and plants, and laced with an occasional Australian term (gig, two-up, petrol) for the child to add to his vocabulary.

Developing imagination. A child who hears Grandma's story read by one who has a sense for the rhythm will soon be reciting sections on her own. This book could easily lead to others, fiction and nonfiction, on Australia.

Bryan, Ashley. *Turtle Knows Your Name*. New York: Atheneum, 1989.

The little boy has a very long name, Upsilimana Tumpalerado. Eventually he can remember all of it, and on that day his delighted Granny takes him to the beach, where they dance his name dance. As always when there is a name dance, Turtle swims to the surface to hear the name, and then dives to the bottom to spell it out in shells on the ocean floor. But though Upsilimana Tumpalerado knows his name, it is too long for his friends, and they still call him Long Name. One day Granny challenges Upsilimana Tumpalerado to tell her *her* name, and he goes searching to find one who knows it—Turtle, of course.

Both the colorful illustrations and the story are full of joy in this retelling of a West Indian tale. Upsilimana Tumpalerado must have a firm sense of his place in the world, with his name written on the bottom of the sea, a Granny who patiently teaches him to

221

remember it, and villagers who respond to his questions by circling around him, dancing and singing.

Identity. Remind the child of the various traditions his family and society have developed to impart the same sense of place and foundation.

Burningham, John. *Hey! Get Off Our Train*. New York: Crown, 1989.

The boy and his stuffed dog go to sleep after a day of playing with the train. In a dream sequence they go for a train ride through the night, stopping for such diversions as playing ghosts in the fog and going for a swim. Each time they return to the train, a new animal has climbed aboard. The boy challenges each with "Hey! Get off our train," but each pleads for sanctuary—the elephants are being killed for their tusks, the seals find less food in polluted waters. Each ends the plea with "and soon there will be none of us left"—so of course all are allowed to join the group on the train. When the boy's mother wakes him for school, she tells him the house is full of animals—all have come home with him.

Drive to understand; Moral concerns. Burningham's book is included in this list because environmental issues are among the moral concerns that gifted youngsters may worry about more deeply and earlier than most children. The train metaphor may help children to conceptualize the problem. No solutions are offered here, but discussion about what the child and his family can do to help the environment is a logical follow-up, and will reassure the child that there is something he can do.

Demi. *The Empty Pot*. New York: Holt, 1990.

Ping lives in China, and even in a land where everyone loves flowers, he is known for his skill in growing things. One day, to choose a successor, the Emperor gives every child a seed. In a year the children are to return with the plants from their seeds, and the new Emperor will be chosen. Ping plants his seed hopefully and cares for it tenderly, watering and transplanting and providing the best soil, but he fails—nothing grows. He must return to the Emperor with an empty pot. The Emperor is delighted with Ping's honesty in a surprise ending.

Demi's delicate illustrations evoke old China and suit the folkloric quality of the story—a memorable introduction to another time and place for a discerning child.

222

Identity; *Moral concerns*; *Perfectionism*. In talking about the book, mention that Ping is not only honest but also courageous, willing to admit failure. In this he is encouraged by his father, who assures him that he has done his best. Our best is enough, if honestly done, even though we seem to fail.

Drescher, Henrik. *Looking for Santa Claus*. New York: Lothrop, Lee and Shepard, 1984.

Maggie lives with her aunts, who force her to work for them and who hate Christmas. On Christmas Eve they send her out to dig Blossom, the cow, out of the snow. Blossom invites Maggie to go looking for Santa Claus, and together they fly off around the world, picking up a cossack in Russia, a shepherd in Switzerland, and a sheik in Egypt. When they return home the aunts welcome the guests and cook a Christmas dinner.

Drive to understand. This is an unconventional Christmas story with a European flavor—Drescher was born in Denmark. The book demonstrates the international character of Christmas without sentimentality.

Gerrard, Roy. *Sir Cedric*. New York: Farrar, Straus and Giroux, 1984.

Finding life at the castle a little boring, Sir Cedric heads off in search of adventure. In the middle of the forest he meets Black Ned, who challenges Cedric to a duel. Cedric wins, rescuing the maid Matilda. At the feast announcing their wedding, Black Ned appears with an army. Cedric meets the challenge, and his army wins the battle in time for tea.

Developing imagination. All this is told in verse, accompanied by illustrations at once rich and charming. Both text and illustrations incorporate a subtle, droll humor which will be appreciated by sophisticated young readers.

Handforth, Martin. *Where's Waldo?* Boston: Little, Brown, 1987.

Waldo hikes to a variety of interesting places—a museum, a fair, the seashore, a railway station—each place illustrated in a double spread, teeming with people and miniature stories. The reader is invited to find Waldo at each location, and Waldo's postcards invite us to find other people and events on each page, too. At the end, however triumphant we may feel about our success in finding Waldo, we face one last challenge: Waldo says that on his travels he has lost his camping gear, one item at a time. Can we find it?

Developing imagination. Like books illustrated by Peter Spier, Richard Scarry, and Mitsumasa Anno, this one is filled with detail, encouraging careful observation and story telling. Adult and child will find new interest with each viewing.

Heine, Helme. *Friends*. New York: McElderry, 1982.

First published in Germany, this picture book shows three friends—a mouse, a rooster, and a pig—as they spend a day together, defining friendship as they share their adventures. "Good friends always stick together," "Good friends always decide things together,"—even, at the end of the day, "Sometimes good friends can't be together."

There is humor in the illustrations, and a touch of European landscape.

Relationships with others. Each of the friends' definitions of friendship can be explored, with examples from the child's experience as a test of validity.

Hoban, Russell. *The Sorely Trying Day*. Illustrated by Lillian Hoban. New York: Harper and Row, 1964.

Sometime in the 1890s, Father comes home after a sorely trying day to find his family in an uproar. Mother has had a trying day too, what with the four children, who are "striking one another and speaking unpleasantly in loud, harsh voices," and the dog, who has chased the cat to the top of the grandfather clock. In sentences polite and civil, parents and children begin to explain the sequence of events, tracing the trouble to the cat. Dog, cat, and mouse join in the untangling of the story, and then the narrative goes back up the chain to children and parents, with new and more plausible details added with each confession and apology.

The delightful humor is in the impossibly high level of civility and the completely recognizable sequence of events. The level of vocabulary will appeal especially to bright children.

Relationships with others. The lesson that tension can be relieved by a simple apology, each one taking his/her share of the blame, is worth elaboration. Mostly, this is a book for enjoyment, for laughing at ourselves, and for adding "I've had a sorely trying day" to the family phrase book.

Hutchins, Pat. *Titch*. New York: Macmillan, 1971.

Titch has an older sister and a bigger brother, and they have larger bicycles, noisier musical instruments, and higher-flying kites than Titch does. But more exciting than Pete's large spade and Mary's fat flowerpot is Titch's tiny seed, which "grew and grew and grew."

The lesson is clear: potential counts more than size, and young children who are constantly trying to keep up will be reminded of their own potential by this simple story.

Identity. What else grows besides seeds into plants? What will *you* be like when you get bigger?

Relationships with Others. How can big children help little children? Is there anyone smaller than you whom you can help by being kind?

Lionni, Leo. *Frederick*. New York: Random House, 1967.

Frederick is a field mouse who sits alone while the other mice store food for the winter. When they chide him for not working, Frederick responds that he *does* work: while they gather food, he is gathering sun rays, colors, and words. The others are reproachful, but in the winter when they are cold and hungry, Frederick is able to warm and nourish them with his words evoking the sun and the colorful flowers. Frederick is a poet, and the mice know that he offers more than food.

The torn-paper illustrations and the simple wisdom in the story make this book a favorite. Some children will empathize with Frederick's day-dreaming and his avoidance of tasks, but they may learn to value "alone time," which may very well be a new concept for them, needing reinforcement from an adult. Frederick's quiet acceptance of himself as he is, even though it sets him apart from the others, is a quality some gifted children have even at this age. For them, it is good to see the other mice learn to value Frederick's special contributions to the group.

Differentness; *Developing imagination*; *Using abilities*. What makes it all right for Frederick not to work with the others? Can the child tell you when she feels like Frederick, thereby identifying her own need for time to reflect?

Lionni, Leo. *Pezzettino*. New York: Pantheon, 1975.

Pezzettino ("little piece" in Italian) is so small that he is sure that he must be part of somebody else. In his search for the larger creature of which he must be a part, Pezzettino discovers that he too is made up of smaller pieces. He is not part of anyone else; he is complete in himself.

It is easy for a child to identify with Pezzettino, small and unsure of his place in the world. In addition, the child's imagination will be stimulated by Lionni's colorful, abstract illustrations.

Identity. Talk about what Pezzettino learns: that regardless of his size he is a whole person. List other examples (pets, plants). Why is it hard to be small for Pezzettino? For anyone? Discuss what Pezzettino means when he says "I am myself!" and why it makes him so happy.

Lobel, Arnold. *The Turnaround Wind*. New York: Harper and Row, 1988.

A group of people going for a walk are caught in a turnaround wind, which "seemed to turn the whole world around and around and upside down." From then on, the book must be read both upside down and right side up, and each picture shows two people, thrown together in the wind—one upside down and the other right side up, blended together in one drawing.

Developing imagination.Children will enjoy the challenge of seeing each picture in two ways. Older children may wish to try drawing two pictures in one.

McCloskey, Robert. *Time of Wonder*. New York: Viking, 1957.

McCloskey's book evokes in words and pictures a child's experience of late summer in Maine. Weather is a factor to be reckoned with, and the children in the story pick up the adults' apprehension about the approaching hurricane, but also observe their parents' knowledgeable preparation for it and their sturdy survival of the storm. Coziness and family security are the themes. Awareness and enjoyment of nature pervade the book, along with respect for its power and wonder at its mysteries. Where *do* hummingbirds go in a hurricane?

Although it is full of action, the book is also quiet and thoughtful, acknowledging the moods of children, whether at play in the sunshine, singing to cover fear in a storm, or experiencing a bittersweet farewell as they leave for another school year.

Developing imagination. What are special places for you, like the coast of Maine for the children in the book? How does it feel to know you are standing where other children stood hundreds of years ago? Or to wonder over the age of a fossil? What other places or events or objects have caused you to wonder? What do you find to wonder about on a simple walk near your house?

MacDonald, Golden. *The Little Island.* Illustrated by Leonard Weisgard. Garden City, N.Y.: Doubleday, 1946.

Life on the little island in the ocean includes spiders and chuckleberries, lobsters and seals, kingfishers and gulls—and a kitten who comes to the island one day and learns the secret of how an island is really a part of the land.

The lyrical prose and award-winning illustrations make this book a delightful way for children to learn what an island is.

Drive to understand. The kitten reflects the child's sense of wonder, imagining what she cannot see: the island connected to all the land underneath the sea.

Milne, A. A. *The World of Pooh: The Complete Winnie-the-Pooh and The House at Pooh Corner.* Illustrated by E. H. Shepard. New York: Dutton, 1957.

The World of Pooh is a fine gift for the fourth birthday of a child who already has plenty of experience with books—but do not begin at the beginning when you read it to a child of this age. The dialogues in the introductory material and Chapter One do not label the speakers, causing difficulty for young listeners trying to follow without benefit of punctuation. Rather, plunge right into one of the stories—each chapter stands on its own. Your child will learn them all and develop favorites, and the characters will become part of her imaginary menagerie.

Identity; Relationships with others. This is a wonderful bedtime reader, full of wisdom, humor, and acceptance of self and others.

Scarry, Richard. *Richard Scarry's Best Counting Book Ever.* New York: Random, 1975.

Because Willy Bunny has nothing to do, Father suggests that he count whatever he sees during the day and report to Father in the evening. Willy and his friend Sally count up to ten watermelons and then review before going on to the teens. After they count 19 pigs having a picnic, the counting goes on by tens to 100 fireflies that evening. Each page shows the correct numbers of items for child or adult to count, and the items themselves beg to be examined for identification, small visual stories, and humor.

Discussion of this book provides familiarity with the sounds of number words and the order of counting, as well as the opportunity to see objects in manageable groupings. Ninety carrots are shown five on each plate, for example, and there are enough plates in the double-page picture to see exactly how many carrots it takes to make 90.

Drive to understand. Preschoolers will not necessarily count to 100 independently because of this book, but they will be introduced to mind-stretching numbers concepts—which is better.

Sewall, Marcia. *The World Turned Upside Down: An Old Penny Rhyme.* Boston: Atlantic Monthly Press, 1986.

> "To see a good boy read his book is no news;
> But to see a goose roasting a cook is strange indeed!"

Following this pattern, Sewall illustrates a series of ridiculous and impossible situations—just right for a preschooler who can see, since she knows how silly these pictures are, how much she already knows about the world.

Developing imagination. Since this old rhyme is placed in a rural setting, many children will learn more about reality as they discern the ridiculous on each page. For a child of the right age and awareness, this book can be delightfully challenging and humorous.

Sharmat, Marjorie Weinman. *I'm Terrific.* Illustrated by Kay Charao. New York: Holiday House, 1977.

Jason Everett Bear tells himself and others how terrific he is, but this gains him no friends. So he changes his approach: instead of doing everything right, he does everything wrong, annoying others in the process. Finally he decides he is neither terrific nor terrible; he can be just Jason Everett Bear. His friends welcome Jason Everett Bear just as he is.

Arrogance; *Identity.* This is one of those books that provide catch-words that parent and child can use to identify different moods and behaviors long after the book is read. Develop the idea of being "terrific" (showing off) or "terrible," and how anyone can change from one to the other depending on what kind of day she is having. Be sure to talk about being just Jason Everett

Bear—just yourself—and help the child identify when she is doing that so she can begin to recognize how it feels.

Relationships with Others. Can your child recognize when other children are being "terrific" (showing off), or "terrible" (behaving badly because they feel bad about themselves), or just being themselves? If he can begin to watch for this, it will be a big step toward understanding and empathizing with others.

Sharmat, Marjorie Weinman. *The 329th Friend.* Illustrated by Cyndy Szekeres. New York: Scholastic, 1979.

Bored with himself, Emery Raccoon invites 328 friends to a picnic lunch, but they are all so busy talking to each other that no one talks to him. So Emery takes his lunch inside and converses with himself as he eats, finding that he is not so boring after all. When he goes back outside, his guests are looking for him, and the party ends successfully.

Emery has learned that he is a good friend for himself, and that makes it easier for him to feel that he is liked by the others—a double boost for his self-concept.

Aloneness. Reinforce Emery's discovery that he is not boring. How is Emery a good friend for himself? When are you a good friend for yourself?

Identity. Talk about what Emery has learned about himself, and about the positive traits the child has, naming reasons other people like her and how she knows they do.

Relationships with Others. In talking about Emery's liking himself and being liked by others, help the child to see the link between the two. It might also be possible to discuss the link between being bored and being boring. When you are unhappy with yourself, how do you treat other people? Why is it easier to be a friend when you are pleased with yourself?

Steptoe, John. *Stevie.* New York: Harper & Row, 1969.

Robert's mother babysits a little boy, Stevie, whose mother works. While Robert is in school, Stevie plays with his toys. After school, Stevie trails along after Robert like a little brother and disrupts his play with his friends. Robert resents Stevie, but when Stevie's family suddenly moves away, Robert remembers the good times he had with Stevie.

Relationships with others. Discussion should bring out the fact that we all have strong and weak points, and it's best to look for the good in others—while we can still be friends with them.

Van Leeuwen, Jean. *Amanda Pig On Her Own.* Illustrated by Ann Schweninger. New York: Dial, 1991.

Four stories about Amanda, whose older brother Oliver has just begun school. Amanda misses him but then learns that she is never *all* alone, and learns to be happy entertaining herself. She also learns how to feel better when sick in bed, the disadvantages of a messy room, and what a Bad, Sad, Mad Day is like. Young readers will recognize the feeling of frustration when nothing goes right.

Aloneness. Beginning readers can read this on their own, and it is a good book to remember when a child feels alone, or a room is a mess, or a day seems to go all wrong.

Identity. While Amanda learns to entertain herself and what it is like to have a bad day, she is also learning that she can handle daily difficulties—she is more capable than she thought. So is every child, but often it is not pointed out to them in so many words. Use this book to clarify your child's awareness of her own growth, connecting recent specific examples from events at home or preschool to Amanda's experiences.

Wittman, Sally. *A Special Trade.* Illustrated by Karen Gundersheimer. New York: Harper and Row, 1978.

When Nellie was very little, Old Bartholomew took her for walks in her stroller, then helped her learn to walk and finally to rollerskate. Now Nellie is in school, and Bartholomew, who is also older, is in a wheelchair. Nellie takes him for walks, treating him just as kindly as he treated her. They are good friends, having made a special kind of trade.

Relationships with others. How does Nellie know just how to take Old Bartholomew for a walk? What trades can you—and do you—make with friends, old or young?

Early Elementary

Kindergarten — Grade Two

Alderson, Sue Ann and Ann Blades. *Ida and the Wool Smugglers*. New York: McElderry, 1987.

Ida and her family are new settlers on an island off the west coast of Canada, raising sheep and farming. But there is a problem—smugglers from the mainland occasionally steal the farmers' sheep. One day, Ida's mother asks her to take bread to their nearest neighbors, the Springmans, who have a new baby. Although brother John thinks Ida is too young, she is the only one free to go, and she sets off through the meadow so she can see her pet ewe and the twin lambs on her way. When she hears the whistles of smugglers signalling to each other, Ida has to find a way to save the ewe and her twins.

Identity. Using this simple story of bravery and responsibility, with lovely illustrations evocative of the past, parents can talk about how children had a role to play in helping families and neighbors, and can ask a variety of questions. What do children do now to help? What do you do in your family to make things go more easily for everyone? What are you old enough to do that makes you proud—as proud as Ida was to hold the Springmans' new baby?

Aliki. *Feelings*. New York: Greenwillow, 1984.

This is not a story, but a book showing on each page a different familiar childhood event—a birthday party, a space capsule created of wood blocks and then destroyed, getting lost in a store, being bored—with the characters commenting on their positive and negative feelings.

Aloneness. Identify lonely or alone situations in the book (such as boredom). What do you do when you feel like that? What else could you do?

Identity. A calm, objective discussion of both good and bad feelings based on the book can help a child recognize and accept her own feelings later, when emotions may run so strong that rational discussion is not possible: How would you feel if this happened? Why? What would you do? Are there other times when you feel the same way? How do you act when you feel that way? Is it all right to feel that way? Do other people ever feel the same way you do?

Relationships with others. This book can be used to help children focus on how other people feel as well as on how they themselves feel. How can you tell what these people are feeling? How can you tell when your friends feel angry, lonely, happy? What do you do then?

Anno, Mitsumasa. *Anno's Journey.* Illustrated by the author. New York: Putnam, 1981 [c1977].

This wordless book shows a man journeying on horseback through a medieval European landscape. The reader who looks carefully can identify a fair, a duel, a foot race, a ping-pong game, visual jokes—the book is full of details to observe and discuss.

Drive to understand. A child can pore over this book for hours, still finding something new. An adult can enrich the experience by questioning: What are they doing? Tell me a story about this. What do you think this is?

Anno, Mitsumasa. *Topsy-Turvies.* Illustrated by the author. New York: Walker-Weatherhill, 1970.

This is another of Anno's visually rich, wordless books, full of double-page spreads of optical illusions, mathematical impossibilities, and incongruities to tease and expand the imagination. Children will need time to look—silently.

Drive to understand. Adult input should be designed to reinforce the wonder and the open-minded approach required, and to foster an appreciation of the variety of possibilities Anno presents.

Baker, Jeannie. *Where the Forest Meets the Sea.* New York: Greenwillow, 1987.

A boy and his father spend a day on the beach between an Australian rain forest and the Great Barrier Reef. The boy ventures into the rain forest, which his father says has been there one hundred million years. He wonders about the age of the forest and the creatures who have lived there, and the collage illustrations reveal outlines of animals and people from the past, superimposed on the present-day forest. Back on the beach, the boy wonders about the future—will the forest remain? Will it be there when he returns? Again the illustrations display shadow outlines, this time of tourists, cars, and hotels obliterating the view of sea and sky.

The illustrations provide a photographically realistic view of a rain forest, while including the element of imagination. The ecological concern, of course, is very real, as a final note confirms.

Developing imagination; Drive to understand; Moral concerns. Adults working with gifted children can use the book for information (the rain forest), to stimulate imaginative thinking (what animals and people lived right *here* in the past? will live here in the future?) and to focus on environmental concerns.

Bang, Molly. *Dawn.* New York: Morrow, 1983.

Dawn's father tells her the story of how, shortly after he found and rescued a wounded Canadian goose, a young woman magically appeared and began to weave light, strong sails for the ships he built. He married her and they had a child, Dawn; the sails the woman made for their family boat were especially fine. A wealthy client demanded sails like them; she protested that it would take too much out of her to make more such sails, but when her husband insisted, she relented. Just as the sails were nearly finished, he impatiently opened the door of the room where she worked—and saw the Canadian goose, pulling out its breast feathers and weaving them into sailcloth. At his appearance a flock of geese flew into the room and carried her off. At the end of her father's story, promising to find her mother and bring her back in the spring, Dawn she sets off in the small boat her father had made for the three of them.

Developing imagination; Drive to understand. Ask the child to imagine a sequel to Dawn's story. Or point out that *Dawn* is based on the Japanese tale of the Crane Wife, and suggest comparing the two stories.

Bang, Molly Garrett. *Tye May and the Magic Brush.* (Adapted from the Chinese.) New York: Greenwillow, 1981.

Tye May is a poor orphan who longs to paint. One night in a dream she receives a magic brush from a woman who tells her to use it carefully. With her brush Tye May paints birds and animals that come to life. Soon she paints for the poor: a loom for a weaver, an ox cart for a farmer. A greedy landlord, and then the Emperor, want Tye May to paint for them. She pretends to cooperate with the Emperor, but his greed causes disaster for him and his court. They say Tye May still goes from village to village, painting for the poor.

Using ability. This is a read-alone book about the wise use of gifts. Why does the brush work well for Tye May and cause such trouble for the Emperor? What *is* the wise use of gifts—what does the woman mean when she says, "Use it carefully"?

Baum, Arline and Joseph. *Opt: An Illusionary Tale.* New York: Viking Kestrel, 1987.

This collection of optical illusions is united in a story of a dragon visiting the castle of Opt for a birthday party. On each page is at least one optical illusion; explanations are given at the end, followed by suggestions for creating original optical illusions.

*Developing imagination.*This is a book to arouse curiosity and stimulate careful observation, as well as awareness of optical illusions all around us and how they happen.

Brown, Ruth. *If At First You Do Not See.* New York: Holt, Rinehart, and Winston, 1982.

The caterpillar goes off in search of food, but each time he thinks he has found a meal, he discovers that he has stumbled onto one creature or another who does not want to be eaten. At last a scarecrow puts the caterpillar in his pocket where he can rest. When he wakes, the caterpillar has become a butterfly.

The illustrations carry the story. On each page the text continues around the margins, so the book must be turned; when it is upside down (if the reader looks carefully), the creature who is reluctant to become dinner appears. Imbedded in the right-side-up picture of the grass or flowers that looked so good to the hungry caterpillar is an upside-down picture of a man or a witch, but we must work a bit to find it.

Developing imagination. In Brown's book, the child's imagination is called into play to make sense of both story and pictures.

Bulla, Clyde Robert. *Daniel's Duck.* Illustrated by Joan Sandlin. New York: Harper and Row, 1979.

Growing up in a Tennessee mountain cabin, Daniel wants to learn to carve like his brother Jeff, who carves so well that his proud parents say someday he may carve as well as Henry Pettigrew, a man widely known as the best wood-carver in

Tennessee. Daniel's father gives him wood and a knife, and Daniel thinks for some time before he finally carves a duck looking backward. At the spring fair, where the family hopes to sell the handwork they have made all winter, people stand in silence before Henry Pettigrew's carved deer, but they laugh when they see Daniel's duck. Mortified, Daniel seizes the duck and runs to throw it in the river. He is stopped by an old man who quietly explains that there are different kinds of laughter. People laughed at Daniel's duck because it made them happy. The duck is good, says the man—Henry Pettigrew.

Differentness. Daniel's differentness is represented by his interest in carving animals—merely for the sake of their beauty—while his practical brother carves useful dishes. It is Daniel's divergence that leads him to carve the duck looking backward. It would be worthwhile also to mention Henry Pettigrew's understanding. Daniel's work is better understood by older people than by children, indicating that he will "fit in" better when he and his peers are adults.

Sensitivity. Daniel displays two kinds of sensitivity, one through his period of thoughtfulness before beginning to carve, the other through his assumption that the laughter was derisive. The first can be positive and productive; the second type of sensitivity can be damaging if not understood and counteracted.

Burningham, John. *Time to Get Out of the Bath, Shirley.* Illustrated by the author. New York, Crowell, 1978.

While Shirley's mother carries on a typical maternal nagging monologue about neatness and cleanliness on the left-hand page, Shirley, who is taking a bath on the right-hand page, imagines herself riding her rubber duck down the bathtub drain and into a wonderful world of castles and kings. Riding an inflated rubber animal in the river flowing by the castle, Shirley unseats the king himself in a joust—and then she is ready to return to the real world and the bath.

Aloneness. Shirley uses her imagination to provide herself with some alone time, even with her mother in the room. Why does she do this? Do you ever want to be alone? What are things you can do best alone?

Developing imagination. The book is a celebration of the imagination of the child as well as of the value of imagination in dealing with humdrum routines and concerns. How does Shirley make her trip? Where can you go in your imagination? Can you make up stories? When do you find time to do this?

Identity. Daydreaming like Shirley's, a normal experience for children, is sometimes difficult for task-oriented adults to tolerate. In discussion, the adult should be accepting not only of the daydreaming, but also of Shirley's need—and right—to tune out her mother's mundane monologue.

Carrick, Carol. *What Happened to Patrick's Dinosaurs?* Illustrated by Donald Carrick. New York: Clarion, 1986.

While Patrick and his older brother Hank rake leaves, Patrick tells his story of how dinosaurs disappeared. Dinosaurs, he tells Hank, used to do everything for people—built their houses and roads, even put on shows to entertain them. They wanted to teach people, but the people were interested only in lunch and recess—so the dinosaurs built a space ship and left.

Developing imagination. For children at the dinosaur stage, who probably know something of scientific theories about the dinosaurs' disappearance, this book is a counterpoint in fantasy. How satisfying to make up a story to explain a mystery, especially a happy story to explain a sad mystery! Patrick's story, used in conjunction with nonfiction about dinosaurs, can help children separate fact from fiction and see that each has its place. What other mysteries can we explain by making up stories?

Using ability. Some young readers, eager learners frustrated by classmates who are interested only in lunch and recess, may be interested in following up on the point of Patrick's theory. If you have a child who relates to this aspect of the book, ask him to describe where Patrick's dinosaurs went, what they are doing there, and how the people receive them in a place where they want to stay. You may hear a version of what the child would like to find at school.

Carrick, Donald. *Harald and the Great Stag.* New York: Clarion, 1988.

Harald lives in medieval England. The son of a farmer who works the Baron's lands, he is a friend of the Baron's huntsmen. From them Harald learns that the Baron plans a hunt for the Great Stag. Having just seen the Stag for the first time, Harald is awed by the animal's nobility, and he resolves to confound the Baron and his companions by blurring the trail. He is almost caught by the hunters and, hiding in a tree, knows how it feels to be hunted.

An old hunter turns the dogs away from Harald's tree, but Harald does not dare descend until dusk. At last he learns that the Stag has eluded the hunters—and that the old hunter, too, is a friend of the Stag.

This beautifully illustrated story not only introduces some of the mores of the Middle Ages in England, it also shows a boy coping in his own way with a moral issue—something of which gifted children are more aware than most, and at an earlier age. Harald and the old hunter stand out against their society, questioning what is readily accepted by most. The happy ending is not permanent, but the bond between Harald and the hunter is, as is Harald's knowledge that he is not alone.

Moral concerns. Ask about the value and the risks in taking a stand. Is Harald right or wrong? What difference does it make that he had looked the Stag in the eye? How does knowing the old hunter help Harald? How will it help him in the future?

Carroll, Lewis. *Jabberwocky*. Illustrated by Kate Buckley. Niles, Ill.: Albert Whitman, 1985.

Kate Buckley illustrates Lewis Carroll's famous nonsense poem from *Through the Looking Glass* as the story of a boy who bravely slays a fearsome beast and returns home to a joyful reception from his father, who has warned him about just such creatures. The simple story line will appeal to preschoolers, as will the words of Carroll's poem, which sound as though they ought to make sense but don't quite.

The illustrations suit the words. Buckley's creatures look almost but not quite like recognizable animals. The slithy toves, gyring and gimbling in the wabe, are especially endearing. The final illustration shows boy-hero and father headed toward home against an evening sky, leaving the mome raths outgrabing still—a return from imaginative adventure to secure reality.

Developing imagination. To avoid confusion, clarify to preschoolers that both words and animals are imaginary, just for fun. This is a thoroughly delightful book; enjoy it.

Cendrars, Blaise. *Shadow*. Translated and illustrated by Marcia Brown. New York: Scribner, 1982.

The French poet Blaise Cendrar's poem, "La Feticheuse," evokes an image that goes far beyond that cast by an object between the earth and the sun. It incorporates the idea of spirit, both haunting and enchanting, and the mystery of the African jungle. Brown's illustrations capture the mood of the text, conveying an eerie—but not at all frightening—sense of awe of the unknown that Shadow represents.

Developing imagination. The text, translated as it is from poetry, offers a challenge to young listeners and readers to comprehend it both intellectually and emotionally. The illustrations are original and abstract, enhancing the text to add to the total experience of the book.

Clifton, Lucille. *Everett Anderson's Friend.* Illustrated by Ann Grifalconi. New York: Holt, Rinehart and Winston, 1976.

This is the story of how Everett Anderson finally admits that new neighbors can be a pleasant surprise, even if the family does have all girls, including Maria, who can beat him at races. Eventually, Maria is even welcome to play with Everett and Joe and Kirk.

Told in verse, the story has gaps which the child can fill with his own inferences.

Relationships with others. Maria provides clear evidence that the way to have a friend is to be one. Preschoolers can understand her natural friendliness toward Everett in spite of his rejection of her—and the happy result.

Clifton, Lucille. *My Friend Jacob.* Illustrated by Thomas di Grazia. New York: Dutton, 1980.

Sam tells the story, explaining that Jacob is his best friend. Jacob helps Sam shoot baskets and carry things at the grocery store, and he writes a birthday card for Sam all by himself. Sam teaches Jacob a new skill: to knock before entering.

Sam is eight and black; Jacob is seventeen, white, and mentally handicapped. This is a gentle story which implies but does not preach acceptance and empathy. Friendship is based on giving and receiving, not necessarily on similarity, and both Sam and Jacob are able to give and receive.

Relationships with others. How do you know that Jacob is Sam's best friend? How do you know how Jacob feels about Sam? Do you have a friend who is very different from you in some way? How do you show that person that you are his or her friend?

Cooney, Barbara. *Island Boy*. New York: Viking Kestrel, 1988.

A simple story of the life of Matthais Tibbetts, born the first of twelve children in the first family on Tibbetts Island (a fictional island off the coast of Maine) around the turn of the century. The family flourishes on the island, but eventually all return to the mainland—even Matthais leaves the island to serve as cabin boy and then master on a sailing vessel. After fifteen years, though, Matthais returns to the empty house, bringing his bride, Hannah. Their three daughters leave when they are grown, but after Hannah's death, Annie and her son Matthais return. Life continues on the island as the grandfather, daughter, and grandson sell vegetables and milk to vacationers on nearby islands. In good time, Old Matthais, the Island Boy, dies during a trip to the mainland on rough seas. Young Matthais may stay on the island—we do not know. We do know that Old Matthais has lived a complete, fulfilled and successful life.

Cooney's illustrations set the mood for this description of a life of hard work whose reward is simple enjoyment of family and the pleasures of making good use of the abundance provided by land and sea. Without preaching, Cooney speaks of these basic values and the satisfaction they bring. Her story is a strong statement of the richness to be found in a sense of family, a sense of place.

Drive to understand. For children who have no experience with living on an island, or with the northeast coast of our country, *Island Boy* provides a narrative of a way of life similar enough to their own to facilitate understanding, but in a different time and place.

De Paola, Tomie. *Tomie de Paola's Book of Poems*. New York: Putnam, 1988.

Gathering poems for young children from classic to modern, Tomie de Paola has collected works by Lewis Carroll, Langston Hughes, Jack Prelutsky, Eve Merriam, X.J. Kennedy and many others, and then has added his own artistic talents to produce this book. It is recommended here as an example of many fine books of poetry—an important ally in any effort to enhance and encourage the imagination of young children.

Developing imagination. Especially for younger children, poetry is better enjoyed than analyzed.

Dorros, Arthur. *Abuela*. Illustrated by Elisa Kleven. New York: Dutton, 1991.

Rosalba tells of a day in the park with her *abuela* (grandmother). Rosalba imagines flying over New York City with her *abuela*, seeing the harbor, the airport, the streets and office buildings, the Statue of Liberty. Rosalba's narrative is sprinkled with terms in Spanish, her *abuela*'s language, offering just enough challenge to invite an English-speaking child to become fascinated with the words. The illustrations are joyous, colorful, and rich in details to explore.

Developing imagination. Invite the child to imagine with you what you would see if you flew together over a familiar place. For a young child, begin with a small space, such as her own block; enlarge the area for older children.

Drive to understand. This is a delightful book to introduce a child to New York City and to another language. A glossary of Spanish terms is included.

Dragonwagon, Crescent. *Home Place*. Illustrated by Jerry Pinkney. New York: Macmillan, 1990.

Hiking in the woods, a family comes upon remnants of a vanished homestead—daffodils, a chimney, a stone foundation. Digging just a little, the girl discovers a marble and part of a china doll. A family has lived here, and the hikers imagine how they lived, trying to reconstruct the ordinary daily events in the lives of unknown people long gone.

*Developing imagination.*The book stretches our awareness of our own lives to include lives much like ours, lived generations ago, evoking wonder about how things change and remain, and adding meaning to daily concerns about the weather and a family meal—concerns that do not change over the centuries.

Drescher, Jean. *Your Family, My Family*. New York: Walker, 1980.

Not a story, this book presents the great variety of family constellations we have today: adopted children, fathers keeping house, single-parent families, commune arrangements, foster homes, grandparents as parents. The book will reassure a child in a nontraditional home and will broaden the definition of family for children from traditional homes.

Identity. In discussion, reinforce ideas that a family is people living together, sharing chores and caring for one another, and that the child has a role in making it work.

Relationships with others. To help children understand and accept family arrangements that are different from theirs, this book is a good introduction to the various kinds of families in our culture. Which family is most like your own? Which ones are like families of friends of yours? How do families help people get along with each other?

Emberley, Michael. *The Present.* Boston: Little, Brown, 1991.

Arne Hansen, the handyman, needs a birthday gift for his nephew Tove, who lives in nearby Silkborg. A day's shopping in Brundby Market yields a wonderful (if rusty) 17-blade pocket knife. Cleaning it, Arne is so impressed with what it can do that he wonders if it is just the right present for a 12-year-old boy. He decides to fix up an old bike instead. Riding the bike to Silkborg, he enjoys himself so much that he begins to wonder if *it* is just the right present. The puzzle is easily settled in the end, to everyone's satisfaction.

Developing imagination. Told with gentle humor and with tolerance of the weaknesses in human nature, this story is illustrated with equal humor.

Gardner, Beau. *The Look Again . . . and Again, and Again, and Again Book.* New York: Lothrop, Lee and Shepard, 1984.

A graphic designer, Beau Gardner has created a series of designs each of which can be viewed from all four sides (or from a bird's-eye view) and be seen as at least four different objects. As the child turns each picture around and his perception of the design changes from one object to another, he will almost be able to feel his mind stretching.

Developing imagination. These continuing changes can be discussed: How does the design change from a teddy bear's foot to a pipe bowl? What actually changes? How does the child's mind do that? What other things can his mind do?

Goble, Paul. *Iktomi and the Berries.* New York: Orchard, 1989.

Iktomi is the Lakota (Sioux) name for the trickster character in native folklore. In this story, retold and illustrated by Paul Goble, Iktomi dresses in his finest clothes to go hunting, thinking of how his relatives will praise him for the meat he will bring back to them. Instead of returning in triumph, however, he misses seeing the prairie ducks, scares the ducks away when he falls into the river, and nearly drowns through foolishness when he tries to gather berries reflected in the water.

The humor is in the contrast between his fine regalia and his ineptitude—between show and substance. Goble points this out by showing in italics the comments listeners are expected to make as the narrator tells the story, indicating that they know Iktomi well and see through his pomposity. Thus the children learn to look through the surface to the quality that lies below, and learn also how foolish it is to boast.

The story can be used for discussion if we don't strain too hard for parallels. Iktomi, a stereotpyical folkloric character, will not change, but children will—a fundamental difference. Ask a few leading questions and let children draw their own conclusions.

Relationships with others. Where does Iktomi place blame when things go wrong? What foolish things does he do? Why, despite his foolishness, do people like him enough to continue telling stories about him?

Godden, Rumer. *The Mousewife.* Illustrated by Heidi Holder. New York: Viking, 1982.

A house mouse yearns to know more than hunting for food, and steals time to gaze out of the window at the garden, the fields, and the woods. A newly-captured dove in a cage tells her of wind, corn, clouds. She frees the dove and, seeing him fly away, is saddened by the thought that he will tell her no more. But now she can see the stars for herself; she no longer needs the dove's help. She remains a mousewife, but with a difference.

Some gifted children will be able to identify with the mousewife's yearning to know, to learn what is beyond her horizon, and also with the sadness of recognizing the limitations placed upon her by circumstances she cannot control. To some, it may be simply a story. In talking about the book, ask first for a general response; then base further discussion on what you learn from the child's answers.

Differentness; Drive to understand. Will the mousewife be happier now that she has talked with the dove, or less so? Would it have been better if she had never met him? Is it worth learning new things if you can't use what you learn? Why or why not?

Godden, Rumer. *The Story of Holly and Ivy*. Illustrated by Barbara Cooney. New York: Viking Kestrel, 1985.

Ivy is an orphan who goes looking for an imaginary grandmother at Christmas. Holly is a doll in a toyshop who wishes for a girl to own her. Mrs. Jones wants to celebrate Christmas so much that she decorates a Christmas tree for the first time, and Mr. Jones is the policeman to whom Peter, who works at the toyshop, turns when he discovers that he has lost the key. Holly, Ivy, and Mrs. Jones are united, thanks to Peter, on Christmas Day, and each wish is granted.

This story is told from three alternating points of view—Holly's, Ivy's, and Mrs. Jones'—so the reader must hold three separate stories in mind until they merge.

Drive to understand. In addition to this intellectual challenge, this is a heartwarming story with an implied appreciation for home and family.

Hall, Donald. *The Man Who Lived Alone*. Illustrated by Mary Azarian. Boston: David R. Godine, 1984.

The man who lived alone builds himself a camp near the farm of relatives, where he had lived and worked as a boy. He is very much an individual, growing and canning his own vegetables, hunting for meat, working in town for a few days each year for cash to pay his taxes. He makes friends of an owl, and takes pride in his mule. He can do anything with his hands: solder, build a house or a shotgun, shoe a horse or mule. He likes to keep his own hours, and often works all night. His aunt and uncle, and then his cousin and her husband and daughter, are close enough for company when he wants it, and he often helps them out.

The man who lived alone is alone but not lonely; rather, he is resourceful, affectionate and generous. His life is not typical but it is self-sufficient and he is content. This book's unusual theme provides assurance that spending time alone is not necessarily negative, and in its non-judgmental reporting it exemplifies tolerance for a different way of life.

Aloneness. A reading of this book can lead to a conversation about people we know who live alone, or who spend a great deal of time alone, and are happy doing so. The idea is simply to indicate to the child that being alone can be done well, and is potentially a positive experience.

Hall, Donald. *Ox-Cart Man.* Illustrated by Barbara Cooney Porter. New York: Viking, 1979.

The ox-cart man lives in New England at a time when embroidery needles still come on ships from England. In October, he and his family load all of the produce of their farm that they can sell onto the ox cart and he walks ten days to Portsmouth. There he sells everything, even the cart and the ox. He buys a few necessities and walks back home, where he and his family begin preparing for next October's trip. While the ox-cart man carves a new yoke and builds a new cart, his wife spins flax into linen, his daughter embroiders the linens, and his son makes brooms.

The story is about the self-sufficiency of the farm family, with everyone sharing in the work that sustains them. The illustrations carry much of the story, providing details for discussion as well as evoking the New England seasons and the well-regulated, productive life that results from the family's work.

Drive to understand. The family makes use of everything available to them, some of which will be new to contemporary readers. For example, what does the farmer actually do when he splits shingles to sell? What does the child know about spinning flax into linen, making maple syrup, and shearing sheep?

The book can also be enjoyed simply by examining the pictures and discussing the many details of the hardworking family's life.

Heller, Linda. *The Castle on Hester Street.* Philadelphia: The Jewish Publication Society of America, 1982.

Julie is visiting her grandparents, listening to her grandfather tell stories about his journey from Russia to America. Grandfather's stories are fanciful, full of magic and wealth and fame. Grandmother counters with her stories of the realities: crowded ships, Ellis Island, and hard work as they raised their family.

Drive to understand. Together they give Julie—and the reader—a taste of Jewish immigration and the undauntable spirit that sustained the newcomers as they made their places in their new home: for Julie, a gift of her heritage; for non-Jewish children, a telling of history that incorporates painful fact, unquenchable humor, and the spirit of a people.

Hill, Elizabeth Starr. *Evan's Corner*. Illustrated by Nancy Grossman. New York: Holt, Rinehart and Winston, 1967.

Living in a two-room apartment with a family of eight, Evan wants a space of his own. His mother suggests that he choose a corner for his own place, and Evan adds a picture, a plant, and a turtle. When his brother Adam asks why he wants a corner of his own, Evan says, "I want a chance to be lonely," and when Adam asks if he can come into Evan's corner, Evan helps him choose a corner for himself. But Evan is not entirely happy in his corner, and his mother understands why: "Maybe you need to step out now, and help somebody else."

Evan's story illustrates simply and beautifully the need to balance time alone and time with others, a lesson that gifted people must learn over and over. This book introduces the concept in terms a preschooler can understand.

Aloneness. Why does Evan want to have a chance to be lonely? What is good about being alone? How does he know when he has had enough time alone? What do you do when you need time alone? What do you do when you have had enough?

Drive to understand. Especially for children not familiar with cities, the illustrations in this book reveal the profusion of inner city life in details of home, streets, shops, and playgrounds. Evan is able to cope with it, and he is part of a stable, loving family.

Relationships with others. Why is Evan not completely happy in his corner? Will he want to go back there after he helps Adam decorate his corner? Why is it important to step out and help somebody else? How can someone who enjoys being alone also be a friend?

Hise, Barbara. *A Different Kind of Boy*. Illustrated by Stanley Tang. Phoenix, Arizona: Resources for the Gifted, 1979.

Eric is different because he hears music in his head. His parents are amused at first, then worried; his friends don't know he is different until he mentions the music; his teachers do not like it when he listens to the music instead of to them. The music becomes sad, and when Eric decides not to be different anymore, it stops altogether. Everyone else is happy, but Eric misses the music. Finally, wishing to have his music back, Eric hears it once more. Now he knows he wants to be a different kind of boy.

While this book can help gifted children accept their differences, it also raises the question of denying or using one's ability. It is reminiscent of E. L. Konigsburg's *(George)*, in that the child stifles imaginative activity, and then it gradually returns. In *(George)* the inner voice becomes integrated into Ben's personality as he matures; here the music returns when Eric wills it to do so.

Identity; Using ability. A Different Kind of Boy can be used with any age from early elementary up, stressing the metaphoric quality of the story with older students. The following questions are arranged roughly in the order in which they might be addressed to students from early elementary grades to senior high: Why is Eric happier when he hears the music? Why is it better for him to be different than not? Why is he able to will the music back? Is there any danger that he—or anyone in a similar situation—would not be able to cause the inner experience or talent to return? What would happen then? Do you know of any adults for whom this might be the case? How can we prevent closing off our inner experience? What are the risks in closing off, and in staying open? What are the rewards?

Hoban, Tana. *Shadows and Reflections*. New York: Greenwillow Books, 1990.

This wordless, plotless book is simply a collection of photographs of buildings, animals, and people, showing them in shadow and reflection. Discuss this visual treat first with book in hand—what do we see in the picture, what do we see that is *not* in the picture?—and then again on a walk, looking for the beauty of shadows and reflections around us.

Developing imagination.

Honeycutt, Natalie. *The Best-laid Plans of Jonah Twist*. New York: Bradbury, 1988.

Fourth-grader Jonah is not good at making plans, but for his friend Granville, planning is a strength. Granville's plan to cause Jonah's mother to let Jonah keep one of Granville's kittens seems to be working. However, his plan to avoid having to work on a project with Juliet Fisher fails, so the three must cooperate on a report on elephant seals. Juliet is the fourth grade busybody and has no friends, as Mrs. Lacey points out when she asks Jonah and Granville to give her a chance. Meanwhile Woz the hamster disappears, and Todd, Jonah's older brother, is sure the kitten has killed it. And Mr. Rosetti, an elderly neighbor, is missing, but no one is concerned except Jonah.

There are no dramatic changes here, only a slight shift in Jonah's and Granville's attitude toward Juliet, who displays negative characteristics typical of gifted children, especially girls. (She is a good student whose bossiness, blunt honesty and focus on ideas outrank her interest in interpersonal relationships.) The two boys develop tolerance for Juliet and respect for her ability, despite her direct and somewhat prickly manner.

Relationships with others. How did you feel toward Juliet at the beginning of the book? At the end? Explain the change, if any. Will Jonah and Granville and Juliet be friends from now on? Why or why not? If so, what changed? If you know someone like Juliet, how do you act toward her? Were you surprised to hear she had been crying? Did it change your feeling about her? What makes her bossy? Will that change? What could make it change?

Hunter, Mollie. *The Knight of the Golden Plain.* Illustrated by Marc Simont. New York: Harper and Row, 1983.

Sir Dauntless, the young Knight of the Golden Plain, spends a Saturday dreaming about imagined exploits. After banishing witches and killing dragons, he rides toward the castle, which comes to life at his approach. The lovely princess, Dorabella, cannot speak because the demon magician, Arriman, has caused her voice to leave her in the form of a golden bird, which he keeps caged in the middle of the Dark Forest. Sir Dauntless braves the dangers of the Forest, frees the golden bird, and reduces Arriman to a scarecrow. Then, although he has promised Dorabella he will return, he realizes it is time for tea, and he returns home. As he does so, the castle returns to sleep. Dorabella's father, Sir Veritas, promises his daughter that Dauntless will return, and Dauntless, arriving home for tea, resolves to return to the castle next week, to show himself "a loyal knight, as well as a brave one."

Mollie Hunter, who has been called Scotland's most gifted storyteller, found that her three grandsons delighted in this story, which "began as a small exercise in language."

Developing imagination. The story implicitly gives permission to fantasize, to dream of great deeds, and to spend a day imagining.

Isadora, Rachel. *Ben's Trumpet*. New York: Greenwillow, 1979.

Ben plays an imaginary trumpet as he listens to the musicians from the Zig Zag Jazz Club. He plays for his family and himself, until other boys tease him for having no trumpet. The trumpeter for the Jazz Club sees that Ben has stopped imagining himself playing, and invites Ben to the Club, where he begins teaching him to play. Stunning black and white illustrations capture the art-deco style of the twenties, and the pages seem to vibrate with the music.

The intensity of his desire to be a musician sets Ben apart. Alone and different, he is vulnerable to the taunts of other children, especially when he allows his imagination to take over. But it is just this that catches the attention of a potential mentor, who may make all the difference.

Creativity; *Differentness*; *Intensity*. Does your child know people like Ben (adults or children) who have interests so strong that they seem different from most people? If not, can you help the child meet such people? Point out that those who succeed in difficult fields, like music, are often as dedicated as Ben. The difference is positive, although it is not always viewed that way by children.

Isadora, Rachel. *Willaby*. New York: Macmillan, 1977.

Willaby likes to draw. She draws so much that she forgets to do her math, although she also likes math. She even draws on the playground during recess. When Miss Finney is sick, Willaby forgets to write a get-well card, even though she likes Miss Finney, and draws a fire engine instead. Then she worries that because she forgot to sign the picture, Miss Finney will think Willaby did not like her enough to send her a card—but of course, Miss Finney recognizes the drawing as Willaby's.

The child who becomes intensely interested in a favorite activity will understand Willaby, and discussion of this book may help both child and adult to put his interest in perspective.

Developing Imagination. Discussion about the importance of developing one's imagination might include considering how much time people who excel in a particular activity should spend on it. What does the child like to do so much that people don't understand how much time she spends on it? What could help them understand?

Identity. Questions to consider include why Willaby wants to draw more than most people, whether it is all right for her to draw so much, and the advantages and disadvantages of strong interests for people who have them.

Kellogg, Steven. *Best Friends*. New York: Dial, 1986.

Kathy and Louise are best friends. They share everything—until Louise's aunt and uncle take her to a mountain resort for the summer. Kathy misses Louise, but when Louise's card sounds as though she is having too much fun to miss Kathy, jealousy and anger are added to Kathy's loneliness as she waits for Louise to return. Kathy is cheered by anticipation of the arrival of puppies, due after Louis returns. The new neighbor has promised Kathy the first spotted puppy—but the first pup is brown, so it goes to Louise. When it is clear there will be no more pups in this litter, Kathy's hurt is magnified—but Louise offers to share the brown puppy.

Louise displays the generosity of friendship on two occasions, returning with gifts for Kathy and sharing the puppy. Kathy experiences a turmoil of negative feelings related to friendship—jealousy, anger, alienation—but she also shows fairness and maturity in recognizing that Louise would take good care of a puppy, and in not alienating Louise by expressing her hurt and anger. The friendship is saved through Louise's warm generosity and Kathy's patient forbearance. The illustrations are worthy of comment, too: they are humorous, telling stories in detail and facial expressions that illuminate the text.

Relationships with others. Discuss the element of chance: Louise has an aunt and uncle who invite her; the only pup happens to be brown. This summer Louise is lucky, but sometimes chance runs the other way. Is it fair to be angry or jealous when someone is simply lucky, right now? How can we learn to rejoice with the other in her happiness while we wait for our own luck?

Knowlton, Jack. *Maps and Globes*. Illustrated by Harriett Barton. New York: Crowell, 1985.

Beginning with ancient maps drawn on clay or silk cloth and Polynesian stick chart maps, the author moves quickly on to Magellan's voyage and the advent of more accurate globes. In the section on geographical terminology, he introduces and defines words like *latitude* and *longitude*, *elevation* and *depth*. Then he demonstrates various kinds of maps: physical, political, and specialized maps that show features such as metal deposits and stagecoach lines. He concludes by suggesting a visit to the library to explore atlases.

Barton's illustrations are clear and closely tied to the text, which goes directly to the point, providing much information cleanly and efficiently. Providing satisfying initial information while at the same time opening the door for future learning, *Maps and Globes* is a model nonfiction book.

Drive to understand. Many concepts are introduced which the child may wish to explore further, and the invitation to the library makes it clear that there is more to learn.

Kraus, Robert. *Owliver.* Illustrated by Jose Aruego and Ariane Dewey. New York: Windmill Books, 1974.

Owliver wants to be an actor. His mother encourages him, but his father wants him to be a doctor or a lawyer. Owliver acts out all of these options, but in the end he becomes a fireman!

In a light, humorous way, this book introduces a dilemma that is more familiar to the adult than the child, and will remind the adult of the futility of making a child's decision, as well as of the critical role of parental encouragement.

Identity. Point out how important it is for people to be what they want to be, to make their own decisions. Even among children, this is important. Is it important for the child to accept the decisions of playmates or siblings?

Leaf, Margaret. *Eyes of the Dragon.* Illustrated by Ed Young. New York: Lothrop, Lee and Shepard, 1987.

Leaf's story is based on the Chinese legend of two dragons painted on a temple wall who came to life and flew away when the painter added their eyes. In this version, the great artist agrees to paint a dragon on the village wall, on the condition that the village magistrate accept what he paints. The magistrate agrees, but when the dragon is finished he insists that eyes be added. Reluctantly, the artist paints eyes on his dragon, then takes his money and immediately flees the village under a darkening sky. Slowly the dragon comes to life and rises into the air, leaving the village wall crumbling behind.

Drive to understand. Artist Ed Young was born in China, and his illustrations add drama and immediacy to the story. The book offers a colorful glimpse into life in another time and place, made readily accessible here to American readers.

LeGuin, Ursula. *Leese Webster*. Illustrated by James Brunsman. New York: Atheneum, 1979.

Soon after spinning her first web and admiring the traditional, practical design, Leese asks herself, "I wonder why a web can't be a little different now and then?" She experiments with new patterns, taking ideas from the old carpet and paintings in the ruined castle that is her home. Other spiders scorn her creations, but Leese does not mind. When the castle is renovated to become a museum, cleaning women find the webs, which are assumed to be tapestries and are displayed behind glass. Leese is thrown outside where she continues to spin, enchanted by the additional beauty of dew on her webs in the morning sun.

Creativity. Leese's question, "Why can't it be different?," is one gifted preschoolers should be encouraged to ask. Leese not only models independent thinking, she carries through, making the best of meager resources. She can be used as an example when adults wish to stimulate divergent thinking.

Lindgren, Astrid. *Pippi Longstocking*. Translated by Florence Lamborn. Illustrated by Louis S. Glanzman. New York: Viking, 1950.

A series of vignettes tells about Pippi, who has come home to Villa Villekulla after sailing with her father; she lives alone in the family home and is wonderfully free. Very strong, with no parental restrictions and the freedom to do just as she likes, Pippi goes from one adventure to another, following her own unique logic, to the amusement of neighborhood children and the huge enjoyment of the reader.

Developing imagination. Pippi provides fantasy material and plenty of independence and divergent thinking for beginning readers, girls and boys alike. Adults who met Pippi decades ago still light up when they talk about her, putting Pippi Longstocking in the same category as Caddie Woodlawn, a timeless heroine.

Lobel, Arnold. *On Market Street*. Illustrated by Anita Lobel. New York: Greenwillow, 1981.

Like the Anno books, this one is to be pored over for the detail in the illustrations. In content, it is simply an alphabet book with such commodities as apples, books, clocks, and doughnuts for sale on Market Street, but each page presents a picture of a person made up of gloves, hats, ice cream, and so on.

Developing imagination. The drawings and the rich colors may prove inspirational. Give the child some time with this book, and then ask what he could draw for Market Street.

McDermott, Gerald. *Anansi the Spider: A Tale from the Ashanti.* New York: Holt, Rinehart, and Winston, 1972.

Anansi the Spider is a folk hero to the Ashanti people, a rogue who escapes trouble through his wits, rather like Br'er Rabbit. In this colorfully illustrated tale, Anansi's sons, each with a special talent, come to his rescue when Anansi is lost and swallowed by a fish. An argument ensues over which son should receive the reward, a shining white ball. Since the spiders cannot reach a decision, Nyame, the God of All Things, takes the ball into the sky where it shines forever as the moon.

The illustrations are characteristic of McDermott's work, brilliantly colored geometric shapes creating distinctive images. Children love the story and will ask for it again and again.

Drive to understand. Anansi is a good introduction to non-European folklore for preschoolers.

Nabb, Magdelen. *Josie Smith at the Seashore.* Illustrated by Pirkko Vainio. New York: McElderry, 1990.

Three stories tell of Josie, who lives in England, and the day she and her mom and her gran go by train to the sea. Josie plays in the sand, eats a picnic lunch, swims when the day warms up, rides a donkey led by the donkey man, gets lost, and finally leaves the shore before the tide comes in.

The slight story line is familiar enough for comfort, but her day at the shore bears subtle differences from the American child's experience in a day at the beach. English terms add interest to the text, although some have been removed from the original for this American edition. Josie is lively, warm-hearted, and courageous—a girl any child would want for a friend.

Drive to understand. This book gives a sense for similarities and differences between English and American experiences of the same adventure.

Nolan, Dennis. *The Castle Builder*. New York: Macmillan, 1987.

A boy builds a magnificent castle by the shore, and then as Sir Christopher he walks inside. He explores the castle, tames a dragon, and defends his castle from invading Black Knights. As the wind cools and the waves rise, Sir Christopher finds that he has no power to save his castle from the sea. But the boy who built it rescues Christopher, and plans to build a bigger castle tomorrow.

The Castle Builder demonstrates the power of the imagination, illustrating the value of the adventures we create over those merely watched on TV.

Creativity. What adventures does the child imagine as he creates with blocks, crayons, sand, or impromptu drama? Share some of your own imaginings with the child.

Rappaport, Doreen. *The Boston Coffee Party*. Illustrated by Emily Arnold McCully. New York: Harper and Row, 1988.

Based on a Revolutionary War incident related by Abigail Adams in a letter to John, this is a story of Sarah Homans and her mother, who led a group of women in protest against a merchant who hoarded coffee in order to sell it at high prices.

This I Can Read Book shows young readers how people who care about injustice can make a difference. The children may need some background, however. In discussion, be sure the child knows this is a true story, and that he understands the issues. Explain why items like coffee would be scarce in wartime, and how hoarding drives up demand and thus prices. Define new words such as patriots and merchant, if necessary. Point out that the women were patriots who cared enough about winning the war to spend time sewing shirts, but the merchant only wanted to make money on the war shortages—explaining the animosity between the women and Merchant Thomas. In fact, not all colonists agreed that they should be fighting for freedom from England; the merchant may have been one of those who disagreed.

Drive to understand; Moral concerns. Why were the women so angry? Did they have a right to be angry? Was this a good way to express it? War brings out strong feelings and causes people to do things they would not ordinarily do. What evidence do we see of that now?

Sarton, May. *A Walk through the Woods*. Illustrated by Kazue Mizumura. New York: Harper & Row, 1976.

> The poet, her dog and her cat take a walk through a spring woods. Different moods are shown by the dog: "Speed . . . Speed is what I need!" and the cat: "A walk is a quiet thing. Don't wait for me. I'll be along, wild and alone, in my own good time." Each enjoys the walk in his or her own way, and while they stay separate, each also enjoys knowing the others are there.

> *Developing imagination; Introversion*. Talk about what they see on their walks, what you and your child see on your walks (birds, flowers, rocks, insects), and about the joy of walking and observing which can be as much fun as running and shouting with friends.

Sendak, Maurice. *Outside Over There*. Illustrated by the author. [New York]: Harper & Row, 1981.

> A fantasy told with pictures as much as with words, this is the story of Ida, who rescues her baby sister from the goblins, who turn out to be babies, too.

> Ida is intuitive, resolute and brave, a girl of about six who knows her own mind and does what needs to be done. The illustrations are full of details to be pored over and discussed.

> *Identity*. The impact of this book is emotional rather than intellectual. The strengths in Ida's character may speak for themselves, but adults might wish to reinforce the child's awareness by mentioning what is admirable about Ida, how her baby sister and father feel about her, and why. Perhaps a time can be recalled when the child showed some of Ida's qualities.

> *Developing imagination*. With its fairy-tale quality, this book is recommended for its potential to stir the child's imagination, both visually and verbally.

Sharmat, Marjorie Weinman. *Gladys Told Me to Meet Her Here*. Illustrated by Edward Frascino. New York: Harper and Row, 1970.

> Irving is to meet Gladys for an afternoon in the park, but Gladys is not there. As he looks for her, Irving experiences a typical succession of feelings: worry, memories of Gladys' demonstrations of friendship, awareness of her importance to him, frustration, anger, and fantasies of revenge. Finally he returns to the meeting place, where Gladys is waiting with two popsicles.

The clock in the tower tells us that the whole process has taken ten minutes.

Not all of Irving's feelings are positive, but all are truly part of maintaining a friendship.

Relationships with others. How do we know Irving and Gladys are good friends? At the end of the story Irving says, "Hello, Gladys," and she replies, "Hello, Irving." What will they say next? What should they say, to stay friends? What other little problems can easily be forgiven, to keep a friend?

Simon, Norma. *All Kinds of Families.* Illustrated by Joe Lasker. Chicago: Whitman, 1976.

This picture book shows nuclear families and extended families, emphasizing that even when people don't live together, they are still part of a family. Divorce is not mentioned, and adoption is mentioned just once, but the concepts are implicit in the definition: "A family can be a mother, a father, and children who are growing up. A family can be a mother and her children, living, loving, working and sharing. A family can be a father and his children, living, loving, working and sharing. People in a family help each other and take care of each other."

This book and discussions based on it will give a child a warm feeling of belonging to his own family, and a sense that, whatever his family constellation, it fits nicely into the whole human family.

Identity. Which pictures remind you of our family? Why? (These questions are better asked by family members than by teachers or librarians. If this book is being used at school, it would be better to discuss it in very general terms with a group of students.)

Relationships with others. This book can be used to help children accept family patterns that are different from their own as well as understand the difficulties all families experience. Thus it can help them better understand how their friends may feel about their families. Problems of family life are gently portrayed in the illustrations, and much discussion could be based on them: What do you think is happening? Why? How do these people feel? Why?

More questions will arise from the children's responses.

Sing a Song of Sixpence: Every Child's Book of Poems. Selected by Beatrice Schenk de Regniers and others. Illustrated by nine Caldecott Medal artists: Marcia Brown, Leo and Diane Dillon, Richard Egielski, Trina Schart Hyman, Arnold Lobel, Maurice Sendak, Marc Simont, and Margot Zemach. New York: Scholastic, 1988.

    The Caldecott artists invited to illustrate this new edition of *Poems Children Will Sit Still For* (1969) were carefully matched with poems in the category assigned to each: rhymes, weather, spooky poems, nonsense, people, animals, feelings. While familiar poets are included (David McCord, Carl Sandburg, Eve Merriam, Marchette Chute, Robert Graves, John Ciardi, Karla Kuskin), they are most often represented by less well-known poems rather than the old stand-bys so often anthologized. The result is a fresh presentation, rich both visually and poetically.

    Developing imagination. This book is designed for home as well as classroom use. In sharing it with a child, simply enjoy the poetry.

    Drive to understand. For more analytical moments, notice differences in the illustrators' styles. To acquaint the child further with the illustrators, compare their work here with other books listed in the biographies in the section at the end of the book called "About the Artists."

Smith, Janice Lee. *The Kid Next Door and Other Headaches: Stories about Adam Joshua.* Illustrated by Dick Gackenbach. New York: Harper and Row, 1984.

    The kid next door is Nelson, and in these five stories Adam Joshua and Nelson learn how to overcome significant personality differences in order to be friends—beginning with "The Kid Next Door," in which they share their treehouse despite Adam Joshua's messiness and Nelson's neatness. In "A Dog Named George," Adam Joshua learns that a dog is worse than a baby sister and not as good as a friend, but he loves George anyway. Nelson doesn't. When Adam Joshua learns that Nelson has outgrown Superman in "The Superman Kid," he thinks this is another difference between them—but then he looks from his house into Nelson's room and sees Nelson playing Superman in solitary dignity. The boys join forces to fight back in "A Visit from Cynthia" when Nelson's cousin turns out to be tough and mean; and in "Nelson at Night" Adam Joshua learns to cope with personal habits very different from his own when Nelson stays for the night.

Adam Joshua and Nelson provide a primer in how to be friends though different, as Adam Joshua learns to appreciate the good and accept the difficulty in having Nelson as his best friend. Nelson isn't perfect, but then Nelson wouldn't think Adam Joshua is perfect, either. And "if you needed a friend who made you happy sometimes, and sometimes made you mad, and kept you trying hard to be a friend yourself, Nelson worked out fine."

Relationships with others. Why do Adam Joshua and Nelson keep trying to be friends? What do they gain, besides their friendship?

Stolz, Mary. *Go Fish.* Illustrated by Pat Cummings. New York: HarperCollins, 1991.

Eight-year-old Thomas lives in Florida with his grandfather. On this long summer day, observing Thomas' restlessness, Grandfather puts a marker in his book and suggests fishing. Later Grandpa cooks dinner, and then they sit on the porch and watch the sunset while Grandpa tells another story of their African heritage.

The action is simple—deceptively so; but Thomas' mind is always moving, remembering what Grandpa has taught him, questioning, stretching to understand how old Grandpa's fossil fish is, how long ago his ancestors lived in Benen. Grandpa is a patient teacher, and the bond between the two is strong.

Developing imagination; Drive to understand. The book is recommended for the quality of the conversations between Thomas and Grandfather, both remembered and current, and for the sense of wonder, both described and evoked. How *can* we understand millions of years, and recognize what a small part of history is represented by the time span we know? Even as adults we return to the effort to understand, an effort that never fails to stretch our minds and spirits. Children can benefit from being introduced to this practice of wondering by an adult who shares it with them.

Swann, Brian. *A Basket Full of White Eggs: Riddle-Poems.* Illustrated by Ponder Goembel. New York: Orchard, 1988.

Swann's riddle-poems are based on the folk literature of Italy, Yucatan, Mexico, Lithuania, the Philippines, Alaska, Turkey, Africa and Arabia. They are simple, provocative, and lovely lines posing always the same questions: What am I?

Goembel's stunning illustrations suggest in color, language, and costume the country of origin of each poem; they invite the child to look long and to feel the mood evoked by each double page spread.

Developing imagination; Drive to understand. Answers are given on the last page, but even after each answer is known the book merits more looking. For all children, it will encourage looking at the world with more attention, and some will want to try creating their own riddle-poems.

Viorst, Judith. *Alexander and the Terrible, Horrible, No Good, Very Bad Day.* Illustrated by Ray Cruz. New York: Atheneum, 1972.

The youngest of three brothers, Alexander goes through a day that includes finding nothing in his cereal box (his brothers find treasures in theirs), having the only cavity when they go to the dentist, and learning that the store has sold the last sneakers of the color he wants. The day goes from bad to worse, and the only solution seems to be to move to Australia. But, says his mother, some days are like that—even in Australia.

In spite of Alexander's awful day, when he rolls over to go to sleep the reader knows that tomorrow will be better. Some days are indeed like that, and even young children can learn that when they have a day like Alexander's, it does not mean something is wrong with them.

Relationships with others. Parents can talk about their own bad days. Recognizing the phenomenon and learning that tomorrow probably *will* be better is a step toward maturity.

Viorst, Judith. *Rosie and Michael.* Illustrated by Lorna Tomei. New York: Atheneum, 1974.

Michael tells why Rosie is his friend, and Rosie, in parallel terms, tells why Michael is hers. There is no plot here, but a lot of understanding of what friendship is: tolerating imperfection, plotting (and accepting) friendly pranks, sharing fears and sorrows, keeping secrets, forgiving mistakes, tolerating idiosyncracies.

For a gifted child who feels rebuffed and is puzzled about how to be a friend, discussion could grow out of each page of this book. What exactly are Rosie and Michael doing for each other here? The analytical power of the intellectually gifted youngster should help her to generalize, or to follow adult generalizations, from the situations Viorst presents.

Relationships with others. Do you know any friends who treat each other this way? Does anyone do this for you? When did you last do this for someone else? Can you plan to do this for someone tomorrow? Tell me how it turns out.

Ward, Lynd. *The Silver Pony.* Boston: Houghton Mifflin, 1973.

In 80 pictures, this wordless book tells the story of a lonely midwestern farm boy who escapes to the wider world via his imagination. A winged pony takes him on flying rides, and on each trip they find some other lonely child living his or her particular life: fishing through the ice, struck by a devastating flood, keeping pigeons on a city rooftop, shepherding in the West. Each child originates from a different ethnic group. The bond the farm boy has with them is loneliness, and his ability to give something to them on his imaginary flights.

Creativity; Introversion. This book would best be used by a child looking through it alone first, and then telling an adult the story portrayed by the pictures. The adult can bring out themes of the common experience of loneliness, the similarities between the children, and the fact that the lonely farm boy has something to give. Each child will tell a slightly different story, revealing his or her own feelings, and discussion can arise from that story rather than from a preconceived list of questions.

It is important to spend time with this book. If the reader yields to the temptation to go through it once quickly, much will be lost.

The Silver Pony is listed also in the Upper Elementary section. Your knowledge of the children who will enjoy the book will help you decide when the book should be presented.

Weisner, David. *Free Fall.* New York: Lothrop, Lee and Shepard, 1988.

The plot line is scant in this wordless picture book. A boy merely sleeps and dreams, waking in the morning to his familiar room. The strength is in the surreal illustrations, which for adults call up a wealth of associations: *Alice in Wonderland, Gulliver's Travels,* the art of Dali.

The jacket carries a brief poem describing a dream—an optional text which can be used to follow the pictures, which do progress from one to another in a dreamlike way. It is a journey of strange but familiar images, with a safe return. *Free Fall* is a Caldecott Honor Book for 1989.

Developing imagination. A child can follow the poem of choose to make more (or less) of the pictures, according to his or her experience and imagination.

Willard, Nancy. *A Visit to William Blake's Inn: Poems for Innocent and Experienced Travelers*. Illustrated by Alice and Martin Provenson. San Diego: Harcourt Brace Jovanovich, 1981.

This collection of poems about a visit to an inn hosted by poet William Blake is enhanced by pictures of the inn's interior, with one wall cut away like a dollhouse so readers see everything on several floors and the roof. Each poem creates an imaginative world of its own, but all are tied together by the mystical spirit of William Blake and the poetry he wrote 200 years ago.

Developing imagination; Drive to understand. Willard's poems should be read aloud and enjoyed. Some lines could be memorized for the sheer pleasure of knowing them by heart. The illustrations can be examined for the unexpected surprises on every page. A few poems written by Blake could be read aloud, too. Willard has used some of Blake's rhythms, and children will enjoy comparing them.

Williams, Karen Lynn. *First Grade King*. Illustrated by Lena Shiffman. New York: Clarion, 1992.

The first day of first grade, Joey King is eager to learn to read and to have homework like his brother David, who is beginning third grade. Joey likes his teacher and becomes a friend of Madeline, whose vision is impaired but who faces challenges head-on. A major challenge is Ronald, who is repeating first grade and who teases Madeline—calling her Four-Eyes—and Joey, derisively calling him the king. Then Mrs. Fulks is absent for a couple of weeks, and the substitute teacher, who turns out not to equal her reputation for meanness, arranges a trust game. Joey is astonished to learn that Ronald fears Joey as much as Joey fears him, and the two become friends.

The author has caught the details of starting school so well that older children will remember their first weeks of first grade and empathize with Joey and Madeline. Madeline is especially well-drawn, frank about her vision and tough without being aggressive. Joey responds thoughtfully to his predicament, and learns to stand up for himself by adapting what his parents and brother say about others to his own situation.

Relationships with others. How did your feelings about Madeline change after the school nurse explained her eye problem? About Ronald when you learned he had been held back? If there is someone you don't like or don't understand, how would more information change your behavior toward that person?

Moral concerns. Should Joey have told Mrs. Sullivan about Ronald? Why or why not?

Wilt, Joy. *A Kid's Guide to Making Friends: A Children's Book about Social Skills*. Illustrated by Ernie Hergenroeder. Waco, Tex.: Word, 1979.

This book introduces concepts that can be useful for children who feel awkward with other children or who do not make friends naturally. In three chapters (What Is a Friend?, How to Make a Friend, How to Keep a Friend), it offers specific attitudes and behaviors that foster friendship. Interspersed are questions relating each point to the reader and his own potential friends.

Introductory pages indicate a religious orientation which is not mentioned in the body of the book, so parents and teachers can use it or ignore it. The text will seem plodding to a gifted child, and adults may choose to use the book freely rather than page by page. It is recommended as a good summary of concepts relating to friendship.

Relationships with others. The points made are numbered and repeated for clarity. Once they enter the vocabulary of a family or a classroom they can be recalled whenever pertinent.

Winthrop, Elizabeth. *Luke's Bully*. Illustrated by Pat Grant Porter. New York: Viking, 1990.

Shy, quiet Luke and red-haired, confident Jane have always enjoyed a good friendship, but now in the third grade they are in separate classrooms. Luke sits next to Arthur, who grabs the reading book they are supposed to share, reads aloud so slowly Luke's hands twitch, and demands the cupcakes from Luke's lunch. Arthur also follows Luke home, and Luke despairs when his mother invites Arthur to come over every Tuesday. But rehearsing for the Thanksgiving play, Luke discovers a key to Arthur's problems. The guidance of teachers and his mother have kept Luke open to helping Arthur, and now the two can become friends.

Characters are deftly drawn, raising *Luke's Bully* above didactic bully stories. Quiet children will identify with Luke's wish to be in his hiding place under the stairs reading his animal book, and the friendship between Luke and Jane demonstrates how people with differing personalities can complement each other in a comfortable friendship.

Relationships with others. Questions can center around the "bully" phenomenon. Why is Arthur a bully? Why does he choose Luke to tease? Would you handle the situation as Luke does, or differently? Why does it help to know why someone behaves as he does? If you know someone who acts like a bully, how can you try to understand?

Moral concerns. Should Luke have told Mr. Robbins what was wrong?

Wisniewski, David. *Elfwyn's Saga.* New York: Lothrop, Lee and Shepard, 1990.

Elfwyn (beloved of elves) is born blind because of a curse a rival Viking, Gorm the Grim, has called down upon her father, Anlaf. The Hidden Folk deplore the curse and care for her, and she grows up seemingly with second sight. When Gorm brings a large crystal into Anlaf's hall to sew discontent, only Elfwyn recognizes the danger it presents to her people. Her action causes her blindness—the curse—to be lifted.

Telling an original story that is based on Icelandic history and legend, this book, with its cut-paper illustrations, is a visual and conceptual delight, a challenge to young readers and listeners.

Drive to understand. Themes for discussion are both factual (Viking history, Icelandic history, the aurora borealis) and legendary, the ancient theme of good and evil.

Yolen, Jane. *The Seeing Stick.* Illustrated by Remy Charlip and Demetra Maraslis. New York: Crowell, 1977.

Hwei Ming, the emperor's daughter, is blind, and when the emperor sends a message over the land asking for help in curing her, an old man from the south comes with his seeing stick. As he travels he whittles the story of his journey on the seeing stick, and after he tells Hwei Ming about his journey, he helps her to "see" the carvings on the stick with her fingertips. He continues to teach her to see through her fingers, and she teaches other blind children to see as she does, to "grow eyes on the tips of [their] fingers"—like the blind old man.

Yolen's story is told as a folktale and does not mention until the last page that the old man who takes such a long journey and carves with such skill is also blind. The story provides inspiration for finding ways around difficulties that cannot be changed, as well as an example of the power of imagination.

Developing imagination. More than discussion, an appropriate response to this book might be to encourage children to try growing eyes on the tips of their fingers. What can they sense by feeling faces, flowers, pets, fabrics, surfaces of all kinds? If they had never *seen* what they are feeling, how would they perceive them by touch?

Zolotow, Charlotte. *A Tiger Called Thomas*. Illustrated by Kurt Werth. New York: Lothrop, Lee, and Shepard, 1963.

When Thomas moves to a new neighborhood, he decides people might not like him, so he does not try to make friends. At Halloween, in his tiger costume, he is surprised to find that neighbors, adults and children, call him by name and invite him to come back. He decides maybe they *do* like him—and he likes them.

This is a good book for a shy child, or one who does not take the initiative in building friendships because he or she feels unaccepted. Thomas does nothing toward friendship. He is quite passive, yet he is accepted by people who are clearly willing to be his friends.

Relationships with others. Why does Thomas think his new neighbors might not like him? (There is no answer in the book, so this question asks for the child's perception of how Thomas feels.) What could he have done to make friends earlier? Do you know anyone like Thomas?

How can you be a friend to him or her?

Upper Elementary

Grades Three to Five

Alexander, Lloyd. *The First Two Lives of Lukas-Kasha*. New York: Dutton, 1978.

> Lukas is a vagabond and a scamp in an unspecified town in 15th-century Persia. A wandering magician's trick transports him to Abadan, where he is immediately greeted as king. It soon becomes obvious that he is only a puppet king, and Lukas finds himself caught up in palace politics and then in the imminent war with the neighboring country of Bishangar. Refusing to use bloodshed to solve problems, Lukas manages to bring peace, growing up considerably in the process.

> This is a light and lively story, with the gradual maturing of Lukas handled so deftly that it is quite natural and believable that a vagabond could act like a king. Nur-Johan, the Bishangar captive who turns out to be Queen, presents a contrast to Lukas in her youthful purpose and determination, yet Lukas can teach her how to recognize when using one's wits is more effective than her direct and literal approach might be.

> *Identity*. Point out places in the story when you knew Lukas was growing up. Describe Lukas and Nur-Johan, and how their backgrounds determine their character and behavior. How did each change? Lukas says of his having been sent to Abadan, "I'll have to make my own sense" of the situation. That's a profound statement. Are there situations in your life that are hard for you to explain or understand? Have you made your own sense of them? Could you? How does Lukas do it?

> *Moral concerns*. What decisions did Lukas make that showed maturity?

Base, Graeme. *The Eleventh Hour*. New York: Abrams, 1989.

> For his eleventh birthday, Horace the Elephant plans a party. He invites eleven guests, whips up a feast of eleven party treats, and plans eleven games. The guests arrive early and play games until the hour appointed for the feast: 11:00. Then—surprise and mystery!

But there have been clues. Each luscious illustration contains clues—and red herrings—in the form of anagrams, clocks, riddles, hidden creatures, mirror writing, and jumbled messages. In a sealed section at the end of the book Base reveals the clues, all the while encouraging the reader to deduce the answer through careful observation.

Drive to understand. This book cannot be assigned to just one age group. The verse, illustrations and story line will have great appeal to older preschoolers, and early elementary students must read to figure out the clues. Children of middle elementary age are fascinated by codes of any kind, and will certainly enjoy the intricacy of Base's concoctions. Some clues—Egyptian cartouches and Latin inscriptions, for example—are probably beyond most readers of any age without explanation. Every reader will find plenty of challenge here.

Billington, Elizabeth T. *Part-time Boy*. Illustrated by Diane de Groat. New York: Frederick Warne, [no date]

Ten-year-old Jamie does not mind being different. In fact, he enjoys wearing unconventional clothes like cowboy boots and a Tyrolean hat. In contrast to his boisterous older brothers, Carl and Paul, he doesn't talk much—which worries his mother but not his father. And Jamie enjoys being alone, although he is aware of his mother's concern. This summer Mattie Swenson, another individualist and instructor at the Natural Science Center, invites Jamie to help her at her country home. There Jamie meets a neighbor boy his age who also does not talk much, and realizes he has made a friend without talking. Mattie's friend Mike, an archaeologist, teaches Jamie some advanced soccer skills. Spending the summer with others who are comfortable with his quietness, Jamie makes friends and gains confidence. When he returns home his soccer skill gives him something in common with his older brothers.

This is a gentle, thoughtful book. The question of whether Jamie is too quiet is handled lightly, and the presence of others who understand or prefer quiet themselves is reassuring, as is Jamie's ability to join his brothers' game. Discssion could focus on the experience of being a quiet person, or on understanding others who are quiet.

Differentness; *Identity*; *Introversion*. What are reasons why people are quiet? What pleasures are there in being quiet and alone, different from pleasures of being with a group? We all need some balance of alone time and time with others, but most people prefer one or the other—which do you prefer? What can you accomplish when you are alone that you cannot when people are around? Do you know someone with whom you can share a comfortable silence, not feeling you need to talk? Why is that so with those people?

Blos, Joan W. *Brothers of the Heart: A Story of the Old Northwest 1837-1838*. New York: Macmillan, 1985.

Shem Perkins's family moves to Michigan in 1837, when statehood opens up the land. He is fourteen, called "the fiddler's crippled son" because he had been born with a malformed leg and foot. That summer he leaves home and finds work in Detroit, then is sent on a winter expedition to Mackinac Island and the wild western shore of Michigan. Left alone in a cabin, he expects to die. But Mary Goodhue, an old Indian woman known for healing, finds him. Nearing the end of her life, she stays with Shem and teaches him, and eventually shows him how to return home.

As in her earlier book, *A Gathering of Days*, Blos captures the rhythms of the language of the time in this well-researched novel. She also tells the story of Shem's inner growth in a few short but difficult months, as he transcends his disability. When he returns to southeastern Michigan, she says, "His stride was unashamed"—the limp not vanished by any means, but so outshone by Shem's personal strength, courage, and purpose as to be unnoticed.

Drive to understand. This book can be read for understanding the lives of early settlers in a new state, for appreciation of Native American values, and for its tale of wilderness survival.

Identity. Why was Mary Goodhue able to help Shem overcome his difference when his parents could not? What traits do Mary's husband and Shem have in common? What traits do you have that enable you to compensate for other, less desirable traits?

Brink, Carol Ryrie. *Caddie Woodlawn*. New York: Macmillan, 1935.

Caddie is eleven in 1865, growing up in a pioneer family in Wisconsin. A tomboy, she fords the river and runs through the fields with her brothers, while her older sister, the sedate Clara, learns more lady-like ways. From her father Caddie learns to repair clocks and to respect the Indians who still live near the Woodlawn farm, and she risks her father's anger in a sudden decision to ride to the Indian camp to warn them of danger. From her father she also learns to value the wisdom of strong women, and to aspire to become one.

Brink's novel is a compilation of stories the real Caddie Woodhouse told to her granddaughter, the young Carol Ryrie. Caddie is remembered, her story is loved, by many grown women who saw themselves in the active, assertive Caddie when they were young readers.

Identity. How has Caddie's unusual childhood helped her to become a strong and good woman? What people do you know who are like Father, Mother, Cousin Annabelle, Tom, Caddie's teacher? What are you learning from other people in your life?

Moral concerns. Caddie faces some choices in the course of this book that could lead to discussion of decision-making. Ask what those decisions are and why Caddie chose as she did.

Bunting, Eve. *The Man Who Could Call Down Owls.* Illustrated by Charles Mikolaycak. New York: Macmillan, 1984.

The man calls down owls by waving his willow wand toward the moon, and the boy Con is always among those who watch. The owls sail down silently, settling on nearby branches and even on the man's hat and cloak. Then one night a stranger watches, and the next night he appears again, this time in the old man's cloak. Con sees the large beautiful white snowy owl for the first time that night, and knows the old man will not return. Eager for the power to command the birds of the air, the stranger has killed the old man and taken his hat, cloak, and willow wand; but these do not instill the old man's power. The owls come to him only to scratch and claw until he flees. Finally the owls settle on Con's shoulders and hover around him, filling the night with love.

The death of the old man is off-stage, understood implicitly, and not frightening. The language conveys the mystery and quiet awe surrounding communication between humans and other life forms—clearly the man's power is in love, not coercion, though the stranger fails to see this. In fact, owls are called down by imitations of their call, not by wands, but Bunting captures the wonder felt by the watchers, and the silence of the wand adds to the mythical quality. This book could be discussed with older youngsters as well, making the point that the appearance of power is not equal to the real thing.

Identity. What power enables the man to call down owls? Why does the stranger not have that power? What does power—or "personal power"—mean? Why did the owls settle on Con's shoulders?

Byars, Betsy. *Summer of the Swans*. Illustrated by Ted CoConis. New York: Viking, 1970.

Since their parents' divorce, Sara and her older sister Wanda and younger brother Charlie have lived with Aunt Willie. Charlie has been mentally handicapped since he was ill at three, and Sara is fiercely protective of him. At fourteen, she is also concerned about her moods, her appearance, the size of her feet, and Joe Melby, who seems to have taken Charlie's watch. Then Charlie gets lost and in the search for him, which Joe joins, Sara develops a new perspective.

The characters are especially well drawn in this book, and Sara and Joe in particular will stand as models of empathic and caring behavior in situations where impatience might be expected. Byars' descriptions of Charlie's thinking can help children who have been ignorant or afraid of the mentally handicapped to develop a sympathetic understanding. This understanding can be generalized, with sensitive guidance, to a tolerance and valuing of all others who are not so quick as a gifted child.

Relationships with others. How do the different characters treat Charlie? (Include negative treatment.) How did you feel about the different ways he was treated? How can we understand those who tease? How and why does Sara help Charlie? Why is she able to understand how he feels so well? Is there someone you know who needs your help? Are you the kind of person who offers help when it is needed? Why or why not?

Carrick, Carol. *Stay Away from Simon!* Illustrated by Donald Carrick. New York: Clarion, 1985.

Living on Martha's Vineyard in the 1830s, Lucy fears Simon, the older boy who does not come to school because he cannot learn. One day in a snowstorm Simon follows Lucy and her younger brother, Josiah, home, and Lucy takes a shortcut through the woods to avoid him. After she realizes she is lost,

Simon suddenly appears in the storm, takes Josiah on his back, and walks on. Not knowing what else to do and swallowing her fear, Lucy follows. When she is at the point of exhaustion, her father appears on horseback through the snow: Simon has been taking them home. From her parents' understanding and kindness toward Simon, Lucy learns some sympathy, and when she takes hot cider to the barn, where Simon has insisted on sleeping, she learns why he was following—he had learned from Lucy's song, "One, two, buckle my shoe" how to count to ten, and he wanted to show her.

Carrick wrote this book to help children overcome fear and misunderstanding of the mentally disabled, who would be in school now, but were shunned and outcast then. By highlighting that contrast she also illumines the continuing tendency, especially among children, to draw back from those who are different. Some adults may object that this book teaches children not to avoid strangers. But Simon is not a stranger; he is well known in Lucy's community. He is only different.

Drive to understand. How did her parents' comments change Lucy's attitude toward Simon? (Information helps to reduce fear.) In what other ways are people different, causing distrust? What information would help?

Relationships with others. Should Lucy have feared Simon? Why or why not? Can you suggest better ways for her to handle the situation?

Ceserani, Gian Paolo. *Marco Polo.* Illustrated by Piero Ventura. New York: Putnam, 1977.

This is a visually arresting account of Polo's life, his visit to China, and his friendship with Kublai Khan. The story is especially pertinent for gifted children since both Marco Polo and Kublai Khan were able to pursue their intellectual curiosity in particularly spectacular ways. Their relationship is an example of a friendship based on a "meeting of the minds."

Marco Polo is a good book to read and discuss methodically, with a globe available. Describe how difficult it was to travel across the desert and around India by sea, when there were few or no other travelers, and comment on the courage required to explore the unknown as Marco Polo did.

Drive to understand. What was most important to Marco Polo; what did he value? How was he able to accomplish so much? What did he give up to achieve what he did?

Conly, Jane Leslie. *Racso and the Rats of NIMH.* Illustrated by Leonard Lubin. New York: Harper and Row, 1986.

In this sequel to her father's popular book, *Mrs. Frisby and the Rats of NIMH,* Conly continues the story of Jenner, one of the dissenting rats from the earlier book. Jenner has left the rats to return to the city, and from there his restless son Racso sets out to join the colony the rats of NIMH have founded at Thom Valley. Insecure about how he will be accepted, and endowed with a false sophistication from life in the city, Racso resorts to lies and boasting to win a place in the colony. The quiet competence, humility, tolerance of hard work and cooperative spirit of the other rats gradually have an effect on Racso. As they work together to prevent a dam from flooding their valley, Racso learns how to contribute to the group effort, and eventually he becomes the hero he has wanted to be.

Racso displays the bravado many uncertain children exhibit. Both those who are like Racso and those who are annoyed by children like him will understand how Racso feels about his own behavior. Discussion can emphasize how important the patience and understanding of others is in changing Racso.

Identity. Why does Racso lie, steal, and boast? What is more effective behavior when joining a new group? Why is it hard to do? What qualities in Nicodemus help Racso? Do you know someone who has those qualities? What is that person's effect on you?

Relationships with others. What situations can make anyone feel as Racso does about himself? How does this affect how people get along with others? What can help?

de Beer, Hans. *Kleiner Eisbär, Wohin Fährst Du?* [Little Polar Bear, Where Are You Going?] Monchaltorf: Nord-Süd Verlag, 1987.

In elementary German, this lively book tells the humorous story of Lars Eisbär, who inadvertently floats south on an ice floe. Landing on a foreign shore, Lars befriends a hippo and enjoys playing with him until there is an opportunity to journey north on the back of a migrating whale. Lars returns to his very own iceberg, to find his Vater waiting for him and eager to hurry Lars off to find his Mutter.

The story is suitable for preschoolers, but the challenge presented by the language makes the book a treat for older children as well. With help from the illustrations, a German dictionary, and an adult who remembers a bit of German, children of upper elementary age can approach Lars Eisbär's story as a puzzle to be solved.

Drive to understand. Curious, verbal youngsters may want to go on to other stories in German—or French, Hebrew, Italian, Japanese, Latin, Russian, Spanish. Familiar children's stories, such as *Winnie-the-Pooh* and some of the Laura Ingalls Wilder books, have been translated from English into some of these languages. Look in the children's section of a good bookstore for more ideas of foreign language books for young readers.

Dickinson, Peter. *The Weathermonger.* Boston: Little, Brown, 1969.

Set five years into the future, this science fiction story tells of an England propelled back to the Middle Ages by the Changes, unexplained forces that caused the people to reject machinery and rely on magic and superstition. Because he has disobeyed authorities by maintaining the motorboat he had before the Changes, Geoffrey, the Weymouth weathermonger, is to be drowned with his sister, Sally. They escape to France in the boat and are sent back to England to find the source of the Changes. Their search leads them to a medieval forest near the Welsh border where they confront a reawakened Merlin and learn how the Changes originated.

This well-written book is a good introduction to science fiction and fantasy, containing elements of each. It is clearly a "boys' book," combining adventure and love of machinery.

Drive to understand. More seriously, it raises questions about the environmental impact of machinery. What are the relative advantages and disadvantages of the Middle Ages and the present? Can we manage to have the best of both?

Dutton, Sandra. *The Magic of Myrna C. Waxweather.* Illustrated by Matthew Clark. New York: Atheneum, 1987.

Bertha is starting out badly in fifth grade at McKechnie School. She is already teacher's pet and now the principal appoints her Clean Plate Monitor for Health Day. But Bertha's Fairy

Godmother—Myrna C. Waxweather, a very unusual sort of Fairy Godmother—comes to the rescue, giving Bertha hints and props to bolster her confidence. Using her mind of her own, despite the pressure at McKechnie to conform to rules, Bertha cracks the system—and the other students see her as one of them.

The humor in this book is based on hyperbole, with the oppression by rules and teacher and principal grossly exaggerated. Underlying this, however, Bertha has a serious problem—she is new, and she is the pet, and the other students are unaware of her discomfort with the situation. It takes courage and inner strength to break the mold she's being forced into, and Myrna C. Waxweather helps Bertha to summon both, to do her own thinking, and to act as if she had a mind of her own.

Relationships with others. In discussion, students may need time to talk about life at McKechnie School before they are ready to talk about Bertha's problems. Then: why is it hard to be teacher's pet (or favored in any way, such as with academic ability)? What can students do about it if they don't have a Fairy Godmother? What exactly did Myrna C. Waxweather do for Bertha? How can we substitute for a Fairy Godmother in real life?

Evans, Cheryl and Anne Millard. *Usborne Illustrated Guide to Norse Myths and Legends.* Illustrated by Rodney Matthews. Tulsa: EDC Publishing Co., 1986.

With brief introductory sections on the history of the Norse people and on myths and religion, this informative book establishes a context that helps an analytical reader develop an understanding of how myth related to the lives of the people. The body of the book features two-page retellings of Norse myths, reinforced by a wealth of colorful illustrations. A map of Europe sets the myths in geographical context; a Who's Who and a listing of names and places provides a very useful glossary.

This book is a fine introduction to a body of mythology that has lent more to our culture than we normally recognize. It can be used as a basis for role-playing, as a beginning point for more reading of Norse myths and of other mythologies, and as a starter for a discussion.

Drive to understand. How and why are Norse myths different from Greek and Roman, or African, or any other mythology? What does the Norse mythology tell us about the beliefs of the people? About the warrior image of the Vikings?

Ferris, Jeri. *What Are You Figuring Now? A Story about Benjamin Banneker*. Illustrated by Amy Johnson. Minneapolis: Carolrhoda Books, 1988.

Benjamin Banneker (1731-1806) was a freed black man, a Maryland farmer who studied astronomy, clocks, and mathematics—matters of great interest at the time he lived, when ships sailed by the stars and there were only two books in many homes: an almanac and the Bible. His formal schooling lasted only four winters before he had to work full time on the farm. But when he was twenty, he borrowed a watch, took it apart to analyze how it worked, and reassembled it. Then he used his drawings to build a clock of wood, and became famous as the man who built his own clock. With his study of astronomy and skill at math, he became a surveyor—so well-known that he was appointed by President George Washington and Secretary of State Thomas Jefferson to assist Pierre L'Enfant in laying out the streets of Washington, D.C. He decided to write an almanac, which required hundreds of mathematical calculations to predict the phases of the moon and eclipses; his almanac was known for its accuracy. Only after age sixty did he stop farming his 100 acres to devote himself to math and astronomy, still living in his cabin with his wooden clock.

Always he hungered for conversation concerning ideas about books, math problems, and what was happening elsewhere in the world. The emphasis on this, plus the fresh writing style and the fact that the author causes us truly to care for Banneker, recommends it for intellectually curious readers.

Drive to understand; Using ability. What quality kept Banneker going when he had no one to talk to? How was his family important to him? With whom do you talk about books or math or other favorite subjects? Why is it important to have someone to talk to about these things?

Fitzhugh, Louise. *Harriet the Spy*. Illustrated by the author. New York: Harper & Row, 1964.

Harriet spends her after-school time spying on neighbors. She keeps a notebook filled with comments, not always flattering, on them and on her classmates. Shortly after Harriet's nurse, Ole Golly, leaves the family to get married, the other sixth graders discover Harriet's notebook and form a plan to get revenge. The loss of Ole Golly and her two best friends cause Harriet to respond with the sturdy independence that got her into trouble in the first place. Her parents and teachers help her use her keen powers of observation and her writing ability in positive ways. Gradually, Harriet softens enough to apologize, and her friends return.

Harriet is a prickly person who comes to realize at the end of the book that she is intelligent. She has never known what to do with her precocious insights, and has used her ability in negative ways. The problem is really only pointed out, not solved, in this book.

Relationships with others. Why is Harriet's notebook so important to her? Why does she write so many stinging comments? How does her intelligence get her into trouble? How can it help her get out of it? If you were writing a sequel to this book, what would you have Harriet do to make and keep friends, but still be herself? When is it all right not to be popular?

Using ability. Harriet has been using her special ability in ways that have given other people good reason to dislike her. Do you know anyone who does this? Why do people behave that way? What are the disadvantages? What do they need from others to help them change? What can they do for themselves to change? What will enable Harriet to use her ability more positively?

Fleischman, Paul. *The Half-a-Moon Inn.* Illustrated by Kathy Jacobi. New York: Harper and Row, 1980.

Aaron Patrick's mother leaves him at home alone for the first time when he is twelve—he was born mute, and until now has never been away from her. She has taught him to read and write, but she worries because he cannot call for help. A blizzard keeps her away too long, and Aaron sets out over roads he has never seen to search for her. Lost, he finds that his writing is of no use—no one he meets (in what is apparently 18th-century England) can read. He is turned into a servant boy by the pickpocket proprietress of Half-a-Moon Inn, and escapes only through his wits.

This is part fantasy, part mystery, and much suspense, heightened by the drawings—all elements that children of this age love to find in fiction.

Drive to understand. The setting and Aaron's muteness add interest and information to this challenging adventure story.

Fritz, Jean. *Where Do You Think You're Going, Christopher Columbus?*
Illustrated by Margot Tomes. New York: Putnam, 1980.

This lively biography tells much more than that Columbus discovered America in 1492. Fritz follows Columbus on all four of his voyages, describing his bravado and stubbornness, his successes and failures, and providing along the way glimpses of the late 15th-century European view of the world.

The contrasts are instructive. Columbus was a good seaman but a poor governor. He returned to Spain from his first voyage to a royal welcome, but from 1493 to the end of his life he faced one disappointment after another. Although he was clearly intelligent, the qualities that carried him through difficulties were persistence and faith in what he was doing. This book offers a way of demonstrating the importance of these characteristics to gifted students who may be relying on native intelligence alone.

Drive to understand; Using ability. What words would you use to describe Columbus's character? What qualities made him a good explorer? A poor governor? Why do we hear only of his successes? Do you know of other famous people who failed as well as succeeded? What characteristic was most important to Columbus's success? Do you share any of his traits? What are the advantages? Disadvantages? How can you enhance the advantages and overcome the disadvantages?

Galbraith, Judy. *The Gifted Kids Survival Guide for Ages 10 and Under.*
Illustrated by Priscilla Kiedrowski. Minneapolis: Free Spirit, 1984.

Written to help students understand what the label "gifted" means, this book explains what giftedness is and how it relates to some of the frustrations that gifted children experience in school, with peers, and at home. It includes reassuring information and practical help for making friends and fighting boredom.

The book is written *to* children in a comfortable conversational tone. The format makes extensive use of graphics to add impact, and the writing style is informal. Children respond well to both, so they are able to make use of the information and suggestions; however, the dominant value of the book may well be the assurance it offers to gifted children that they are not alone.

Identity. Five sections of the book cover various issues of identity for gifted children. Adults may wish to select sections of the book that seem especially pertinent. It may also be wise to give some thought to whether group or individual discussion would be best.

Relationships with others. Getting along with others is discussed in sections on friends, coping with teasing, and "gifted grief at home."

Goble, Paul. *Death of the Iron Horse.* New York: Bradbury, 1987.

On August 7, 1867, a group of Cheyenne derailed a Union Pacific freight train in Nebraska to protest the railroads' incursions into their territory. Goble's telling gives the story a mythic quality. After the derailment, the Cheyenne plunder the freight cars, taking not money but all they can carry of goods their people can use.

Simple but beautiful illustrations recall the destruction caused by conflict, with the majestic expanse of the West as a backdrop. The story is told as an old man, remembering years later, might have told it to his grandchildren, from the Cheyenne point of view.

Drive to understand. Since this story is based on fact, discussion can lead to further exploration of the disruption of the various Native American cultures.

Moral concerns. The book can be used as a springboard for discussion that examines both sides. Were the Cheyenne wrong? How can we determine whether they were or not? Consider the story from the point of view of the men on the freight train. Were they wrong? In what way? Who was stealing what, and why, and with what justification?

Goffstein, M. B. *Two Piano Tuners.* Straus and Giroux, 1970.

Since her parents died two years ago, Debbie has lived with her grandfather, the great piano tuner Reuben Weinstock. He wants Debbie to become a great pianist, but Debbie wants to be a piano tuner like him. When Grandpa's friend, pianist Isaac Lipman, comes to town for a concert, Grandpa hopes Isaac's music will inspire Debbie to want to play the piano. But when Isaac plays, what Debbie hears is that Grandpa has tuned the piano so well that at the end of the concert it is still in tune. Debbie's persistence and Isaac Lipman's understanding encourage Grandpa to promise he will teach Debbie to tune a piano. She will become a great tuner like him.

The value of this book is in the pursuit of excellence which shines through in Isaac, Grandpa, and Debbie—an intense interest in something beyond themselves, and a personal humility before the act of creating great music. Debbie has watched Grandpa so intently that she knows the tuning pattern by heart, and all the tuning instruments required. Like a protege, she is aware of her craft on a professional level at an early age. Gifted children with interests other than music can transfer the quality of Debbie's interest to their own field; children who are studying piano will follow the details of tuning and of the concert Debbie attends. This is indeed a special book, with appeal to special readers.

Intensity; Using ability. Why does Debbie get up before Grandpa at the end of the book? Do you do anything that interests you, makes you happy, as piano tuning does Debbie? If not, what *might*?

Greene, Bette. *Philip Hall Likes Me. I Reckon Maybe.* Illustrated by Charles Lilly. New York: Dial, 1974.

Eleven-year-old Beth Lambert is the second best student in her class, but Beth sometimes suspects it is only because she lets Philip Hall be first. In fact, when some of the men in town offer to pay for part of her college education, Beth rises to first place. The friendly—and sometimes argumentative—rivalry between Beth and Philip continues throughout the book, against a background of rural and small town Arkansas.

Each chapter is a story unto itself in this book, a typical pattern in books for young children. Together they provide a greater understanding of the lives of black children in the rural south, of typical elementary-school boy-girl rivalries, and of some of the dilemmas posed by giftedness. Beth is an assertive, saucy girl whose impetuosity sometimes gets her into trouble—and she is appealing in her recognition that this is so.

Relationships with others. In what ways does Beth grow up a little in the year the book records? What does she learn about getting along with others? What do you do to be a good winner? Loser? How could you do better?

Using ability. What does Beth learn about being first? Philip, about being second? What is wrong with "letting" someone else win—for you, for the other person, for the relationship?

Greene, Constance C. *A Girl Called Al.* Illustrated by Byron Barton. New York: Viking, 1969.

Al(exandra) has an extraordinary IQ, but she doesn't work to capacity and is a nonconformist. She explains all this when she meets the narrator (a girl of Al's age who is never named) shortly after she moves into the same apartment building. Al is also lonely and defensive regarding her weight and her parents' neglect. The narrator introduces her to Mr. Richards, the building janitor, and he very gently works to help Al lose weight and to relieve her loneliness.

Giftedness is mentioned just once, but is clear in Al's conversation and insights. The emphasis of the book is on the gradual development of sensitivity to the feelings of others, on the common courage of people facing loneliness, and on the way in which friendship can compensate for lost family ties. This book is better used with third and fourth graders than with older gifted children.

Aloneness. What sets Al apart and contributes to her loneliness? What does she offer to the narrator and her family and Mr. Richards? What does the narrator offer Al? How will Al become less lonely over time?

Identity. Why is it important to Al to think of herself as a nonconformist? How does her nonconformity increase her problems? How does it help her with them? How does her intelligence help her to cope? How do you know she is lonely, even though she never says so?

Relationships with others. Al is a very strong character, clearly the leader in the girls' relationship. Discussion can begin with this relationship: What do the two girls have to offer each other despite their differences? What does Al need from other people? Would you be willing to give it to her? What would make it difficult for you to do so?

Gripe, Maria. *Hugo and Josephine.* Translated from the Swedish by Paul Britten Austin. Illustrated by Harald Gripe. New York, Delacorte, 1962.

Shy and timid, Josephine is teased at school because her father is the vicar and she has made the mistake of carrying her books unfashionably in a knapsack. School is easy, but social life is hard until Hugo Anderson joins the class. Hugo is quietly, rationally, imperturbably independent, always out of step, always polite, and always making perfect, if unexpected, sense. He finds it odd, for example, that the teacher talks and the children speak only to answer her questions: "There's no sense in our answering, when we don't know anything. We're the ones who ought to ask questions." When he realizes how distressed the teacher is because he has not followed his reading lessons, Hugo teaches himself to read in a weekend.

Hugo befriends Josephine and gives her confidence, but when he is suddenly absent for an extended time her timidity returns and the teasing resumes. He finally returns with a sensible, unapologetic explanation for his absence, and helps Josephine in her efforts to be accepted.

Many gifted children will recognize the discomfort of feeling out of place and different as Josephine does. Hugo's personality is the strength of the book. He accepts everyone, including himself, and presents a self-contained maturity that commands the respect of all. In addition, the book offers the opportunity to compare school life in Sweden to that in the United States.

Differentness. Hugo represents the kind of aloneness called Being Alone and Different in Chapter One. He stands alone quite naturally and with such integrity that it brings him respect rather than loneliness. To help the child articulate Hugo's strengths, ask him to describe Hugo. Do you know anyone who is like him in any way? Think of a problem you or your class is having—what would Hugo think of it?

Drive to understand. Consider what the story says about a childs life in Sweden. How is Hugo and Josephine's school familiar? How different? What other aspects of life can you compare, based on this book?

Relationships with others. Although Hugo and Josephine are both bright, there is a striking difference in their ability to get along with people. How can Hugo be so comfortable with being so very different, while Josephine is teased if she is only a little different from the other children?

Gripe, Maria. *In the Time of the Bells*. New York: Delacorte, 1965.

Arvid, the 17-year-old king, is a dreamer, no less unhappy on the throne than his people have been to have him as their monarch since his father abdicated to study astrology. To improve Arvid's attentiveness to matters of state, his parents bring to the castle Helge, the son of the executioner, to serve as whipping boy, and Elisif to become Arvid's future wife. At the first public whipping ceremony, an unusual bond develops between Arvid and Helge. Arvid continues, even more strongly, to insist on his need for privacy, and Helge and Elisif are drawn to each other. At last, Arvid names Helge king for a day for the midsummer festival, and a resolution works itself out as he had hoped.

Arvid is a good example of an individualist thinker who needs more time alone than most people. His introspection and self-analysis will strike a chord with gifted people who do not fit the social expectations of their peers. The personalities of Arvid, Helge, Elisif, and her sister Engelke are clearly differentiated without a trace of judgmentalism, each valued for what they are and what they can contribute.

Identity. Arvid knows he is a difficult person to understand. How does he accept that? What advantages are there in being such a person? Could he change it? How?

Introversion. How can one express love for humanity if one does not love people? How does Arvid do this? Is anyone you know like this?

Sensitivity. Arvid thinks that he is insensitive and does not like people. Do you agree? How does his response to the whipping show sensitivity to others?

Haas, Dorothy. *Tink in a Tangle.* Illustrated by Margot Apple. Niles, Ill.: Albert Whitman, 1984.

Tink is convinced her red hair is the reason she gets into one "tangle" after another, all summer and into her sixth-grade school year. Her best friend, Poppy, and several other friends usually get into trouble, too, as they join Tink in her adventures. When Tink is called to the principal's office yet again, Tink's mother comes to school, and the two adults have a serious talk about Tink. The principal recognizes Tink's high energy and her leadership qualities, as well as the potential demonstrated by her ability to tell "spookies." A new program emerges to channel Tink's energy and use her ability, and she begins to believe red hair may not be the problem she thought it was.

Nothing is said about Tink's intellectual ability, but many high-energy students who haven't learned to think through the consequences of acting on their good ideas will identify with Tink. A sub-theme revolves around Jane Ellen, who wants friends but does not know how to make them, with realistic treatment of the efforts of Tink and her friends to accommodate Jane Ellen in their plans.

Identity. For each "tangle," when should Tink have "thought through"? What is a similar experience of yours, when you did think through? One when you did not? When are you most likely not to take time to think through?

Relationships with others. How well did Tink and her friends treat Jane Ellen? What suggestions do you have for improvement?

Heller, Sherri Z. *What Makes You So Special?*. Illustrated by Jon Enten. Phoenix: Thinking Caps, 1979.

Addressed to students who have been assigned to a gifted program at school, this book briefly defines giftedness (the ability to become a good thinker) and then discusses such issues as risk-taking and dealing with friends who were not chosen for the program. The remainder of the book offers constructive ways of coping with boredom in class so that children *use* rather than *waste* ability. The suggestions encourage children to use their creativity to make assignments more interesting, promoting self-motivation and the value of challenging oneself.

Parents or teachers can read this book along with children soon after they have been selected for a school gifted program, discussing and answering questions that arise from each page.

Identity. The section that discusses how children are chosen for gifted programs would be useful in helping children accept and integrate the concept of giftedness into their self-image.

Relationships with others. The section of the book about relating to friends who were not chosen for a gifted program will help to identify and develop attitudes that promote successful interpersonal relationships.

Using ability. It would be ideal if both parents and teachers knew the content of the book, so they could reinforce the ideas in working with the child on school assignments.

Henkes, Kevin. *The Zebra Wall*. New York: Greenwillow, 1988.

At ten, Adine is the oldest of the five Vorlob girls, followed by Bernice, Carla, Dot, and Effie. The new baby's name will begin with F, and the wall in the nursery is ready, newly painted with a mural featuring flowers, frogs, ferns, fish, and a fairy. But this time it is different: Aunt Irene comes for a visit and gives every evidence of staying—in Adine's room. The baby's arrival brings surprises and a change in plans, but the Vorlob family is flexible and up to the challenge.

Unhappy as Adine and her sisters are with Aunt Irene's presence, they manage to hold their tongues and accept their parents' decision to welcome her. Very gradually Adine learns to see the situation from Aunt Irene's point of view, and moves toward her own acceptance.

Relationships with others. What makes Aunt Irene's visit difficult for Adine? How does Adine warm up toward her aunt? What surprised you about Aunt Irene? Think of someone with whom you are not comfortable. What surprises might they have for you if you knew them better?

Hest, Amy. *Love You, Soldier.* New York: Four Winds, 1991.

Katie is seven when the war comes and her father leaves in an olive green uniform. She and her mother stay in their New York City apartment, her mother working in the hospital and Katie spending hours in the public library. Her mother's friend Louise comes to live with them, since her husband Jack is in the army, too, and soon Louise has a baby. Katie loves Rosie—but then the worst possible news comes. Katie's father has been killed in the war. Katie and her mother stay on in the apartment with Louise and Rosie until the war ends and Jack and Louise's brother, Sam, come home. Then there are more changes, which Katie is reluctant to accept. But their elderly neighbor, Mrs. Leitstein, encourages her, saying, "Love is risky, but it's worth it."

The challenges of developing an identity are intensified for Katie, who must learn to adjust, accept, and risk more than most growing children. She is helped in doing so by the love around her—from and for her parents, Louise, Rosie, Mrs. Leitstein, and finally Sam, the cause of the greatest risk. We are confident that despite the loss of her father and the unknown future, Katie will be fine.

Identity. In what ways does Katie grow up from age seven to the end of the book? What and who helps her to grow well?

Hunter, Mollie. *The Mermaid Summer.* New York: Harper and Row, 1988.

Eric Anderson is a Scottish fisherman who does not believe in mermaids until he sees one, and he and his crew are nearly drowned. Knowing the incident is a punishment for having scoffed at mermaids, and fearing more trouble, Eric decides to leave his fishing village and find work on an ocean-going vessel. From far-away places he sends gifts back to his family. When grandson Jon blows the conch shell sent by Eric, the call summons the mermaid. Soon Jon's sister Anna, who especially longs for her grandfather's return, is drawn into a struggle with the mermaid, first for one of her grandfather's gifts, and eventually for the lives of the village fishermen. But Anna and Jon prevail, with a little help from their mother, their grandmother, the Oldest Fisherman, and the Howdy, the seer of the village. They outwit the mermaid, and soon thereafter Eric returns.

This is a satisfying fantasy based on the traditional literature of Scotland. A model of the criteria Hunter has listed elsewhere for good fantasy, it is a story based in long-ago forgotten truth and a happy blend of the unknown and the feared with the real world and the manageable. Many readers can identify with Anna's loyalty and stubbornness, and with Jon's frustration and courage as he follows his younger sister's lead.

Drive to understand. It may be better to avoid emotional questions about folklore and fantasy. Such questioning requires the child to make verbal what is understood at a preverbal level, and might better be left there. Question then for intellectual understanding: Compare Hunter's story to other mermaid stories. Why are mermaids seen as enemies? What would you like or dislike about life in a fishing village?

Jarrell, Randall. *The Bat-Poet.* Illustrated by Maurice Sendak. New York: Macmillan, 1963.

The bat stays awake during the daytime and wants the other bats to do so, too, to see all the wonders he sees. They will not, so he makes up poems to tell them about the day. They do not understand. He tells his poem to the mockingbird, who comments on the rhyme scheme and the meter, but misses the feeling altogether. Only the chipmunk will listen. The bat makes more poems, and finally one about bats that he wants to share with the other bats. But when he goes to the barn to find them, they have gone to sleep for the winter.

Older elementary children will appreciate the story line, which parallels Plato's story of the man who left the security of the cave, and when he returned could not make the others understand his descriptions of the wider world. Both stories can be used to help gifted children understand the uniquenesses of their perceptions, and why they are not always shared by others.

Creativity; *Differentness*; *Intensity*; *Sensitivity*. The bat-poet never found another bat to listen. How did he feel about that? What did he do about it? Have you ever felt that you wanted to say something no one else could understand? How did you find someone to listen? If you couldn't find anyone, what did you do instead?

Juster, Norton. *The Phantom Tollbooth*. Illustrated by Jules Feiffer. New York: Knopf, 1961.

Milo, who is so bored with life that he never knows what to do with himself, drags home from school one day to find a large package in the living room. Opening it, he finds One Genuine Turnpike Tollbooth. Milo assembles it, drives his small electric car up to the booth, and pays the toll. The road beyond takes him to the Kingdom of Wisdom and the two rival cities, Dictionopolis and Digitopolis, founded by the king's quarrelling sons. Two daughters, Sweet Rhyme and Pure Reason, had kept the peace until they were banished. Milo sets off to find the sisters, accompanied by the Watchdog, Tock, and the Humbug. They drive through the Forest of Sight (where the city of Reality has disappeared because people were too busy to look) and the Valley of Sound (which is silent because people became too busy to listen). Beyond the Mountains of Ignorance they find Rhyme and Reason in the Castle in the Air, and return them to the Kingdom of Wisdom. When Milo returns home, he finds his adventures have made him aware of how much there is to see and do in the world—he will not be bored again.

New thinking is called for not only by the symbolism in the plot, but also by the language, which is full of puns and literal interpretations of verbal expressions—as when Milo and his companions inadvertently "jump to (the Island of) Conclusions." Frivolous as it all sounds, Milo does change in the course of the book. The refreshing use of language, the symbolism, and Milo's boredom should all appeal to gifted readers.

Drive to understand; *Using ability*. Describe Milo at the beginning and the end. How did he change? What changed him? How did the trip help him know what to do with himself? Is this book silly or serious? How is it silly? How serious? Why did the author write it? What messages lie behind the story? How did it make you think of words, numbers, and spending time on unimportant tasks in a new light?

Kendall, Carol. *The Gammage Cup*. Illustrated by Erik Blegvad. New York: Harcourt, Brace and World, 1959.

For 880 years the Minnipins have lived in their valley in the Land Between the Mountains, isolated from the world and remembering the story of Gammage, who led them here, and Fooley, who floated away over the mountains in a balloon 440 years ago and returned with a few little-understood but well-revered artifacts. The Minnipins live tidy, well-regulated lives, with only a few exceptions: Gummy, who scribbles poetry; Mingy the Money Keeper; Curley Green, who likes to paint; and Walter the Earl, the only Minnipin who studies history from the few written records rather than relying on legend; now Muggles, who timidly at first but then more boldly thinks for herself rather than following the traditional ways without question. The story starts slowly and builds to an exciting climax as the five outcasts lead the other Minnipins in a brave and successful effort to save their valley from invasion.

Differentness. The theme of nonconformity can lead to discussion about rules—spoken or unspoken—that are difficult for some to follow. What conformities do we expect, like the green doors on (almost) every house in Slipper-on-the-Water? When is it appropriate not to conform to expectations? When is it inappropriate?

Identity. Why does Muggles change from being like everyone else in Slipper-on-the-Water to being just herself? How does she do it?

Relationships with others. How do we treat people who do not conform? What happens to Muggles when she stops following others' expectations and begins saying what she thinks? How does she avoid offending others when she speaks out?

Kendall, Carol. *The Whisper of Glocken*. Illustrated by Imero Gobbato. New York: Harcourt, Brace and World, 1965.

In this sequel to *The Gammage Cup*, the Watercress River floods, forcing the Minnipins in Water Gap to flee upstream. Reaching Slipper-on-the-Water, Glocken, bell-ringer of Water Gap, realizes his dream of meeting the Old Heroes of the

Gammage Cup. Glocken finds them living quite ordinary, settled lives—but the Old Heroes hail Glocken and the four Water Gapians who have fled with him as the New Heroes who will find and repair the source of the flooding. So five very ordinary Minnipins from Water Gap set out on their own adventure, discovering their latent heroism as events require.

The writing is more subtle and demanding than in *The Gammage Cup*, with vocabulary, metaphor, and proverbs to challenge the middle elementary reader. Imagination is called into play as the reader creates the Minnipin world from vivid description. Each of the five, despite insecurities, peculiarities, and weaknesses, manifests true self-sacrificing heroism at one time or another, and they offer tolerance and support to each other as they work to free the Watercress and save their Land Between the Mountains.

Drive to understand. For good readers who love to read, this is an excellent introduction to fantasy.

Koch, Kenneth and Kate Farrell. *Talking to the Sun: An Illustrated Anthology of Poems for Young People.* New York: Metropolitan Museum of Art and Holt, Rinehart and Winston, 1985.

This is a gorgeous book. To give children a sense of the beauty of poetry, Koch and Farrell have assembled English poems from the 15th century to the present, and poems translated from eleven ancient and modern languages. Their poets include Shakespeare, Blake, Rimbaud, Rilke, Lorca, and Li Po. They have sought not children's poetry, but poetry children will enjoy at different times in different ways.

To illustrate this range of poetry, they have selected paintings and other objects from the collection of the Metropolitan Museum of Art. Where the connection between a poem and a work of art may not be clear, a brief comment illuminates.

Drive to understand. In her introduction Farrell refers to "the mood [a poem] puts you in." Visual art also suggests moods, and here the children can experience the effect of both poetry and art, and the different moods resulting from each. In an appendix on helping young people like poetry, she recalls an image from the conductor Leopold Stokowski, in which the world of art is seen as an oak tree whose branches are the different art forms—music, poetry, painting, and dance—all expressions of the human need to create art. This book brings two branches of the oak/art tree together so well that we long to add others. It is a very rich book indeed for the imagination of a growing child, one to keep and reread for all the years of growing up.

Konigsburg, E. L. *From the Mixed-up Files of Mrs. Basil E. Frankweiler*. Illustrated by the author. New York: Atheneum, 1967.

Claudia Kincaid persuades her brother Jamie, who has enough money to finance the project, to join her in running away. Following Claudia's careful plans, they hide in New York's Metropolitan Museum of Art for a week. At first Claudia's reasons for running away are unclear even to her, but as she becomes fascinated by the mystery of a statue the museum has purchased, she realizes what she wants to accomplish before she returns home.

Written with a light touch, this is nevertheless not a frivolous book. It gives much incidental information for children who do not live in New York about the city, the Metropolitian Museum, and art. In addition, it portrays inquisitive children who have had superb educational opportunities and are appealing models for lively intellectual curiosity.

Identity. Why did Claudia want to run away at first? What is her reason by the end of the book? Why does she want to be different? What are some advantages to being different? How could someone like Claudia accomplish the same thing without running away? What does Mrs. Frankweiler mean when she talks about having some days when rather than learning new facts, it's good to "allow what is already in you to swell up until it touches everything"?

Konigsburg, E. L. *Jennifer, Hecate, Macbeth, William McKinley, and Me, Elizabeth*. New York: Atheneum, 1967.

Jennifer and Elizabeth become friends on Halloween of Elizabeth's first year at William McKinley School. Jennifer says she is a witch, and she does some mysterious things that make it seem possible that she is. Elizabeth becomes an apprentice witch, and all winter the girls meet at the library on Saturdays to study witchcraft, planning to make a magic potion that will enable them to fly.

Elizabeth is lonely at first in the new school. Jennifer, being gifted and black, is different and is not included in the school's social life, but she seems unconcerned about it. A subtheme is

Elizabeth's gradual separation from Jennifer's influence, with Jennifer's help, so that the friendship becomes more equal than the original follower/leader relationship.

Aloneness. Do you think Jennifer is lonely? Why or why not?

Identity. Why does it not seem to bother Jennifer that she is not popular at school? Do you think she is happy just as she is? Why or why not? How do you know when Elizabeth begins to do more thinking for herself? Why does this happen?

Relationships with others. Why is Elizabeth uncomfortable at the birthday party? Do you agree with her behavior? Why is she more comfortable with Jennifer? Why does Elizabeth finally pull away from Jennifer? How does this affect their friendship? What does each girl offer to the other?

Leichman, Seymour. *The Boy Who Could Sing Pictures*. Garden City, New York: Doubleday, 1968.

When the King goes to war each summer, the court jester is free to sing in the towns of the kindgom, and this summer he takes his son Ben with him. It is time for Ben to learn to be a jester, and he begins by singing. But Ben has met the townspeople and learned of their troubles, and as he stands in front of them and sees again the great sadness in their eyes, he cannot sing the silly song he had planned. Instead he tries to sing the sadness away, and gradually his song creates images in the sky—images of beauty the burdened people have never seen, have never been able to appreciate. In the fall Ben is asked to sing his pictures for the King, but in the faces of the people of the castle Ben sees no sadness, only blankness. These people have not experienced life enough to know sadness. So Ben sings life outside the castle for them—dying soldiers, blind beggars, freezing children. Ben is arrested for treason, but the people of the kingdom come to the castle to hear him sing once more. When the King sees Ben sing for them, and sees the people as they really are—not on parade day—he knows that Ben sings truth. He will no longer go off to war each summer; he will stay and help his people.

This is a book based on symbol, and can be used with older children for discussion at greater depth (for example, noting the copyright date and linking one message of the book—peace—to contemporary events) as well as with preschoolers, who can discuss some of the concepts involved at a more personal level.

Sensitivity. Why can Ben not sing a silly song in the face of sadness? Why could the people not see the beauty around them? Do we sometimes miss it, too? Ben points it out to the people in the story, but what or who points out the beauty *we* miss? How does a poetic imagination help us with daily routine, sadness, hard reality?

Using ability. How does Ben discover his unusual talent? How does he use it both generously and wisely?

L'Engle, Madeleine. *A Wrinkle in Time.* New York: Farrar, Straus and Giroux, 1962.

Fourteen-year-old Meg Murry, her younger brother, Charles Wallace and Calvin O'Keefe travel through time and space in search of Mr. Murry, a scientist who disappeared while experimenting with a tesseract, a wrinkle in time. When they find him, they must use all their strength to free him and themselves from the force of evil.

Almost all of the characters in this story are very intelligent, and the three children respond in different ways to the difficulties this causes them in relating to others. L'Engle creates a world in which it is psychologically safe to be gifted, in which the characters care for and challenge one another.

Identity. How are the children different from their schoolmates? How does each feel about being different? How do we show that we do or do not value differences among people?

Drive to understand. Like many of L'Engle's books, *A Wrinkle in Time* features an entire cast of gifted characters. They exhibit the drive to understand, as an intellectually curious reader will easily recognize. What is more, they show that it adds meaning and purpose to living. The book is intellectually satisfying to gifted children because of frequent references to math, science, literature, and music. Challenging discussions based on the book could begin with the question, "What do you think about life on Camazotz?"

LeShan, Eda. *What Makes Me Feel This Way? Growing Up with Human Emotions.* Illustrated by Lisl Wiel. New York: Macmillan, 1972.

This book about feelings is written as a conversation with a child. Psychologically sound, it covers typical feelings of children, parents, and teachers, and the behaviors that display or hide the feelings. LeShan discusses the responses of different people to the same feelings, and the importance of recognizing, understanding, and paying attention to our own feelings.

While the concepts presented apply to every child, some are especially apt for gifted children. Among these are preferring study to athletics, showing early concern for world problems, and understanding the importance of using interests and abilities and being oneself.

Aloneness. Adults using this book with children they know well will understand which sections to choose for discussion. The book is useful for talking about the need to have time alone to work on issues that are bothering them, as well as the need to do so in conversation with others.

Identity. A good way to use the book would be for adult and child to read one chapter at a time, noting ideas they would like to discuss with each other. The adult might prefer to be the first reader, to be prepared for questions a child might ask while reading it. (The chapter on "Feelings about Being a Boy or a Girl" mentions masturbation in a low-key, easily discussable way.) A general question to begin discussion would be: Have you ever felt this way? Adults should be ready to reveal times when they have felt this way, too.

Relationships with others. Find sections that discuss issues related to relationships with others and ask the child for her response. What personal experiences does the book bring to mind? She may remember past events that she is now ready to discuss. The book can promote discussion of how she feels about her relationships with classmates and how she is presently coping with situations that bother her. Adults should consider whether this book is better used with groups or with individual children.

Lowry, Lois. *Anastasia Krupnik.* Boston: Houghton Mifflin, 1979.

In her green notebook, ten-year-old Anastasia records her favorite words, important private information, and a list of "Things I Love!" and "Things I Hate!" When she learns that her mother will have a baby boy in March, she adds "my parents" and "babies" to the Hate list, but stops short of running away when her father suggests that she give the new baby whatever name she chooses. Anastasia writes a horrible name in the green notebook. Over the next few months, she considers becoming a Catholic and changing her name, learns how to listen to her 92-year-old grandmother, falls in and out of love, decides she likes her name—and records all of this in the green notebook, occasionally moving an item from the Hate list to the Love list. Eventually even "babies" appears on the love side of the ledger.

Anastasia is a bright, inquisitive, sensitive girl who is doing her best to make sense of the world and the process of growing up. She vaguely dislikes her teacher, without knowing the reason. The reason is clear to the reader when the teacher rejects a poem Anastasia has written that does not rhyme. Later her teacher makes a special effort to be kind, and Anastasia moves her name to the Love list. Anastasia's parents are models of support and understanding for a gifted child. There are no major issues here, only Anastasia becoming more aware of herself through her own efforts and with her parents' help.

Identity. How do *people* get moved from the Hate to the Love list? What do all have in common? Describe the difference between the college students' and Anastasia's attitude toward Wordsworth. Do you know people who have the students' attitude? What are the consequences? (If it seems appropriate, discussion leaders may want to add questions related to Anastasia's knowledge of and attitude toward her own giftedness.)

Macauley, David. *Cathedral: The Story of its Construction.* Boston: Houghton Mifflin, 1973.

By giving specific dates and names, Macauley adds authenticity to this book of fiction—a story of how the people of a French town worked together for 86 years to build "the longest, widest, highest, and most beautiful cathedral in all of France." The illustrations show in exquisite detail how the land was cleared and foundations built, how the buttresses, piers, stairways, vaults, windows, even bells were constructed—and how the village grew around the cathedral over the years. Correct architectural terminology is used, and a glossary provides definitions.

Drive to understand. Cathedral is used here to represent others of Macauley's books (*Castle, Underground,* etc.) which answer questions most curious children have asked, if only to themselves. Macauley writes with respect not only for the object constructed but for the people who do the work, and he never writes down to his audience. His books are a good introduction to serious work in the adult world.

MacLachlan, Patricia. *Arthur, for the Very First Time*. Illustrated by Lloyd Bloom, New York: Harper and Row, 1980.

When he is ten, Arthur goes to stay with Great-Aunt Elda and Great-Uncle Wrisby for the summer because his parents are fighting. In addition, Arthur believes his mother is going to have a baby, which he does *not* want. Life is very different with Uncle Wrisby and Aunt Elda—they live on a farm, so they teach Arthur about nature and farm life. Their pet chicken, Pauline, sleeps in the kitchen and their pig, Bernadette, will give birth to piglets soon. They also have neighbors, including Moira and her grandfather Moreover, the veterinarian. Moira calls Arthur "Mouse" as they become friends, and Arthur learns that her family problems are more troubling than his. Nevertheless, Moira is a positive person who urges the timid "Mouse" to do something—and Arthur does.

This is a story of friendship and of Arthur's growing sense of purpose, nascent self-understanding and eventually the shift in his attitude toward a baby, directly due to his experience with Bernadette's piglets. The book includes Aunt Elda's story, which will remind readers of MacLachlan's later and better-known *Sarah, Plain and Tall*.

Identity. What did Arthur do? Why? How has he changed? So much is unresolved at the end of this book that some discussion can center on what the reader thinks will happen next. How will Arthur be different when he returns to his parents? How will his family be different?

Montgomery, L. M. *Anne of Green Gables*. Toronto: Bantam, 1984 (c. 1904).

As an eleven-year-old orphan, Anne is adopted by a 60-year-old Prince Edward Island farmer, Matthew Cuthbert, and his sister, Marilla. Anne is red-haired, bright, and eager to please, but above all, she is impetuous and imaginative. Despite her best efforts, she is forever getting into trouble. The story follows her for the next five years, through friendships, problems at school, and misunderstandings. As she learns to tame her romantic nature, the reader watches Anne grow mature and thoughtful.

First published in 1904, this book is refreshingly old-fashioned and idealistic in comparison to today's "problem novels." (Some will say too idealistic—how could anyone who has lived through Anne's childhood have survived so well?)

However today's readers may view Anne's efforts to "be good" and Marilla's efforts to avoid spoiling her, the underlying desire to make something good of one's life is a needed example, and well done here. Perhaps it is just the distance in time that allows this book to make the point without preaching.

Identity. Anne has no problems with recognizing and using her intelligence, so she can be a positive example. In what ways are you like Anne? In what ways could you be like her, if you had lived in her time? Who are kindred spririts for you? Might Anne be one? Why or why not?

Naylor, Phyllis Reynolds. *Shiloh*. New York: Atheneum, 1991.

Eleven-year-old Marty Preston is walking through his beloved West Virginia countryside one Sunday when he comes upon a dog—a frightened beagle who clearly yearns to befriend Marty and who follows him home. But Marty's family can't afford to feed a pet, and his father returns the dog to its owner, Judd Travers, whose reputation for meanness is based in part on his mistreatment of his hunting dogs. When the beagle (whom Marty has named Shiloh) escapes and returns to the Prestons, Marty hides him, even from his family, while he tries to find a way to earn enough money to buy the dog. The crisis comes when Shiloh is attacked in his hiding place by a neighboring German shepherd, and Marty's parents—and Judd—discover Marty's secret.

Marty is caught in a dilemma in this Newbery winner because both the law and the weight of local custom conflict with his passionate desire to protect Shiloh from a cruel owner. Although his parents are supportive, they insist that Marty work the problem out on his own. His manner of doing so shows uncommon courage, maturity, and wisdom, along with a need for compromise.

Identity. What is it in Marty that causes him to question rules that others around him follow easily? Imagine Marty in 15 years—what might he do then to protect a dog like Shiloh? How and why might Marty be different from his parents when he is grown?

Moral concerns. Did Marty make any decisions you would not have made? Was his parents' position a good one? Why or why not?

O'Brien, Robert C. *Mrs. Frisby and the Rats of NIMH*. Illustrated by Zena Bernstein. New York: Atheneum, 1971.

Worried about the illness of her son Timothy, Mrs. Frisby goes to Mr. Ages, a wise older mouse, for medicine. Later, when it is clear that Timothy is too weak to be moved from their garden home before it will be destroyed in spring plowing, Mr. Ages sends her to the rats for help. Thus she learns how the rats had been captured and groomed in a laboratory at NIMH, their intelligence enhanced until they learned to read; they finally escaped, and they set up their own civilization under a large rosebush on the Fitzgerald farm. Now they are planning to move again, this time to a remote valley where they can be self-sufficient, no longer dependent on Mr. Fitzgerald's grain. Mrs. Frisby learns also that her husband Jonathan, who had died the previous summer, had been a laboratory mouse who escaped with the rats. He died during an attempt to help them. They are therefore eager to help Mrs. Frisby although they, too, are in danger.

The super-intelligent rats of NIMH are so different from other rats that they want to live differently, according to their own ideas and values, even though they do not entirely agree among themselves on those values. One basic question the book raises is how much separateness is called for by a high intelligence, and why.

Identity. After escaping from NIMH, the rats are uncomfortable with other rats, who edge away from them. If you have experienced this, how do you respond? What are advantages of the rats' separate civilization? The disadvantages? This story is an extreme: what examples of the same impulse to separateness do we see among people? What are the advantages and disadvantages? What compromises are possible? What is your preference?

Moral concerns. Nicodemus and others argue that a life made easy by machinery is too easy, causing the rats to lose a sense of purpose in meaningful work. What do you think? What would be the result if they used their leisure time to learn more? What if people did the same?

Page, Michael. *The Great Bullocky Race*. Illustrated by Robert Ingpen. New York: Dodd, Mead, 1984.

The race is to see who can drive their team of bullocks faster to the south coast of Australia with wagonloads of baled wool:

Donald McDonald and his daughter Alice, or Foxy Murphy and his son Young Wally. The journey takes nearly three weeks, and because it goes through lonely territory in the heat of summer, each team is obliged to help the other when necessary. First the dogs, then Alice and Young Wally, and then even Donald and Foxy, rivals though they are, become friends. In the end, who is to know who won?

The view of Australia given in the story and even more through Ingpen's illustrations is equal in importance to the theme of cooperation and friendship in this Hans Christian Andersen medallion winner.

Drive to understand. Find Australia on a globe, and then look for the towns and rivers on a map. Enjoy the names of the towns—"all the beautiful Aboriginal names"—and play with them. What does Aboriginal mean? How would it feel to be Alice or Young Wally? How are their lives different from yours? The same?

Paterson, Katherine. *A Bridge to Terabithia*. Illustrated by Donna Diamond. New York: Crowell, 1977.

Sensitive and interested in art, Jess is a misfit in his family and in school. When Leslie moves to his rural area of Virginia and joins his class, she frees Jess to play and learn in the country of their imagination, Terabithia. When Leslie is killed in a flooded stream, Jess must face her death and his aloneness. Although he is still different from others, he realizes that he has gained strength from the friendship and can be himself now.

Katherine Paterson wrote this book after the death of a special friend of her own son, and it rings with the truth of the relationship between two sensitive people who find strength and validation in their friendship. Many children can respond to that truth whether or not they themselves have such a relationship, and this book is highly recommended for bright and sensitive upper elementary readers.

Aloneness. Why do Jess and Leslie enjoy Terebithia so much? What other places could serve the same purpose? Do you have such a place? Would you like one? How would you find it? When would you go there? What would you do there? Would you go alone or with someone else?

Drive to Understand. Describe the difference in background between Jess and Leslie. Why is the trip to Washington, D.C. so important to Jess? Have you had any such experience?

Identity. How is Leslie different from the other students at Jess's school? How is Jess different? How does each one feel about being different? What would happen if they tried to change in order to fit in better? If you could meet them, would you like them better as they are, or if they changed in some way? Do you know anyone who seems different from the group, but who is pretty good at being who he or she is?

Relationships with others. How do Jess and Leslie recognize each other as potential friends? What does Leslie offer to Jess? What does Jess offer to Leslie to build a friendship? What do you offer to and gain from special friends?

Using ability. Why is it so difficult for Jess to develop his artistic talent? What will he have to do to be able to use his talent? What traits will help him? What traits do you have that would help you, if you were in his situation? What talent do you have that you can develop? Is it harder or easier for you than for Jess? Why?

Phelps, Ethel Johnston. *The Maid of the North: Feminist Folk Tales from around the World.* Illustrated by Lloyd Bloom. New York: Holt, Rinehart and Winston, 1981.

Phelps has gathered folk tales from Europe, Africa, the Far East, Asia, and North america, the common thread being that the main character in each is a woman who is spirited, clever, or brave—a heroine instead of a hero.

Drive to understand. The feminism is not belabored. These are simply good tales, little-known and therefore fresh and spritely, in the authentic folklore form. They are good reading for both boys and girls.

Rodgers, Mary. *Freaky Friday.* New York: Harper & Row, 1972.

Annabel Andrews and her mother trade places, so Annabel goes through the day in her mother's body and sees herself as others speak to her "mother" about her. She learns that her brother loves her despite her impatience with him, that the housekeeper will not clean her room because it is so messy, that the boy she admires thinks she is ugly and awful, and that her teachers are frustrated with her underachievement.

The book is sometimes hilarious as the reader follows Annabel's thoughts and reactions. The high point is her mother's interview with her teachers, in which Annabel learns that she has a high IQ and that her teachers are concerned about her lack of achievement. When she and her mother resume their own bodies, she finds that her mother has had her braces removed and her hair cut, and has bought Annabel a new wardrobe. Instant transformation from an ugly duckling to a budding beauty—what every adolescent girl would love to have!

Identity. What is it about the interview with her teachers that makes Annabel want to change? How would Annabel describe herself at the beginning of the book? How would you describe her at the end? What *inner* changes take place? Why? Do you know anyone like Annabel? What do you think he or she is like inside?

Using ability. How will Annabel's behavior change as a result of the inner changes that take place in this story?

Speare, Elizabeth George. *The Sign of the Beaver*. New York: Dell, 1983.

When Matt and his father come from Massachusetts to Maine to claim land the father has purchased, they are the first white family to settle in the area. They build a log cabin and plant corn, and then Matt's father goes back to Massachusetts for his mother, sister, and the new baby, leaving Matt alone to tend the corn. When he is caught in a bee swarm, Matt is rescued by an Indian and his grandson, Attean. The old man asks Matt to teach Attean to read, in return for food. Attean is not receptive to reading; his parents have been killed by whites and he has no liking for their culture. But gradually he teaches Matt survival skills, and they become friends and then brothers. When the tribe moves on, Matt is invited to join them. His family has been so long in coming that it seems they might not come at all, so the decision is not easy. Although Matt faces the winter alone, he decides he must stay. Just before Christmas his family arrives, delayed by typhus.

In this good introduction to historical fiction, Matt is introduced to another culture and must recognize that in some ways it is superior to his own. The book can lead to discussion of ways in which all people adapt to their environments and develop patterns that make sense—because they are effective in the situations the people face.

Drive to understand. What does Matt learn from Attean and his family beyond survival skills? What does he teach them?

Sperry, Armstrong. *Call It Courage*. New York: Collier, 1971 [c1968].

When Mafatu was three, his mother was killed at sea. Mafatu survived, but his childhood experience left him afraid of the sea, a coward in the Polynesian world where courage is everything. Rejected by all, Mafatu finally leaves Hikueru, his home island, and sails to a deserted island where he must depend only on himself for survival. While providing food and shelter and building a new canoe, he also kills a shark, a wild boar, and an octopus. Finally he must flee the island, pursued by a band of men from a nearby island. Having so abundantly proven his courage to himself, Mafatu returns home to the welcome of his people.

This fast-paced adventure will hold children's attention and give them a vivid picture of life in another part of the world. Mafatu's journey is the classic quest story, and he sets for himself tasks that correspond to the rites of passage marking the beginning of manhood in many societies. Although younger gifted children can read *Call It Courage* with enjoyment, those in the upper elementary grades are at a more appropriate age to respond to the story of Mafatu's search for identity.

Identity. Why did Mafatu leave Hikueru? Why did he explore the island he found, even though he suspected it might be one of the dark islands? Why did he go to the plateau instead of leaving the island when he heard the drums? Describe Mafatu's character. What traits helped him survive psychologically (survive the teasing and rejection of his people)? Physically (survive the dangers of sea and island)? Do young people in the United States face challenges in growing up that these traits will answer? How can you use the traits Mafatu had or developed?

Tolan, Stephanie. *A Time to Fly Free*. New York: Scribner, 1983.

By the time he is in fifth grade, Joshua Taylor has developed a defensive wall to keep from being hurt by the cruelty of other students to animals, to weaker students, and to himself. But this year, the wall no longer protects him. His teacher is unimaginative and humorless and school is unbearably boring. One day, Josh simply walks out. His parents agree to a temporary leave of absence while his mother looks for a new school, and Josh begins to work with Rafferty, a retired man who cares for injured birds.

Even here, Josh cannot escape the fact of cruelty, and begins to face his own responsibility to accept it and go on in spite of it.

Tolan writes with perception of the feelings of a highly gifted child who does not fit, describing both his stress and the reactions and concern of the adults around him. This book will invite discussion of sensitivity in people and sensitivity to the environment. It will give parents and teachers insight into the feelings of children like Josh that may surprise them.

Aloneness. Why does Josh leave school? Do you understand how he felt? Have you ever known anyone else you think might have felt that way? What clues do you have that make you think so? If such a person cannot leave school, how else can he or she deal with the situation? Is it all right that Josh does not have close friends of his own age? Describe Josh as you think he will be when he is an adult.

Identity. Why is Josh so comfortable with Rafferty and his parents, but not with classmates? Does this bother him? What will he be like when he is grown up?

Using ability. What effect will dropping out of school have on Josh's ability to make good use of his intelligence? What responsibility (if any) does a bright person have to use his or her intelligence? Who determines what is a "good" use of intelligence? In making that decision for yourself, what factors would you consider?

Ward, Lynd. *The Silver Pony.* Boston: Houghton Mifflin, 1973.

Fully annotated in the Early Elementary section, this book can be used with older elementary children, too. The stories they tell about the pictures should be more detailed than those of younger children.

Creativity; Introversion. Discussion can focus on the loneliness of each child the boy visits and what compensations they may have. Children of this age can develop an appreciation of the fact that there are other people like them in the world, even though they may not live nearby. As they grow older, they will have opportunites to meet more people like them.

Yolen, Jane. *The Boy Who Had Wings.* Illustrated by Helga Aichinger. New York: Crowell, 1974.

In ancient Thessaly, Actos is born with wings. His father is ashamed of so different a child, and his mother makes a cape to hide the wings. Actos grows up isolated from other children, never attempting to fly or to let others know he has wings. Then his father is trapped in a snowstorm, and Actos, using his wings at last, is the only one who can find and rescue him. Still his family ignores him, until finally his wings shrivel and drop away—but Actos remembers always the soaring freedom of flight.

The author writes that the inspiration for this story is both mythological and autobiographical. "It might also serve as biography for anyone who has ever been blessed with a gift—whether of writing, painting, or the like. For to be different . . . is not an easy thing when, as a child, you are longing to be like everyone else. I think I have been much luckier than Actos. Though there were times when I would have loved to be average, not a writer, I neither lost my wings nor gave them away. And now that I know that my writing can bring pleasure to others . . . I am grateful and proud of my wings."

Identity. This picture book is recommended here for older children who can discuss symbolism. What different kinds of wings are people born with? How do parents and others avoid or hide a child's wings? What are your wings?

Using ability. What happens to a person who never uses his wings? How can people grow up without losing their wings or giving them away? What adults do you know who only learned to use and enjoy their wings in adulthood—like the author? What are you doing to keep your wings?

Yolen, Jane. *The Sultan's Perfect Tree.* Illustrated with etchings by Barbara Garrison. New York: Parents' Magazine Press, 1977.

The sultan loves perfection, and when a strong wind blows leaves from his perfect tree, ruining its beauty in his eyes, he commands an artist to paint the perfect tree on a screen set before the window. The sultan is satisfied until winter, then until spring—for each season the artist is asked to paint the perfect tree. Finally, the sultan demands an autumn tree, bending and swaying under the weight of its fruit. The artist sighs—he is not a god; he cannot paint movement. Perfection does not move, does not grow. And so the sultan learns to see the beauty in an imperfect, living, changing tree. As the servant girl says, "to be perfect means the end of growing."

Perfectionism. This lovely picture book could be used with early elementary children to introduce the idea of perfectionism,

300

and with older children for a fuller discussion. What do they know that is living, growing, changing, not perfect—and a source of delight? A pet, a sibling, a friend? Parents can point out ways in which they themselves are still growing, not perfect. The Latin origin of "perfect" means "complete"—in what ways is the child still growing, not complete? What are the hazards of perfectionism, of striving for completion as a primary goal?

Yolen, Jane. *Bird Watch: A Book of Poetry*. Illustrated by Ted Lewin. New York: Philomel, 1990.

Yolen's poems about birds reflect varying moods, including humor, thoughts on her preference for winter birds over Christmas lights, and acceptance of the death of a bird that flew into a window. Yolen's poetry, like her prose, gives a child a new way to think about something.

Drive to understand. A final page identifies each bird in the poems and illustrations, with habits and habitats.

Middle School

Grades Six to Eight

Abeel, Samantha. *Reach for the Moon*. Illustrated by Charles R. Murphy. Duluth: Pfeiffer-Hamilton, 1994.

Inspired by the works of an established artist, thirteen-year-old Samantha Abeel has responded with moving, insightful poetry and prose. Charles Murphy's watercolors are realistic but often have mystical overtones; Abeel's writings tell the story or reflect the emotion she perceives in each painting.

The story of how this book came to be is as inspirational as the book itself. Samantha Abeel is not only gifted but also learning-disabled. For the first years of schooling, her inability to comprehend numbers, tell time or make change overshadowed her insight and her verbal gifts. Recognizing Samantha's writing talent, her seventh grade English teacher, Roberta Williams, chose to encourage her strength and to overlook difficulties with spelling, verb tenses, and due dates. At the request of Elizabeth Abeel, Samantha's mother (herself an artist), Williams arranged a summer writing program for Samantha, based on the art of family friend Charles Murphy. The result is not only this book; it is also a success story for Samantha and a demonstration of what can happen when schools, parents, and mentors work together on behalf of a child who does not fit the mold.

Differentness; *Using ability*.

Adderholdt-Elliott, Miriam. *Perfectionism: What's Bad about Being Too Good*. Illustrated by Caroline Price. Minneapolis: Free Spirit, 1987.

Many gifted teenagers are victims of perfectionism, harboring so strong a desire to do everything perfectly that they consider second place or a *B* a failure. Some go so far as to avoid risking that failure by refusing to accept a new challenge or to take an advanced course.

Perfectionism speaks to these students, describing its effects on mind, body, and relationships and then prescribing practical steps toward becoming more realistic about expectations. Counselors, teachers, and librarians will find the book a useful tool for school-based discussions on giftedness, and parents can use it effectively at home. The insights it offers are as important for adults working with gifted youngsters as for the students themselves.

Perfectionism; *Using ability*.

Alexander, Lloyd. *Westmark*. New York: Dutton, 1981. (A trilogy including *The Kestrel*, 1982; and *The Beggar Queen*, 1984.)

A printer's apprentice who flees when his master's press is destroyed as a result of political upheaval, Theo meets a rich assortment of characters in quick succession: a street urchin; two "river rats"; a charlatan and his sidekick, a dwarf; revolutionary students, a cartoonist and a thief; courtiers and royalty—all of whom reappear as the trilogy unfolds. Ruled by a weak king who is controlled by a power-hungry chief minister, Westmark falls into war with a neighboring kingdom as civil unrest builds. The street urchin, Mickle, learns she is Westmark's princess, and Theo grows to love Mickle while he also joins the revolutionary students who help Mickle's army to defend Westmark from the neighboring Regian army. Far from staying in the safety of the palace, Mickle proves to be a fine general. When the war against the Regians is won, however, she and Theo must address the civil unrest within Westmark and a further threat from the exiled chief minister.

This trilogy traces Theo's growth from a young and naive printer's devil to a thoughtful, complex young man who recognizes and regrets his own potential for violence. His loyalties are divided first between the monarch and the rebels who struggle for a republic, then between his natural pacifism and the raging desire for vengeance that rises when a friend is killed. At the same time he tries to understand his motivations—to please one of the leaders, Justin, or to follow his own inner commands.

The writing is deceptively simple, and the plot perhaps too dependent on coincidences, but the ideas are demanding and require a thoughtful response. Intellectual challenge is also provided by frequent shifts in locale as different facets of the story come into play.

Drive to understand. Discussion related to intellectual curiosity will view the story from a socio-political level, looking, for example, at the causes of political unrest. Alexander has based his story on the history of the French Revolution. What are the similarities between pre-revolutionary France and Westmark? Why is Westmark ripe for rebellion?

Identity; Intensity. Readers can interpret the story at a personal level, exploring the development of Theo's character as he grows. His need to prove himself leads to what results for himself? For others?

Moral concerns. What does Theo learn as he struggles with the pacifist and the warrior within his character? What contradictory values or impulses do you recognize within yourself? What can you learn from Theo's experience?

Using ability. How can Florian so steadfastly oppose his background, giving up his birthright? What motivates him?

Anno, Mitsumasa. *Anno's Medieval World.* New York: Philomel, 1979.

With text and pictures, Anno presents the religious beliefs and superstitions that made up the medieval world view. The infant sciences of the time were not understood by many people, and their message was frightening: nothing less than the rejection of age-old convictions about how the world was structured. Anno mentions the burning at the stake of Bruno, who espoused

Copernicus's theory of the universe, and the recanting of Galileo. The book ends with adventurers sailing off to learn whether the world is indeed round.

This book could be used as the basis for discussion not only of the medieval world, the Ptolemaic and Copernican theories, and the blend of science and culture, but also of how it feels to know, as Galileo did, a truth that others cannot yet recognize. In an author's note, Anno speaks of our ability (or lack of it) to feel what Bruno or Galileo felt, having knowledge and unable to convince others of its truth. ". . . it troubles me," Anno says, "to hear it said, lightly and without any feeling, 'The world is round and it moves.'" Through discussion of this book, children can gain appreciation of how hard-won that knowledge is, as Anno hoped.

Drive to understand. How would it feel to live in a world where it is dangerous to have or seek scientific knowledge? Knowledge of any kind? Why is it important for scholars to be able to speak about what they learn, even if it is not popular?

As a picture book, this appears to be for young children, but the ideas can profitably be explored by students of middle school age. Questions for this age might include the following: What cherished beliefs of ours are being called into question by new developments, not necessarily scientific? Are ideas still dangerous? Who are present-day Brunos and Galileos?

Arkin, Alan. *The Lemming Condition.* Illustrated by Joan Sandin. New York: Harper and Row, 1976.

On the day of the great leap into the sea, a lemming named Bubber talks to his friend Crow, who raises questions Bubber can't answer: *Why* would they jump into the water? Can they swim? In his confusion, Bubber turns to Arnold, a lemming he has always admired, and finds Arnold uninterested in the questions. His Uncle Claude assures him there is no problem; it's just something lemmings do. Seeing that he will not learn more from a fellow lemming, Bubber returns to Crow, who flies him to a pond so he can test how water feels. When he realizes he cannot swim, a sense of doom overtakes Bubber. An eccentric old lemming reassures him, saying the race to the sea won't happen because lemmings can't agree on anything: "You couldn't get an agreement on what time to have lunch, never mind a mass suicide." When the run begins, Bubber joins it, more afraid of isolation than of the consequences of the run to the sea, and feeling close to other lemmings for the first time in his life. But when the ocean looms ahead, Bubber stops and hides among rocks so the tide of lemmings will not carry him with it. The next morning he returns to the burrows, where he finds a few surviving baby lemmings who have slept through the run. Foreseeing that the whole process will begin anew with them, Bubber passes by, heading east away from the ocean and telling the young ones he is not a lemming anymore. "What are you then?" they ask. "I'll let you know when I find out," Bubber answers.

Aloneness; *Differentness*. *The Lemming Condition* is a good starting point for discussion of the importance of standing alone and doing your own thinking. Explore the role of each character and what they represent: Arnold, the blindly-followed leader; the old lemming, an ineffective rebel; Crow, the questioner; Bubber, the young seeker. Who are their counterparts in a real-life scenario of following the crowd without thinking? What makes Bubber stop running? Did he make the right decision? Why?

Identity. Could you play the role of the Crow—the questioner—for yourself? If not, who plays it for you? Consider how difficult life will be for Bubber alone. How hard would life be if you made Bubber's choice? Would it be worth it? Where would you find help?

Avi. *The Fighting Ground*. New York: Lippincott, 1984.

Jonathan is thirteen, tilling the fields with his father near Trenton, New Jersey, when the bell from the tavern a mile and a half distant sounds an alarm. It's April 3, 1778; his father is recovering from a war wound, and Jonathan is sent to learn the news—but then, both parents order, he is to return home immediately. Learning that fifteen Hessians are marching from Pennington, and eager to fight, Jonathan disregards his parents' directive and joins the hastily-gathered band of colonists under command of a zealous and not entirely trusted corporal. All is confusion when they meet the enemy on the road; Jonathan flees and is captured by three Hessians. Neither Jonathan nor they know who won the battle, and although they speak only German (translated in the back of the book), making verbal communication impossible, Jonathan begins to feel a degree of comfort with them. They find an abandoned farmhouse for shelter, and when Jonathan enters a shed for a bucket to milk the cow, he discovers a young child, a boy who will not speak to Jonathan but who does, when

Jonathan asks "Mama?," point to where his parents lie shot. In the night, as the Hessians sleep, Jonathan escapes with the boy and runs through darkness, stumbling upon the remnants of the colonial band. A Frenchman in the group speaks to the child, who in a torrent of French tells of his parents' deaths and shrinks from the Corporal, who wants to return to the house to kill the Hessians. The Corporal insists that Jonathan lead the way, but it becomes clear that the Corporal has been there before. It was he who killed the boy's parents because they were informers. In an agony of indecision Jonathan switches loyalties from the Corporal to the Hessians and back, but he is finally forced at gunpoint to aid in the killing of the Hessians. He returns home just twenty-four hours after he left, changed forever.

Chapters are titled by the time, highlighting the brevity of this period that changes Jonathan's life. There is a complete lack of the glory Jonathan had expected; only fear and confusion, and uncertainty as to what the colonists are doing, and why. Germans, Americans, and French are all good and bad by turns—human, sympathetic characters with flaws. Avi has written a story of how war takes over, ignoring human values.

Drive to understand. Discuss the difference between what Jonathan expected and what he found. How does the reality of Jonathan's experience square with what we see of war—or any kind of violence—on television? Analyze how representatives of each nationality are admirable and despicable. What is Avi saying by depicting them in this way?

Moral concerns. How did Jonathan's view of his father change? Did any of your views change as a result of reading this book? Should the Revolutionary War have been fought? Were there other ways of settling the issues? Are there now?

Avi. *The True Confessions of Charlotte Doyle*. Illustrated by Ruth Murray. New York: Orchard Books, 1990.

In the summer of 1832, thirteen-year-old Charlotte Doyle boards the Seahawk in Liverpool to rejoin her family in Providence. Though her father had planned carefully so that she would be accompanied, the other passengers do not arrive. Charlotte, a young lady taught to obey her elders and avoid informal contact with servants, sails with only Captain Jaggery and his rough, rebellious crew for company. She soon realizes that she is in grave danger, and must decide where her loyalties lie.

Because she has to, she learns to be a sailor, doing so well that she earns the crew's respect. The Charlotte Doyle who disembarks in Providence in August is very different from the girl who had left the Barrington School for Better Girls in June.

Appealing to both boys and girls, Charlotte's story is much more than good mystery and adventure, although it is certainly that. Charlotte must change internally, without guidance or model, in order to survive. When she joins her family she is expected to change again, a challenge she will not accept.

Arrogance. Charlotte would not have called herself arrogant, but readers of her story might. What role does arrogance play in her decisions?

Drive to understand. Avi's story offers readers a compelling picture of life in the early 19th century, providing plenty of opportunity for comparisons and further exploration.

Identity. Discussion can center around Charlotte's decisions. Why would she adapt to the sailors' life, yet be unwilling to re-adapt to her family? Which is more truly Charlotte, and why? In ten years, will Charlotte have one life or the other, or a blend? If a blend, describe it.

Relationships with others. What can you learn from Charlotte's ability to get along with the sailors?

Using ability. How would the social rules of her time affect Charlotte's future? Are there situations now that cause people to straddle two lives, two expressions of themselves? How is it done? Is it healthy for them?

Bang, Molly. *Tye May and the Magic Brush.* (Adapted from the Chinese.) New York: Greenwillow, 1981.

This provocative picture book is fully described in the Early Elementary section. Older students, who are coming to terms with the need to accept and use their abilities, can return to this picture book to discuss the magic brush as a metaphor for talent.

Using ability. How does one who has special talents use them wisely? How can we balance giving to others and using our gifts for our own pleasure? Would we make the same choice that Tye May did? What would be the factors in our decision?

Bond, Nancy. *A String in the Harp.* New York: Atheneum, 1977.

Unhappily spending a year in Wales while his father teaches at the University of Aberystwyth, Peter Morgan finds on the seacoast a strange silver object—a tuning key for a harp. The key sings to him, enabling him to see events that happened hundreds of years ago, scenes which eventually Peter realizes are from the life of the 6th Century Welsh bard, Taliesin, to whom the key belonged. As Peter concentrates on Taliesin's story he becomes more distant from his family; his father and sisters, Becky and Jen, become more concerned about him. At last, with his sisters' support, Peter realizes what he must do about the key, and the family is reunited.

The fantasy story of Peter's visions of Taliesin is convincingly counterbalanced by the reality of the area of Wales in which the Morgans live, and the Welsh people who become their friends. Bond's sense for the setting—both geographical and psychological—is sure, and readers will feel that they have gained some important knowledge about the essence of Wales.

Aloneness. Jen thinks perhaps Gwilym isn't "solitary from choice." Why then is he solitary? Is his aloneness something to worry about? If so, what should Gwilym do to improve the situation? What should others do to help him?

Drive to understand. This book is part realism, part fantasy. How can you balance the rational and irrational aspects of the story?

Identity. What differences are there in Jen's and Becky's responses to Peter's behavior? How do they correspond to the reactions of Dr. Owen and Dr. Rhys? Why do these people respond so differently?

Cole, Brock. *The Goats*. New York: Garrar, Straus, and Giroux, 1987.

They are called goats because they are scapegoats, the brunt of a cruel trick at an exclusive but poorly supervised summer camp. Left alone at night on an island, the boy and girl make their way to the mainland and to an empty cabin. They determine never to return to the camp, and for three days they avoid the searchers. During this time they fall in with a group at another summer camp, and these campers treat them with kindness and understanding. They learn to care for and depend on each other, building feelings of trust neither one has known before.

They see themselves as "socially retarded for my age," as the girl puts it, because they do not fit in, but in a short time they learn to relate well to each other—proving to themselves and demonstrating to the reader that those who don't fit in with the crowd do very well if they can find just one person to whom they can talk freely.

Aloneness. To build an understanding of why some people are isolated by the cruelty of others, discuss scapegoating. Why is it that some people are "goats"? What causes a group—a neighborhood, school, or nation—to find goats? What characteristics make individuals vulnerable, likely to become goats? Consider the consequences of scapegoating: What characteristics of scapegoated individuals might make them valuable to society? What affect will this incident have on Laura and Howie as they grow older, and in their adult lives? What changes will have occurred in them? How will it affect their personalities, if at all? What affect will it have, if any, on what they contribute to society? To discuss scapegoating at a personal level, inquire: Do you know any goats? Can you see beneath the surface to what they have to offer? Do you ever see yourself as a goat? How can you grow beyond it?

Relationships with others. To use this book to help children discover ways to cope with beign alone, ask: Are some people "socially retarded" for their age, as Laura says she is? If so, how does this happen and what can one do about it? What was the difference that made the second set of campers kind to Laura and Howie? What did Laura and Howie learn that would help them get along better with others?

Conford, Ellen. *And This Is Laura*. Boston: Little, Brown, 1977.
Everyone in Laura's family has a special talent except Laura. Even when she learns that she is psychic and gives a credible performance as the second lead in a school play on short notice, her feelings of being ordinary and therefore unworthy persist. When she finally expresses her sense of inadequacy to her parents, they point out that she is an all-A student. They both explain that she is valuable to them as a person, not for her gifts. Her gifts are for her to enjoy, not for them to use as a basis for loving her.

Laura is an example of a sibling unsure of where she fits in a gifted family. Not recognizing or appreciating her own talents until circumstances or other people point them out, she is like many gifted girls who minimize the quality and importance of their abilities, limiting what they accomplish because of a low self-concept.

Identity. In what different ways does Laura recognize each of her gifts?

Relationships with others. If you were Laura, would you be convinced by her parents' reasons for loving her? Why or why not? Why is it especially difficult for people who have a lot of talent to know why other poeple like them?

Using ability. What difference will it make to Laura to have learned about her ability? What difference will it make to others?

Cooper, Susan. *The Dark is Rising*. Illustrated by Alan E. Cober. New York: Atheneum, 1974.

On his eleventh birthday Will Stanton learns that he is one of the Old Ones, called to struggle through the ages against the Dark. The Dark is rising this Christmas season, in one of a series of attempts to dominate the world. Will's task is to search for the six Signs that the Old Ones will need in the final battle against the Dark. His search takes him to distant places and bygone centuries, while he learns under the tutelage of Merriman Lyon to use the powers of the Old Ones. Throughout, he remains an eleven-year-old boy, living in the warmth of a large family.

Drive to understand. A Newbery Honor Book, this well-written fantasy is excellent for good readers, challenging in its structure as Will travels from one century to another and meets some of the same characters in each.

Cresswell, Helen. *Ordinary Jack*. New York: Macmillan, 1977.

Jack is the only ordinary member of the extraordinary Bagthorpe family. Father writes scripts for BBC, Mother writes an advice column, and siblings William, Tess, and Rosie all have several "strings to their bows," a circumstance which is highly valued in the Bagthorpe clan. With Grandma (irascible), Grandpa (selectively deaf), Uncle Parker and Aunt Celia (poet and potter) and their daughter Daisy (arsonist), life is always interesting if not chaotic. Jack's only claim to fame is his hapless dog, Zero. Uncle Parker decides that Jack will become known as a Prophet and helps him set this up, advising Jack to stage Mysterious Impressions and Visions, building to Rosie's birthday party, when the vision of the red and white bubble and the Great Brown Bear comes true.

The zany humor is sure to appeal to bright readers. In addition to good characterization and dialogue, *Ordinary Jack* provides some insights into the quirks—good and bad—of creative people.

Identity. This book is for sheer fun. It would be difficult to base a serious discussion on it, but it can provide a way of laughing with Jack as he faces the universal dilemma of finding his niche.

Danziger, Paula. *The Cat Ate My Gymsuit.* New York: Dell, 1974.

Shy, overweight Marcy Lewis is propelled into the small group of student leaders when a favorite teacher is dismissed and Marcy proves her ability and willingness to speak out in the effort to have the teacher reinstated. To her amazement, Marcy finds that Joel, the smartest, most self-assured boy in the class, likes her—and that Joel's family life, like hers, is not entirely happy. As the students work together they come into conflict with some of the adult community, including Marcy's father, but Marcy's self-confidence grows.

It may be necessary to point out the copyright date and give some background on Marcy's mother's discomfort with speaking her own mind, since she may not seem credible to some readers, but that will not be a major problem for students. The characters line up so clearly on one side or other of the issue of firing the teacher that it is easy to discuss the real theme of the book: standing up for one's own beliefs against following the majority, a good theme for middle school students to consider.

Aloneness. How does one decide when to be part of the majority, and when to be different? Is it worthwhile to be different? For Marcy? For you? Under what circumstances?

Identity. What makes shy Marcy speak up when Mr. Stone announces Ms. Finney's leaving? Why is Joel so self-confident? What does he mean when he says that when he grows up he wants to be Joel Anderson?

Relationships with others. Marcy finds herself in a situation that gives her a chance to know other students better and gives them a chance to know her. How does that happen? What role does Marcy play in making it happen? In your own situation, what could you do to make it happen if you needed to? What are the rewards?

Dickinson, Peter. *Eva.* New York: Delacorte, 1988.

Eva Adamson is fourteen, living in a future when burgeoning population has caused humans to take over the earth, crowded into high rise buildings in sprawling cities and rarely seeing a tree or an animal. Her father does research with the few remaining chimpanzees, all in captivity, and when Eva is critically injured in an accident her parents consent to an experimental attempt to save her life—transplanting Eva's brain into the body of a chimpanzee named Kelly. Her human mind survives but receives some of Kelly's genetic memory, and Eva becomes more comfortable in social groupings of chimps than of humans. Persuaded that humans are giving up—social systems are failing, no one is going into research, long-term planning has lost its viability—a brilliant young rebel arranges for Eva and a group of chimps to escape to one of the few remaining natural tropical forests.

Several controversial and discussable themes permeate this disturbing book: the effects of overpopulation on the earth's ecology, the ethical questions of the use of animals in research, the impact of the media on human initiative, the loss of will to communal progress.

Drive to understand. The basic question of the book concerns what it is to be human. Have we somehow gone beyond the best that is human, to our detriment? Has the human race peaked?

Moral concerns. If we could start over again, as Eva's chimps may, what changes would you make? In history? In human nature? In what ways do we have the potential to make these changes? How can we prevent, even now, the future Dickinson projects?

Dixon, Paige. *May I Cross Your Golden River?* New York: Atheneum, 1979.

When he is 18, Jordan Phillips learns that the uncharacteristic weakness in his wrist and knee signal the onset of amyotrophic lateral sclerosis, the fatal muscular degeneration known as Lou Gehrig's disease. Jordan and his large and loving family must face his death within a matter of months. They do so with sensitivity, humor, and a heart-warming support for one another and for Jordan that never becomes sentimental or maudlin.

Dixon has created a remarkable family unit in which each member actively pursues his or her own talents while contributing uniquely to Jordan's care. The humor in the book, intelligent and original, is especially fine. Jordan and his family use a variety of elements of life to come to terms with death. For Jordan, the natural beauty of his Colorado home plays a significant part. The birth of his nephew, Jordan's godson, implies what Jordan calls the going-on-ness of life.

The book provides an opportunity to consider the acceptance of death and the value of life, and the warm family life provides both emotional depth and a safe environment for pondering these themes—so difficult to grasp, especially for teenagers. Far from depressing, this is rather an uplifting and triumphant book.

Drive to understand. How has the book helped you to think about death? To develop new values in life? Who is your favorite character, and why? What has the book added to your thinking about the importance of caring for other people?

Douglass, Frederick. *Narrative of the Life of Frederick Douglass, an American Slave.* New York: New American Library, 1968. (Written in 1845.)

Born a slave in Maryland in 1818, Frederick Douglass escaped to the north twenty years later. He had taught himself to read and write but was otherwise uneducated. Nevertheless, leaders of the abolitionist movement recognized his intelligence and eloquence, and by 1841 he was a public speaker for their cause. Later he became Recorder of Deeds for the District of Columbia and United States Minister to Haiti. This narrative is the story of his years in slavery, telling how he was passed from one owner to another, how and why he was beaten, what happened to his family and friends, and how a kind mistress taught him the alphabet and a few words before her husband forbade her to continue, saying that reading would make him unfit to be a slave—thereby firing in Frederick the determination to learn to read. The fact that he gives no details of his escape, fearing that the information would close the route to freedom for fellow slaves, creates for the modern reader a startling sense of immediacy and authenticity.

Drive to understand; Moral concerns. The contrast between the appalling descriptions of slavery and the clear evidence of Frederick's sensitivity, intellect, and ability to articulate epxeriences and feelings is deeply moving. The book is valuable both for understanding slavery and as the autobiography of a gifted writer who fought against overwhelming odds to realize his capacities.

Ferris, Jeri. *Native American Doctor: The Story of Susan LaFlesche Picotte*. Minneapolis: Carolrhoda Books, 1991.

Susan LaFlesche (1865-1915), daughter of Omaha Chief Iron Eye, was sent to the Elizabeth Institute for Young Ladies in Elizabeth, New Jersey; to the Hampton Institute in Virginia; and to Women's Medical College in Philadelphia. She returned to the Omaha reservation in Nebraska to work as doctor, interpreter, and political leader for her people. In telling Susan's story, Ferris includes much information about Native Americans' difficult transition from traditional to European ways, and she gives an unflinching portrayal of white domination, including the illegal purchase of native land (making farming impossible for Native Americans) and the greed-motivated sale of alcohol.

Not fictionalized, this is a biography, with historical records used as sources for quotations. The illustrations are photographs taken during Susan's lifetime.

Using ability. Susan had many advantages, but she also faced many obstacles. What personal qualities helped her overcome them in order to make good use of her abilities and her opportunities? What elements in her environment, family, and background were helpful to her? If you had been Susan, what would have been most difficult for you? How would you have handled it?

Fox, Paula. *The Village By the Sea*. New York: Orchard Books, 1988.

While her father has heart surgery, ten-year-old Emma is sent to stay with his sister, Aunt Bea, and her husband, Uncle Crispin. They live on Long Island in a house on the shore, a childless house where Emma is lonely until she meets Bertie, the girl next door. Emma and Bertie spend days building a village from shells, twigs, anything natural they find on the beach. Emma's stay remains difficult because of Aunt Bea, who is cold and unpredictable—not at all like Emma's father, Bea's much younger half-brother. Emma gradually pieces the family story together in conversations with family members and Bertie, and is finally able to forgive even Aunt Bea's most incomprehensible act.

The challenge in this book is the psychological study of Aunt Bea—and the requirement that the reader, too, piece together the family story from clues dropped in conversation. The tension and suspense are psychological—this is an introspective mystery, not an action book; it is about getting along with others by developing a sophisticated understanding of human behavior.

Relationships with others. Why is Aunt Bea hard to get along with? Could you have forgiven Aunt Bea as Emma does? If so, what kind of thinking and understanding would lead you to forgive her? What examples of understanding and forgiveness do you see in the people around you? Adults? Children? Can you remember a time when understanding a destructive act helped you to withhold anger?

Galbraith, Judy. *The Gifted Kids Survival Guide for Ages 11 to 18.* Minneapolis: Free Spirit, 1983.

Written for gifted students from ages 11 to 18, this book speaks directly to junior and senior high school students. Compiling contributions from over 300 gifted teenagers, the author describes the frustrations of growing up gifted and offers suggestions for dealing with them: what to do when bored in class, tips for making friends, steps to improve educational opportunities, how to handle stress, and techniques for setting goals. With extensive use of eye-catching graphics and a fast-paced, breezy style, the book will appeal to teenagers.

There is a wealth of material for discussion. One approach would be to choose a paragraph of particular relevance and ask general questions: What do you think of this? Is this a problem for you? Have you tried this? How did it work?

Differentness; Identity. For discussions to clarify self-concept, the first five sections of the book will be useful since they all deal with identification of the gifted.

Relationships with others. To build discussion of getting along with others, use the two sections on friends, the one on teasing, and the one on getting along with parents.

Using ability. Sections of the book pertaining to full use of one's potential are those on how to make school more challenging, perfectionism, stress, and goal setting.

Gardam, Jane. *Bilgewater.* New York: Willow Books, 1977.

Marigold, nicknamed Bilgewater, grows up in an isolated environment: the English boys' boarding school where her widowed father is a master. Her best friends are the other masters—who are her father's friends—and Paula, the matron who is a substitute mother for her. Dyslexia adds to her isolation and masks her intelligence for years. By the time she is 17, she has overcome it and is suddenly encouraged to take the entrance exams for Oxford and Cambridge. At the same time a childhood friend returns and draws her into a social life, and two of the boarding school boys begin to notice her, with mixed results. All of this plays a significant role in her slowly growing self-confidence. Marigold, her father, and Paula are memorable individuals, and the surprise ending contributes to a book well worth reading.

The many British terms add to the challenge and interest without being a barrier to good reading. Characters and setting are well drawn, and Marigold's intelligence and wit come through plainly—to the reader, if not to her.

Aloneness. Marigold had more time alone as she was growing up than most children have. How was this an advantage to her? What would she have said if you had asked her this question when she was 15 or 16? What would she say now?

Identity. How does Marigold's self-concept affect her behavior? How accurate is it? Does she like herself? Do you like her? Why or why not? What do Terrapin and Boakes see in her? How does her appearance affect the kind of person she becomes? How does our appearance, or our perception of it, affect the kind of people we all become? How do all of these questions apply to you?

Relationships with others. How did Marigold make it difficult for other people to know her? How do we all do that? What are the consequences? What are some remedies?

Garfield, Leon. *Smith*. Illustrated by Antony Maitland. New York: Pantheon, 1967.

A street urchin and pickpocket in 18th century London, Smith steals a document from a man who is then murdered by men seeking the document Smith has pilfered, but which he cannot read. The murderers pursue Smith. In his flight, he meets and guides home a blind judge who takes Smith into his home. The suitor of the judge's daughter accuses Smith of the murder, and Smith goes to Newgate Prison. With the suitor's help, Smith escapes, but he has been led into a trap. As Smith tries to protect his friend the judge, he discovers that he is being betrayed by a highwayman he has always admired. Eventually the tangle of shifting friends and enemies is straightened out, the suspense lasting until the very end.

Drive to understand. This exciting murder mystery, like all of Garfield's work, is well-written, challenging fare for good readers. Garfield provides a far better picture of the dangerous realities of the streets and highways in 18th century England than any nonfiction description could. Most of the characters are rascals or worse, presented sympathetically but with no excuses offered for their behavior—good background for discussion of the social implications of poverty and the diversity of human character.

Garner, Alan. *The Stone Book.* London: Collins, 1976.

Mary takes a lunch to her stonemason father, climbing to the pinnacle of a church steeple to give it to him. Unable to attend school, she has not learned to read, but she asks him for a book. That evening, her father takes her to a mine, leading her into the hill and directing her to follow a path too narrow for him, as his father had directed him when he was still small enough to go. There Mary learns from markings on the rock something of her own heritage. Then he carves her a book of stone in which her imagination can roam free. Although Mary cannot read, it is clear that her mind is open to wonder, as is her father's, in spite of the narrowness of their existence.

The first of four books about four generations of a family living near Manchester, England, this is a good introduction to the atmosphere and literary style of Garner's books. Tension and mood build quickly through spare, precise language. Much is felt and suggested but left unsaid between the characters and for the reader.

Creativity; Using ability. This is a book to ponder more than to discuss. Mary travels to height and depth. It is in depth and silence that she learns the most. What is the relationship between imagination, creativity, the spirit of wonder—and formal education? What has her father given to Mary? What experience of yours compares?

Identity. Why is knowing our family history part of determining who we are? What difference will it make to Mary?

Greene, Bette. *Summer of My German Soldier*. New York: Dial, 1973.

Patty Bergen's parents are cold and distant, her father physically abusive to her. Living in a small Arkansas town during World War II, the twelve-year-old experiences the loneliness that results from this emotionally barren home, as well as from the lack of friends to match her own highly verbal, quick-thinking nature. Only when visiting her maternal grandparents in Memphis, where the family's Jewish traditions are honored, does Patty feel at home. When Anton Reiker, a German soldier, escapes from a nearby prisoner of war camp, Patty hides him in the apartment above the Bergen garage. The son of a history professor at the University of Goettingen, Anton had been a medical student in Germany before the war. He sees both beauty and value in Patty, and he is the first person she has met whose wide-ranging interests and good educational background provide companionship for her. Anton risks his safety in a bid to protect Patty from her father's beating, but he must leave to avoid detection and danger for Patty and Ruth, the family housekeeper who also protects Patty.

This book offers many themes for discussion: physical abuse, low self-esteem in both Patty and her father, the importance to Patty of Anton's caring for her and seeing good in her, and the distinction that must be made between "German" and "Nazi." And, of course, prejudice—against Germans, Negroes, and Jews. Of all the characters in the book, Anton—the German soldier, the enemy, the POW—and Ruth, the housekeeper, are the most prejudice-free, and the most sympathetic.

Aloneness. What qualities set Patty apart from others in the story? Why do some people see good in her? Why do others not? How do the reactions of others determine Patty's behavior? In what ways is she independent of their reactions? What is the basis of the courage that enables her to hide a POW?

Drive to understand. Explore the story of Anton's father's choice to be quiet and live—the evidence that there was opposition in Germany to Hitler's military policies.

Moral concerns. Consider the prejudice in the story against Germans, Jew, and Negroes. Who is prejudiced against whom? Explain why.

Hahn, Mary Downing. *Daphne's Book*. New York: Clarion, 1983.

Jessica is dismayed when her seventh grade English teacher pairs her with Daphne in a book writing and illustrating contest, but Mr. O'Brien will not change his mind. Daphne is the best artist and Jessica the best writer in the class, and together he expects they will produce something really good. Jessica is losing her friendship with Tracey, and she is convinced that working with the silent and unpopular Daphne will accelerate that loss. As she gets to know Daphne, however, Jessica finds herself more comfortable with her than she was with Tracey. The two girls allow their imaginations to work, creating a fantasy world out of which comes their book. As their friendship grows, Jessica visits Daphne at the home she shares with her younger sister Hope and their aging grandmother. The grandmother's health and mental state are rapidly deteriorating, but Daphne fears that she and Hope will be sent to an orphanage if anyone knows this. Finally the situation becomes so bad that Jessica tells her mother, breaking her promise to Daphne. Daphne's grandmother is sent to a hospital, where she dies, and Daphne and Hope go to a children's home. Daphne and Jessica are reconciled when Jessica visits to tell Daphne their book has won the contest, and learns that Daphne and Hope will go to live with relatives of their mother whom the social worker has located.

The behavior of Daphne's grandmother and the old house in which Daphne lives are in disturbing contrast to Jessica's family, which is comfortable and stable even though her parents are divorced and her mother about to remarry. Despite the differences, Jessica and Daphne come together because they find they can talk to each other better than to anyone else. They are alone but for this one friendship, and for the moment, it is enough.

Aloneness. What reasons might Mr. O'Brien have for pairing Jessica and Daphne, other than their talent? Why are they not popular? What qualities do they have that compensate for lack of popularity? Predict their futures.

Relationships with others. Why are Jessica and Tracey moving apart? Why does Jessica want to hide her growing friendship with Daphne? What qualities in Jessica help her to be able to learn from this situation? In Jessica and Daphne's friendship, what does each girl learn about herself? Who benefits most from the relationship?

Hamilton, Virginia. *The Planet of Junior Brown.* New York: Dell, 1971.

Junior Brown is obese, an artist and a musician. The adults in his life are his mother (who wants Junior to be cultured but is not able to understand his art or listen to his music), his piano teacher (who is demented, but Junior cannot afford to recognize that), his absent father, and Mr. Pool, the school janitor. There is also Buddy, a fellow student who has no family and who is part of an underground network that helps homeless boys to survive in New York City. Buddy and Mr. Pool watch Junior slip toward insanity, and they are able to begin to help him back to reality.

This well-written book offers challenging reading and at least two themes that would be useful for gifted students to discuss: the frustration of Junior's talent, symbolized by the silent pianos; and the challenge of getting along with others, exemplified by Buddy, a leader who progresses from teaching his boys to live for themselves to teaching them to live for others. In spite of his strength, it is clear that Buddy also needs help—a reminder that we are interdependent, not self-sufficient.

Relationships with others. Why does Junior need Buddy? What does he offer to Buddy? How do Nightman and Franklin help each other? Identify a leader whom you follow. What do you offer to that person?

Using ability. What does Junior need in order to to use his artistic and musical talents? What does Buddy need?

Hentoff, Nat. *Jazz Country.* New York: Harper & Row, 1965.

Tom Curtis is sixteen, the son of a prominent New York corporate lawyer. He wants to be a jazz musician, perhaps more than he wants to go to college, but when he attempts to get into the real world of jazz he is told that he has not paid his dues, that his life has been too easy, too white. Nevertheless, the black musicians see promise in Tom, and he is able to learn from them, not only about music but about the realities of life as a jazzman. Tom finally faces the question of college versus jazz when he is invited to join a band.

The references to the mid-60s, when racism was the predominant prejudice, add to the authenticity of the book, and the issues surrounding racial prejudice are well presented. In addition, this is a good choice for young musicians who are drawn to music as a career. It clearly raises questions about how one should use talents without finally answering them.

Identity. What personal traits make it possible for Tom to be accepted by Godfrey and the others? How does prejudice affect Tom? Mary? Fred Godfrey? Dudley? In what different way does each respond to it? How are their identities shaped by prejudice? By their response to it?

Using Ability. How does racial prejudice (their own and others') affect the ways in which the various people in this book (black and white) are able to use their talent? What prejudices do you have, not only toward other races, but toward occupations, regions of the country or world, social classes, other differences? In what ways are you limited by your prejudices? How are you working to overcome them?

Hunt, Irene. *Across Five Aprils.* Illustrated by Albert John Pucci. Chicago, Follett, 1964.

Telling the story of a southern Illinois family through the five years of the Civil War, this book depicts the pain of families and communities divided by loyalties to North and South. Jethro Creighton is nine when the war begins, and within a year he has the responsibility of managing the farm that feeds the family members still at home. Through letters, the family follows the sons at war; they face danger and hatred because one son has joined the Confederate Army.

A minor theme is the growth of Jethro, whom his unlettered mother recognizes as having special talent. Encouraged by the schoolteacher before he goes off to war, and by the newspaper editor in a nearby town, Jeth follows the war through newspapers and atlases and works to improve his crude country speech. He will be the first of the family to go to college.

Drive to understand. The book presents many ideas for discussion. In talking about giftedness, include the distinction between intelligence and education, the need to look behind poor speech patterns for a good mind, and the value of an education to those who cannot take it for granted.

Relationships with others. For what reasons do some people in this book criticize others? What is your own response to the criticisms, at the beginning of the book and at the end? In real life, what are your reasons for sometimes looking down on other people? What can you do to develop your own tolerance for people who are different from you? Is it worth the effort? Why or why not?

Using ability. What does Matt mean when he says the replacement teacher has a "mean and pinched-in mind"? How does Shad encourage Jethro to learn without school? Give examples of people who have expansive minds. How can you cultivate that for yourself?

Hunt, Irene. *The Lottery Rose*. New York: Scribner's, 1976.

When seven-year-old Georgie wins a rosebush in a grocery store lottery, it brings to life the beautiful gardens in books, which represent to Georgie a safe haven from his alcoholic mother and her boyfriend's beatings. When the neighbors finally call the police to stop a beating and Georgie is sent to a residential school, he takes his precious lottery rose with him. Georgie knows that Mrs. Harper's lovely garden across the street from the school is the perfect home for his rosebush, but when he plants it there without permission, Mrs. Harper is so angry that he fears her, even though he learns to love her father, Mr. Collier, and her mentally handicapped son, Robin. Georgie's old school file labels him "retarded," "destructive," and "incorrigible," but in the accepting environment of the new school with Mr. Collier teaching him to read and Robin looking up to him as a friend, Georgie begins to relax and give as well as receive love and trust. Eventually, Georgie learns to trust Mrs. Harper, and then a tragedy brings them even closer.

With a background in psychology, Hunt writes with knowledge and sensitivity about the strong and conflicting feelings of a victim of child abuse. Robin is depicted with love and respect, and Mrs. Harper's anger and grief are shown in ways that young readers can understand. No one in the book enjoys a perfect life, but the story shows how interdependence can lift people above the limitations of circumstance.

Relationships with others. What does Georgie need from other people? What does he give to them? Ask the same questions for Robin and Mrs. Harper. Why is it hard to ask others for that which we need? Who in the story gives without being asked? Do you know someone who does this? Do you know what you need from other people? What you give to others?

Using ability. Why does Georgie think he will never be able to read? Why can he learn so much more easily at his new school than at the old one? What factors, other than intelligence, affect how well children do in school? (For broader understanding, encourage children to name more influences on success in school than those in this story.) Do you know anyone who is not doing

322

as well in school as he could? What does he need to be able to do his best?

Hunter, Mollie. *A Sound of Chariots*. New York: Harper & Row, 1972.

This is the story of Bridie McShane's growth, from the time of her father's death when she is nine until she leaves home and school to go to work at 14. The first half is a flashback that establishes the close relationship between Bridie and her father and develops his character. He was an Irish socialist, intelligent but uneducated. Bridie is like him in appearance, in love of learning and language, and in passion for life. The second part, telling of her adjustment to his death, is almost surrealistic in its evocation of her new awareness of symbols of death and her realization that she, too, will die. She develops a heightened sensitivity to life and begins to write poetry. She also learns to hide her strong feelings and her precocious powers of observation and analysis in order to avoid censure.

Hunter's writing style is challenging and the imagery is beautiful. This, along with the subject matter, make it an excellent choice for gifted readers.

Aloneness. Bridie makes friends at the Wishart school by giving up time for herself and by stifling her leadership qualities. Why would these choices be difficult for some people? Why are they possible for Bridie? How does she compensate for the loss? Have you made similar sacrifices? How do you compensate?

Using ability. Bridie is told, "Creativeness, my child, is all out-going." Do you agree? What examples of your own creativity are out-going? Bridie's mother says, "Don't be proud of any gifts you have, dearie. Be grateful for them, remembering they are a trust from God that you must render back some day." How do you feel about the responsibility gifted people have because of their gifts? How does this apply to you?

Relationships with others. Bridie develops into "two separate people," one a chatterbox and one an observer, and then she is lonely. Is this a good way to handle the problem Mr. Purves describes as grownups not liking her insight? How else could she have done it?

Hunter, Mollie. *The Stronghold*. New York: Harper and Row, 1974.

The eighteen year old Coll, crippled at the age of five during a Roman slave raid on his village in Scotland's Orkney Islands, has perfected a plan for a series of strongholds that will enable his people to withstand future raids. However, in the competition between Nectan, chief of the village, and the Druid priest, Domnall, Coll's voice of reasonable compromise cannot be heard. The manipulations of Taran, an islander returned from slavery, heighten the tension and lead to the choice of Nectan's daughter Fand as a sacrificial victim. Coll and his brother Bran, a student of Domnall, cooperate in an effort to save Fand. As a result, Coll becomes Master of the Stronghold, directing the building of his fortification and then participating in its defense when the Romans raid again.

Hunter's story is based on her visit to the brochs of the Orkney Islands, the remains of the strongholds built around the time of Christ. They are alike in plan and structure, yet unique to this part of the world—the product of one brilliant mind, Hunter reasons. Her story is good historical fiction, good adventure, and an example of careful, persistent thought. Coll is obsessed with his idea, and has the good fortune of seeing it come to fruition.

Intensity; Using ability. Why does Coll persist so long in pursuing his dream? What other motivations might cause others to do the same? What are disadvantages of being so persistent? How does Coll overcome them?

Imaginary Gardens: American Poetry and Art for Young People. Edited by Charles Sullivan. New York: Abrams, 1989.

This is a collection of poems by American poets illustrated with paintings, drawings, and photographs by American artists. The book covers all of American history, from the colonial to the modern period. Some of the poets included are Benet, Bly, Dickinson, Eliot, and Silverstein—a range of writers—and the artists include Audubon, Benton, Calder, O'Keeffe, and Andrew Wyeth. Altogether they present a rich panorama of American artists, both literary and graphic, to give the young reader an idea of the work of people whose names he may have heard—or will hear in the future.

Drive to understand.

Kaufman, Gershen and Lev Raphael. *Stick Up for Yourself! Every Kid's Guide to Personal Power and Positive Self-Esteem.* Minneapolis: Free Spirit, 1991.

This book is written to students and is accompanied by a teacher's guide. General issues of self-esteem, labeling feelings, naming future dreams (and how to get there), and developing relationships with others are especially useful. The difference between role power and personal power, for example, can be a helpful concept as hypercritical youngsters learn how to be effective in their criticism of authority figures.

Identity. Information on self-esteem could be adapted to the particular needs of highly able children learning to come to terms with exceptional talent.

Relationships with others. This book includes useful information on building good relationships with others as a necessary step toward developing self-esteem.

Using ability. The section on naming dreams and how to get there offers suggestions that can be helpful in making good use of an outstanding ability.

Kelly, Eric P. *The Trumpeter of Krakow.* New York: Macmillan, 1966 [c1928].

Joseph Charnetski is fifteen in 1461 when his father's house and fields are destroyed; he flees with his parents to the busy medieval city of Krakow. Here they meet the alchemist and scholar, Kreutz, and his niece, Elzbietka. Kreutz finds lodging for the family and work for Joseph's father as a trumpeter in the church tower. But those who destroyed the Charnetskis' home have followed them to Krakow, seeking the Tarnov Crystal, which has been the responsibility of the Charnetski family for generations. Kreutz, too, is in danger. One of his students is systematically hypnotizing him to gain the secret of turning base metals into gold.

The setting of this book is one of its strengths, giving a picture of Krakow as a medieval center and of the 15th century as a time of transition from superstition to science. The story is suspenseful, and the subplot raises questions about the moral uses of knowledge.

Drive to understand. What situations can you name in which scientists are asked now to work for gain rather than for knowledge?

Moral concerns. What is the responsibility to society of anyone with unusual knowledge, ability, intelligence?

Using ability. How valid are the arguments Tring uses to persuade Kreutz to do the experiments Tring wants him to do? In Kreutz's position, what would have been your attitude toward the general interest in making gold from base metals?

Konigsburg, E.L. *Father's Arcane Daughter.* New York: Atheneum, 1976.

Winston Carmichael has grown up taking care of his younger handicapped sister, Heidi, but now Caroline has returned. Their father's daughter from a previous marriage, Caroline had been kidnapped and was presumed dead. Through her efforts, both children develop in ways that would not have been possible without her, but the question always remains: Is this really Caroline?

This is a sophisticated mystery with a challenging structure of flashbacks featuring unidentified speakers. Caroline's role as change agent can lead to discussion of ways in which we are all potential change agents for others.

Identity; Relationships with others. Why was it important for Heidi to know that she was gifted? What was more important to Heidi's and Winston's adult success than their intelligence?

Using ability. Why was Caroline so important to both children? Winston says that Heidi has the makings of a brave soul but lacks the focus. What does he mean? What happens when people are unable to fulfill their potential? What characters in the book had special gifts? What gifts? What else did they need if they were to be able to use their gifts?

Konigsburg, E. L. *(George).* New York: Dell, 1970.

Ben Carr is a very bright sixth grader who has an imaginary friend, George, living inside him. George is both Ben's worse self and his better self. He makes the outrageous comments Ben would never dare say, and he sees long before Ben is willing to recognize it that William, the senior Ben admires so much, is leading Ben into trouble. George becomes Ben's conscience, but Ben does not want to listen, and for a while Ben is totally out of touch with George—until Ben himself sees trouble and begins to change.

This is a humorous book with a serious message: it is important to stay in touch with our inner selves. As Ben grows older, his voice "becomes indistinguishable from George's." It is sometimes easier for gifted children to accept themselves as they get older; Ben has integrated George into his own personality.

Aloneness. How do you listen to your conscience or your inner self? Do you have any particular way or place or time for doing that? How could you develop one?

Differentness. What role does George play in Ben's life? Why has Ben developed George? Why has George stayed so long? (Adults may wish to reassure children that many gifted children have imaginary playmates; usually they disappear when the children begin school.) Why does George leave, or stop talking to Ben? Did you want him to come back, even though the psychiatrist said it was good that he had gone? Why? Why does he come back? What does this sentence mean: "Ben's own voice had deepened by then, and it had become indistinguishable from George's"?

Identity; Intensity. How did being gifted cause a predicament for Ben? How did it help him cope? Are you ever in difficult situations with people older than you? How do you feel about it? What abilities do you use to cope? What are differences between George and Ben? Which do you like better? Why? Is there sometimes a difference between what you think inside and the "you" that other people see? What are the advantages and disadvantages of that?

Using ability. Read aloud the section about using skills to "collect attention" and "buy friends" (page 52 in the edition noted). Why is it tempting for Ben to do this? How can people who do this learn not to? What help do they need from others? Read about "not-knowing gracefully" (page 53 in the same edition). What does George mean by this? What do you not-know gracefully? What does Ben learn about using his intelligence well?

Latham, Jean Lee. *Carry On, Mr. Bowditch.* Illustrated by John O'Hara Cosgrave. Boston: Houghton Mifflin, 1955.

Nathaniel Bowditch grew up in Salem in the age of sailing ships. He had a quick mind, especially in math, and it was clear that he should go to Harvard. But there was no money, so instead he was indentured for nine years. People who recognized his brilliance offered the use of their libraries, and Nat never stopped learning. He taught himself languages, mathematics, and astronomy, and when he went to sea he learned navigation. Soon he was teaching others, and before he was 30 he had written a book on navigation which is still a standard text.

This biography is a story of both physical and intellectual adventure. In addition, it includes several themes related to giftedness: Nat's thirst for learning and the necessity of persistence; the eagerness of uneducated sailors to learn and Nat's commitment to teaching them; and his commitment to accuracy and the importance of risking a new approach, trusting new knowledge rather than traditional methods. Nat's zest for learning and disregard for obstacles shine throughout the book.

Drive to understand. This story could be read simply for the pleasure of learning how Nat navigated through days of fog, finding harbor through the sheer power of mathematics.

Identity. People think of Nat as a "brain." What is your response to that?

Using ability. Have you ever felt as though you are "stumbling on other people's dumbness. And—you want to kick something"? What traits does Nat have that enable him to overcome that while continuing to use his brain? What can you learn from Nat?

L'Engle, Madeleine. *The Arm of the Starfish.* New York: Ariel Books, 1965.

Adam Eddington has been hired to work in the island laboratory of Dr. O'Keefe the summer after high school, and he finds himself caught in an international struggle for the information from Dr. O'Keefe's experiments. Each side seeks to enlist Adam, and he must decide for himself which group to support.

In one of her warm and loving large-family settings, L'Engle raises the issue of the moral use of information as well as of one's intelligence. The plot is tightly written and suspenseful, and will lead to discussions of good and bad use of intelligence and knowledge, the need to learn to trust one's own instincts, and the awareness that intelligence alone is not enough.

Moral concerns. What guides Adam in deciding which side deserves his allegiance?

Using ability. What qualities does Adam have besides intelligence? What qualities must he develop in order to play his role effectively? In what ways does he succeed in developing these qualities? In what ways does he fail?

Levitin, Sonia. *The Return*. New York: Atheneum, 1987.

In the early 1980s, drought and famine made life hard for all Ethiopians, and the persecution of Ethiopian Jews grew so threatening that some fled. In 1984-1985 a secret airlift transported thousands of Ethiopian Jews to Israel. Based on that event, Levitin tells the story of Desta, her brother Joas, her sister Almaz, and her betrothed, Dan. As part of a larger group they flee on foot into the Sudan in the hope of reaching Jerusalem. Desta becomes the leader of the group. Through loss, suffering, and endurance, her courage grows.

The Return is recommended for thoughtful readers for several reasons. Writing in the first person, Levitin captures the rhythm of her characters' speech and thought, and maintains it. She smoothly depicts the development from girl to young woman, as Desta considers her responsibility to her family, grows in self-awareness, and faces the conflict between education and early marriage. The major characters—Desta, Dan, Aunt Kibret—are well-rounded, showing real complexity. The book fosters an awareness of the larger world, as Desta meets with fortitude difficulties most readers never know. In fact, most readers will not have known of the historical event, the airlift, on which the book is based. Desta and her family have shown us real people behind the starvation-dulled faces we see on television.

Drive to understand. Learn more about Ethiopian Jews. What is their history in Ethiopia? How have they fared since 1985? Learn more of the drought areas in Africa, and how war plays into drought as a cause of starvation.

Moral concerns. Discuss Hagos, the boy who has grown up without family in the refugee camp, and the importance of knowing one is part of a family, a community, or religious group that embraces common values. Even when separated from all that is familiar, Desta and the others find that their background of common values impart the essence of humanity. What values would you take to a POW or refugee camp?

Lewis, Barbara A. *The Kid's Guide to Social Action*. Minneapolis: Free Spirit, 1991.

In the hands of an encouraging adult, this very practical guide can provide an answer to the anquish some bright and sensitive children feel as they become aware of all the wrongs in the world. Written by a teacher who guided her students to make a difference (their efforts resulted in the cleanup of a hazardous waste site and in the passage of two new laws in Utah), *The Kid's Guide to Social Action* gives concrete suggestions *kids* can use to bring about change. Lewis includes tips on "power skills," including interviewing, speaking, surveying, petitioning, fundraising and campaigning. There is a section on changing or initiating legislation, and a long list of resources.

Moral concerns; Using ability. Throughout are stories of kids who have taken action, individually or in groups, and have been heard. Although there have been failures, which are freely acknowledged, the book is upbeat and the message is clear: there is something we can do. This would be a good book for a religious education program, as well as for homes and schools.

Relationships with others. The guidelines given here for effective advocacy can be generalized as tips for getting along with authority figures.

Lipsyte, Robert. *The Contender.* New York: Harper and Row, 1967.

Alfred Brooks has dropped out of school. He lives with a widowed aunt and her daughters and works in a small grocery store in Harlem. His best friend, James, is using drugs and spending time with older boys who jeer Alfred about his dead-end job. Only Henry, crippled from polio, has a kind word: Henry suggests that Alfred come to the gym where Henry works to learn to box. After James and his new friends are caught attempting to break into the grocery store, Alfred does go to the gym, where Mr. Donatelli begins by telling Alfred what is ahead of him: no guarantees of championship, but a great deal of hard work before he can even be a contender. "Everybody wants to be a champion. That's not enough. You have to start by wanting to be a contender." Despite discouragement and threats from James's new friends, Alfred does become a contender, and then uses his new self-confidence and self-discipline to reach out to others.

Drive to understand. This award-winning book is tightly written, offering in brief vignettes a picture of the difficulties of growing up in a ghetto.

Using ability. What are the positive influences in Alfred's life? The negative? Why does he choose in favor of the positive? What events discourage him, and what keeps him going? How is boxing helpful to him? In what areas would you like to be a champion? Are you a contender yet? If not, what steps will you take to become one? What will discourage you, and how will you keep yourself going? Who are your models and possible mentors? Whom can you help?

McCaffrey, Anne. *Dragonsong*. New York: Atheneum, 1976.

Menolly is growing up on the island of Pern during a time of threadfall, of spores periodically falling from the sky and consuming all living matter not under shelter. Her father is head of a fishing village which is protected from threadfall by tradition and by the dragons that live on the island. However, the main theme is not the conflict between dragons and threadfall, but that between Menolly's unusual musical gifts and the tradition, strongly held in her own village, that says women cannot become Harpers. Forbidden her music, Menolly flees the safety of the village to live alone, escaping threadfall as she can. When she is caught without shelter in a threadfall, she is rescued by a dragon and its rider and taken to a weyr to recover. There she finds shelter, friends, and finally a recognition of her talents and encouragement to use them.

This is not the high fantasy of Cooper or LeGuin, a mighty struggle between good and evil, but a tale of a more insidious struggle much closer to our daily reality. Menolly's gentle enemy is the tradition-bound close-mindedness of Yanus, her father, who is a good man, a solid and reliable leader, a hard worker—but not a man of vision, one who cannot consider change. Her mother, Mavi, accepts and reinforces Yanus's rule; only Menolly's brother, Alemi, understands her, but he has no power to help. The Harper Elgion, who serves the role of village pastor, is a force toward enlightenment, but change will be too slow for Menolly and her passion for music.

Drive to understand; Moral concerns. Where do we see too close a following of tradition, superstition, and slowness to change affecting our world? In what ways does it prevent people from growing? What balancing forces (like Alemi, Elgion, and the weyr) do you see?

Intensity; Using ability. What experience in your own life helps you understand the strength of Menolly's desire to use her music? Was she right to leave the Sea Hold? What else could she have done?

Matas, Carol. *Lisa's War.* New York: Scribner, 1987.
Matas, Carol. *Code Name Kris*. New York: Scribner, 1990.

Based on interviews with friends and family in Denmark, Canadian writer Matas recounts events of the Danish resistance to the German occupation during World War II. In *Lisa's War* the story is told by Lisa, thirteen at the time of the invasion in April, 1940. Her older brother Stefan quickly joins the underground resistance movement, and Lisa feels sure her parents are involved, too, although the movement is so tightly organized that each resistance fighter knows only a small group of others, and underground activities are not discussed among the family members. Soon enough Lisa finds a way to join Stefan and his friend Jesper. At first her assignments are small but important—and risky—tasks like distributing leaflets bearing accurate information about the war, but later she is trusted with more dangerous work, such as helping to set explosives to blow up a factory that provides war materiel for the Germans. One day word comes that the Jews of Denmark will be rounded up and deported to concentration camps, and the resistance movement brings all of its organization to bear on the immediate problem of gathering the Danish Jews—including Lisa's family—and getting them to the coast for rescue. The story of how the fiercely independent Danes protected their Jews and smuggled over 90% of them into neutral Sweden is seen through Lisa's eyes, as she and Stefan and Jesper continue their resistance activities until Stefan and Lisa must clamber aboard the last little boat for the perilous trip to safety.

Matas continues the story in her second book with Jesper, who tells us how under his code name, Kris, he continued in the resistance, was captured, and escaped. Fearing recognition by the Nazi officer—a Dane who had once been like a big brother to him—Jesper went underground, hiding his identity, not returning to his parents' home, and working for an underground newspaper. In 1944 Stefan returned to Denmark on a special mission, and Stefan and Jesper worked together until they were captured. Jesper tells this much of the story as he attempts to retain his sanity in prison. The two friends face a moral dilemma and finally escape as their prison is bombed. Still, they agonize over the decision they must make, realizing that they have learned to hate, and have even killed. Are they becoming like the Nazis?

The extensive World War II literature for young adults has not had much to say about the role of the Danish resistance movement. Now Matas presents this stirring story in a plot enlivened by adventure, enriched by friendship and deepened by the raising of moral questions related to acts of sabotage, which arise in both books—the central question being whether in pursuing activities that sometimes cause deaths, the resistance fighters have sunk to the level of their enemies.

Drive to understand. At the end of *Lisa's War* Matas credits a German, G. F. Duckwitz, with providing the secret warning that told the Jews of Denmark that it was time to flee—at the risk of his own life. How does this information change your perception of human character as it is depicted in these historical events?

Moral concerns. Have Susanne and Lisa in *Lisa's War*, and Jesper and Stefan in *Code Name Kris*, become like the Nazis, as they fear? If you think not, what is the difference? What saves the resistance fighters from the condemnation we feel for the Nazis?

Relationships with others. What is the role of friendship in these stories? What have Jesper and Stefan learned about human weakness—in Frederik, and in themselves?

Moser, Don. *A Heart to the Hawks.* New York: Atheneum, 1975.

At 14, Mike Harrington is an amateur biologist, a collector of small wild creatures, and a sophisticated student of the pond near his home. But in this summer of 1947, the post-war building boom is reaching his pond and he is powerless to stop it. He tries various means to save the pond and woodland, and then resorts to violence in what he knows will be a futile gesture.

This book should appeal to boys, even those who are scientists first and readers of literature second. They will respond to the friendship between Mike and Corcoran, to their unpolished curiosity about girls, and to Mike's high idealism, his imaginary episodes of life as a lone naturalist, and his need to achieve some measure of acceptance of what he cannot change. The reader believes that as Mike grows older, he will learn more effective ways of bringing about change.

Aloneness. Is Mike too much of a loner? Why or why not?

Arrogance. Mike says he hates "stupid people." What ways have you found to deal with people who don't understand you or your interests? What effective ways have you seen others use?

Relationships with others. What do you think will happen in Mike's relationship with Angelina? How will Mike have to change in order to become effective in protecting the environment?

Using ability. What is your interpretation of the Robinson Jeffers quote on page 196? ("Give your heart to the hawks for a snack of meat, but not to men!") How does it apply to Mike's life? Can you apply it to your own? What do you think Mike will be doing in 10 years? What steps must he take to get there from here?

North, Sterling. *The Wolfling*. New York: Dutton, 1969.

Growing up in rural Wisconsin in the 1870s, Robbie Trent leads a rigorous life, lightened by the companionship of his pet, a wolf cub, and by the friendship of his teacher, Hannah Hitchcock, and his neighbor, the Swedish-American naturalist Thure Kumlien. His hard-working and demanding father expects Robbie to end his education at the eighth grade and work for him until he is 21. Robbie must buy his time from his father if he hopes to continue his education, and he is encouraged by others to do so. He needs this encouragement, because it is difficult for him to see a way out of the obligation imposed by his father.

The story is based on the life of the author's father, with the historical accuracy documented in a separate section. It is particularly useful for discussing the difference in values between parents and children, and the need for children to be encouraged by other caring adults. Robbie's father is not uncaring, and he is sympathetically depicted as careworn with the shortsightedness that often goes with a daily struggle for a livelihood.

Drive to understand. How does Robbie feel about his father? What causes his father to feel as he does about Robbie's education?

Using ability. Why is it important for Robbie to continue his education? What traits does Robbie need to develop in order to do so? Do you think he will succeed? What traits does he already have that will help him? If you were in Robbie's situation, what person do you know who would help you as Thure Kumlien and Hannah Hitchcock helped Robbie?

O'Dell, Scott. *My Name Is Not Angelica*. Boston: Houghton Mifflin, 1989.

When she is fifteen, Raisha and others from her African village are captured by another tribe and sent to the Caribbean island of St. John to be sold as slaves. Raisha, renamed Angelica, becomes a house slave, but the others, including Konjo, who is Raisha's betrothed and their village leader, endure much harsher conditions working in the fields. Konjo soon escapes to head a group of runaways in planning a revolt. Joining the escapees, Raisha witnesses the climax of this small band's role in a general slave revolt.

Based on the slave revolt of 1733-34, this book meets the high standards we expect in O'Dell's work. Raisha is strong, independent, and self-sufficient, like young women in other O'Dell books. The book is well-researched, and the reader feels both the justice and the hopelessness of the cause. The oppressing whites are shown with some sympathy, too, enmeshed in a system that inevitably enslaves the masters. This is a fine historical novel for the upper elementary grades, clarifying the issues and telling the story on a very human level.

Aloneness. What examples do we have here of people standing alone for something they believe is right? What gives them the inner strength that enables them to be so brave?

Drive to understand. How is Raisha like Karana in O'Dell's *Island of the Blue Dolphins* and like Bright Morning in his *Sing Down the Moon*? What common threads do you see in O'Dell's books about conquered and oppressed people? How can you tie these themes to current events?

Moral concerns. Why did some whites respond to slavery like Governor Gardelin and some like Preacher Gronnewold? What justifies the disobedience of authority that culminates in rebellion? When is rebellion *not* justified?

Oneal, Zibby. *The Language of Goldfish.* New York: Viking, 1980.

For someone who resists change, adolescence can be frightening. Carrie Stokes is frightened, but she doesn't know why. She is most comfortable on Saturday mornings in her art teacher's home, but when confronted with symbols of growing up like junior dancing class, she has brief spells of dizziness. Finally she loses touch with reality enough to need a psychiatrist. The combination of her talks with him and her art work, plus her acceptance of an unexpected change in her art teacher, bring Carrie to an acceptance of change in herself.

Gifted in math as well as in art, Carrie has the advantage of being in the advanced math class; nevertheless, she feels out of step. The critical times come when she is forced to do something she is not ready for, by people who expect her to act 13 before she is ready to do so. She must be herself and have some control over her own rate of growth.

The book offers insight into the pressures placed on young people to grow up at the rate society dictates, into the necessity of being oneself despite external pressures, and into the experience of psychotherapy—something about which young people probably need more information than they have at present. It also brings out the fact that people respond to the same situation in different ways, for entirely legitimate reasons.

Aloneness; *Introversion*. Why does Carrie withdraw from friends at school? How does she spend the time by herself that she gains by withdrawing? Is withdrawing or the wish to be alone good for her? What are you reasons for your answer?

Differentness; *Identity*. Why did Carrie respond the way she did to the pressures of growing up? Can Carrie's story help you to be more tolerant of responses you may not understand in people around you? In yourself? What does Carrie learn about herself? What does she do to help herself to get better? What are her strengths to help her cope with being different? Your strengths?

Relationships with others. How do other people help Carrie to get better? What does Carrie do to allow them to help her? Have you ever been in a situation in which others could have helped if you had allowed it? Why is it difficult to accept help? What are the rewards for people who can do it?

Paterson, Katherine. *Come Sing, Jimmy Jo*. New York: Dutton, 1985.

Eleven-year-old James Johnson belongs to a family of professional country music singers. Their new agent, upon hearing the child sing, urges him to join the family on stage. His feeling for the music helps James overcome his initial fear, but it is not so easy to become comfortable with the new identity that goes with performing. He does not want to become "Jimmy Jo" instead of James, does not want school friends to know that he appears on television each Friday night, and is not happy about the rivalry his popularity sets up between him and other members of the Family.

The stability in James's life comes from his grandmother and his father. Family relationships and tolerance of difficult personalities are well portrayed. Grandma encourages James to sing, saying "You got the gift... It ain't fittin' to run from it ... The Lord don't give private presents." James's challenge is to use his gift and remain himself.

Identity. Why is it so important for James to remain *James*? Why does it not bother his mother to change herself for the sake of publicity? How would you feel if you were James? Why? Why does James feel that he betrayed Grandma? Do you agree that he did? What could you say to help him feel better about that?

Using ability. How is James's gift a "burden" to him? ("Sometimes the gift seems more like a burden.") What are his rewards for singing? Are they worth the sacrifices? Identify a gift or talent of yours. What would be the sacrifices and rewards of developing it fully? Do you want to? How? Discuss Grandma's statement that "The Lord don't give private presents." To what extent do gifted people have a responsibility to use their gifts? If you think there is no responsibility, what other reasons are there to use gifts?

Paterson, Katherine. *Jacob Have I Loved.* New York: Crowell, 1980.

Growing up on an island in Chesapeake Bay, Louise is convinced that everyone despises her and loves Caroline, her beautiful, musically talented younger sister. Not until she is 17 does Louise recognize that she is gifted intellectually and capable of doing anything she chooses. Others are willing to help, but she must make the choice.

A Newbery winner, this complex book has several themes other than giftedness, and a thoughtful teenager will find much here to think about: sibling rivalry, responsibility for one's own decisions, tradition-breaking and respect for tradition, going one's own way despite feeling uncomfortable about being different.

Differentness. How could Louise have responded more helpfully to her feelings of being different?

Identity. How do Caroline's and Louise's pictures of themselves affect their behavior? Their decisions? How accurate are their pictures of themselves? How does being gifted affect each girl's childhood? What difference does it make (in personal happiness, in career choice, in the way you treat other people) to know you have a special ability?

Relationships with others. Louise has what might be called a prickly personality. What makes her that way? How does her personality complicate her life? What role does her giftedness play? What can happen to people like this as they become adults? What keeps Louise from turning into a prickly adult? If you could talk to Louise as a teenager, what advice would you give her?

Using ability. Why is Louise able to make use of her intelligence? What is the turning point for her? What would be other possible turning points for someone like Louise? How might the book have ended so that Louise would take more command of her own future?

Peck, Robert Newton. *A Day No Pigs Would Die.* New York: Dell, 1972.

Robbie tells of his 13th year growing up in a Shaker family in Vermont, and especially of his father, who was both illiterate and wise. Rather than a plot, Peck offers a series of vignettes that reveal the daily concerns of a rural community in which a Shaker family is even more traditional than most.

Rob grows up knowing he is different and valuing his own family even as he sees the disadvantages of their way of life. Rob is different because of his religion, not because of giftedness, but the principle is the same: to recognize and value the strengths of his family and himself, and to be able to accept both himself and his father in spite of their differentness.

Differentness. What factors help Rob accept his and his family's difference? Is this story outdated, or is it relevant today? How? Generalize: What are the advantages and disadvantages of being different? How can people decide how and when to accept being different?

Identity. How is growing up a Shaker an advantage to Rob? How is it a disadvantage? Will he overcome the disadvantages? How? What does Rob admire in his father? What do you admire in Rob? In his place, what would you have done differently? Would you have rebelled? When? Why? Was Rob wrong not to?

Rand, Ayn. *Anthem.* New York: New American Library, 1946.

In a future collectivist society, Equality 7-2521 is out of place because he is more intelligent than most. Assigned to be a Street Sweeper, he discovers a tunnel which becomes a hiding place where he writes and experiments, eventually discovering electricity. When he presents his discovery to the Scholars, they reject him and he flees to the Uncharted Forest, finding there an abandoned house from the Unmentionable Times (the 20th Century). Here he finds manuscripts and reads in them his heritage, including the forbidden, lost word: ego, I. Recognizing the possibilities of individualism, he resolves to begin a new life and a new political order.

This novel was written for the purpose of extolling individualism over collectivism. Middle school students with lively intellectual interests are enthusiastic about it. They understand the political message, see a need for balance between the individual and the community, and identify with Equality's urge to know and his frustration at being repressed.

Differentness. How can people who are different cope in our society without leaving, as Equality did?

Identity. Does anything like the Scholars' rejection of Equality's idea ever happen to students in school or to teenagers in their families? How do they react?

Moral concerns. How can people like Equality, who are different from or brighter than others, manage to be themselves and yet fit into a community?

Relationships with others. Do you agree with Equality that "we have no need of our brothers"? Under what conditions might Equality recognize the need for other people?

Using ability. Can you explain why Equality so strongly wants to study and to experiment? What personal qualities make him able to do so, while others cannot, although they may wish to do so?

Rhue, Morton. *The Wave.* New York: Delacorte, 1981.

Based on a real incident in a California high school, this is the story of a teacher's attempt to demonstrate to a history class how it felt to live in Germany under Nazism. Within a short time, the students and even the teacher are caught up in The Wave, their experimental totalitarian organization, which requires its members to obey their leaders without questioning. It spreads to include students outside the history class until the teacher realizes that it has gained a momentum of its own and that he must stop it somehow. It is clear that this will hurt some of the students, especially Robert, an underachiever who is rebelling against his brother's success, and for whom The Wave is a born-again experience. The story is told largely from the point of view of Laurie, an *A* student and editor of the student paper, who questions the group and finally writes an editorial exposing its dangers.

Rhue does well at presenting The Wave from various points of view so that the reader begins to understand how such a group can be attractive, and to whom. The saving grace is Laurie's insistence on thinking for herself, and her mother's support as she stands alone for what she sees as right.

Aloneness. How does Laurie keep fighting, even after David and Amy desert her? What qualities does that take? Do you have them? How can one develop them?

Identity. What is happening to the teacher in the course of the experiment? To Robert? How is Laurie different from the others in the book, causing her response to be different from theirs? How does all this relate to a sense of identity?

Moral concerns. Why does Laurie take the Hitler film "too seriously"? Why and how do good people like David become involved in a group like The Wave? How could that involvement be avoided?

Relationships with others. What role does the need to belong play? Why does Robert become so deeply involved so easily? How can young people work to develop healthier relationships with friends?

Using ability. What characteristics does Laurie have that make it logical for her to fight The Wave? Why is it important for her to use those characteristics? What would have happened to The Wave and to her if she had not?

Richter, Hans Peter. *Friedrich*. Translated from the German by Edite Kroll. New York: Holt, Rinehart and Winston, 1970.

The story is told through a series of vignettes of the friendship between the narrator, a Christian boy, and Friedrich, a Jewish boy in Germany from 1925 to 1942. Friedrich's family lives in the apartment above the narrator, and the two families are distant friends. As pressure against Jews builds, the landlord arranges an attack on Friedrich's family, and his mother dies as a result. Eventually his father is arrested, and Friedrich finds a hideout elsewhere. Seeking a picture of his parents, he returns to the narrator's family's apartment just as the air raid siren sounds, but the landlord will not allow Friedrich into the air raid shelter. When they return to the house they find Friedrich sitting on the stoop. He has been shot and killed.

From the early picture of joy and spontaneous fun between Friedrich and his mother as they play in the snow, the book moves relentlessly to the final scene, bringing the enormity of the Holocaust down to one family and one boy. This is an excellent example of the growing body of literature written to acquaint young people with the events of World War II in Germany, different from many others (thus more representative of the reality) in that Friedrich is not a survivor. The value of this literature lies in the importance of educating a new generation of leaders about these events and, insofar as can be understood, the structures that allowed them to occur.

Drive to understand; Moral concerns. This story in itself will not provide enough information for a full discussion. Rather, it provides the emotional impact that prepares students to look at the situation from both sides. Discuss the growing reluctance of the narrator's family to help Friedrich's family. Include discussion of similar hostilities elsewhere in the world. Aim for some understanding of circumstances that might cause, or prevent, a recurrence in any country.

Sebestyen, Ouida. *Words by Heart.* Boston: Little, Brown, 1968.

Lena's Papa has high hopes for his daughter, so he moves his family from the post-Reconstruction South to the more open West, where a black family may have a better chance. But Papa's willingness to work brings resentment from Mr. Haney, who loses his job to Papa, and Lena learns that not everyone rejoices with her when she wins the scripture-reciting contest. It is clear that prejudice here is merely more subtle than it is in the South, and the family will still need extraordinary fortitude to survive.

Racial prejudice is the theme of this book, with Lena's giftedness adding emphasis to the need of blacks for opportunities to grow and develop. Talented blacks can see a version of their own struggle in Lena's story, and all talented students can recognize Lena's and her father's acceptance of the responsibility to use one's gifts, even against difficult odds.

Differentness. What does Papa teach Lena that will help her to survive? What else do you think she will need to get through the next few years?

Identity. If you were in Lena's position, do you think you could make it? What would be your greatest asset? Your greatest liability?

Using ability. What did Papa teach Lena, both by what he said and by the way he lived? Is there anything in that which could be useful to you? If your own life is easier than Lena's, how might that make it more of a challenge for you to grow up to be a productive person, making full use of the abilities you have? How are you doing so far?

Speare, Elizabeth George. *The Witch of Blackbird Pond.* Boston: Houghton Mifflin, 1958.

Kit Tyler grew up with her grandfather in Barbados, but upon his death in her sixteenth year, she sails to Connecticut to live with an aunt whom she has never met. Kit does not fit in with the Puritan Connecticut of 1687, but she finds a few kindred spirits: Nat, first mate of the ship in which she sailed; Prudence, a downtrodden child hungry to learn; and Hannah, the outcast Quaker who lives by Blackbird Pond and who is thought to be a witch. Kit's friendship with Hannah leads to the accusation that Kit herself is a witch.

Characterization is excellent in this book. Kit is accepted if not understood by her Puritan relatives, and she comes to respect her stern uncle's fairness and sense of justice. Several characters—Kit, her uncle, Hannah, Nat, the young minister-in-training, and even Prudence—provide examples of standing alone for their own beliefs and the consequences (both difficulties and rewards) of doing so. The book also offers examples of ways people need and support each other.

Differentness. Consider each of the people who take a stand for their beliefs. What characteristics do they have that put them in this position? How do they find the strength or courage they need; what sustains them?

Drive to understand. This book is often read simply for the insight it gives into the lives of the New England colonists.

Moral concerns. How would this story have been different if the people of the village had been asked questions of Hannah before deciding she was a witch? How can we avoid similar pre-judging—that is, prejudice?

Relationships with others. Consider instances in which one person supports another even without liking what that person is doing. Have you ever seen someone offer that kind of support to another? Why do people do this? Have you ever done it yourself? Can you think of an opportunity to do so? What would be the consequences, both positive and negative?

Spiegelman, Art. *Maus: A Survivor's Tale.* New York: Pantheon, 1986.
Spiegelman, Art. *Maus: A Survivor's Tale, II: And Here My Troubles Began.* New York: Pantheon, 1991.

In his first book, the son of survivors of Auschwitz tells the story of his parents' meeting and the early years of their marriage in Poland, until they arrived at Auschwitz and were separated. The second volume continues the story with their experiences in Auschwitz and after the war, including insights into long-term psychological effects of the Holocaust on one survivor, Vladek Spiegelman, and on his relationship with his son. (Spiegelman's mother, Anja, committed suicide in 1968, leaving no note.)

Spiegleman bases his story on taped discussions with his father and tells it in cartoon form, drawing Jews as mice, Nazis as cats, Poles as pigs, and Americans as dogs. The scene alternates between Poland in the 1930s and 40s and Rego Park, New York, where Art interviews his aging father and tries to maintain their uneasy relationship. The harrowing wartime experiences of Polish Jews, combined with evidence of the lasting impact on Vladek Spiegelman's personality, told with simple words and cartoon illustrations, create a vivid impression of the terror of those years like no other literature of the period.

Drive to understand. What new information or feelings about the Holocaust do you gain from this story? What part does the cartoon treatment play in your new understanding?

Moral concerns. Does the cartoon format trivialize the subject matter? Why or why not?

Relationships with others. Describe Vladek Spiegelman in a brief character sketch. Why is he so complex a person? How did Vladek's experiences affect his personality, which affected his relationship with his son, which affected his son's personality? Relate this domino concept to other intergenerational relationships you know.

Sutcliff, Rosemary. *Flame-colored Taffeta.* New York: Farrar, Straus and Giroux, 1986.

Although she is best known for her fiction of early medieval England, Sutcliff writes here of the 18th Century, a time of smugglers and intrigue revolving around efforts to crown Bonnie Prince Charlie. Twelve-year-old Damaris lives on a farm near England's coast, and when she finds a wounded smuggler—or spy?—she and her friend Peter must contrive to keep him hidden and safe while, with the help of old Genty, the Wise Woman, they nurse him back to health.

The plot is well-constructed and suspenseful; this book really is hard to put down. Discussion could focus on the historical events surrounding Bonnie Prince Charlie, and other literary—and musical—treatments of the same story. Or it could lead to other fiction set in the 18th Century, such as Leon Garfield's books, *Smith* and *The Sound of Coaches*.

Drive to understand. What differences do you see in the rural world Sutcliff presents and Garfield's urban setting? What similarities? Analyze differences in the authors' writing styles, and the suitability of each style for their subjects. What emotional effect does each writer's work have on the reader?

Sutcliff, Rosemary. *The Sword and the Circle*. New York: Dutton, 1981.

For her retelling of the Arthurian legends, Sutcliff draws stories from several sources and weaves them into a whole—a collection of stories of Arthur and Guenever, Lancelot, Gawain, Tristan and Iseult, Merlin, and others, all of the Fellowship of the Round Table. Sutcliff has written often of this period and others in British history, and her sense for language and place enhances the tales to create an experience of wonder and imagination for sensitive readers.

Drive to understand. The author's note will intrigue readers who want to know more of origins—who was the historical Arthur? Her stories come from history, poetry and legend; some readers may want, now or later, to read the earlier versions. Especially inquisitive readers may also want to compare Sutcliff's retelling of the Arthurian legends with others.

Tolan, Stephanie S. *A Good Courage*. New York: Morrow, 1988.

Ty (short for Tie-Dye Rainey) and his mother, Jasmine, are on their way to Florida for yet another new start when a TV ad for the Kingdom, a religious community, catches her attention. Jasmine fits in immediately; Ty is skeptical but unconcerned, since he is sure her interest in the Kingdom will flag in a few weeks, as it has elsewhere. But here parents and children are separated, and in the few moments he has to talk with his mother, Ty realizes she is settling in for longer than he can bear to. Children are carefully controlled, and while they are not beaten, there are enough incidents of unhealthy treatment and dangerous punishment that

Ty finally escapes and goes to the police to complain of child abuse. The police return with Ty to the Kingdom, where the leader, Brother Daniel, acts his part so smoothly that Ty's story is not believed. Help comes from an unexpected source, however, and Ty escapes again, this time with his new friend Samarah. An old friend, a father-figure, meets them and takes them back to the Home Place, the commune where Ty and Jasmine had most recently stayed.

Tolan has the courage to write on controversial topics, and she treats them with an even hand. As our empathy with Ty and the other children grows, the sense of being trapped causes revulsion but not too much fear. Characters are well-rounded: even Brother Daniel, who could be portrayed as a dictator, is seen in a softer light by the end of the book. Religion is treated with respect.

Aloneness. How is Ty required to stand alone in the Kingdom? In what areas does he change his thinking, while maintaining a core of self?

Identity. Distinguish between physical and mental control. How does Ty retain his own way of thinking? What is the source of his strength? Why is his mother so easily swayed? In what ways does Ty grow and change? What does he learn?

Voigt, Cynthia. *Building Blocks.* New York: Atheneum, 1984.

Brann Connell has grown up believing that his father is weak, indecisive, and ineffectual. In a time-warp experience, he spends a day with his father as a boy, seeing his father's childhood home and family and watching how ten-year-old Kevin coped with a situation too difficult for Brann to comprehend. He returns to his own time with a better understanding not only of his father, but also of his father's traits, which represent a strength Brann lacks.

Voigt reveals a sensitivity to different personality styles that can help gifted children recognize, even look for, something of value in people they have not been able to understand. This book suggests that there is much to know about others for those who look below the surface and are open to another's experience.

Identity. How are Brann and Kevin different? What strengths of Kevin does Brann discover? What caused Kevin to become the person he is now? Choose one of Kevin's traits and discuss how it can look like a weakness from one angle, a strength from another. Do you know anyone like Kevin, with a characteristic that can be both bad and good? Do you have any such traits?

Relationships with others. How will Brann's experience change his future relationship with his father? Can you choose someone you have difficulty understanding or with whom you are impatient and imagine a story like this told about that person? How does it change your feeling about him or her? How does the experience help Brann understand himself better?

Voigt, Cynthia. *Jackaroo.* New York: Atheneum, 1985.

Gwyn is a sixteen-year-old innkeeper's daughter in medieval Wales, to judge from the names. Times are hard, and although the innkeeper is prosperous and his family better off than most, Gwyn feels intense sympathy for the poor, so distant from the concerns of the ruling lords. In this hard winter a lord and his son stop at the inn, and when they leave suddenly, they request a servant for each of them. Gwyn and the manservant Burl attend them, but the four are separated in a blizzard, and Gwyn and the lordling spend many days snowbound in an abandoned stone cabin. Gradually they become friends despite the awkwardness of the lord/servant relationship, and the lordling teaches Gwyn to read. Cleaning the cupboards of the stone cabin one day, she finds an old pair of thigh-high leather boots, a plumed hat, and a tunic—the costume worn by the legendary Jackaroo, who rides to aid the people in difficult times. Gwyn has never believed the legends, but she finds the costume useful. In its disguise she is able to dispense some of the gold pieces, given to her by the lord when she returned his son safely to him, to people who desperately need help. However, riding as Jackaroo enables Gwyn to feel fully her strength and independence, until she realizes she cannot follow the narrow choices open to her at the inn or in the nearby village.

Voigt captures language patterns and medieval mores and restrictions well, describing vividly the lives of common people living in a period most literature depicts only through the eyes of the nobility. Many readers will identify with Gwyn's sensitivity to the needs she sees around her and the sense of differentness it engenders. The love story of Gwyn and Burl is slow and subtle, a long friendship developing before Gwyn recognizes it as love.

Differentness; *Sensitivity*. Why is Gwyn so much more aware of others' needs than most people in the story? Why is Burl aware? What restrictions did medieval living patterns impose on "different" people, like Gwyn and Burl? If the Earl had not intervened, what could they have done? What restrictions do present living patterns and unwritten rules impose on people like them? What options do such people have now?

Identity. How did playing Jackaroo help Gwyn to clarify her own identity? Why was it dangerous? What was Win warning her about? How would you have advised her about marriage? Why?

Voigt, Cynthia. *The Runner*. New York: Atheneum, 1985.

In this prequel to *Homecoming*, Voigt tells the story of Bullet—Samuel Tillerman—at seventeen, a high school junior in 1967. The war in Vietman is a distant struggle, not nearly as threatening as the conflict in Bullet's home, where his father's tight control has already sent Bullet's older brother and sister away for good. Only Bullet and his mother are left, she to endure and Bullet to mark time until he, too, can leave. The discipline of running hardens Bullet—but running also brings him into contact with Tamer, an older black student. Tamer and Bullet's boss force him to look at himself with the same insistence on truth that he turns on the rest of the world.

The book is beautifully written and demands much of the reader. Those who have read *Homecoming, Dicey's Song*, and *A Solitary Blue* will gain greater understanding of the children's grandmother, Abigail Tillerman. Those who have not read any of Voigt's *Homecoming* series will want to start here.

Drive to understand. What is Bullet's major inner conflict? Leaving his mother? Coaching Tamer? Facing his prejudice? Why do you choose the one you do?

Identity. Of the men Bullet knows, who is the best mentor for him, and why? What qualities make him so?

Moral concerns. Why would Bullet urge Tamer to stay out of Vietnam but not do so himself?

Wersba, Barbara. *Crazy Vanilla*. New York: Harper and Row, 1986.

As a twelve-year-old, Tyler Woodruff learns that his older brother, Cameron, is gay. Now, at fourteen, Tyler is still coming to terms with the loss of Cameron (who moved out of the house in the face of their father's intolerance), his mother's alcoholism and his parents' incompatibility. Tyler does not fit into the wealthy crowd at his private school, and he has no one with whom to share his passion for wildlife photography—until he meets Mitzi, a year older and different from Tyler in nearly every way. But Mitzi, too, is a loner, a fine wildlife photographer, wise enough to be able to help Tyler sort out his feelings about Cameron. Their relationship is brief, but it is a saving one for Tyler.

This story exemplifies the importance of having even one person who understands our interest, intensity, and passion for whatever it is that engages and motivates us. For Mitzi, that role had been played by Garrett Smith, her mother's former boyfriend. For Tyler, it is Mitzi, and even though the relationship ends, the knowledge of Mitzi's understanding will carry Tyler through the next few difficult years, until he can make choices that will put him in contact with more compatible people.

Differentness. What will Tyler be doing over the next five years? How will his friendship with Mitzi help him? How did they get past outward differences to recognize their real similarities? What attitudes (Tyler's, Mitzi's, their mothers') helped? What can you do to adopt such attitudes?

Introversion; Intensity. Is Tyler too much of a loner? What advantages are there in being a loner? What disadvantages?

Wojciechowska, Maia. *Shadow of a Bull.* Illustrated by Alvin Smith. New York, Atheneum, 1964.

Manolo's father was once the greatest bullfighter in Spain, and everyone expects Manolo to be like him. When Manolo is almost 12—the age when his father first fought a bull—a group of men who have been watching him since his father's death begin training him to become a toreador. Manolo is not sure that he wants to be a bullfighter, and he assumes that his fear means that he lacks courage. He sets for himself the task of learning to be brave. Two people help clarify his hopes for the future: Juan, who passionately longs to become a bullfighter, and the doctor who has spent his life repairing bodies broken in the bullring.

Manolo is trapped by the expectations of others and confused by his own definition of courage. The decision he eventually makes reflects both self-knowledge and moral courage.

Drive to understand. This well-written story conveys the historical tradition behind bullfighting with respect, and it raises the inevitable questions without giving a definitive answer. Manolo's answer, as it should be, is for only himself, leaving room for discussion.

Identity; Intensity. How does Manolo feel about himself? How would you describe him to someone else? How does Manolo define courage? How does he show it? How would you have defined it before reading the book? After reading the book? Do you see examples of moral courage in others? In yourself?

Using ability. What advice would you give Manolo? Manolo's mother says that what his father did was "for himself, most of all for himself." Is that all right, or is it selfish? Why? What does Manolo do for himself? Is it selfish? What do you do for yourself that is not selfish?

Senior High

Grades Nine to Twelve

Auel, Jean. *The Clan of the Cave Bear.* New York: Crown, 1980.

This popular novel features several characters who stand out in their prehistoric clan because of their special abilities. The medicine woman of the Clan of the Cave Bear cares for a five-year-old girl from an unknown clan who was orphaned when an earthquake swallowed her home. As she grows, the differences between the Cro-Magnon Ayla and the Neanderthal Clan people become apparent. The Clan is deeply traditional, relying on a mixture of instinct and knowledge from past ages. Ayla displays flexibility, intelligent curiosity, a drive toward individuality, and a willingness to take risks that put her at odds with the Clan people.

These differences between Ayla and the people who surround her are analogous to the differences a highly talented student may sense between himself and many of the people around him. Understanding how Ayla feels and seeing her responses to the situation should help him understand and respond constructively to his own situation.

Identity. How does Ayla come to recognize her differences? How does she feel about them? What is her self-concept, and how does it affect her behavior? How does it change as she learns more about herself?

Relationships with others. How does Ayla compromise her abilities in order to fit in with the Clan, and how does she decide when not to compromise? What mistakes does she make? Can you go on from this to draw a set of criteria to determine when compromise is adaptive, and when it is nonproductive? What would be Ayla's definition of personal integrity? What is yours?

Becker, Jurek. *Bronstein's Children.* Translated by Leila Vennewitz. New York: Harcourt Brace Jovanovich, 1988.

Hans was an East German Jew, just finishing at the gymnasium and preparing for the university, when he discovered his father and two other men torturing a former Nazi concentration camp guard they had captured. The book alternates in time between the present, as Hans recalls the events leading up to his father's death, and flashbacks to the two-week period when the guard was held captive, a year earlier. The small cast of characters includes Hans's girlfriend Martha and her parents, who take Hans in after his father dies; and his sister Elle, who is in a mental institution due to sudden violent outbursts dating back to the Nazi period.

The story line is deceptively simple, the structure demanding, the mood somber. The questions raised are serious ones. They can be asked as limited to the Nazi period, but then asked again in broader terms, as they apply to victims in other situations, perhaps even to readers' own lives.

Aloneness. Hans is lonely, alienated, left to work out his solution by himself. How does he do it? Why does it take so long?

Identity. Who are the victims? How long does one remain a victim? How does one stop being a victim, and how much control does one have?

Moral concerns. How does one gain control over one's own life and destiny? How gather the strength and courage to act?

Berman, Phillip L., editor. *The Courage of Conviction.* New York: Ballantine, 1985.

As part of his own search for a sustaining and sustainable system of belief, Berman invited thirty-three well-known contemporary men and women to write an essay answering two questions: What do you believe? How, emphasizing your occupation(s), have you put those beliefs into action? The resulting essays are somewhat uneven in quality but honestly and carefully written. The range of beliefs in itself is thought-provoking and informative. Contributors include Steve Allen, Joan Baez, Mario Cuomo, Jane Goodall, Madeleine L'Engle, and Benjamin Spock.

Drive to understand. The wide range of responses provide a compelling demonstration of the variety of beliefs by which thoughtful people guide their lives, and offer models for young people.

Identity. Possible responses to this book include asking readers to answer the two questions themselves, finding essays with which they agree or disagree, and selecting statements from the essays to begin a discussion.

Moral concerns; *Using ability.* Berman's second question might be worded, "How do your moral concerns effect your occupational choice?"—a good question for young adults who are making college and career choices.

Bielenberg, Christabel. *Christabel.* New York: Penguin, 1989 [copyright 1968].

In 1932, Christabel and Peter Bielenberg were married in Hamburg, Germany. She was English and Irish, in Hamburg to study voice, and Peter was a law student planning to enter the family practice. They watched as Hitler rose to power, and Peter's circle—men who but for the war would have been leaders of Germany's next generation—first opposed Nazism and then joined in a plot to assassinate Hitler. Several were hanged when the attempt failed. Peter was imprisoned, and Christabel braved an interview with a Nazi officer in a successful attempt to win his release. In 1968, in Ireland where they now live, she transformed her diary into this very moving book.

Christabel saw World War II unfold through both English and German eyes, and she writes very perceptively but also with a light, sometimes witty, touch. She presents convincingly the complexity of German society, making it clear that not all Germans were Nazis, and expressing the frustration she and Peter and their friends felt at not being able to persuade the Allies that there was an opposition to Hitler within Germany. Her story reads like a novel, full of personal anecdotes, especially of her life in Bavaria, where she and their sons finally went for safety. This book offers not answers but a personal account from a unique point of view, making the World War II experience accessible to modern young adult readers.

Drive to understand. How might the outcome of the war have been different if Adam's mission to gain Allied support for opposition movements within Germany had succeeded? Discuss the possibilities if the Allies had not demanded Germany's unconditional surrender but had offered compromise, as the author suggests. Discuss the story of Christabel's Nazi gardener, in which she illustrates how and why Nazism appealed to some Germans. How have your views of World War II, Nazism, and the Germans changed as a result of reading this book?

Moral concerns. Discuss Christabel's comment that she was "born and bred in a country where communal activities and also communal protest belonged as much to a way of life as cricket or Christmas pudding" (p. 25). What is the importance of communal activities and protest? What productive forms can protest take?

Bradbury, Ray. *Fahrenheit 451.* New York: Ballantine, 1953. "Author's Afterword," 1979.

In Bradbury's imagined future, firemen have become those who create fire, the censors who burn books (which have a conflagration point of 451 degrees Fahrenheit). In doing so they are merely carrying out the will of the majority, who long ago scorned books, turning to the pseudo-world of television. Books, after all, cause dissension, since they don't agree with each other; and in any case the populace is more docile when kept in the state of intellectual numbness induced by video. But Montag is a fireman who questions. After his wife makes a suicide attempt (a common occurrence in this world), he brings down the books he has hidden in the attic and begins to read, looking for answers and meaning. In due time the firemen arrive to burn his house and books, and Montag becomes a fugitive. As the war that has threatened throughout the book descends on the city, Montag finds himself welcomed by a group of other questionners and dissidents, each carrying the treasure of a remembered book in his brain.

The "Author's Afterword" is a protest against publishers' attempts to remove passages thought to be offensive from Bradbury's works as they were considered for use in high school anthologies—effectively censoring this book on censorship. The Ballantine Del Rey edition of 1979 restored lost sections and printed the Afterword—all of which is worth discussion in itself. Here, in addition to censorship, Bradbury anticipates the rampant growth of restrictions on thinking, speaking, and writing that resulted from the move toward "politically correct" expression.

Drive to understand. Follow Beatty's history of the end of books. What looks familiar? How far have we gone toward the future Bradbury predicts? Will the end of the Cold War (which Bradbury did not foresee) change any of his forecasts?

Moral concerns. What is the role, the danger, and the future face of censorship in our time? What are the differing roles of the public and the government? How does censorship affect the development and appropriate use of your abilities? What are sources of censorship in your life? What is your personal responsibility regarding censorship?

Finally, have you read the works the men have memorized? They make a good reading list.

Buck, Pearl S. *The Exile*. New York: Reynal and Hitchcock, 1936.

Based on the life of the author's mother, this book is more a character study than a novel. The story spans the adult life of Carie, a missionary to China from 1880 to about 1920. There are several strong threads in the book: Carie's concern for the role of women, America as the golden land, China in its pre-Revolutionary period, Carie's search for meaning in life and her inability to find it in the 19th-century version of God, and her turning to action rather than preaching as a result. Carie is bright, and she struggles against her "faults" of impetuosity, warmth, exuberance, humor and love of beauty. She is a practical idealist, rearing her children with a fierce energy and determination to teach them the best that is American as she sees it, in her memory and from afar.

Differentness; Identity. The book is recommended especially for gifted girls trying to define the roles they want to play, and for young adults, both male and female, who are questioning traditional religion.

Moral concerns. How does Carie reconcile her idealism with the realities of her world? How is she able to question the idea she has been taught of God and act as a missionary at the same time? What similar paradoxes have you encountered or are you likely to encounter in your own life? How can they be reconciled?

Using ability. Although Carie lived at a time when there were more restrictions on women than there are now, her story still has relevance. What universals are there in the restrictions placed on her by her role in the society she lived in? To what extent did she surpass the roles most women played at the time? What attitudes and actions enabled her to make the use she did of the talents and interests she had?

Chatwin, Bruce. *Utz*. New York: Viking, 1988.

Kaspar Utz, the lone descendant of his wealthy grandmother, is able to bear life in Prague under Communism rather well. Through various understandings with the authorities, Utz retains and even augments his collection of Meissen porcelain. The narrator, an English historian of the Northern Renaissance, meets Utz on a research trip to Prague in 1967, just before the "Prague Spring" of 1968, and returns in the late 80s, years after Utz's death (but before the collapse of the Iron Curtain) to learn the fate of the Meissen collection. He pieces together more of Utz's story, especially the role of his servant Marta, but the reader is left to conjecture about the Meissen.

Written by an English writer and based on Eastern European history and culture, this book will prove a serious challenge to American high school students, but it is worth the effort. Some background reading on August the Strong, the history of Meissen porcelain, and Dresden will add to the pleasure and enable motivated readers to follow the story easily, preparing them to consider the philosophical questions raised in this brief novel.

Drive to understand. Consider the aspects of Western society that disgusted Utz: What causes the difference between his attitude and that of those who wanted to emigrate? How does his attitude toward the Western world square with his passion for porcelain? What is Chatwin saying about materialism? What implications, if any, do you see for the blending of Eastern and Western European (and American) culture after the events of 1989? What do you think happened to the Meissen collection? What *should* have happened to it? Why?

Moral concerns. Utz says the collection ruined his life. If so, in what way? Is Utz's fascination with porcelain a form of idolatry, in your view?

Cole, Brock. *Celine*. New York: Farrar, Strauss, Giroux, 1989.

Celine is a junior in a Chicago high school, an artist living with her twenty-two-year-old stepmother while her irresponsible father is on a European lecture tour. Jake is a young boy in the apartment across the hall whose artist father is separated from his mother. Celine copes with these disparate people as well as with typical high school problems—the paper on Holden Caulfield, the friend who uses Celine as a cover to attend a forbidden party, the unwelcome boyfrind—with a sense of humor tinged with a fine edge of irony and devastatingly clear self-awareness.

It is the writing rather than the plot that will appeal to mature readers of *Celine*. Cole provides a sample of the thinking of a talented high school girl as she deals gamely, without pretension or illusions, with the realities of daily living, the shortcomings of herself and others. Despite the distractions, we know Celine will prevail, if only because of her clear sense of herself as an artist.

Identity. Questions might include inquiry into the role art plays in integrating Celine's life. What, if anything, does or could play such a role in your life?

Using ability. Explore the importance of knowing we do something well, of pursuing something outside ourselves that helps us keep perspective, as art does for Celine. What other qualities in Celine help her to stay on top of things? In you?

Cormier, Robert. *I Am the Cheese*. New York: Pantheon, 1977.

Adam Farmer tells the story of a bicycle ride from Massachusetts to Vermont in search of his father. Interspersed between chapters about the ride are documents recording a therapist's interviews with Adam, during which his memories slowly tell the story of his childhood in a happy family with a terrible shadow looming over it. Adam's father, a reporter, had provided information on organized crime to the government, and since then his family's life has been ruled by the governmental agency that protects witnesses who have put their lives in danger. They have been given a whole new identity. Adam discovers that he isn't even Adam Farmer, that he was born Paul Delmonte. Finally he realizes that Brint, his "therapist," is trying to cause him to remember further information, information Adam's father never gave him. It becomes impossible to know whom to trust—and the chilling sense that this is so grows until by the end of the novel it is the point of the story.

This book is recommended for good readers because it is challenging—with flashbacks, alternating settings and shifting loyalties—and because it presents new ideas and information which raise questions about the role of government in citizens' private lives. It lends itself to conjectural discussion.

Moral concerns. Should Adam's father have given the information? What is Brint's motive? Mr. Gray's? How could the system be handled better?

Coupland, Douglas. *Generation X: Tales for an Accelerated Culture.* New York: St. Martin's Press, 1991.

Andy narrates this story of himself and his friends Dag and Claire, all in their late twenties, living in Palm Springs on the proceeds of their various low-paying jobs—all the work they can find despite their good educational backgrounds. They no longer believe in a future that will enable them to live as well as their parents do. Only Tyler, who represents a younger, business-oriented generation, is optimistic. The book is a collection of vignettes about these three, plus stories they tell to each other. What meaning there is is to be found in their stories. The ending introduces a different tone, a saving event for the formerly pseudo-sophisticated Andy, administered by the most real and natural people in the world—mentally handicapped children who are treated lovingly.

The plot line is slim, but we have a striking picture of the frustrations and vexations of the generation that follows the Baby Boomers. Their conversation is intentionally, relentlessly shallow, as they purposely and desperately avoid looking at real values, out of fear of discovering emotional and moral bankruptcy.

Using ability. Does the author express any experience, fear, or resentment of yours? If you are more idealistic than Andy, Dag, and Claire, why is this so? How do you reveal or express your idealism? What forces, in addition to economic conditions, have created Generation X? What will change it, if anything? How will your generation be different? Do you expect to have the opportunity to use the ability you have? How can you make the most of it?

Curie, Eve. *Madame Curie.* Translated from the French by Vincent Sheean. Garden City, N.Y.: Doubleday, Doran, 1937.

Gathering letters, family stories, and her own memories, Marie Curie's daughter wrote this biography shortly after her mother's death. She tells of Marie's childhood in Russian-occupied Poland and of her intellectual isolation while she worked as a governess to send her sister to medical school in Paris. When she was 24, Marie was finally able to go to Paris for her own studies. The book tells of her marriage to Pierre Curie, of their partnership in the discovery of radium, of the lonely years of dedicated work after his death, and of the honors she at last endured, having no talent for the life of the celebrity.

The book is a rich source for high school students whose interests are intellectual in nature. It presents the different worlds of well-educated children growing up in Poland, and the life of scientists in Paris at the turn of the century. Most stimulating for many readers is the glimpse of the excitement of intellectual life in Europe at that time; it made demands on Marie and Pierre which they gladly met. Marie's life is a ringing statement of the connection between hard work and accomplishment, as well as of the passionate absorption of a gifted adult in her work. Both she and Pierre were happiest in their laboratory, but they also had warm relationships with family and colleagues.

Drive to understand. This book is listed here because of the picture it provides of intellectual life in both Eastern and Western Europe before and after World War I. For gifted students whose only experience with meeting intellectual needs and interests has been the American high school of the 1990s, this view of Europe can be both stimulating and inspiring.

Intensity. Discuss the contrast between play during Marie's youth in Poland and work during her adulthood in Paris. Did she make a bad choice, in your view? Why or why not?

Using ability. How did Marie's childhood and youth prepare her for her life work? How did specific incidents lead her to her career choice? How important was the influence of her family?

Delisle, James R. and Judy Galbraith. *The Gifted Kids Survival Guide II: A Sequel to the Original Gifted Kids Survival Guide (For Ages 11-18).* Ed. by Pamela Espeland. Illus. by Harry Pulver, Jr. Minneapolis: Free Spirit, 1987.

This sequel to the 1983 book responds to young peoples' requests with more specific information about giftedness, testing, and intelligence. A long section offers ways students can take charge of their own education, and there are pointers on making and keeping friends. Delisle brings his work on suicide among gifted teenagers to this book, too, discussing this difficult topic with frankness and suggestions for prevention.

The first book is listed in the Middle School section since it is logically read first, but each book can be useful to students throughout the teen years.

Achievement. In a section on aptitude and achievement, the authors point out the relationships between the two and explain what achievement tests do and don't mean.

Arrogance. In discussing how students can ask for appropriate educational programs, sample conversational ploys are presented that can be generalized to help young people understand how they can avoid sounding arrogant.

Perfectionism. A segment on perfectionism offers suggestions for mastering this potentially destructive characteristic.

Relationships with others. A long section includes the importance of learning to suffer fools gladly and the distinction between popularity and friendship.

Dixon, Jeanne. *The Tempered Wind.* New York: Atheneum, 1987.

Gabriella is a dwarf. At seventeen, she tells the story of her life: living during the early years with her parents, who had kept her confined to the house "for her own good," then with an aunt who sent her to school at last, but did not know how to help her make friends—until through the mail Gabriella finds work as a chore girl on a Montana farm. On her way from St. Louis to Montana she meets an itinerant preacher, also going to Montana, who is kind to her. Dreams of love support her while she lives with the troubled Shevala family, finally finding her niche as a teacher in the country school. When her preacher returns she finds that she has learned to discern among various kinds of love, and she knows herself well enough to choose well.

The book is well-written, with sharply defined characters, suspense, and lack of sentimentality. Gabriella is both bright and handicapped, and she looks at the world unflinchingly—with hatred at first, and then, very gradually, in response to love. Her intelligence helps her to understand and defend herself against the taunts of others, but her defenses are self-destructive, as she clearly explains in retrospect. Verbally adept people who have used their sophistication and vocabulary to taunt those who taunt them will recognize the dynamics of hurt and rage which Gabriella displays and finally overcomes.

358

Identity. When Gabriella tells about school, she says all she thought about then was "me, me, me." What people and events cause her to begin thinking about others? How does this help her learn more about herself, and grow? Can you generalize your response to Gabriella's story to other people with other differences?

Relationships with others. Reread the story of Gabriella's interview with Miss Rasmussen, head of the school she attends briefly in St. Louis, in which Miss Rasmussen makes it clear that making friends is Gabriella's responsibility, despite her difference from the others. Do you agree with Miss Rasmussen? What ideas would you add to the conversation? What could Gabriella have done to improve the situation? What might the others at the school have done? What kind of help does Gabriella need? How does this apply to situations and people you know?

Eco, Umberto. *The Name of the Rose*. Translated from the Italian by William Weaver. San Diego: Harcourt Brace Jovanovich, 1980.

Set in a 14th century monastery in northern Italy, this acclaimed mystery novel is told by Adso of Melk, a Benedictine novice assigned to serve William of Baskerville, a Franciscan monk whose mission it is to arrange talks between emissaries of the two popes—one in Rome and one in Avignon. This mission, however, is merely the background for the more immediate problem Brother William faces: finding the causes of the mysterious deaths, one each day, of the monks in the Italian abbey where the talks are to take place. This mystery centers on the library, where manuscripts are kept in a labyrinth forbidden to all but a few, so that William and Adso must explore it by night.

Eco is a philosopher, historian, aesthetician, and semioticist, and his story is laced with discussions that range over all of these fields. In addition to unravelling the mystery, then, the reader's mind is challenged by the theology, the logic, and the politics of the 14th century, amid the confusion of Italian civil and ecclesiastical intrigue just after Dante's time.

Drive to understand. Readers may wish to discuss questions which are raised or implied in the text. For example, Adso comments, "I had always believed logic was a universal weapon, and now I realized how its validity depended on the way it was employed . . . [it] could be especially useful when you entered it but then left it" (p. 262). In a discussion of the allegorical value of the legend of the unicorn, he says, "Higher truths can be expressed while the letter is lying" (p. 316). In Adso's final discussion with William, they consider the role of laughter and of evil as a perversion of good (p. 491-2). If both leader and readers note such quotations as they read, they will gather plenty of material for discussion when they meet.

Faulkner, William. *The Sound and the Fury*. New York: Random House, 1929.

This "tale told by an idiot" is related in four parts, the first told by Benjy, the mentally handicapped son of an old Mississippi family. Subsequent narrators are Benjy's brothers: Quentin, who tells of the day he committed suicide, and Jason, whose meager (and partly ill-gotten) savings are stolen by the brothers' niece, last of the family, when she runs off with a sideshow pitchman. The story, then, is of the decline and finally the demise of a family which traced its lineage to a Civil War general and a governor.

The book is technically complex, employing not only multiple narrators but shifting time sequence and Faulkner's stream-of-consciousness writing style. An American classic, it challenges and rewards good readers. It is worth reading if only for the pleasure of recognizing fine literature—some sentences are brilliant jewels describing internal experience. Beyond seeing it as a work of art, however, thoughtful high school students will find that it helps to focus questions of value, of what is to be done with one's life.

Drive to understand. The Sound and the Fury can be recommended to college-bound students with an interest in literature, as an example of Faulkner's writing.

Using ability. Consider each of the major characters: Jason III and Caroline; their children Quentin, Candace, Jason IV and Benjy; Candace's daughter Quentin; and the cook, Dilsey. What are the elements of decay, and their origins? What elements work against decay, bending toward maintaining or advancing the family's viability? Which are inevitable, and over which do individuals have some measure of control? In your own life, can you identify negative and positive forces that may determine your future? Do you have any control? How are you using the opportunities you have to make the most of your circumstances?

Frankl, Viktor E. *Man's Search for Meaning: An Introduction to Logotherapy*. Translated from the German by Ilse Lasch. Boston: Beacon, 1962.

The first part of this book tells of Frankl's experience in Auschwitz and other concentration camps, where he spent three years as a slave laborer. A psychiatrist, he focuses on the psychological reactions he observed in himself and fellow prisoners. From his experiences came logotherapy, sometimes called the Third School of Viennese Psychiatry, after Freud and Adler. (Frankl speaks of the will to meaning, in contrast to Freud's will to pleasure and Adler's will to power.) The final third of the book gives a brief explanation of logotherapy.

This will be a useful book for young adults concerned with developing a philosophy of life, and may be especially helpful for those who experience existentialist depression. A few ideas which may be particularly intriguing: While existentialist philosopher Jean-Paul Sartre says that we invent ourselves, Frankl asserts that we do not invent the meaning of our existence, we detect it. He speaks of the existential vacuum which often manifests itself in boredom. And he speaks of the need for each person not to ask the meaning of life but to ask the meaning of his or her own life: "to life [we] can only respond by being responsible." In contrast to Maslow, Frankl believes that human existence is self-transcendence rather than self-actualization. (There is some evidence that Maslow would have added self-transcendence to his pyramid had he lived longer.)

Drive to understand. There is much material here for thought and discussion; the book can be read again years later for more depth. Adolescents will respond to those ideas for which they are ready. Leaders may do well to let them pose the questions for discussion.

French, Michael. *Us Against Them*. Toronto: Bantam, 1987.

Seven students in a small town in the Adirondacks have formed a club for mutual support against the boredom of small town life. When their clubhouse is torn down to make room for a highway, they go backpacking in the mountains for a few days, under the leadership of Reed, one of their number. Most of them have some reason to be distrustful, fearful, or at least not admiring of adults, but it is Reed's determination to avoid adult domination that gradually drives them all, not entirely willingly, to stay in the mountains until the adventure turns sour and then dangerous. The negative side of Reed's strong leadership takes over, and Marcy, Devon, and the rest finally realize that being independent is more complex than merely avoiding adults.

This is an adventure story in which characterization plays a more important role than action. We learn enough of the home lives of the club members to have some understanding of their reasons for reacting as they do. The character of Reed—almost pathologically self-sufficient, with an outer toughness concealing inner cowardice and self-deception—is especially well-developed. The theme of negative leadership and of following a leader versus standing alone for one's convictions offers good material for discussion.

Aloneness. What motivates Reed, Marcy, and Devon, and why?

Arrogance. How do you recognize and resist strong but misguided leadership?

Moral concerns. What finally gives Marcy the courage—or is it cowardice?—to tell the truth? Which quality, courage or cowardice, causes the twins to leave the cabin? Who betrays whom, Devon or Reed? How do you decide? If you were in the club, at what point would you have made your decision, and what would it have been? What in your background or belief system would motivate you and support you in your decision?

Fuller, Iola. *The Loon Feather.* San Diego: Harcourt, Brace Jovanovich, 1968 [1940].

Oneta, daughter of Tecumseh, grows up on Mackinac Island, at the confluence of Lakes Michigan and Huron, in the early years of the 19th century, when Mackinac was a fur-trading center where French and Indian cultures met. Her French stepfather sends her to school in Quebec, and when Oneta returns to Mackinac at 24 she has learned to see the best in each culture and to understand reasons for conflict between them. Eventually she chooses her Indian heritage, but she does so by serving as a bridge for her people from the old ways to the new.

In the person of Oneta, this unusual book gently compels the reader to look at two conflicting cultures with respect and understanding for each. Fuller masterfully evokes the natural beauty and atmosphere of a specific place, and the story is set in an accurately depicted historical period. Nevertheless, the theme of accepting the differences of others is a universal human challenge which Oneta and others meet with dignity and a sustaining sense of self. The book is recommended for its challenge to readers to hold two conflicting views at once, stretching their minds and sympathies.

Drive to understand. What qualities do you admire in Oneta? In Martin Reynolds? What knowledge of Native Americans have you gained from this book? What attitudes have changed as a result of reading *The Loon Feather*? What new understanding have you gained of other historical clashes of cultures? What applications are here for your own life?

Golding, William. *The Lord of the Flies*. New York: Coward-McCAnn, 1954.

A group of British boys is stranded on a coral island during an atomic war. Two leaders emerge immediately: the fair-minded Ralph, whose efforts focus on keeping a fire going to attract rescuers, and the militant Jack, who becomes a hunter and scorns efforts toward rescue. There is also the thoughtful Piggy, who is not a natural leader but whose insight guides Ralph. As the days wear on, memories of civilization fade, and the boys adopt primitive ways related to the hunt, painting their faces for camouflage and dancing to stir up blood lust. Horrible accidents occur as these practices continue unrestrained, and the boys gradually divide themselves into followers of Ralph or of Jack, with the majority following Jack. The boys—and the reader—long for adult supervision, but of course, the world's adults are busy destroying each other. Rescue comes at last, but not before the author's point about the dark side of human nature has been made.

Neverthless, this is not a depressing book. However overwhelmed they are by numbers, Ralph and Piggy never give up their faith in the group process or their search for what is right. Therefore the human spirit is not destroyed by the reversion to savagery of the other boys—one independent spirit can make all the difference.

Arrogance. What role does arrogance—the assumption of one individual that he is superior to others—play in this story?

Moral concerns. How does Ralph keep going in the final hunt? Why does he not align himself with Jack to save himself? What less dramatic examples do you see of the same behavior around you, or in the newspaper? Have you ever kept going when you were alone but right? What enabled you to do so?

Relationships with others. Describe and analyze Piggy's attitude toward being teased. How is it useful to him? How would you use his example to encourage an elementary school child to cope with teasing? (This question can be used to help high school students find a way to understand and accept painful teasing remembered from their own childhood.)

Hesse, Hermann. *Demian: The Story of Emil Sinclair's Youth.* New York: Harper and Row, 1965 (c 1925).

As the subtitle suggests, *Demian* is really not so much about Max Demian as it is about Emil Sinclair. Beginning with an incident that occurred when he was ten years of age, Sinclair recounts the "steps that I took to reach myself," ending with his first year of university and the beginning of World War I. In these years there are long periods when he has no contact with Demian at all, but each renewal of the friendship is highly significant for Sinclair's development. One other person, the musician and religious seeker Pistorius, is also important, both for what he teaches and for the fact that Sinclair must grow beyond him.

This psychologically-oriented account of the growing up of a highly sensitive, introspective boy has appealed to thoughtful young people since its first appearance. Sinclair is tormented by issues of right and wrong, good and evil; he tries desperately to understand how to live his life. "I wanted only to try to live in accord with the promptings which came from my true self. Why was that so very difficult?" In a time when it is difficult even to learn to *hear* the promptings from one's true self over the raucous demands of advertising and peer pressure, this book can be both a stimulus and a solace for those who march to their own drumbeat.

Aloneness. Why does Sinclair separate from his parents, even though it was a loving home? In what way does he return? How does this apply to you?

Identity. Such a personal book calls forth responses on a very personal level. Several themes may be drawn out in discussion: What is your interpretation of the "mark of Cain"? What is your experience of a *daemon* or fate? What objections might others raise to these concepts? How would you discuss them with those who might consider them elitist? Why was Pistorius not suitable as a long-term mentor? How does Sinclair's story help you understand yourself?

Intensity; Introversion; Sensitivity. Students who give evidence of these characteristics may enjoy this book because they see themselves in Sinclair.

Moral concerns. What is your interpretation of Demian's assertion that "Others sense their own laws within them; things are forbidden to them that every honorable man will do any day in the year and other things are allowed to them that are generally despised"?

Using ability. Sinclair says, "Each man had only one genuine vocation—to find the way to himself." Do you agree? How does this pertain to career choice?

Hesse, Hermann. *Steppenwolf.* Translated from the German by Basil Creighton, updated by Joseph Mileck. New York: Bantam, 1963 [c1927].

Harry Heller, a lonely intellectual of 47, calls himself the Steppenwolf—wolf of the Steppes—in acknowledgment of the animal, uncivilized part of his nature. Loneliness and existential suffering have become the dominant forces in his life, bringing him to the point of suicide. Then he meets Hermine, a beautiful young woman who takes him in hand, teaches him to dance, and introduces him to the life of the dance halls in the Germany of the 1920s. The story culminates in a masked ball, reminiscent of a Faustian revelry, which becomes mystical and symbolic. Harry emerges with a resolve to re-enter the game of life, this time to learn to laugh.

Even at 47, Harry still struggles to balance his intellectual interests—writing, classical music, and political theory—with more common concerns such as dancing, jazz, people, and laughter. The two parts of the story represent extremes: too sober and depressing until he meets Hermine, then happy and wild to the point of unreality. Suicide, loneliness, and Harry's inability to fit in are themes throughout the book, yet the overall impact is not depressing because Harry learns that neither intellectualism nor socializing is sufficient in itself. There must be a balance, and he will continue to try to find it.

Steppenwolf is not easy reading and should be recommended for older, mature, high-potential students who are likely to be dealing with similar issues. Ask students to identify themes they would like to discuss as they read the book.

Drive to understand. Themes for mind-expanding discussion include the concept that some people are "the suicides," or "those who see death and not life as the releaser"; Harry's dream of his interview with Goethe; his view of the bourgeoisie and of the immortals; Pablo's opinions on music versus Harry's; and Hermine's last talk with Harry, summarizing the views of both of them.

Identity. Consider with students the implication that Harry takes himself too seriously, that he needs to laugh at himself. If they have seen the film "Amadeus" compare and contrast Harry and his idol, Mozart, concerning laughter and taking oneself and one's work too seriously.

Introversion. Discuss Steppenwolf's search for balance between his natural introversion and his need to be with people.

Relationships with others. How can others be helpful to Steppenwolf? How might they be damaging? How should he act to make the most of relationships with other people?

Hunt, Irene. *William.* New York: Scribner, 1977.

Eight-year-old William and his sisters Amy and Carla would have been left alone when Mama died, if she had not established a bond with Sarah, a teenager who has come to live in her aunt's house until her baby is born. Then the three children and baby Elizabeth become a family headed by Sarah—but the arrangement is threatened when Amy and Sarah quarrel. Through it all William grows and matures, and when Sarah has the opportunity to study art in Chicago, he is able to accept her departure.

Though told from the point of view of William, this book is at least equally interesting for Sarah's story: an artist and an unmarried teenage mother, burdened with too many responsibilities and distrustful of the conventional world, she nevertheless plays her role well, providing essential support to the younger children while using this period of several years to gather her own forces.

Using ability. Discuss Sarah's reasons for not wanting to go to art school. Why does she finally go? What would you have done? What has she gained from her time in Florida? In what ways is she conventional and unconventional? Where do you fall on this scale? How does Sarah's position on the conventional-unconventional continuum affect her potential to use her talent? How does your position affect yours?

Hunter, Mollie. *Cat, Herself.* New York: Harper and Row, 1985.

Catriona McPhie, a young teenager, is a Scottish "traveller," one of a tightly-knit group who rove constantly from one place to another, living by skills passed from father to son, mother to daughter. Cat loves the travelling life, but she rebels against the confined roles assigned to women. Moreover, lacking a son, her father teaches Cat to hunt, poach, and pearl. Possessing these male skills, Cat is different even within a group that is different, and she is determined to be Cat, herself, even in marriage. Charlie Drummond understands this, at least in part, and when they marry, it is with the knowledge that she may someday leave him to follow her dream.

The strengths of this book are in the descriptions of the travellers and their way of life, leading the reader to see the people behind the veil that initial prejudice may throw over them. In the character of Cat the theme is clearly that of a woman's right to independence, and Cat carries that theme well. This book can be useful in discussing with talented young women the options they have as they make educational decisions that affect their future achievement level.

Differentness; *Identity*. How does Cat's differentness help to form her sense of identity? How is it helpful to her?

Using ability. Should Cat have married Charlie? What options does she have? In what ways will Cat and Charlie need to grow for the marriage to last? What compromises will be required for Cat to realize her dream? What options do you have at this point in your life? What decisions will you have to make to keep those options available?

Hunter, Mollie. *Hold on to Love.* Cambridge: Harper and Row, 1983.

In this sequel to *A Sound of Chariots* (reviewed in the Middle School section), Bridie McShane is living in Edinburgh with her grandparents, working in the family flower shop while she strives to become a writer. In her night school English class she meets Peter McKinley. Their friendship grows into love, but when Peter becomes possessive, Bridie fears their relationship might threaten her independence and hinder her freedom to write. Under the shadow of World War II, they argue and finally reconcile, as the two of them confront the issues her talent presents to them.

This well-written love story can be recommended simply as that. In addition, Bridie's belief in her talent and her commitment to it can be a model for high school girls of high ability in any area. Bridie never gives up on her ambition, even teaching herself not to say "I want to be a writer" but to call herself a writer now, in the present tense. Even in the pain of separation after her quarrel with Peter, her faith in her own future gives reassurance that she was right to insist that Peter not treat her as a possession.

Identity; Intensity. What is the source of Bridie's faith in herself and her talent? How can young people gain and nurture such confidence?

Using ability. What characteristics typically associated with creative talent does Bridie have that make her life more difficult? Easier? What qualities in Peter and Bridie attract them to each other? How would her life have been different if Bridie had subordinated her ability to her relationship with Peter?

Kerr, Barbara. *Smart Girls, Gifted Women.* Columbus: Ohio Psychology Publishing, 1985.

This is nonfiction, a report of a research study done by Kerr as the result of a high school reunion. The gifted women in her class asked her to find out why they were pursuing typical careers or homemaking, instead of being the world leaders they had been told they would be.

In a readable style, Kerr discusses the developmental history of most gifted girls, the barriers to intellectual achievement, the family-career conflict, and ways in which gifted girls can be helped to aim higher. She includes several short biographical sketches of eminent women that illustrate her findings.

Gifted teenaged girls should read this book as part of their task of recognizing how their intelligence affects their choices over the next few critical years. It may make them uneasy about choices they have already made that could limit their futures, and it will be quite natural for them to set the book aside unless they talk with women who are old enough to give living examples of what Kerr is describing.

Identity. Where in the book do you see yourself? Your friends? Your mother or other older relatives? What changes would you like to see in the pattern? What obstacles do you see?

What suggestions would you have for young women who want to overcome the obstacles?

Using ability. What critical decisions will you be making in the next few years that determine whether you can make maximum use of your abilities? What planning can you do to keep your options open as long as possible? What are the patterns of decision-making by gifted women that you should be aware of in yourself?

Lagerkvist, Pär. *Barabbas.* Translated by Alan Blair. New York: Random, 1951.

Swedish intellectual Pär Lagerkvist has written a fictional account of the life of Barabbas after he was selected to be freed, and Jesus crucified in his stead. Stunned and inarticulate, Barabbas listens to Peter describe the crucifixion from his point of view, then goes to the tomb on Easter morning to see the stone rolled away. He finally leaves Jerusalem to rejoin his band of thieves, but finds that he no longer belongs. Years of slavery follow, and when he is taken to Rome he becomes aware of the Christians there. Still inarticulate, he is drawn toward them, and finally joins them in his own way, without their knowledge or consent; he remains alone to the end.

This fine book demands the best of the reader, and offers a journey inward. It can lead to discussion on many levels. One useful approach is the question of Barabbas's aloneness, so fundamental as to put the loneliness most of us experience in a different perspective. Also important is the potential the book has to help focus the religious questions many inquisitive people begin to raise in the senior high years.

Drive to understand. It might be helpful to talk of Barabbas not as a person but as an archetype: the Barabbas story. What is universal here? How does he represent—potentially—the experience of all of us? What does his story tell us about being human? Is the Barabbas story a necessary part of the Jesus story? How? What do we learn of our own potential in pondering the Barabbas story?

Introversion; Moral concerns. These two categories, too, might be useful points of departure for discussion, depending on the students and the context.

Langone, John. *Thorny Issues: How Ethics and Morality Affect the Way We Live*. Boston: Little, Brown, 1981.

    In a book for the high school reader, Langone explores ethics in several pertinent areas: medicine, war, capital punishment, business and government, science and technology, the press, and human rights. In each case he presents the issues and abiding questions, only occasionally giving clues as to the "right" answer. He makes it clear that far from being a matter for philosophers only, ethics and morality should be concerns for everyone who wishes to live responsibly.

    Both the book and related discussion will help to focus the thinking of gifted adolescents who are already debating these issues internally. The book makes clear, and discussion can affirm, the responsibility we all have to think these issues through and to make what impact we can on decisions regarding them. Idealistic and sometimes cynical gifted young people need to hear the assertion that we can do something about these problems, and that they can and must contribute.

    Questions abound in the book. Each chapter will provide material for several discussions. The leader might consider covering one chapter at a time, rather than hoping to discuss the entire book in one session. Some sections, especially those on medical ethics and war, may be depressing for idealistic young adults, and discussion should confront the depression or discouragement. The adult leader would do well to have thought through his or her own answers before discussing the book with a teenager.

    Drive to understand; Moral concerns.

LeGuin, Ursula K. *Very Far Away from Anywhere Else*. New York: Atheneum, 1976.

    Owen Griffiths tells his story, of being "a bright little jerk" and how he deals with being different. When he was in junior high he tried to conform, but now that he is sixteen, he knows that conforming for the sake of conformity will not work for him, although he is still not comfortable being himself. Natalie Fields is. She is also a gifted musician, self-sufficient and self-directed. Owen learns from Natalie, and when the friendship shows signs of turning into love he learns even more, especially about taking charge of his own future.

This book shows several facets of being alone and different because of unusual talent, and how two people cope with it, although they are also different from each other.

Aloneness; Introversion. What is the difference between Owen's kind of aloneness, and Natalie's kind? Natalie likes herself better than Owen does. How has she learned to do that? What difference does it make in her life? Does it make her less alone?

Identity. How does Owen feel about himself when he says he was a bright little jerk? Have you ever tried to conform, as Owen did, and found it not right for you? What will happen to Owen's and Natalie's sense of being different as they grow older? Describe how you think of them as adults. What are they doing now that will cause them to grow into the kind of people you describe? Describe yourself as an adult. What characteristics do you have that will bring about the person you describe?

Using ability. How does Natalie make decisions about her future? And Owen? What changes does Owen make in this book? What has he learned?

Moliere, Jean Baptiste Poquelin. *The Misanthrope*. Woodbury, N.Y.: Barron's Educational Series, 1959. (Written in 1666).

Set in Moliere's contemporary and fashionable 17th century Paris, this drama is one of the masterpieces of the great French comedian. Alceste values sincerity in communication with others so highly that he is uncomfortable with the flattery that is considered good manners in courtly drawing rooms. He becomes quite fanatical about it, ignoring and hurting well-meaning friends and finally resolving to withdraw from society altogether because in his eyes it is so dishonest.

Moliere's genius is to draw the comedic and the serious very close together, so this comedy offers material for thoughtful discussion. However, high school students may need some background to understand the excesses of the French court at that time. If the play is only read, the comedy will not come through nearly as poignantly as it does on the stage.

Arrogance. What role does, or should, tolerance for human weakness play?

Intensity. How far can one sensibly go in standing up for his values? How much is Alceste losing?

Relationships with others. Is Alceste justified in hurting others for his beliefs? How do we know whether and when to sacrifice honesty for politeness? How might he have avoided the way the play ends?

Perfectionism. What standards do you feel very strongly about? In what ways do you compromise? Should you?

The Music of What Happens: Poems that Tell Stories. Selected by Paul B. Janeczko. New York: Orchard, 1988.

In this collection of story poems, some are clearly narrative and some more symbolically so, requiring the reader to interpret, teasing out the story lines. There are good examples here of why poetry is sometimes the vehicle of choice for a writer. The collection includes many recent poems which are unlikely to be in a literature anthology. They appeal to high school students for their down-to-earth quality and directness of language, with ordinary working people speaking of hard realities.

Drive to understand.

Peace and War: A Collection of Poems. Chosen by Michael Harrison and Christopher Stuart-Clark. New York: Oxford U.P., 1989.

These are not all war poems, but a collection arranged to trace both individual and universal experiences of war. The compilers begin with poems expressing a heightened awareness of the beauty and joy of life. Next they offer poems that deal with war—at first indirectly, with poems about preparations for war, and then directly, as they move on to poetic description of war itself, and the emotions that accompany it. Finally they turn to peace, gathering poetry about the relief and sad wisdom that follow the turmoil of war. The poems they have selected come from over 2000 years of literature, reinforcing the universality of the experience of war and its aftermath.

Drive to understand.

Peck, Richard. *Remembering the Good Times.* New York: Delacorte, 1985.

At sixteen, Buck Mendenhall looks back over the last four years to tell the story of his friendship with Kate Lucas and Trav Kirby. Coming from different backgrounds, they are brought together by the transformation of their rural area into an affluent suburb. Together they face the stresses of adolescence in a too-rapidly changing world. It is Trav, the brilliant and wealthy one, who finally cannot cope with the combination of pressure at home and mediocrity and neglect in the new school.

This book is rich in characters, relationships, and issues for discussion, but paramount is the suicide of bright, intense, sensitive Trav. Discussion of suicide is difficult but worth the effort. Leaders should be prepared with their personal answers to the questions they ask, however incomplete those answers may be.

Identity. Trav and Kate both have talent. What are the differences that make Kate stronger? Do you agree with Kate: "I'll never trust anything again. I'll never believe in anything or anybody. You can count on that"?

Using ability. Why did Trav kill himself? Whose "fault" was it? How might it have been prevented? What could Trav have done to prevent it? How do you answer the questions he raised about "deteriorating conditions" and the lack of challenge in school?

Peyton, K. M. *The Beethoven Medal.* New York: Crowell, 1971.

In this second Pennington book, following *Pennington's Last Term*, Patrick Pennington is studying piano on a scholarship and working as a bakery delivery boy when Ruth Hollis meets him. Ruth is puzzled by the gulf between Pat's working class background, his aggressive, rough manners, and his jail record—and the other world he enters as a potential concert pianist. The conflicts within Pat are not resolved by the end of the book, and the relationship between him and Ruth seems likely to continue, at least for a while.

The book presents a strong portrait of the lengths to which a gifted person may have to go to develop a gift. Pat is an example of one who has made a firm commitment to his talent, but is still tormented by the negative aspects of some of the very characteristics that, put to constructive use, could make him a concert pianist. A complex person, Pat is not entirely explained in this book, nor is Ruth, whose relationship to Pat seems to be rather slavish without sufficient reason given for that. The book can nevertheless be useful for dicussion. It is demanding reading for younger readers, partly because of British slang. The toughness of Pat and his friends may make the book appealing to some readers.

Achievement. If Pat succeeds as a pianist, what factors would be the cause of his success? If he fails, what factors?

Identity. There are two distinct sides to Pat. Which do you think is real? What reasons do you have for your answer? What factors will determine which side of himself Pat develops? What responsibiity does he himself have in the determination?

Using ability. What must Pat do to stop the cycle of behavior in which he appears to be caught? What evidence do you see that he will be able to do so? What evidence to the contrary? Can you give other examples of people with negative traits that threaten to cancel out the realization of their talents?

Pirsig, Robert M. *Lila: An Inquiry into Morals*. New York: Bantam, 1991.

The author of *Zen and the Art of Motorcycle Maintenance* continues to state his Metaphysics of Quality in the form of a novel. The story line in *Lila* has Phaedrus sailing down the Hudson River, hoping to get to Florida before winter. In a bar in Kingston he meets Lila, who joins him and becomes a focus for some of his metaphysical musings. In this book it is Lila who slips toward insanity as Phaedrus watches with concern.

The real stuff of the book is the wide-ranging philosophy, and *Lila* is suitable only for those who will be intrigued by that—the story line is too slight to hold interest by itself. But those who would like an informal glimpse of philosophy at work can watch Phaedrus's mind roam as he explores such topics as the state of anthropology, Indian versus Victorian morals, European values versus late-20th-century American values, and religion and science.

Drive to understand. Phaedrus's musings provide plenty of discussion starters. To avoid too much leader domination, readers could be asked to jot down page numbers when they find a discussion they would like to pursue with the leader. Or they might be encouraged to follow one theme—the Victorian theme, or the anthropological, for example—throughout the book. Victorians specialized in manners, 20th-century intellectuals in causes. What's next? Another recurring topic is the opposing roles of society and the intellect. How does this conflict affect you? How does your response to it compare with Pirsig's? He says intellectual patterns have won. Do you agree?

Moral concerns. Are Victorian moral codes returning? If we do not return to Victorian values, what will replace them?

Reade, Charles. *The Cloister and the Hearth.* New York: Random. First published in 1861.

Erasmus, the great Dutch humanist, scholar and theologian, was born probably in 1466, apparently out of wedlock. The 19th-century British writer Charles Reade wove a long and carefully-researched novel around the imagined lives of Erasmus's parents. In Reade's fiction, the young Gerard Eliasson and Margaret a Peter are cruelly separated after an interrupted marriage ceremony, and Gerard, a gifted scribe and illustrator, flees Holland to seek his fortune in Italy, home of the arts. When he is told, falsely, that Margaret has died, he turns to the priesthood in despair. The real love story unfolds later, after Gerard returns to Holland and, finding Margaret and their son there, relives the anguish of separation. The young Erasmus grows up knowing both parents, though Margaret and Gerard continue to live separate lives, caring for each other from a distance and working together in providing for the poor people in their community.

This is a long book (913 pages in the Modern Library edition) to be read not for a deadline, not to finish the book, but for the pleasure gained in the reading—a summer book, with much food for thought. Wonderfully versatile, Reade writes equally convincingly of the raw danger in medieval foot travel and of subtle psychological change; of theological reflection and domestic strife; of friendship among men and among women. The language he employs is an early form of modern English, sprinkled with bits of Latin, Greek, French, and German, in sentences graced by rhythm and framed in long cadences—a luxuriant style in refreshing contrast to the short, choppy sentences of many 20th-century novels. There is humor, based on understatement, and controlled outrage at the social injustices of the day. Altogether this is a compelling picture of conditions in the late medieval period, bringing the 15th Century to life in the reader's imagination. Highly recommended although it is out of print, *The Cloister and the Hearth* is both a challenge and a pleasure, worth the effort of locating through interlibrary loan if necessary.

Drive to understand. Erasmus appears in the book, but only as a child. A follow-up might be to read about Erasmus, read something by Erasmus, and then look for foreshadowing—has Reade attributed to Gerard any stirrings of ideas which Erasmus brought to fruition, perhaps in his correspondence with Martin Luther?

Moral concerns. Can we separate the 15th century attitudes Reade describes from the 19th century attitudes in which he was steeped—attitudes toward women, toward the Church, toward Germans, French, Italians, Dutch?

Sagan, Carl. *The Dragons of Eden: Speculations on the Evolution of Human Intelligence.* New York: Random, 1977.

High school students who enjoy conjecture may be interested in this popularized version of brain structure and function. For example, they might find challenge in—or wish to challenge—Sagan's suggestions regarding the link between the development of the neocortex and the Genesis story. As the subtitle points out, Sagan is here presenting "speculations" rather than hard science, and the book must be read in that spirit. However, the book is sufficiently grounded in science to hold the interest of a reader open to questioning.

Drive to understand. Discussion could easily be based on questions and responses to Sagan's speculations that occur to the reader while reading. Suggest that readers note questions and comments as they read, and bring them to the discussion.

Smith, Huston. *The Religions of Man.* New York: Harper & Row, 1958.

The son of missionaries to China and a professor of philosophy at Massachusetts Institute of Technology, Huston Smith has written descriptions of seven great religions: Hinduism, Buddhism, Confucianism, Taoism, Islam, Judaism, and Christianity. His aim is to convey "the meaning these religions carry for the lives of their adherents." Accordingly, he writes little of doctrine and less of history (both of which are to be found in a good adult encyclopedia), but reveals for each "why and how they guide and motivate the lives of those who live by them." In the final chapter he presents a sound argument for accepting the validity of each faith for the people who follow it.

Drive to understand. Senior high students who are beginning their personal religious search find this book useful, especially appreciating Smith's objectivity, which frees them to reach their own conclusions. The objectivity is balanced by a respect for each religion and its people—a human perspective which prevents the material from ever becoming intellectualized or dry. Thoughtful young people seeking meaning for their lives will find here seven different broad approaches to the question of meaning which have stood the test of time. Moreover, while acknowledging the triviality and violence to which religion can descend, Smith describes each religion in its highest, most intellectually and spiritually challenging form. Readers will find stimulus for thought in each religion, and will gain a greater understanding for its followers.

Stone, Bruce. *Been Clever Forever.* New York: Harper and Row, 1988.

Stephen Douglass is an intelligent, divergent thinker, who as he enters senior high already has one major debacle on his record which caused a teacher to lose his job. The first week of tenth grade, the biology teacher, N. A. Truelove, sarcastically selects Stephen for use as a specimen, encouraging the class to document Stephen's cleverness. Later, in a rage, Truelove vandalizes the classroom. Stephen, the only witness, is blamed. As the story spins out Stephen is asked to help get Truelove fired, to help Truelove escape gracefully, and to be a cause celebre for activist student Peggy Klecko, who pushes him into running for class president. Stephen is pulled in all directions. His parents are supportive but divorced and immature. Thus Stephen is surrounded by adults who are as unsure as he is about what to do next.

This is one of a few books which face giftedness head on, labeling it and showing how a gifted person fails to meet the varied expectations of others. It is indeed cleverly written, demonstrating some of the negative qualities of cleverness: the humor is brittle, and feelings are in a shell. Stephen's father is an example of a gifted underachiever, a perfectionist who has not yet succeeded as an adult—though he may in the future. All three major adult figures, Stephen's parents and teacher, betray a sense of emptiness at 40; yet we view them with sympathy, and the book ends on a realistically positive note. Perhaps the best summary of the ambiguities portrayed in the book is from Nu Tran, Stephen's friend who perceptively describes him as "unusual to know but very worthwhile. Sometimes may be a puzzle with many solutions, to himself I think sometimes too."

Achievement. Discussion could start with Stephen's father's story. How could it have been different? How much of a factor is the war in Vietnam? Giftedness? Other factors? What did he need in addition to top grades? How will his story end?

Arrogance. Stephen describes the news show interview as though he were an outside observer. What are the dangers of this facet of cleverness? What are likely consequences of hiding behind cleverness? Is this arrogance?

Identity. Why does Stephen never tell us how he feels? On the few occasions when we know how he feels, how do we know? How would Jamie describe Stephen? What recommendations or predictions would she make for him? In what ways do you think he should change? Why? How could he accomplish it?

Using ability. In a gifted person, what function does cleverness play? If it is a negative role, how can that be changed?

Storr, Anthony. *Solitude: A Return to the Self.* New York: The Free Press, 1988.

A Clinical Lecturer in Psychiatry at Oxford, Anthony Storr suggests that post-Freudian psychological theories place too much emphasis on interpersonal relationships as a sole foundation of human happiness. He argues instead that, especially for the creatively gifted, solitude may be essential to a contented, productive life. Certainly, the desire for solitude is not to be thought of as pathological. "If it is considered desirable to foster the growth of the child's imaginative capacity, we should ensure that our children . . . are given time and opportunity for solitude" (p. 17). "The capacity to be alone . . . becomes linked with self-discovery and self-realization . . ." (p. 21). Storr explores the role of solitude in learning, thinking, creativity, and self-knowledge, as well as in grief work and religious insight, and he suggests that individuals can find life's meaning in interests and ideas as well as in intimate relationships. Indeed, for some gifted individuals at some times, ideas may be more important than relationships.

Chapters on solitude and creativity late in life may not appeal to teenage readers, but Storr's extensive use of biographical material to illustrate his point undoubtedly will. The book should prove reassuring to those unusual students, the highly gifted in particular, who are more comfortable alone than with others.

Aloneness; Introversion. How do you feel about alone time? How do those around you feel about it? How well do you use it? If you need more, how would you get it?

Relationships with others. In your own life, what is the present balance between interests and relationships? Are you happy with the balance? How would you change it?

Using ability. What implications does this idea of balance between ideas or interests and interpersonal relationships have for your career choice?

Tate, Joan. *Tina and David.* Nashville: Nelson, 1973.

Tina is a shy girl with not much color in her life. Nevertheless she becomes a lifeline of human communication for David, who had been traumatized as a child and who is so terribly shy that for him speaking is very, very difficult, sometimes impossible. Tina's shyness prevents her from asking him to speak; since she accepts him as he is, he becomes comfortable enough to speak to her.

Despite his silence, David is clearly intelligent, but he has been hampered in his development by the loss of his parents and then his grandmother. His extreme loneliness symbolizes how lonely we all are, how much a small word or touch can mean. There seems to be nothing special about Tina, so the story demonstrates that all of us, even those who appear ordinary, can offer much to each other without knowing it. It leaves us with a sense of how vastly important we are to each other, and how easily we overlook that in daily life, allowing ourselves to be turned aside by the defenses others set up. *Tina and David* strips away the daily defenses, leaving David starkly vulnerable. Tina is sensitive to his defenselessness and does not violate it. Their story makes it clear that to need is not weakness—David is needy but tough; and to be needed does not require what we usually think of as strength—Tina is needed, although in some ways she is weak. To need and be needed is merely human.

Relationships with others; Sensitivity. If you met Tina or David in the factory, would you want to know them better? What people do you know who might be worth knowing better? Is there anyone in your class who is quiet, whom you might try to get to know? What *in you* makes that difficult? Or are you the quiet person others don't know well? How can you help them get to know you? Have you ever been thought standoffish when you were really shy? Do you know anyone who seems aloof who might be merely shy? What can be done about that? To whom might you be important?

Thomas, Elizabeth Marshall. *Reindeer Moon*. Boston: Houghton Mifflin, 1987.

Set in Siberia 20,000 years ago, this novel of prehistory tells the story of Yanan, who is thirteen years old when the story begins. Gathered in family groups of about a dozen people, traveling on foot, following the animals to summer and winter hunting grounds, and subject always to sudden death through injury, illness, or childbirth—or slow death through starvation—Yanan's people focus first on finding food and secondly on the complex social fabric of their lives. Thomas depicts well the dependence of these hunter-gatherers on the animals of the plains they roam—lions, tigers, horses, deer, wolves, mammoths—and assumes that there is a consequent intimacy of the spiritual lives of animals and people. Much of the novel focuses on the spiritual lives of the people, and the interweaving of personal and spiritual relationships creates an absorbing story line, despite the repetition of the relentless search for food.

Courageous, headstrong, and alone, Yanan comes of age without her parents' guidance, and she makes some fatal errors in judgment. Readers will recognize the impatience, impetuosity, and moodiness of adolescence, despite the millenia which separate Yanan and today's young people—who face essentially the same questions.

Drive to understand. What gives meaning to the lives of Yanan's people? What can we learn from this fictional version of paleolithic life that helps us define what is essentially human? From this perspective, discuss the role of material goods in defining what it is to be human. In the same light, consider the role of knowledge, which has increased so much; the role of developments in religion since 18,000 B.C.; and the changes in our relationship to animals.

Thomas, Joyce Carol. *Marked by Fire*. New York: Avon, 1982.

Growing up in the black community of an Oklahoma town, Abby Jackson learns wisdom and strength from her mother, from Mother Barker, from the rural rhythm of nature and the sudden devastation of a tornado, and from the cruelty of some of her neighbors. After an assault, she stops using her lovely singing voice. Mother Barker and her mother help her gradually to regain her sense of self, and she reaches adulthood with a deep, sure sense of her own uniqueness, and a commitment to use her healing abilities, as well as her voice, for others.

The style moves imperceptibly betwen prose and poetry. Evocations of the rhythms of speech in the singing and story-telling of the women of the community are especially powerful. There is a haunting quality in the writing style and in the person of Abby herself that makes this a beautiful book to read.

Identity. Abby's parents are Patience and Strong. How does Abby develop and use these qualities? Why are they especially useful for a sensitive person like Abby? Are you aware of using or developing them in your own life? How do you know when to use which?

Relationships with others. What examples are there in the book of acceptance of human failings? Is it a strength or a weakness to be so accepting? Why? How is it related to Abby's acceptance of her special talents?

Using ability. Will Abby become a doctor? Should she? Why or why not?

Tillich, Paul. *The Dynamics of Faith.* New York: Harper & Row, 1957.

Tillich examines the phenomenon of faith objectively, analytically, and apart from specific doctrinal content, so that although he is one of this century's great Christian theologians, followers of other religions, too, can read this book for greater understanding of their experience of their own faith. Defining faith as "ultimate concern," he considers what faith is and is not, the symbols of faith, and types of faith. Sections on mythology and humanism as they relate to faith may be of particular interest to gifted high school students.

Drive to understand. This book is suggested as an introduction for questioning young people to religious thinking at its highest and most challenging—therefore potentially most interesting—level. Whether they are among those who take religion seriously or those who question whether religion has any value at all, or those who read simply for exposure to a new field, interested high school students would do well to meet Tillich. This book is a good introduction to his thought.

Tolan, Stephanie S. *The Last of Eden*. New York: Warne, 1980.

Mike (Michelle) Caine tells of her sophomore and junior years at Turnbull Hall, a private boarding school on the shores of Lake Huron which she regards as a perfect Eden. Mike is a writer, and her roommate, Marty, is an artist; their strong friendship is based on their shared commitment to their arts. The new art teacher, Priscilla Kincaid, inspires Marty to greater effort and achievement than ever before. But Kincaid's husband, a history teacher, is so attractive that another sophomore, Bits, develops a crush on him. When Bits begins a rumor that the relationship between Marty and Priscilla Kincaid is a homosexual one, both Mike and Marty learn what it is like to be at the center of a vortex of tension, suspicion, and lies, testing all of their friendships. The furor is finally glossed over before the end of the school year, and the Kincaids leave Turnbull. The next fall a new student, Sylva, identifies the strongest friendship in the class—Mike and Marty—and determines to make her mark by breaking it up. She does so by convincing Marty that her strong feelings for Priscilla Kincaid had indeed been more than those of a sensitive student for her mentor. Finally Marty and Sylva both leave Turnbull, and Mike is left to rebuild relationships with her old friends. Turnbull is an Eden no more, but Mike is beginning to realize she must rely first of all on her own strength.

Themes for discussion related to building a personal identity are the balance between depending on others and on oneself for stability, and the teen-age search for a sexual identity. The theme of homosexuality is skillfully handled, open-ended, leaving room for education and discussion. Since no one in the story is clearly homosexual, the topic can be discussed from a relatively non-threatening theoretical angle, making this book a good way to begin discussion on this difficult subject.

Identity. What people and events cause Mike to begin seeing herself as an individual? How does her writing help? What similar people, events, and skills do you find in your life? Why was Bits's rumor so destructive? Tolan wrote this book in 1980—how might the girls' response be different now?

Relationships with others. What are the sources of interpersonal stability in Mike's life? Why do her friendships survive the rumors? What contributions do others in the story make to demonstrate fidelity in friendship? Can you identify people in your own life who play the role of Scovie?

Using ability. Are the difficulties Marty experiences as the result of success with her art inevitable? What is the price paid for the pursuit of excellence in an art—or elsewhere? Why do many, like Marty, believe it is worth it? What do you think?

Tolan, Stephanie S. *No Safe Harbors.* New York: Fawcett Juniper, 1981.

Amanda Sterling is the sixteen-year-old daughter of the wealthy mayor of a town on the Ohio River. Her ten-year-old brother, Doug, is a precocious loner, intent on rock-hunting, and her mother represents the proper mayor's wife, an activist in correct causes. Amanda has just met Joe Schmidt, who is working at the marina because his father refused to sign the college financial forms when Joe insisted on studying English rather than something practical. When Amanda learns that her father is guilty of accepting a bribe, her problem of rejecting her father is comparable to Joe's problem of rejecting his.

Both Doug and Joe are gifted, and some of the problems of giftedness are explored through them. They cope in different ways. Doug has given up on having friends his own age; Joe tries to learn to like rock music. Amanda's difference from her friends is evidenced in her values: Her friends assume and accept her father's guilt. Amanda eventually accepts him, but not what he did.

Identity. What are the advantages of Doug's way of coping with being different? The disadvantages? Reread the discussion about dealing with feeling different (beginning on page 64 in the noted edition). What would you add to that? What does it say that you have not considered before?

Using ability. For both Doug and Joe, it is very important to be able to make the best possible use of their intelligence. What are the advantages to people who are able to do that? What are the disadvantages to those who cannot? In your own life, what steps must you take to become one who can make maximum use of intelligence or talent? How well are you doing at it right now?

Turner, George. *Brain Child.* New York: Morrow, 1991.

David Chance is raised in an Australian orphanage in the mid-21st century. As an adult, he learns that his father is alive, one of the survivors of a genetic experiment that produced four sets of four siblings each, with each group extraordinarily superior in a different area. The novel revolves around the mystery of the C group, so intellectually brilliant that they could not communicate in any meaningful way with *homo sapiens*, and why they all suddenly died, committing suicide by force of will, one day while still in their late teens. As David investigates the events leading up to their deaths, he is drawn closer to the only family he has—but finds it far more disturbing and even dangerous than welcoming.

George Turner is one of Australia's best-known writers of science fiction, and *Brain Child* is only the third of his many books to be published in the United States. This novel raises questions about the nature of very high intelligence. While C group's intelligence is so extreme as to be other worldly, it suggests discussion that can explore at a safe distance issues that concern very bright students.

Drive to understand. What can individuals of very high intelligence do about their need to communicate with others?

Moral concerns. Turner's book presents other issues for discussion, too: the moral implications of genetic research, or of any research on human subjects; questions related to the role of politics in science, and what happens when politics is in control, and the problems arising when scientists pursue research before thoroughly considering possible outcomes.

Vinke, Hermann. *The Short Life of Sophie Scholl.* New York: Harper and Row, 1980.

Born in Germany in 1921, the child of enlightened, progressive parents, Sophie Scholl enjoyed a childhood rich with books, music, and outings until Hitler came to power in 1933. Sophie joined her brother Hans at the University of Munich in 1942, just as he and a group of close friends were founding the White Rose, an organization for students who opposed Hitler, the war effort, and Nazism—a very dangerous position. Sophie eagerly joined as the group wrote, printed, and distributed leaflets calling for the downfall of Hitler. In February 1943, Sophie and Hans were arrested and executed for high treason, as were several of their friends.

Although the story of the White Rose has been told in Germany in film and in print, it is relatively unknown in the United States. Vinke's book tells Sophie's story through narrative interspersed with letters, memoirs, the words of those who knew her, and her letters and drawings. She combined a strong, unswerving moral sense with introspection and shyness. Sophie and her friends read and discussed Socrates, St. Augustine, Mann, and Heine, and they enjoyed music and studied art and graphics design. They did these things not to appear to be intellectuals, but in order to grow up, looking for answers to the questions life posed for them. They questioned seriously, took life seriously—but also sang, danced, hiked, swam, and enjoyed nature as well as art.

Drive to understand. Discuss Hans's conflict with his father over political issues, and with the Hitler Youth. What do these conflicts tell you about the social and political climate in Germany during the pre-war period? What do Sophie's thoughts on patriotism add to this picture? Was what the White Rose did "unreasonable and foolhardy" (p. 213) under the circumstances? How can you explain why they did it? What can today's young people learn from the Scholls and the White Rose?

Identity. What was the impact of the books she read on the development of Sophie's identity? What did religion mean to her? There was a dichotomoy between the rational and the emotional aspects in Sophie's nature. How did she integrate the two? What can you learn from this?

Intensity. Consider Sophie's words, "We carry all our standards within ourselves, only we don't look for them closely enough. Perhaps because they are our severest standards" (p. 211). What are the standards within you? What are the advantages of not looking for them closely enough? The disadvantages?

Moral concerns. Sophie's parents provided everything a bright and sensitive child needs to develop into a strong individual, and this book is exceptionally rich in examples of what it can mean to stand alone for one's convictions. Discuss these quotes from the interview with poet Ilse Aichinger: "This hope made it possible for us to go on living in those days, even though it had nothing to do with hope of survival" (p. 207), and "You have to see a future *within yourself*" (p. 208). Aichinger comments about Sophie "making a decision against herself" (p. 213). How does this happen? When is it necessary? Who else has done so? Why? What were the results?

Voigt, Cynthia. *Izzy, Willy-Nilly.* New York: Atheneum, 1986.

Izzy is a sophomore, a pretty, popular cheerleader, when she accepts Marco's invitation to a party, not because she especially likes him, but because he is a senior. Marco drinks too much, and the accident on the way home results in the amputation of Izzy's right leg. As she recuperates, Izzy watches her friendships change. Marco never calls, even to apologize. Lauren, who plans to be a model, withdraws from Izzy, overwhelmingly appalled at physical imperfection. Suzy's habit of lying becomes a too-familiar brand of false friendliness. Even Izzy's strong and loving parents, who deal efficiently with the practical aspects of her handicap, are not available to recognize her emotional vulnerability. Only Roseamunde, who is seen as weird and is rejected by Izzy's popular group, comes forward as a friend who can accept and reflect what Izzy is experiencing, though she does so awkwardly at first. The daughter of an artist, Roseamunde is more intellectual than the others and different in her own right—and she says exactly what she feels, a trait that enables her to reach Izzy in her isolation. When Izzy returns to school she finds that she is still popular, but now she is on her way to becoming an individual.

Voigt offers an absorbing story line with a psychological depth that continues to merit thought and discussion long after the reading is done. A teacher, she records the high school atmosphere accurately, and even the weaker characters are sympathetically drawn. Roseamunde, with the social awkwardness combined with the sensitivity, maturity, penetrating insights, and direct honesty characteristic of many bright and introspective people, is especially memorable.

Identity. What does Izzy learn about herself from Roseamunde? From the accident? In what other ways can high school students become individuals, beyond the high school scene? Why is it so important to Izzy that Roseamunde is so direct? Why does Roseamunde seem rough, and Izzy smooth, in being honest? Why is Roseamunde more developed as an individual by the age of fifteen than Izzy?

Relationships with others. What did Roseamunde see in Izzy that led her to believe she could be a friend? What do Roseamunde and Izzy have in common with each other that they do not share with Lisa, Lauren, and Suzy? What can they continue to learn from each other?

Vonnegut, Kurt. *Slaughterhouse-five*. New York: Delacorte, 1969.

Twenty-four years after the city of Dresden, "the Florence of the Elbe," was firebombed by the Allied Powers, Vonnegut published this novel based on his experiences as a prisoner of war and survivor of that masssacre. As is fitting for an event too awful to look at straight on, the narrative dances around the bombing, foreshadowing the terrible event we know is coming but then glancing off to focus instead on the story of Billy Pilgrim, the chaplain's assistant who plays Vonnegut's role. Billy is a time-traveler; his consciousness shifts easily from awareness of present to past and future scenes of his own life. His understanding of time as a continuum (whatever has been always is) rather than as made up of discreet moments is enhanced when he is kidnapped and taken to the planet Tralfamadore to be exhibited in a zoo. His story parallels the events leading up to the firebombing, setting it in a context of confusion and chaos.

The form of this novel is a kaleidoscopic mix of events, places, and people, not a chronological narrative at all—emphasizing the impossibility of comprehending Dresden through a logical, linear approach. It can only be approached sideways, out of the corner of one's eye. Today's students may need to be reminded that the book first appeared during another event that challenged comprehension: the Vietnam Conflict.

Differentness. Discuss Billy's differences in seeing what others do not see, and how he copes with that.

Drive to understand. Vonnegut's method of telling the story could be considered now in light of left brain/right brain or random versus sequential thinking. What does this approach tell us that a historical chronology would not? For what other subjects would this style be appropriate? What do you consider sequentially, and what holistically or spatially? Why?

Moral concerns. What does the historical event of Dresden have in common with other 20th century massacres? How does it differ? What have we learned?

Webb, James T., Elizabeth A. Meckstroth, and Stephanie S. Tolan. *Guiding the Gifted Child.* Columbus: Ohio Psychology Publishing Co., 1982.

Although this book is subtitled *A Practical Source for Parents and Teachers*, it is such a clear explanation of the major emotional difficulties a gifted child faces that teenagers are able to gain much self-understanding from it. Stephanie Tolan's "Open Letter to Parents, Teachers and Others: from Parents of an Exceptionally Gifted Child" is especially recommended for highly gifted young adults. If they identify with RJ, they may begin to understand why they felt as they did in elementary school.

This acceptance of their younger selves can be a cathartic experience for them, and the beginning of a new level of self-acceptance and understanding.

Teenagers and adults can read this book separately, each noting page and paragraph numbers they would like to consider further, and then meet for discussion.

Aloneness. The chapter on depression should interest people who are concerned about aloneness in the life of a gifted child.

Identity. The first three chapters will help young people develop a better understanding of their identities as gifted persons.

Relationships with others. The chapters on communication of feelings, peer relationships, sibling relationships, and parent relationships all offer information that will promote discussion of getting along with others.

Using ability. Chapters that relate to making maximum use of potential are those on motivation, stress management, and discipline.

Achievement; Identity; Intensity; Moral concerns; Perfectionism. Each of these issues is mentioned in this book.

Wolfe, Tom. *Bonfire of the Vanities.* New York: Farrar, Straus and Giroux, 1987.

Sherman McCoy is a Wall Street whiz of the high-flying '80s, a junk bond Master of the Universe, until he stumbles over the belief that he deserves to have ever more. An accident in the Bronx, with his mistress in his car, brings Sherman devastating publicity—which grows inexorably into notoriety—and acquaints him with reality as harsh as his upbringing has been privileged.

Wolfe skillfully draws a wide range of characters, and requires the reader to remember each throughout the long novel as he pulls the cast closer together toward the final court scene. Sherman undergoes psychological changes that provide a good beginning for discussion.

Arrogance. How does the tone of the book change after Sherman is stripped of arrogance? What is the effect of this on you as the reader?

Identity. Sherman is a decent person who shrinks from anything he considers to be ill-bred. What acts are moral or immoral in his view? Where is the line between morality and a good upbringing?

Moral concerns. Why does Sherman have difficulty regarding the tapes? Would you? Why or why not? How could this theme be treated with someone like you as the main character? What temptations could cause you to rise so high and fall so far?

Using ability. In order to have become a "Master of the Universe," Sherman must be of above-average intelligence. Why then does he get into so much trouble? What are the uses and limits of high intelligence as a guide for living?

Wolff, Tobias. *This Boy's Life: A Memoir.* New York: Atlantic Monthly Press, 1989.

Prize-winning fiction author Tobias Wolff turns to nonfiction for this story of his boyhood, which is also the story of the masking and creation of an identity. Born in Alabama in 1945, he moved with his mother to Washington State after his parents separated, when he was ten. "Jack," as he calls himself, spends most of his teenage years in Seattle and then in a small mountain town, now with a volatile stepfather. He is a discipline problem; his friends are unsavory; an almost schizophrenic split develops between who he believes he is and how others see him. A very strong core of undeveloped self-knowledge enables him to avoid being defeated by the difficult circumstances of his life: self-knowledge and a renewed contact with his older brother, who had stayed with the father when the fmaily separated. We do not see the completion of his growing up in this book, but we see a major act of deception (which stops short of self-deception, however) that gives him an escape from the limitations of his early years.

This Boy's Life raises questions about who we are, who we think we are, who others think we are, and who we may become. One of Wolff's achievements is to make it possible to see with unusual clarity the lines between those four facets of self-understanding and self-creation. Evidence of the dichotomies in his self-perception appear throughout the book; toward the end of the book we see introspection directly related to this theme.

Achievement. How does high potential complicate Wolff's boyhood?

Identity. Describe Wolff as he is, as he thinks he is, as others see him, and as a potential adult. Now do the same for yourself, and then for some other person you would like to understand better. How do the circumstances of your life make your development of identity a different task from Wolff's? How does the book help you understand anyone you know?

Moral concerns. Reread the paragraphs on his relationship with Arthur in the story of the grudge fight (p. 217-218). How does he use the words "citizen" and "outlaw"? What prevents Wolff from "trying to be a citizen"? Which is the better route, and the cost of each? How are you choosing and why?

Wolitzer, Meg. *Sleepwalking*. New York: Random, 1982.

Claire is one of three Swarthmore freshmen who are so interested in the poetry of women who have committed suicide (Sylvia Plath, Anne Sexton, and in Claire's case, "Lucy Ascher") that they become known as "the death girls." Julian, an upperclassman, is intrigued by Claire, but their relationship is weakened by Claire's involvement with Lucy Ascher and the death girls. Finally, Claire decides that she wants to be closer to Lucy than she can be simply by reading her poetry, so she goes to Lucy's parents' home and asks for work as a housekeeper. There, Claire gradually begins to comprehend the impact on her and her parents of the death of her brother several years earlier. At the same time, her presence helps Lucy's parents to resolve their own grief. In the end, it is one of the other death girls and Julian who help Claire make the decision to return to Swarthmore and her own life.

Flashbacks tell the stories of Claire's and Lucy's childhoods, so we can piece together the similarities and differences. Several themes invite discussion: relationships between parents and daughters, the importance of friends, handling aloneness, coping with death and grief, and, of course, suicide. This discussion should be planned with sensitivity to the needs of the reader(s).

Aloneness. Why was Lucy so alone? Why did she kill herself? Why is Claire so interested in Lucy? What difference between them explains why Lucy committed suicide and Claire does not? Were Lucy's parents at all responsible? How did Claire's childhood and her parents affect who she is now?

Using ability. Lucy Ascher was obviously a gifted poet. Did she commit suicide because of this? How could her suicide have been prevented by her? By others? How do you feel about Claire's leaving school to pursue her obsession with Lucy Ascher?

Yevtushenko, Yevgeny. *The Poetry of Yevgeny Yevtushenko, 1953 to 1965*. Translated from the Russian by George Reavey. Bilingual edition. New York: October House, 1965.

A leader of the rebirth of Russian poetry after Stalin, Yevtushenko writes with a forceful, fresh honesty. His work is imbued with youthful idealism combined with maturity—perfect characteristics for poetry to be recommended to sensitive young adults.

In addition, his subject matter is both informative and moving: his home town in Siberia, his longing to travel, his love of the Russian people, his eagerness to overcome bureaucratic restrictions, and the effects of the Russian Revolution on ordinary people. Throughout the book is a boundless enthusiasm for living tempered with an awareness of the poet's responsibility to speak the truth.

Aloneness. Poems relating to aloneness include "There's Something I Often Notice," "I Don't Understand," and "People Were Laughing Behind a Wall."

Drive to understand. Poems that will lead to a greater understanding of the Russian Revolution include "Weddings," "Babii Yar," "Moscow Freight Station," and "Honey."

Identity. Poems especially recommended for high-potential young adults dealing with issues of identity include "Prologue," "Irreconcilable," and "The Angry Young Men."

Using ability. Poems in this collection pertaining to using one's full abilities include "Others May Judge You," "The Concert," "A Career," and "Let Us Be Great!"

CHAPTERS ONE to SEVEN

Index of Subjects

H

I

J

CHAPTER EIGHT

ANNOTATED BIBLIOGRAPHY

Index of Authors

408

CHAPTER EIGHT ANNOTATED BIBLIOGRAPHY

Index of Titles

CHAPTER EIGHT

ANNOTATED BIBLIOGRAPHY

Index of Categories

Preschool

Kindergarten — Grade Two

Differentness

Drive to Understand

Identity

Intensity

Introversion

Grades Three — Five

Grades Six — Eight

Grades Nine — Twelve

CHAPTER

EIGHT

ANNOTATED

BIBLIOGRAPHY

Index for All Ages

The following books can be used with various age groups: